WOODWORKING

Tools, Fabrication,

Design, and Manufacturing

WOODWORKING
Tools, Fabrication,
Design, and Manufacturing

ROBERT LENTO

Professor of Industrial Education
City College of New York

PRENTICE-HALL, INC., *Englewood Cliffs, New Jersey 07632*

Library of Congress Cataloging in Publication Data

Lento, Robert (date)
  Woodworking : tools, fabrication, design, and
manufacturing.

  Includes index.
  1. Woodwork. I. Title.
TS843.L43   684'.08   78-17620
ISBN 0-13-962514-3

Editorial/production supervision and
    interior design by Virginia Huebner
Page layout by Martin J. Behan
Cover design by Edsal Enterprise
Manufacturing buyer: Cathie Lenard

Printed in the United States of America

10 9 8 7 6 5 4 3 2 1

Prentice-Hall International, Inc., *London*
Prentice-Hall of Australia Pty. Limited, *Sydney*
Prentice-Hall of Canada, Ltd., *Toronto*
Prentice-Hall of India Private Limited, *New Delhi*
Prentice-Hall of Japan, Inc., *Tokyo*
Prentice-Hall of Southeast Asia Pte. Ltd., *Singapore*
Whitehall Books Limited, *Wellington, New Zealand*

For Kathy, Guy, Maryalice and Janet

CONTENTS

chapter **TEN**

PRODUCTION   **486**

INDEX   **529**

PREFACE

This book is designed for the beginning woodworker—whether self-taught or a student in a structured school setting. It provides information in detail and in depth in those areas which most directly confront the novice: the use of handtools and power machinery. More advanced and specialized areas, such as cabinetmaking and building construction, are dealt with in introductory chapters which give the reader an overview of the area. Wood lamination is treated in detail because many woodworkers have little experience with this technique.

The illustrations clarify and support the text. Step-by-step instructions are given where necessary to provide detailed guidance to the novice. Such "how-to-do-it" material should also serve as a point of departure for the mature and more advanced craftsman.

The first chapter is devoted to problems and concepts that are basic to the development of a craftsman-like approach to woodworking. The true craftsman must understand wood as a material and realize its impact on design.

The second chapter introduces the common handtools and briefly describes their capabilities.

The third chapter presents a generalized procedure for the fabrication of a project after the project design has been developed, thus bridging the gap between tool use and project fabrication.

The fourth and fifth chapters discuss power tools. Where possible, power equipment is related to appropriate handtools.

Chapter 6 introduces cabinetmaking. This section applies much of the information presented earlier in the book.

In Chapter 7, which discusses wood lamination and solid woodbending, various types of molds are described including a unique variable laminator that can produce a variety of angular shapes.

Chapter 8 is devoted to wood finishing. Emphasis is on a systematic analytical approach to the subject. Easy to apply, fast drying finishes are featured.

Chapter 9 deals with light frame building construction. Basic information is covered beginning with site development and ending with roof installation.

Finally, Chapter 10 describes the industrial methods and equipment used in manufacturing and relates them to line production in the typical industrial arts class.

ACKNOWLEDGEMENTS

The author thanks the following associations and manufacturers who helpfully provided illustrative materials for this book.

Adjustable Clamp Company
Baxter D. Whitney and Sons, Inc.
Bostitch Division of Textron, Inc.
Culley Engineering and Manufacturing Company, Inc.
Danckaert Woodworking Machinery Co.
Danly Machine Corp.—Onsrud
De Vilbiss Company
Dry Clime Lamp Corp.
Diehl Machines
Ekstrom Carlson and Company
Forest Products Laboratory
Greenlee Tool Company
Goodspeed Machine Company
Handy Manufacturing Company
H. K. Porter Company Incorporated
Kurt Manufacturing Company—Carver Division
The Coated Abrasive Division of the Norton Company
Powermatic Houdatile Inc.
Rockwell Manufacturing Company, Delta Power Tools Division
Stanley Tool Company
St. Paul Machinery Manufacturing Company
J. L. Taylor Manufacturing Company
Tennewitz, Inc.
Wisconsin Knife Works Inc.
The Warren Group
Weyerhaeuser Company

ROBERT LENTO

New York, New York

WOODWORKING

Tools, Fabrication,
Design, and Manufacturing

DESIGN AND MATERIALS

DESIGN

The beginning woodworker, and sometimes even the experienced craftsman, tends to be more concerned with the "nuts and bolts" of fabricating a piece rather than with its overall design or organization. As a result, even well-made pieces frequently lack the look of well-designed commercial products. One of the most common reasons for this situation is the lack of any real identifiable style in the pieces produced (Fig. 1-1). Some commercial producers of medium- and low-priced furniture make a basic cabinet, like a dresser, in several styles. Even such commercial work is generally recognizable in terms of the style it is attempting to represent. The worst work of the nondesigner resists any clear classification.

The first and most basic problem for the aspiring craftsman is therefore to seek out designs which have a clearly recognizable style. This statement suggests that craftsmen should copy good designs. In fact, the statement recognizes the reality that a great majority of woodworkers will and do copy existing pieces. The student of design should begin by studying universally recognized, well-designed examples of various styles of work. Such work can be seen in museums and in a variety of publications devoted to subjects such as interior decoration and design itself. Unfortunately, the designs in many woodworking project books suffer from the same problem that the

Fig. 1-1. No identifiable style

novice designer confronts, that is, a lack of recognizable style. In addition, many of these pieces are not well designed from a functional or visual point of view.

Recognizing Good Design

What is a good design? A simple answer is, one that the viewer likes. Unfortunately, though personal preference is very important in the choice of a design, it does not always guarantee that such a choice is a wise or informed one. It is very possible that a piece of furniture or a car that is well designed will not be liked by a particular person. In fact, that is the very reason varieties of furniture styles and automobile models exist. Designers attempt to satisfy a variety of tastes. A well-designed product will meet certain standards or measures of design that will be recognized by most informed, knowledgeable viewers.

To determine whether or not a useful object, like a chair or table, is well designed, we can use at least two approaches. The first deals with how successfully the object does what it is supposed to do. For example, how efficiently does a chair support a human form? This element of design is known as *function*. Obviously, purely decorative pieces such as paintings or sculpture have a very limited function, whereas useful objects such as furniture have a function that is a very important part of their design. One of the useful statements about design is the one that says *form follows function*. This does not mean that any object which is functional, which does the job it is supposed to do, will automatically also be well designed. For example, a wooden orange crate of the right height can function as a seating device, but most of us would agree that it is visually unsuccessful as a chair design.

A second approach that can be used in analyzing a design is therefore a visual one. Does the object have visual appeal? Does it look right? In terms of the *form-follows-function* statement, we might ask the questions: Does the chair function efficiently as a chair? Does it add to the visual appearance of the setting it is in? If it does perform its function well, but is unbalanced looking or otherwise ugly, then the design is not a complete success.

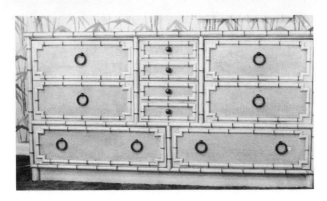

Fig. 1-2. Symmetrical balance

Balance

In attempting to analyze a design, or in creating a design, we note that certain identifiable characteristics are present in an effectively visual piece. For example, the cabinet in Fig. 1-2 exhibits *symmetrical* balance. When this cabinet is divided in half vertically, each half of the piece is a mirror image of the other. This kind of formal balance is very common in nature. Thus a symmetrical approach is an easy way to design pieces that will have balance. Most geometric solids are symmetrical and, of course, have balance. Cubes, cones, and cylinders are examples of such forms. In cabinetmaking these basic shapes are among the most common cabinet shapes.

Informal Balance

Informal balance or asymmetrical balance is another approach used by designers to achieve a balanced design. Figure 1-3 shows a wall unit that is not symmetrical. Dividing it vertically down the center will not result in a mirror image on each side of the dividing line. However, in spite of this lack of symmetry, the unit seems balanced and at rest. Why? One way to analyze

Fig. 1-3. Informal balance

this unit is as follows: The long, thin, vertical carving appears to be balanced by the lower vase with its spreading dried flowers. In addition to the use of the mass or the visual weight of forms in such asymmetrical balance, pattern, color, and texture can also be used in a similar way.

Proportion

In the preceding examples, we tended to consider flat surfaces and areas because we were looking at pictures. It is important to remember that these areas have a mass or volume which affects their balance value. *Proportion* is really an important part of balance, especially when one object is placed in a group with others. For example, if a very large lamp is placed on a small table, we would probably say the lamp is out of proportion to the table or that the scale of the lamp is too large for the table. In the case of a table top, we might note that the table is too long for its width. In other words, the length and width are out of proportion to each other. A table with a very thick, massive top, perched on long, thin spindly legs, might be described as having a top that is out of proportion to its legs or base. When the proportions of a piece are good, the piece will generally be balanced.

The novice designer can use the proportions of existing pieces as a guide in determining whether or not the proportions of a similar design are suitable. Another helpful device is to construct a mock-up of the proposed piece with cardboard or other similar materials. This full-sized model of the piece can be helpful in judging its proportions.

Continuity—Harmony

Most objects are composites, made up of assembled parts of many forms. In Fig. 1-4 the table is made up of legs, rails, and a tile top. The design works because its parts promote a feeling of continuity or harmony, that is, the parts seem to belong together. One way the designer achieved harmony in this piece was to round many of the parts and to curve the lower rails.

Fig. 1-4. Composite form

Fig. 1-5. Sofa leg-arm joint illustrates "honest" use of materials

This repetition of curves promotes *harmony*. In fact, *repetition* is one of the devices used for that purpose. Another device used in this piece to promote continuity is the repeated use of square, or almost square, spaces.

Woodworkers have many factors working for them in producing harmony in wooden pieces. A cabinet made of one kind of wood will naturally have continuity and harmony. Most cabinets tend to be geometric shapes, and their parts (e.g., drawers and doors) are related geometric shapes.

Emphasis

Artists use emphasis, that is, they make certain parts of their work stand out, to attract the viewer's eye. In furniture design a part that provides emphasis often has a practical or functional value. For example, drawer pulls attract the eye and often act as emphasizers. They also allow the cabinet user to open the drawers.

The sofa leg-arm joint shown in Fig. 1-5 directs the viewer's attention to that point and therefore lends emphasis to the design. In this case we might describe this joint as being an example of the *honest use of materials*.

Honest Use of Materials

To use materials "honestly" means not to make something look like something it isn't. For example, a wood-grained plastic laminate, like Formica®, on a table top is not representative of the honest use of materials. The designer is attempting to fool the eye by making the plastic look like wood. If the plastic laminate were a solid color or had some pattern that was obviously not wooden, it would be a more honest design. The honest use of materials overlaps slightly into the area of taste or preference because certain established styles of furniture are not honest in their construction. Thus joints are made so as not to indicate the method of joinery used.

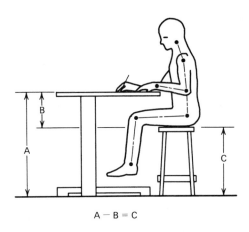

A − B = C

Fig. 1-6. Using body size in functional design

Nevertheless, the concept of honest use of materials is important and should be understood by the serious designer.

Most of what has been discussed relates to the visual aspects of a design; however, the functional aspects of a design are also very important. The heights of tables and chairs, for example, are critical to their comfortable use, and commercially made pieces can provide information about optimal heights. Another practical method is illustrated in Fig. 1-6. In deciding how tall to make a coffee table, the designer can measure the sofa which will be used with the table. The seat height of the sofa would be a suitable height for the coffee table (Fig. 1-7). Other factors influencing design include joinery, materials, finish, and type of construction to be used.

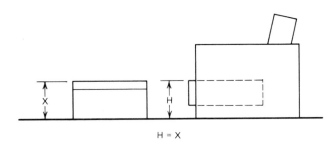

H = X

Fig. 1-7. Relating pieces in design

How then does the craftsman or novice go about designing a piece? The simplest way is to find an existing design and reproduce it with or without modifications. Another approach, after determining the functional requirements of the piece, is to design the piece on paper from "scratch."

Functional Requirements

A good way to begin to determine the functional requirements of a piece is to assign a functional name to the piece. Is it to be a coffee table? an end table? a desk? Even this first basic step delimits the design to some extent. If it is to be a coffee table, for example, its height should be related to the height of the sofa it is to rest in front of.

Stylistic Requirements

In developing the total design, the craftsman can begin to block out basic geometric shapes and forms which will satisfy the functional requirements of the piece (see Fig. 1-8). The block sketches should be approximately to scale, and the geometric shapes can be thought of as frames or enclosures inside of which the final form of the piece will take shape.

At this point in the development of the design, the designer might begin to consider which style category the piece will fit. For example, if the piece is to be colonial, it may have raised paneled doors, scalloped trimming, and distinctive brass hardware. If it is to be contemporary, it may have an angular shape and an unornamented appearance (see Figs. 1-9 and 1-10). These refinements in design can be sketched on tracing paper, which can then be superimposed on the basic form developed in the first step.

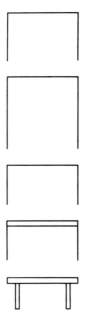

Fig. 1-8. Blocking out a design

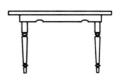

Fig. 1-9. Colonial style table

Fig. 1-10. Contemporary style table

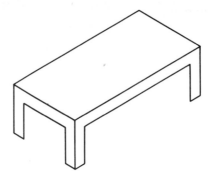

Fig. 1–11. Cardboard mockup

Mock-Ups

At this stage a full-sized blocked-out cardboard model of the piece can be constructed. This model (Fig. 1–11) can more easily be evaluated for important features such as proportion. Once the basic shape and proportions have been determined, more detailed plans can be developed.

Working Drawings

Complex pieces usually require detailed planning which can most easily be accomplished by making detailed drawings. Ideally, the drawings of the proposed piece should be full-sized. Full-sized drawings do not require dimensioning, and measurements can be taken directly from them. If a mock-up has not been constructed, the full-sized drawing can help the designer to determine factors such as proportion. And, finally, templates and patterns can easily be reproduced from full-sized drawings by simply tracing the desired parts and then transferring the tracing to the material for fashioning (Fig. 1–12).

Fig. 1–12. Tracing made from original full size drawing

There are situations where it is difficult, or at least inconvenient, to make full-sized drawings. A chest of drawers, for example, would require a very large sheet of paper and jumbo-sized drafting tools. When this is the case, scale drawings can be substituted.

The most common type of working drawing is the orthographic projection, which consists of at least two views and in many cases three or more views (Fig. 1-13). This type of drawing shows details in scale size and shape.

The drawing should contain enough detailed information so that the viewer can completely understand the construction of the piece. Extensive use of hidden outlines should be avoided because this tends to be confusing and difficult to interpret. Cutaways and revolved or removed sections are easier to interpret.

Although the working drawing should be complete in its details, the craftsman may want to leave certain final decisions until later when the piece is almost completed. For instance, the shape of a table top can be determined after the leg-rail system exists and the basic rectangular shape of the

JOINT REQUIREMENTS: MATERIAL: ½" Basswood

#1 = Through dowel one side, blind dowel on the second side.
#2 = Dado, #3 = Dovetail, #4 = Masonite back set in rabbet 1/8" material
#5 = Door, fit into opening, hardware student choice

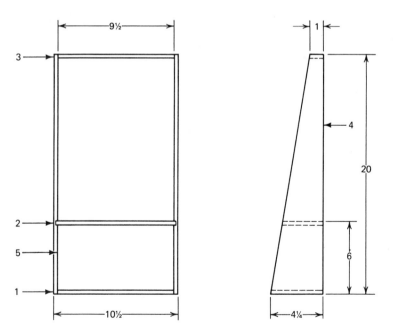

Fig. 1-13. Orthographic drawing

Fig. 1-14. Trying cardboard tops on completed base to determine final top shape

unfinished table top has been made. Then a cardboard top or tops can be tried on the table to determine the final shape and size (Fig. 1-14).

The process described above can be followed by a designer who has never worked with wood; however, the results are likely to be unrealistic in terms of what can be done with wood as a material. For this reason the designer who is a craftsman is more likely to design efficiently for the material whose limits and qualities he understands.

WOOD AS A MATERIAL

Availability

Wood has enjoyed unparalleled popularity as a material for the craftsman since the earliest times. This has been true for two major reasons: wood is readily available and relatively easy to fashion. Even in this era of advanced materials technology, wood is still used widely for a variety of purposes. Among the commonly used natural materials, it is the only one which is renewable. All other materials exist in definite, limited quantities.

Ease of Fastening

In terms of fashioning, the ease of using wood arises from the simplicity of the tools which can be used to shape it and the variety of methods which can be used to join it. Joinery, and/or glue, and simple hardware can effectively fasten wood. In the case of metal, holes must be drilled, tapped, or riveted. Welding requires high temperatures and a high degree of skill to accomplish.

Dimensional Stability

Wood is made up of cells which are very much like soda straws in shape, though of course they are microscopic in size. These long and narrow cells tend to expand or swell when they absorb moisture and to shrink when they give up moisture. This expansion and contraction affects the diameter of the cells much more profoundly than the length. This is the reason wood expands and contracts much more across the grain (in width) than it does with the grain (in length). See Fig. 1-31. In width, wood is less stable. A rule of thumb is to allow 1/8 inch per foot of width for expansion and contraction in furniture construction.

Permanence

Under ideal conditions, when protected from insects and moisture, wood can last for thousands of years. Furniture found in burial vaults in the Near East has been found in nearly perfect condition.

One of the reasons for the durability of wood is its resistance to corrosion. Unlike many metals, wood does not oxidize rapidly. When exposed to the atmosphere, it wears away at a very slow rate, approximately 0.125 inch every 50 years.

Fire Resistance

Although wood is used as a fuel, in thick cross-sections, it does not burn rapidly. A thick log takes many hours to burn when it is thrown on a fire. When wood reaches approximately 550°F, it begins to decompose at the rate of about 0.03 inch per hour. During this process, charcoal is produced which acts as an insulator against heat. Unlike metal, wood does not slump or sag when it gets hot (Fig. 1-15).

Fig. 1-15. Steel beams bend during fire. Wooden beam, although damaged, still provides support. (*Courtesy U.S. Forest Service Laboratory, Forest Service, U.S. Dept. of Agriculture.*)

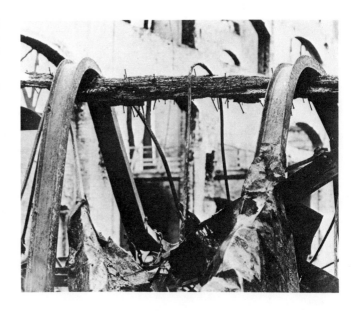

Heat Conductivity

Because of its structure, wood is a good heat insulator. The heat loss of other common building materials compared to that of wood is as follows:

Brick—6 times the heat loss of wood
Glass—8 times
Concrete—15 times
Steel—390 times
Aluminum—1700 times

Dynamic Loading Strength

Structures made of concrete or steel have no ability to support loads greater than their design strength under momentary impact. For example, a bridge deck made of steel or concrete, designed to support 500 pounds per square inch, cannot support a truck tire that bounces over a rock and, for an instant, applies more than 500 pounds per square inch to the road surface. A wooden structure can support double its design load for a momentary impact.

Ecological Advantages

Wood has many ecological advantages. No energy other than the direct energy of the sun is used to produce wood. Other materials, such as concrete and steel, require large amounts of heat energy, usually derived from oil or gas, in their production.

Wood is also biodegradable; it eventually decays and returns to the soil.

Cell Structure of Wood

Wood is composed of three types of cells: *vessels, tracheids,* and *fibers.* Vessels are very short cells with thin walls, and their principal function is to conduct sap (Fig. 1–16). Fibers are very long, thick-walled, and narrow. Their narrow diameter prevents them from acting as sap conduits, but their length and strong thick walls make them useful as support and strengthening materials in the wood. Tracheids are in-between fibers and vessels in terms of their structure and function; they can conduct sap and also help provide strength for the tree. Tracheids make up most of the woody material of conifers, which are believed to have developed before the broad-leafed hardwoods. The hardwoods contain all three types of cells, with each type performing specialized jobs, but with the tracheids performing both strengthening and sap-conducting functions.

The great length of the tracheids makes them highly suitable for paper making, where the long fibers mat well to form the paper body. Hardwoods

VESSELS

Fig. 1-16. Magnified view of the cellular structure of a tree. Fibers or cells form just under the bark, divide, and gradually develop thicker walls that are composed almost entirely of cellulose. A single fiber is shown at right

are not suitable for this purpose because they contain relatively smaller numbers of these cells.

Tree Growth

A tree grows by adding new cells to the sticky layer of wood just under the bark (Fig. 1-17A). This cambium layer forms the annual rings of the tree as it develops. Horizontal sap movement is provided by the cells that make up the medulary rays of the tree (Fig. 1-17G). The cells close to the cam-

Fig. 1-17. Section through a log. (A) Cambium; (B) Inner bark; (C) Outer bark; (D) Sapwood; (E) Heartwood; (F) Pith; (G) Medullary rays

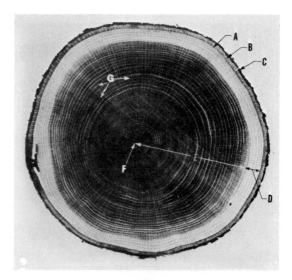

bium conduct the sap of the tree and provide support for it. Food is not stored here. Because this wood conducts sap, it is called *sapwood*.

As the tree continues to develop, adding new layers of sapwood, the wood near the center of the tree gradually loses its sap- and water-carrying function. It is then known as *heartwood* (Fig. 1-17). The heartwood is usually darker than the sapwood. This darkening occurs because the extractives in the heartwood change chemically. It is most dramatic in walnut, where the heartwood is deep brown and the sapwood is almost white; by contrast, in many softwoods almost no color change occurs.

Earlywood and Latewood

In woods such as fir, the grain pattern is made up of contrasting colored woods (Fig. 1-25). One is very dark and dense, while the wood next to it is light and relatively soft. The light, soft wood is earlywood. The earlywood forms in the spring when moisture is abundant and growing conditions are ideal for rapid growth. This early or springwood is made up of tracheidal cells that have thin walls and large interiors for the efficient flow of sap.

Later in the summer the latewood develops. The cells in this material have thicker walls and are more dense. In the case of fir, they appear darker and are harder.

Classification of Woods

Woods can be divided into two broad categories: hardwoods from deciduous trees and softwoods from coniferous trees.

Hardwoods. The term *hardwood* is misleading because not all hardwood trees produce woods that are hard. In general, hardwoods are those trees whose leaves are broad and are termed deciduous trees or angiosperms. These trees have true flowers and their seeds are enclosed in a "fruit." Maple trees are an example. In the spring they produce a kind of flower that later develops into a seed (Fig. 1-18) which is enclosed in a pod. Wood from

Fig. 1-18. Maple leaf and maple tree seed pods

Fig. 1-19. Pine cones

broad-leafed trees tends to be hard, although there are some exceptions to this rule. Hardwoods generally lose their leaves in winter.

Softwoods. Softwoods come from needle-leafed, cone-bearing trees known as *coniferous* (cone-bearing) trees or *gymnosperms*. They have exposed seeds, usually in cones, and their leaves remain on the tree year-round. In general, these woods are softer than most hardwoods, which come from broad-leafed trees. Among the exceptions to this rule are long-leafed pine and Douglas fir. These two woods are harder than basswood or aspen (Fig. 1-19).

Specific Characteristics of Wood

The characteristics described above are the general properties of wood which account for its widespread use, especially as a construction material. The craftsman is also interested in its working qualities.

Wood is formed as the tree grows. Each year the tree adds a new layer of material, which increases its trunk diameter and its height (Fig. 1-20). The density of the layers is determined by several factors, including the species of tree, the environment, and the time of year.

Grain. Because layers of wood are added to the trunk as it grows, a grain pattern develops (Fig. 1-21). The grain pattern is most pronounced on the face of the board. Although some pieces have a grain pattern that parallels the edges of the piece, most have nonparallel patterns (Fig. 1-21). In cutting the wood, the best results are obtained when the cutting edge cuts with the grain (Fig. 1-22). Cutting against the grain is likely to produce broken fibers or splitting. Thus, one of the most important facts which the craftsman needs to know is grain direction.

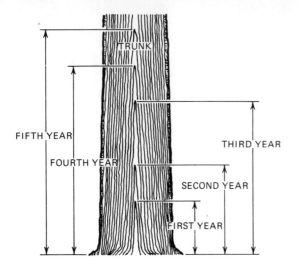

Fig. 1-20. Annual increases of tree trunk diameter and tree height

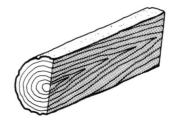

Fig. 1-21. Plain sawed log showing end and face grain

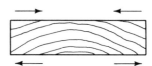

NO CHANGE OF GRAIN DIRECTION ON AN EDGE

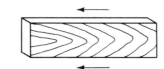

CHANGE OF GRAIN DIRECTION ON AN EDGE. AVOID SELECTING THIS TYPE OF MATERIAL

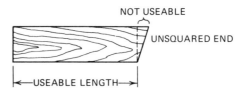

NOT USEABLE

UNSQUARED END

USEABLE LENGTH

Fig. 1-22.

When wood fails under stress, it tends to split along grain lines. Therefore, in Fig. 1-23, piece a will fail under a much lighter load than piece b would. The more parallel the "slope of the grain" is to the edge, the greater the strength of the wood when it is loaded, as shown in Fig. 1-24 (d) and (e).

Grain also plays a role in the finishing of wood. Some woods, like oak, are very open grained. This openness appears as small depressions in the surface of the wood. In most cases these depressions must be filled to avoid

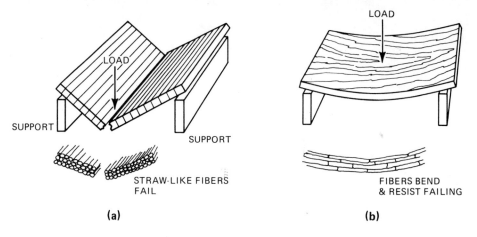

Fig. 1-23. Grain direction and failure resistance

a pitted, finished surface. The grain pattern or figure is one of the factors that adds to the beauty of wood.

The direction of forces applied to a piece of wood directly affects the way the wood reacts to the load. In Fig. 1-24 (a), (b), and (c), three pieces of wood are shown, looking in the direction of their end grain. The degree of deflection under a given load applied in the direction of the arrow is highest for a, intermediate for c, and lowest for b. This information is useful in selecting a given piece of wood for a specific application.

Fig. 1-24. Grain slope and failure resistance

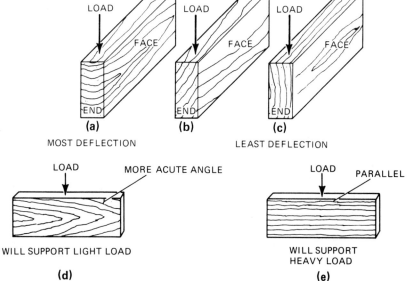

DEFECTS IN WOOD

A defect in wood is any irregularity which makes the wood less useful. These defects can be the result of factors which influence the tree as it grows—natural defects. They can also be caused by improper processing after the tree has been harvested—seasoning and machining defects.

Natural Defects

Knots. Knots are among the most common natural defects. They are the result of the development of a branch on the trunk of the tree (Fig. 1-25). The branch is subjected to great pressure from the trunk as both grow; as a result, the wood in the knot tends to be harder than the surrounding material. In addition, the normal grain pattern of the trunk is disrupted by the growth of the branch (Fig. 1-26). Therefore, because of its irregular grain and hardness, the knot causes problems in machining.

Two basic types of knots are commonly found as defects in wood: loose knots and intergrown knots. *Loose knots*—encased knots—are formed when the tree trunk continues to grow around a branch that has died. When the trunk is cut into boards, these knots usually appear as dark, circular areas in the wood (Fig. 1-26). As the wood dries and shrinks, the knots become loose and often fall out. *Intergrown knots* are formed when a living branch is surrounded by the trunk as they both grow. The fibers of the trunk and the branch are interwoven and intimately connected (Fig. 1-26). When inter-

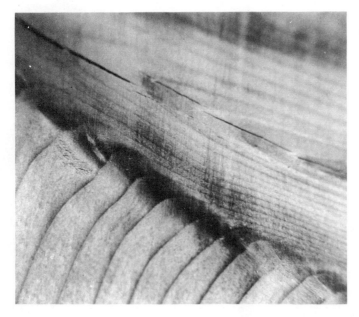

Fig. 1-25. Grain disturbance around knot

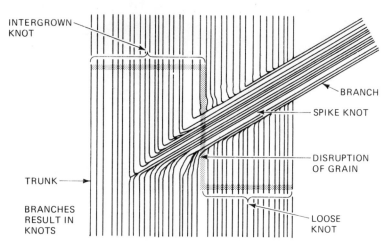

INTERGROWN KNOT

BRANCH

SPIKE KNOT

DISRUPTION OF GRAIN

TRUNK

BRANCHES RESULT IN KNOTS

LOOSE KNOT

Fig. 1-26. Branches result in knots

grown knots appear in wood, they remain in place. Although they are less undesirable than loose knots, intergrown knots do interfere with machining and finishing.

Since the saw that cuts the trunk into boards frequently cuts through the imbedded branches at right angles to the branch axis (Fig. 1-26), the knots appear as circles or ovals. In some cases the saw cuts through the branch parallel to its axis (Fig. 1-25), and then the knot appears as a wedge-shaped defect known as a *spike knot*. These knots are generally larger than other knots and frequently appear at the edges of the board.

Knot frequency. The number of knots in a board depends on several factors, including the species of the tree and the relative location of the board in the trunk during the tree's growth. Woods such as pine tend to have many knots because pine trees are heavily branched. In addition, the lower branches on pine trees tend to die as the tree grows, and they become loose knots. In the diagram shown in Fig. 1-27, notice that the fewest knots are

Fig. 1-27. Knot frequency in tree trunk

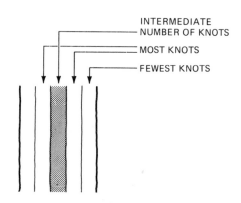

INTERMEDIATE NUMBER OF KNOTS

MOST KNOTS

FEWEST KNOTS

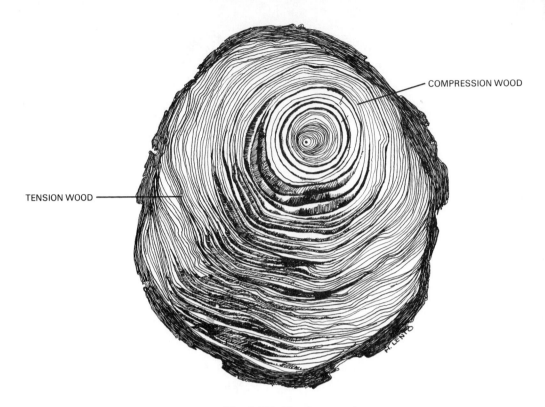

COMPRESSION WOOD

TENSION WOOD

Fig. 1-28. Tension wood

found closest to the surface of the trunk. The area between the heart of the tree and the outer layers of sapwood generally contains the greatest number of knots because this area of the trunk developed when the tree had many lower branches. The innermost part of the trunk contains a moderate amount of knots because of the presence of some branches in this area when the tree was young.

Reaction wood. When various environmental factors cause a tree trunk to develop a curved rather than a straight configuration, the result is *reaction wood*. In the case of hardwoods, the abnormal wood formed above or on the positive side of the bend is called *tension* wood (Fig. 1-28). In softwoods, the wood on the negative side of the bend (Fig. 1-29) is called *compression* wood. Among the changes which take place in reaction wood are increased density, excessive shrinkage in length during drying, and reduced strength. The unnatural curvature of the trunk can also result in increased grain irregularities which make machining difficult.

Pitch pockets. Certain highly resinous woods like pine and spruce sometimes develop voids which fill with pitch. These pockets tend to leak and make finishing difficult.

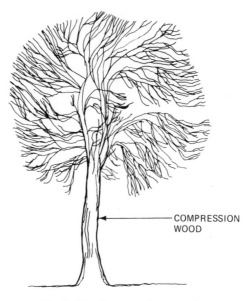

Fig. 1-29. Compression wood

Shakes. Shakes are cracks that appear on the ends of logs or pieces of timber. These cracks are caused by a variety of factors, including wind action or frost. *Heart shakes* tend to develop along the medulary rays of the trunk, whereas *ring shakes* follow the annual rings (Fig. 1-30).

Seasoning Defects

Most wood is unusable immediately after cutting because green wood contains large amounts of water which must be lost before the wood can be used for construction purposes. This water accounts for as much as 200 per-cent of the dry weight of the material. It is normally removed in stages after the wood has been rough-cut into boards. First, air-drying is used; then

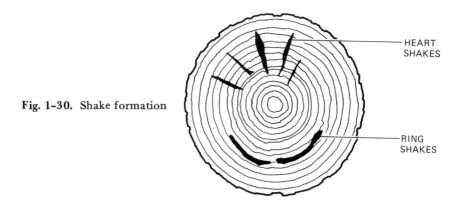

Fig. 1-30. Shake formation

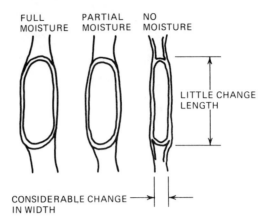

FULL MOISTURE PARTIAL MOISTURE NO MOISTURE

LITTLE CHANGE LENGTH

CONSIDERABLE CHANGE → IN WIDTH

Fig. 1-31. Wood cell shrinkage with moisture loss

kiln- or forced drying removes the remainder of the water, leaving 5 to 15 percent of the original water in the wood. As this water evaporates, most of the changes in the wood take place as the wood shrinks along the annual rings (Fig. 1-31). Some shrinkage takes place radially as well. Many lumber processors coat the ends of the lumber with a sealer to help prevent end checks that can occur even after seasoning is complete.

Warpage. Warping is by far the most common seasoning defect. It occurs when the stresses set up by the difference in radial and annual ring shrinkage are too great. Warping is caused by any uneven drying of the material. Controlled drying through the seasoning process helps to reduce the tendency of wood to warp.

In *cup warping,* the wood cups in the direction shown in Fig. 1-33). If the piece is quartersawed or comes from the center of the log, this type of warping is less likely to occur. In slash-sawed lumber, all of the boards except the one cut from the center of the tree have end-grain patterns as shown in Fig. 1-32. As the wood dries out, the cells lose water and shrink

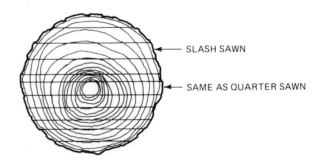

SLASH SAWN

SAME AS QUARTER SAWN

Fig. 1-32. Slash-sawed log

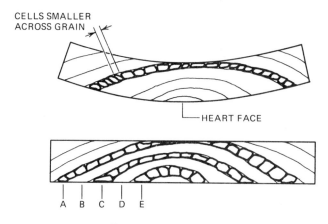

Fig. 1-33. Cup warp

(Fig. 1-33). The number of cells side by side in the portion of the annual ring (E) is relatively small; so this row of cells shrinks a small amount. The other rings become longer and contain many more cells. The longer rings shrink more in total and the result is that the edges of the board bend up away from the rings into the cup warp (Fig. 1-33).

Lumber should be stored flat in a pile so that the weight of the material above it helps to keep it flat. It should also be kept in a location where the moisture in the air is approximately equal to the moisture content of the lumber.

Crooking. In crooking (Fig. 1-34), the face of the board remains flat and the edges of the piece curve.

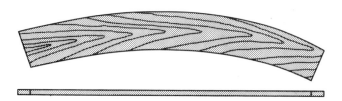

Fig. 1-34. Crooking

Bowing. In bowing, the face of the board bends like a barrel stave (Fig. 1-35).

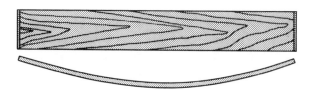

Fig. 1-35. Bowing

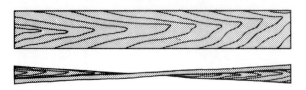

Fig. 1-36. Winding

Fig. 1-37. Diamonding

Winding. Winding is a common defect in which the board twists so that it resembles a propeller (Fig. 1-36).

Diamonding. In square-cut stock, uneven drying causes the piece to change from a square in cross-section to a parallelogram in cross-section (Fig. 1-37).

Defects Caused by Improper Machining

Raised grain. Raised grain is a condition which occurs when summerwood is raised above the adjacent springwood so that the surface appears to be ridged or corrugated. It almost appears as though the wood were sandblasted, causing the softer portions of the wood to be abraded away. Raised grain is caused by surfacing wood that has a relatively high moisture content, above 12 percent. The planer knives crush the harder latewood into the softer earlywood. The earlywood is not really fully cut. Later, the compressed earlywood under the crushed hard latewood absorbs moisture and swells so that it rises above the harder, uncompressed latewood. The result is a corrugated appearance. Dull knives increase the tendency for this condition to develop.

Fuzzy grain. In this case the surface of the wood appears rough and fuzzy. If the cells close to the surface of the wood pick up excessive moisture and are sanded in that condition, the cells rupture and are shredded by the sanding process, producing the fuzzy-grain condition.

Chipped or torn grain. Chipped grain can be caused by planing against the grain of the wood.

LUMBERING AND PROCESSING

One of the first steps in lumbering operations is the building of a rough road into the stand of trees to be cut (Fig. 1-38). Then the trees to be harvested are identified, cut, transported to the mill, and processed into boards. Once this has been done, the green lumber must be seasoned (dried) so that it will be dimensionally stable and suitable for its intended use. It is estimated that the United States consumes 50 billion board feet of lumber yearly.

Fig. 1-38. Building a rough lumbering road. (*Courtesy of Weyerhaeuser Company, Dept. of Public Affairs.*)

Tree Selection

In managed forests, trees are carefully selected and marked for harvesting (Fig. 1-39). This selection takes into consideration the size and quality of each tree, as well as other factors, such as the environmental effect of the harvesting.

Cutting

A tree is generally cut or felled by a lumberjack using a gasoline-powered chain saw (Fig. 1-40). After felling, the tree is limbed and cut into rough lengths suitable for its ultimate use. The logs are taken to the collecting point by tractor or truck (Fig. 1-41), and from this point they are transported to the mill.

Fig. 1-39. Marking trees for harvest. (*Courtesy of Weyerhaeuser Company, Dept. of Public Affairs.*)

Fig. 1-40. Felling a tree using a chainsaw. (*Courtesy of Weyerhaeuser Company, Dept. of Public Affairs.*)

Fig. 1-41. Logs stacked at collection point. (*Courtesy of Weyerhaeuser Company, Dept. of Public Affairs.*)

Fig. 1-42. Mill pond log storage. (*Courtesy of Weyerhaeuser Company, Dept. of Public Affairs.*)

Mill Operations

Many mills employ millponds, often artificially created, to store the logs prior to processing in the mill. The ponds make the moving of the logs easier, and the water keeps the wood from drying out prematurely and helps to protect the logs from insect attack (Fig. 1-42). When logs are required, they are carried into the mill by a conveyor; as they enter the mill, they are cleaned by a high-pressure stream of water (Fig. 1-43). In many mills the bark is stripped from the logs, prior to cutting, by mechanical strippers or by very-high-pressure streams of water.

Fig. 1-43. Log cleaning and bark stripping. (*Courtesy of Weyerhaeuser Company, Dept. of Public Affairs.*)

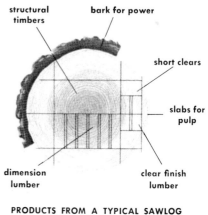

structural timbers

bark for power

short clears

slabs for pulp

dimension lumber

clear finish lumber

PRODUCTS FROM A TYPICAL SAWLOG

Fig. 1-44. Log sawing operation. (*Courtesy of Weyerhaeuser Company, Dept. of Public Affairs.*)

Sawing. The sawing of the logs into lumber is accomplished in a variety of ways. For hardwoods, the entire log is usually converted into lumber; in softwood processing, part of the log may be used for lumber while the rest is used for other purposes (Fig. 1-44). In one type of mill the log is first sawed into a cant (Fig. 1-45). Then the log is positioned on a movable carriage and sawed into boards by circular saws or band saws.

Most lumber is slash- or plain-sawed because this method produces the smallest amount of waste. Quartersawing is sometimes practiced because it results in lumber that is much more resistant to warping. The term "quarter-sawed lumber" originates from the practice of quartering logs and then sawing boards from the quarter as shown in Fig. 1-46. This results in boards whose faces display edge grain, and whose ends have grain at right angles to the faces of the board (Fig. 1-47). Most quartersawed lumber which is cut

SAWING DIRECTION

Fig. 1-45. Cant

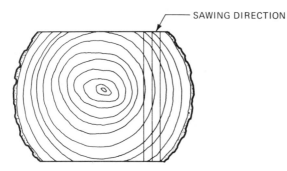

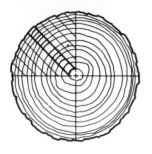

Fig. 1-46. Quarter-sawed lumber

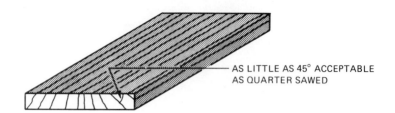

AS LITTLE AS 45° ACCEPTABLE
AS QUARTER SAWED

Fig. 1-47. Grain angle of quarter-sawed lumber

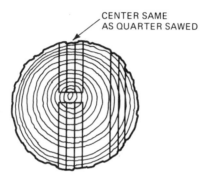

CENTER SAME
AS QUARTER SAWED

Fig. 1-48. Slash or plain sawing

today results from slash-sawing (Fig. 1-48). The center board is the true quartersawed piece, but any board whose annual rings are between 45° and 90° to the face are considered to be quartersawed.

The newly cut boards are ripped to standard widths on an edger saw. Then the boards are cut to standard lengths on trimmer crosscut saws (Fig. 1-49). During this operation many of the defects are cut out.

Seasoning. Newly cut lumber contains large amounts of water. In some cases this water accounts for additional weight equal to two or three times the weight of the dry material.

Air-drying. In air-drying, the lumber is stacked (Fig. 1-50) in protected sheds for a period of time ranging from several months to several years. Stacking leaves open space around the lumber and speeds the drying process. The weight of the lumber highest in the stack on the material below keeps the boards flat and relatively warp-free.

In general, air-dried lumber has a moisture range, by weight, from 12 to 15 percent.

Kiln-drying. Some air-dried lumber is further dried in heated kilns under controlled conditions. This type of drying is more closely controlled and is

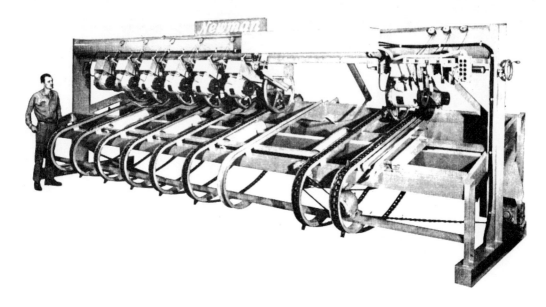

Fig. 1-49. Trimmer cross-cut saws

commonly used for hardwoods that are intended for furniture construction. In the early stages of operation, the humidity in the kiln is kept high to prevent excessive drying-out of the surface of the wood before the interior of the material has had a chance to dry. The entire process can take several weeks (Fig. 1-51).

Final Processing

Most lumber is not used in the rough condition, although hardwoods are frequently sold rough. Softwood lumber is surfaced on both faces and both edges to standard sizes. Other material is shaped into standard shapes (Fig. 1-52) and is known as worked lumber. This process takes place in a mill.

Fig. 1-50. Air drying lumber

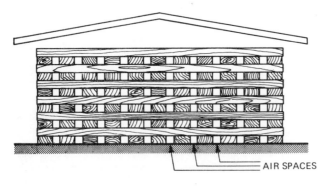

AIR SPACES

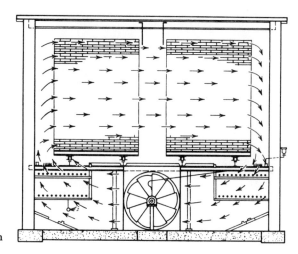

Fig. 1-51. Schematic of kiln

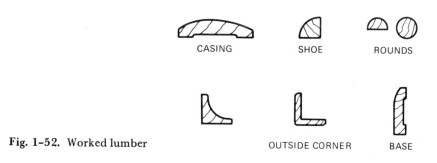

CASING   SHOE   ROUNDS

Fig. 1-52. Worked lumber

OUTSIDE CORNER   BASE

Hardwood Lumber

Hardwood lumber is cut to a greater variety of standard sizes than soft-woods are. Sizes generally range from 4 to 16 feet in 1-foot increments. Hardwood lumber widths are usually specified as being 8 inches or wider. Most hardwoods are rough-sawed to 1-inch thickness and then surfaced down to smaller thicknesses. The buyer generally is charged for the 1-inch thickness. In the case of the most expensive hardwoods, such as walnut, smaller thicknesses are rough-cut for economy.

Softwood Lumber

Softwood lumber is generally cut into lengths beginning at 6 feet and increasing in 2-foot increments up to 18 feet. Thicknesses are similar to those used for hardwoods. The processed lumber is then sorted according to standard grading specifications.

Grading Lumber

Several different sets of standards exist for softwoods. The standards described here are fairly typical of softwood grading.

Softwood grading standards. The term *select* is usually assigned to the best grade of softwood lumber. This grade allows very few minor defects and includes the most expensive lumber. Within the select grade there are three other grades: B and better, C, and D. All of the lumber graded in the select range is suitable for finish woodwork, furniture, and other high-quality uses.

Number 1 and No. 2 common are the next lower grades. Here the minimum acceptable width is 3 inches and the minimum length is 4 feet. Number 1 must yield two-thirds clear material, and No. 2 must yield at least half clear material.

Common grade lumber allows many more defects, including knots. Five grades of common have been established: No 1 common, No. 2 common, and so on. Number 1 common has fewer defects than No. 2; No. 2 has fewer than No. 3; etc.

Grades of hardwood lumber. The standards used for hardwood grading are those that have been established by the American Hardwood Lumber Association. This system is based on the quality of the best face of the piece of material being graded (Fig. 1–53).

The top grade of hardwood lumber is called *firsts*. The two top grades, *firsts* and *seconds,* are usually combined and are known as FAS (firsts and

FIGURE 1–53. STANDARD HARDWOOD CUTTING GRADES*

Grade and Lengths Allowed (ft.)	Widths Allowed (in.)	Surface Measure of Pieces (sq. ft.)	Amount of each Piece that must Work into Clear-face Cuttings (%)	Maximum Cuttings Allowed (no.)	Minimum Size of Cuttings Required
Firsts:† 8 to 16 (will admit 30 per-cent of 8- to 11-ft, half of which may be 8- and 9-ft)	6+	4 to 9 10 to 14 15+	91 $\frac{2}{3}$ 91 $\frac{2}{3}$ 91 $\frac{2}{3}$	1 2 3	4 in. by 5 ft, or 3 in. by 7 ft
Seconds:† 8 to 16 (will admit 30 per-cent of 8- to 11-ft, half of which may be 8- and 9-ft)	6+	4 and 5 6 and 7 6 and 7 8 to 11 8 to 11 12 to 15 12 to 15 16+	83 $\frac{1}{3}$ 83 $\frac{1}{3}$ 91 $\frac{2}{3}$ 83 $\frac{1}{3}$ 91 $\frac{2}{3}$ 83 $\frac{1}{2}$ 91 $\frac{2}{3}$ 83 $\frac{1}{3}$	1 1 2 2 3 3 4 4	Do

FIGURE 1–53. CONTINUED

Grade and Lengths Allowed (ft.)	Widths Allowed (in.)	Surface Measure of Pieces (sq. ft.)	Amount of each Piece that must Work into Clear-face Cuttings (%)	Maximum Cuttings Allowed (no.)	Minimum Size of Cuttings Required
Selects: ‡ 6 to 16 (will admit 30 percent of 6- to 11-ft, one-sixth of which may be 6- and 7-ft)	4+	2 and 3 4+	$91\,^2/_3$ (‡)	1	Do
No. 1 common: 4 to 16 (will admit 10 percent of 4- to 7-ft, half of which may be 4- and 5-ft)	3+	1 2 3 and 4 3 and 4 5 to 7 5 to 7 8 to 10 11 to 13 14+	100 75 $66\,^2/_3$ 75 $66\,^2/_3$ 75 $66\,^2/_3$ $66\,^2/_3$ $66\,^2/_3$	0 1 1 2 2 3 3 4 5	4 in. by 2 ft, or 3 in. by 3 ft
No. 2 common: 4 to 16 (will admit 30 percent of 4- to 7-ft, one-third of which may be 4- and 5-ft)	3+	1 2 and 3 2 and 3 4 and 5 4 and 5 6 and 7 6 and 7 8 and 9 10 and 11 12 and 13 14+	$66\,^2/_3$ 50 $66\,^2/_3$ 50 $66\,^2/_3$ 50 $66\,^2/_3$ 50 50 50 50	1 1 2 2 3 3 4 4 5 6 7	3 in. by 2 ft
No. 3A common: 4 to 16 (will admit 50 percent of 4- to 7-ft, half of which may be 4- and 5-ft)	3+	1+	$33\,^1/_3$ §	unlimited	Do
No. 3B common: 4 to 16 (will admit 50 percent of 4- to 7-ft, half of which may be 4- and 5-ft)	3+	1+	25‖	unlimited	1 ½ in. by 2 ft

*Inspection to be made on the poorer side of the piece, except in selects.

†Firsts and seconds are combined as one grade (FAS). The percentage of firsts required in the combined grade varies from 20 to 40 percent, depending on the species.

‡Same as seconds with reverse side of board not below No. 1 common or reverse side of cuttings sound.

§This grade also admits pieces that grade not below No. 2 common on the good face and have the reverse face sound.

‖The cuttings must be sound; clear face not required.

seconds). According to this standard, firsts must yield at least 91.6 percent material free of defects; seconds must have at least 83.3 percent clear material. The minimum allowable sizes of these boards is 6 inches in width and 8 feet in length.

Select is the term used for the next lower category. In this grouping the lumber must be at least 4 inches wide and 6 feet long. A larger number of defects is allowed and less clear material is required (Fig. 1-53).

Machine grading. Originally all grading was done visually, and it is still done in that manner for hardwoods. For softwoods intended to be used as framing material, the appearance of the material is secondary and strength is primary. Stress grading accomplishes this mechanically; the amount of deflection on the grading machine is related to the strength of the material (Fig. 1-54).

Fig. 1-54. Machine grading of lumber

Board-Foot Measure

When dealers price lumber, the price is quoted for units known as *board feet.* A board foot (bd ft) is actually a measure of volume. It is a piece of wood 1 inch thick, 12 inches wide, and 12 inches long, or its equivalent. Such a piece of material is 1/12 cubic foot (Fig. 1-55).

To calculate board feet, use either of the following formulas:

$$\frac{\text{Thickness (inches)} \times \text{width (inches)} \times \text{length (inches)}}{144} = \text{board feet}$$

$$\frac{T'' \times W'' \times L''}{144} = \text{bd ft}$$

or

$$\frac{\text{Thickness (inches)} \times \text{width (inches)} \times \text{length (feet)}}{12} = \text{board feet}$$

$$\frac{T'' \times W'' \times L'}{12} = \text{bd ft}$$

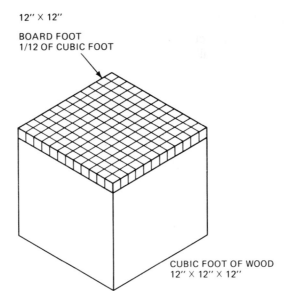

12″ × 12″

BOARD FOOT
1/12 OF CUBIC FOOT

CUBIC FOOT OF WOOD
12″ × 12″ × 12″

Fig. 1-55. A board foot of lumber

Sample Problems

How many board feet are in a piece of lumber 3/4″ × 8″ × 60″?

$$\frac{T'' \times W'' \times L''}{144} = \frac{1* \times 8 \times 60}{144} = 3.3 \text{ bd ft}$$

*Material less than 1 in. thick is considered 1 in. thick.

How many board feet are in a piece of lumber 1-1/8 in. thick, 10 in. wide, and 48 in. long?

$$\frac{T'' \times W'' \times L''}{144} = \frac{1\text{-}1/4* \times 10 \times 48}{144} = \frac{1.25 \times 10 \times 48}{144} = 4.16 \text{ bd ft}$$

*Between 1 and 2 in., thickness is computed in quarter inches. If a measurement is less than a quarter inch, it is rounded off to the next highest quarter inch.

How many board feet are in a piece of lumber 2-1/4 in. thick, 6 in. wide, and 12 ft long?

$$\frac{T'' \times W'' \times L'}{12} = \frac{2\text{-}1/2* \times 6 \times 12}{12} = 15 \text{ bd ft}$$

*Material between 2 and 3 in. thick is rounded off to the nearest half inch. Material over 3 in. thick is rounded off to the next whole inch. See page 50 for determining board feet using the Essex Scale on the framing square.

SHEET MATERIALS

Plywood

Plywood consists of layers of wood (plies) which are glued together so that the grain of each succeeding layer is at right angles to the layer below it (Fig. 1-56). The grain on the outermost layers goes in the same direction. Thus, plywood always has an odd number of plies. The principal advantages of plywood are its great strength and dimensional stability. In addition, the alternating layers limit the amount the material can expand or contract. Plywood is manufactured in large sheets (4 feet by 8 feet is standard). The standard size of the sheets makes plywood especially useful in building construction, where the framing members are commonly on 16-inch centers. A sheet of plywood 4 feet by 8 feet is a multiple of these dimensions (Fig. 1-57).

The veneer which is used to make softwood plywood is usually obtained from a fir log. One method for cutting veneers is *rotary* cutting, shown in Fig. 1-58. Plane and quarter slicing are two methods used for cutting face veneers (Fig. 1-59). After the veneer is cut and dried, it is graded, coated with adhesive, and pressurized in a press until the glue sets. The resulting plywood is then trimmed and cut to finish size.

Most of the plywood produced is softwood plywood. Hardwood plywood is available and is used extensively for cabinet work. Some of the finest plywood of this type comes from Scandinavia and is made of many thin layers of birch veneer (Fig. 1-60). Softwood plywood is available with many different hardwood face veneers glued to the surface.

Plywood types. If the plywood is glued with a water-*resistant* glue, it is known as *interior* plywood. If a *waterproof* glue is used, it is designated as *exterior* plywood.

Fig. 1-56. Plywood construction. (a) Veneer core plywood; (b) Lumber core plywood

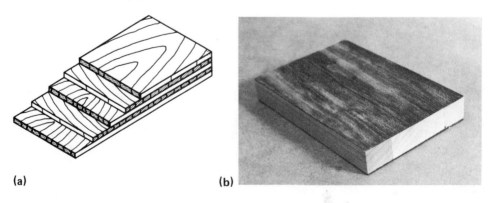

(a)   (b)

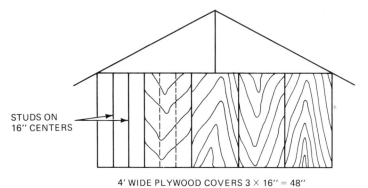

STUDS ON
16" CENTERS

4' WIDE PLYWOOD COVERS 3 × 16" = 48"

Fig. 1-57. Plywood sheathing. 4" x 8" sheets fit studs 16" on center

Fig. 1-58. Rotary cutting of veneer. (*Courtesy of Weyerhaeuser Company, Dept. of Public Affairs.*)

QUARTER SLICED   PLAIN SLICED   ROTARY

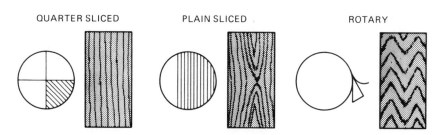

Fig. 1-59. Common methods for cutting veneer

Design and Materials   **37**

Fig. 1-60. Hardwood cabinet grade plywood

In addition to the interior-exterior designation, various grades of softwood plywood are available. The grade is determined by the quality of the face and back veneers used in its production. The letters A, B, C, and D are used to identify the quality of these face veneers. These letters, together with a third letter which indicates the type of glue used, are printed on the plywood to identify it. For example, CDX on plywood indicates that the face veneer is of C quality (A being the highest and D the lowest), the back veneer is of D quality, and the glue used makes the panel suitable for exterior applications. Hardwood plywood is graded with numbers 1 through 4, indicating the best grade and the poorest grade, respectively.

Standard sizes. The standard dimensions for plywood are 4 feet by 8 feet. Thicknesses available are 1/4, 3/8, 1/2, 5/8, and 3/4 inch. Unlike solid-wood lumber, plywood and other sheet materials are sold by the square foot.

Hardboard

This material is manufactured from waste materials. The lignin which is removed from wood during paper manufacture is the basic ingredient used. Together with waste-wood fibers, lignin is compressed under great pressure into sheets. These sheets are usually 4 feet by 8 feet in size and commonly range from 1/8 to 5/16 inch in thickness. Hardboard is dimensionally stable. Hardboard is available in standard sheets or in tempered sheets, which are harder and more resistant to moisture. Most hardboard is smooth on one side and has a rough wafflelike surface on the reverse side. The material is also manufactured with holes, drilled on 1-inch centers, which are useful for hanging tools when fitted with metal hangers manufactured for that purpose (Fig. 1-61). In addition to the common brown standard hardboard, a variety of finishes are available. Wall panels with simulated wood graining are popular in paneling operations (Fig. 1-62).

In general, hardboard is less expensive than plywood. It is widely used in furniture construction for furniture backs and drawer bottoms. The smooth surface of hardboard takes paint well, but the material is difficult to glue and

Fig. 1-61. Hard board (Peg Board) and flake board

fasten. Because hardboard is an abrasive material, carbide-tipped tools are most suitable for cutting it.

Particle or Flake Board

Particle board is manufactured from waste materials of the woodworking industry. The scrap wood from which it is made is reduced to small flakes, combined with an adhesive, and then formed into sheets under pressure. The material is available in sizes and thicknesses similar to those of plywood.

Particle board is very dense and heavy as compared to plywood. It is used extensively in the manufacture of medium- and low-priced case goods. Its greatest advantage is low cost, which is approximately one-third that of

Fig. 1-62. Hard board simulated wood paneling. (*Courtesy of Weyerhaeuser Company, Dept. of Public Affairs.*)

softwood plywood. It is difficult to fasten and does not hold screws very well. When adequate surface area is involved, glue adheres moderately well to its surface.

Most particle board is not suitable for use in wet applications; however, water-resistant material is available. Though this material can be worked with standard woodworking tools, like hardboard, it is abrasive and tends to dull cutting edges quickly. Carbide-tipped tools are most suitable.

GENERAL LUMBERING TERMS AND CLASSES

Rough lumber is material that has been rough-sawed on its faces and edges. Originally a two-by-four was actually 2 inches by 4 inches in size before planing. This size was reduced during surfacing operations. The 2-inch by 4-inch measurement was known as the *nominal* size of the material. Today, a two-by-four is less than 2 inches by 4 inches even in the rough-cut state. See Fig. 1–63 for the actual dimensions of material.

NOMINAL	ACTUAL
1 X 3	¾ X 2½
1 X 4	¾ X 3½
1 X 6	¾ X 5½
1 X 8	¾ X 7¼
1 X 10	¾ X 9¼
1 X 12	¾ X 11¼
2 X 3	1½ X 2½
2 X 4	1½ X 3½
2 X 6	1½ X 5½
2 X 8	1½ X 7¼
2 X 10	1½ X 9¼
2 X 12	1½ X 11¼

Fig. 1–63. Nominal and actual dimensions of standard lumber

Dressed lumber is material that has been made smooth by surfacing and jointing, usually in one operation. The abbreviation S4S means that the material has all four long surfaces, faces, and edges smoothed.

Worked lumber is material that has been shaped. An example would be moldings of various types (Fig. 1–52).

Matched lumber is material whose edges or ends have been machined so that they fit into one another (Fig. 1–64).

SHIPLAP   TONGUE & GROOVE   DROP SIDING

Fig. 1–64. Matched lumber

Timber is generally a piece of material whose minimum width or thickness is 5 inches.

Planks are pieces of material between 1½ and 5 inches thick.

Boards are pieces of material less than 1½ inches thick and at least 4 inches wide.

Flitch is a log which is to be processed into veneer.

SELECTING AND BUYING LUMBER

Softwood Lumber—Framing Material

Ideally, the buyer should select each piece of material personally if possible. Some of the following pointers may be used:

1. Select material that appears to be dry and free of stains. Obvious mold growth indicates that the material has been subject to wetting and should be rejected.

2. Check straightness by sighting along the edge of the piece.

3. Check for flatness. A straightedge can be used to check for conditions such as cup warp.

4. Examine the ends of the piece to see whether checking has taken place. Surface checks should also be looked for.

5. Determine the grade of the material from the seller and then estimate whether obvious defects such as knots and wanes appear to reflect the quality of the material in terms of the assigned grade.

Softwood Lumber—Trimming Material

Material suitable for interior trim work should be top grade and free of obvious defects.

1. Check the relative weight of the material. If it feels heavy, the wood may be sappy and hidden pitch pockets may exist.

2. The checks (items 2 and 3 above) for straightness and absence of warping should be used here.

3. The quality of the exposed surfaces should be examined for finishing. If a transparent finish is to be used, the surfaces should be free of all blemishes.

4. Prefinished worked lumber is available for use in trimming paneling installations. This material may be wood, finished in the usual way or it may be made up of many small pieces joined together with finger joints (Fig. 1-65) and covered with a film of vinyl with a woodlike design printed on it.

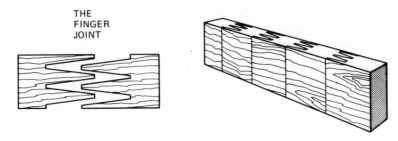

THE
FINGER
JOINT

Fig. 1-65. Finger jointed lumber

If the lumber dealer does not permit the buyer to select the material personally, or if such a selection is impractical, then a known reliable dealer should be dealt with.

Hardwood Lumber

Hardwood lumber is usually not available in local lumber yards, but generally may be purchased through hardwood or cabinet-wood dealers. If sufficient quantities are ordered, these dealers will serve retail customers. Some local lumber dealers can order hardwoods for their customers. In any case, the opportunity to personally select the material will be unlikely. Therefore, it is very important to write clear specifications for the material desired so that the lumber delivered is what the buyer wants.

A good source of suppliers may be found in the various publications that serve the craftsman. Advertisers offer catalogs and other types of information on a wide range of special items not generally available in the local lumber yard.

HANDTOOLS

Handtools were the forerunners of all power woodworking machines. The basic operating principles of many handtools have been directly translated to power tools. Although portable and stationary woodworking machinery is becoming more and more common, handtools still serve an important set of needs. For example, there are situations where a stationary machine is not suitable—such as planing a tight-fitting door. Obviously, the door would be difficult to transport to a jointer. The portable power plane might be used if available, but most carpenters would use a hand plane to complete the job. In this chapter emphasis will be placed on the common handtools. Exotic tools not commonly available will not be considered here.

LAYOUT AND MEASURING TOOLS

Measuring is at best an inexact science. All measuring involves working within acceptable limits or tolerances. In fields such as optics, lenses are polished to tolerances of millionths of an inch. In cabinetmaking, the 1/16-in. tolerance is usually acceptable. In carpentry, even the 1/8-in. tolerance is frequently acceptable. The woodworker should attempt to achieve a high level of accuracy without spending excessive amounts of time on a particular task. In many instances pieces of duplicate size are more important than pieces of a specific size. For example, it is more important for a table to have legs of equal length than legs of a specified size.

Rules

In woodworking, the common measuring device is the rule. Woodworking rules are generally calibrated in sixteenths of an inch. A variety of rules are available to the craftsman, but the easiest to use for bench work are one-piece models. These are made of wood or metal and are available in 1-ft, 2-ft, 3-ft, and 4-ft lengths.

Metal rules have the advantage of durability and thinness. These rules may be used flat (Fig. 2-1), since their thinness allows the calibrations to be close to the surface being measured. One disadvantage of metal rules is that they can damage cutting tools if they inadvertently come into contact with the cutting edges of machines or handtools.

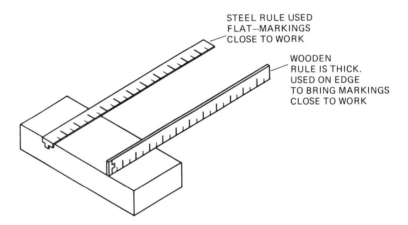

STEEL RULE USED
FLAT—MARKINGS
CLOSE TO WORK

WOODEN
RULE IS THICK.
USED ON EDGE
TO BRING MARKINGS
CLOSE TO WORK

Fig. 2-1. Steel and wooden ruler use

Wooden rules are generally made of hardwood such as maple or boxwood (Fig. 2-2). The better-quality models have metal tips to protect the ends from damage. Wooden bench rules are usually made from one piece of wood and are fairly thick (¼ in. is common). Their thickness makes them durable, but requires that the rule be placed on edge when used for measuring (Fig. 2-1). In this position the calibrations are in contact with the workpiece, and measurements are likely to be most accurate.

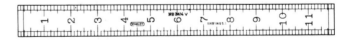

Fig. 2-2. Boxwood rule. (*Courtesy of Stanley Tools.*)

In addition to the obvious measuring function, one-piece rulers are suitable for testing surfaces for flatness (Fig. 2-3) and for straightness. Various types of folding wooden rulers, shown in Fig. 2-4, are also available.

Fig. 2-3. Testing flatness with a rule

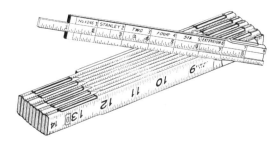

Fig. 2-4. Folding "zig-zag" rule. (*Courtesy of Stanley Tools.*)

PULL OUT
EXTENSION

Fig. 2-5. Inside measuring with folding rule

The carpenter's zigzag ruler, when equipped with an extendable section (Fig. 2-5), is very useful for internal measurements, depth measurements, and for transferring measurements from one place to another. Six- and 8-ft models are available.

Tapes are the most compact form of rule. Their flexibility sometimes reduces their accuracy in measuring straight surfaces, but it also makes measuring curved surfaces possible (Fig. 2-6).

Inasmuch as rules are testing tools, they should be handled with care to maintain their straight surfaces.

Fig. 2-6. Steel tape. (*Courtesy of Stanley Tools.*)

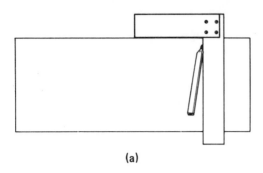

(a)

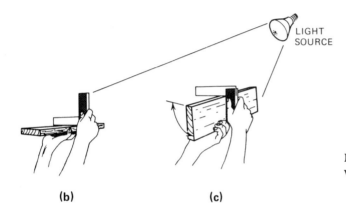

LIGHT
SOURCE

(b)   (c)

Fig. 2-7. Laying out line square to edge
with try square

Squares

Try square. The try square is used to test surfaces to determine whether
or not they are at right angles to each other, to lay out lines at right angles
to surfaces, and to test surfaces for straightness and squareness [Fig. 2-7].
When used for testing squareness, the try square should be held as shown in
Fig. 2-7(c). Note that the piece being tested is held up to a source of light.
When the try square is used for layout, the inside edge of the blade should be
used. The use of this surface helps to prevent the try-square handle from
moving away from the reference edge [Fig. 2-7 (a)]. One hand keeps the
handle against the reference surface, and the other hand holds the marking
implement.

Combination square. The combination square is really several tools in
one. It is a try square with an adjustable blade length; a miter square [Fig.
2-8(a)]; a level [Fig. 2-8(b)]; a plumb tester [Fig. 2-8(c)]; a depth gauge
[Fig. 2-8(d)]; and a marking gauge [Fig. 2-8(e)]. With a divider-head accessory attached, it can be used to locate the center of circles and round
pieces [Fig. 2-8(f)]. With the rule detached from the head, it is a rule and a
straight edge.

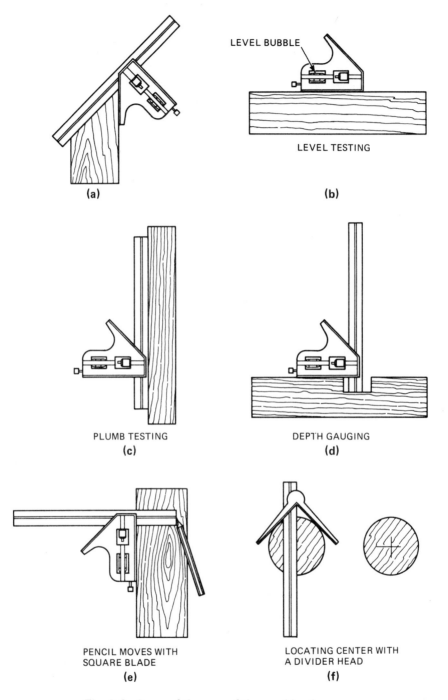

(a)

LEVEL BUBBLE

LEVEL TESTING

(b)

PLUMB TESTING
(c)

DEPTH GAUGING
(d)

PENCIL MOVES WITH
SQUARE BLADE
(e)

LOCATING CENTER WITH
A DIVIDER HEAD
(f)

Fig. 2-8. Some of the uses of the combination square

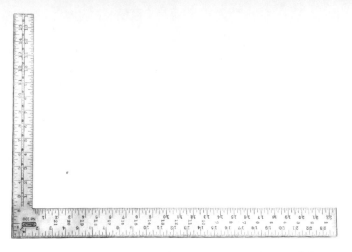

Fig. 2–9. Framing square. (*Courtesy of Stanley Tools.*)

Framing square. The framing square is made from a single piece of metal. It consists of a tongue and blade which are at right angles to each other. The tongue is generally 1½ in. wide and 18 in. long. The blade is 24 in. long and 2 in. wide. The inside and outside corners are known as the *heel* (Fig. 2–9). The broad surface of the square, which has the manufacturer's name on it, is known as the *face*. The reverse face is the *back*.

The edges of the framing square are calibrated in inches. The face has 1/16-in. graduations on its outside edges and 1/8-in. graduations on the inside edges. The back of the tongue is calibrated in twelfths on the outside edge and tenths on the inside edge. The back of the blade has twelfths on the outside edge and sixteenths on the inside edge. On the back of the tongue, in the corner of the framing square, is a scale for hundredths of an inch (Fig. 2–10).

The framing square also has tables imprinted on its face and back. In the middle of the tongue face is the octagon table. On the back of the blade is the Essex board measure. The brace measure table is on the back of the tongue. The use of these tables is described below. Rafter tables are described in Chapter 9.

Fig. 2–10. 1/100's scale on framing square

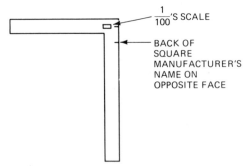

Laying out an octagon using the octagon table. It is sometimes necessary to reduce a piece of lumber that is square in cross-section to an octagon. This may be done using the framing square octagon table, which consists of a row of dots starting under the 2-in. graduation and going almost to the end of the tongue (Fig. 2–11). A total of 65 dots appear, with every fifth dot replaced by a number with a vertical bar between the digits, like 1│0. Each bar replaces a dot and is counted as a dot.

In Fig. 2–12, a square which measures 5 in. on a side is illustrated.

1. Draw diagonals to locate the center of the square: AB and A′B′.
2. Draw a horizontal line CD through the meeting point of the diagonals and a vertical line C′D′ through the meeting point of the diagonals.

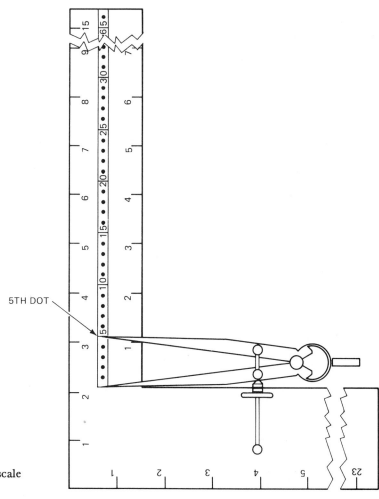

5TH DOT

Fig. 2–11. Octagon scale framing square

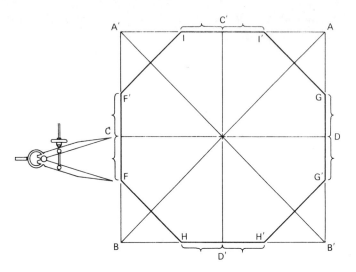

Fig. 2-12. Laying out an octagon

3. Set one leg of a pair of dividers on the first dot of the octagon table (under the 2-in. mark; see Fig. 2-11).

4. Set the other leg of the dividers on the fifth dot of the octagon table. If the square being used were 10 inches on a side, the tenth dot would be used, and so on.

5. Place one leg of the dividers at point C and lay out a space above and below C as shown: F and F'. Repeat this step at point D opposite C, G, and G' (Fig. 2-12).

6. At points C' and D' use the same divider setting to lay out equal spaces on each side of these points: H and H' and I and I'. Now connect H and F, F' and I, I' and G, and G' and H', as shown, and the octagon is complete.

Determining board feet in a piece of lumber using the Essex board measure. A board foot is a piece of wood 1 in. thick, 12 in. wide, and 12 in. long. In buying lumber, the quantity is determined in board feet.

Assume that you have a piece of wood 1 in. thick, 8 in. wide, and 13 ft long.

1. Find the column of numbers under the 12-in. mark on the upper edge of the framing square (Fig. 2-13).

2. Travel down the row of numbers until you reach the number which equals the length of the board you are working with (in this case 13).

3. Travel horizontally to the left until you reach the column of numbers under the 8-in. mark on the upper edge of the square (Fig. 2-13). Eight inches equals the width of the board.

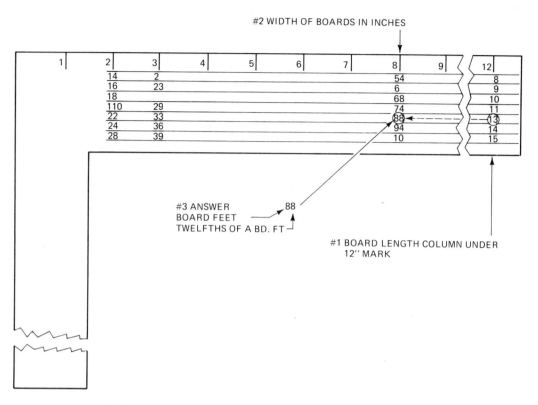

Fig. 2-13. Essex board measure table on the framing square

4. At this point the number 88 is seen; therefore, the number of board feet in this piece is 8-8/12. The right-hand number of the two gives full feet and the left gives twelfths of a foot.

If the board were 2 in. thick instead of 1 in., as in this example, the answer would be doubled. If the board were more than 12 in. wide, you would move to the right in step 2 until the appropriate number was found. Since the largest number in the column under the 12-in. mark is 15, that is the longest piece which can be found in a single step. If a piece 25 ft long were being considered, it would be dealt with as though it were a piece 10 ft long plus a piece 15 ft long.

Brace measure table. The brace measure table on the back of the framing square tongue is used to find the length of a 45° brace running between two members set at a 90° angle to each other [Fig. 2-14(A)]. The information in the table is given in the following form:

$$\frac{24}{24}33\frac{94}{}$$

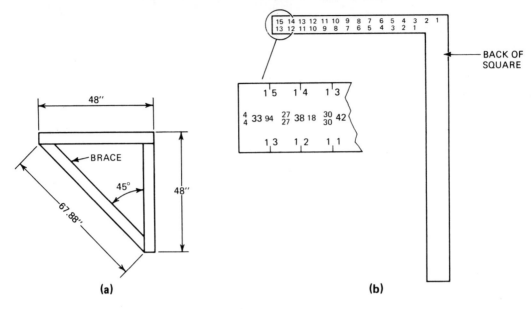

Fig. 2-14. (A) Brace table use; (B) Brace table on framing square

The 24s represent the length of the components (a and b) at right angles to each other being braced. The $33\frac{94}{}$ is read 33.94 and is the length of the brace. In all, 14 sets of braces and components are given in the table. Thirteen have the components equal in length and one has components of 18 and 24 [Fig. 2-14(B)].

The following procedure may be used to determine the length of a brace from the table on the framing square:

1. Determine the length of the vertical and horizontal components to be braced.
2. Find the matching numbers on the back of the framing-square tongue.

(*Note:* If the numbers do not appear in the table, a different method must be used to determine the brace length.)

For example, if the pieces are to be braced at a distance of 48 in. from where they intersect, find the following number in the table under the 8½-in. mark on the upper edge of the square: $\frac{48}{48}67\frac{88}{}$. The 48s represent the distances from the ends of the two components at right angles to the brace (Fig. 2-14A). The length of the brace along its longer outer edge is 67.88 in.

Sliding T Bevel or Bevel Square

The bevel square is composed of a slotted steel blade 6 to 12 in. long, with one end rounded and the other end cut to a 45° angle, and a handle

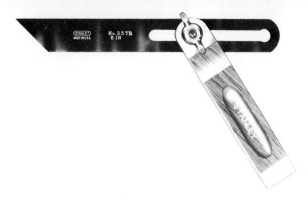

Fig. 2–15. "T" bevel. (*Courtesy of Stanley Tools.*)

(Fig. 2–15). The two parts are fastened together by a thumbscrew or by a pivot screw with a thumbscrew located at the end of the handle. The blade and handle can be set at any angle, and this feature is commonly used to transfer angles. Another common use of the bevel square is to test bevels and chamfers, especially when they are at angles other than 45°.

Dividers and Trammel Points

Dividers consist of two pointed steel legs pivoted at one end and fitted with a locking device to hold the legs apart at a predetermined angle. Dividers are used primarily to transfer measurements. They can also be used as a compass to scribe arcs and circles (Fig. 2–16). For oversized applications beyond the capacity of dividers, trammel points can be used (Fig. 2–17).

Fig. 2–16. Dividers. (*Courtesy of Stanley Tools.*)

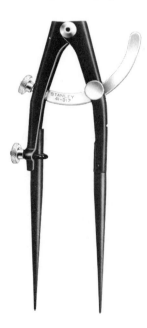

Fig. 2-17. Trammel points on wooden beam. (*Courtesy of Stanley Tools.*)

Level

The carpenter's level consists of a wooden or metal block 12 to 30 in. or more in length, with one or more true surfaces (Fig. 2-18). Two bubble tubes in the device indicate when it is in a level or plumb position. One is set parallel to the long true edge and is used in leveling; the other is set at right angles to the long true edge and is used in plumbing (Fig. 2-19). The level is used to check surfaces for levelness or plumbness or to position pieces in the level or plumb position while they are fastened.

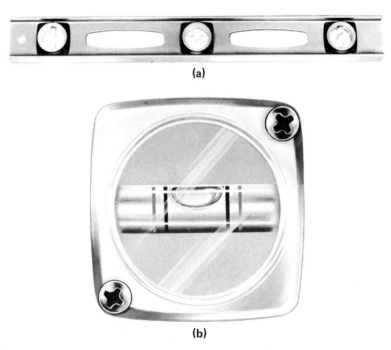

(a)

(b)

Fig. 2-18. Carpenter's level and level vial closeup. (*Courtesy of Stanley Tools.*)

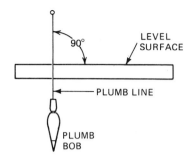

Fig. 2-19. A plumb line is at a 90° angle to a level surface

Plumb Bob

The plumb bob consists of a weighted string. The weight is pointed and is used to check the plumbness of vertical surfaces or to locate a point above or below another point (Fig. 2-20).

Fig. 2-20. Plumb bob. (*Courtesy of Stanley Tools.*)

Marking Gauge

The marking gauge is a metal or wooden device used to lay out lines parallel to edges. It consists of a graduated beam which slides through a hole in the second part of the device, the head. The head can be fastened to the beam by means of a thumbscrew (Fig. 2-21). The marking is accomplished by a metal spur, which is fitted into a hole at the end of the beam.

Fig. 2-21. Marking gauge. (*Courtesy of Stanley Tools.*)

In use, the spur is set about 1/16 in. out from the beam edge (Fig. 2-22). To use the marking gauge:

1. Set the face of the head and the spur at the desired distance. To make small adjustments, set the thumbscrew snugly (not tight) and then lightly tap the end of the beam on a hard surface to increase the distance between the head and spur. By tapping the spur end of the beam, you can reduce the distance between the head and spur. When the desired setting is obtained, tighten the thumbscrew.

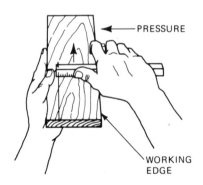

Fig. 2-22. Using marking gauge

2. Place the face of the head against the edge which is to serve as the reference surface.
3. Place the spur on the face of the workpiece, with the spur tilted toward you.
4. Place your thumb behind the spur and hold the head with the other four fingers (Fig. 2-22).
5. While keeping pressure between the head and the reference edge, *push the marking gauge away* from you. If the spur tends to follow the grain of the workpiece, adjust it so that less of the spur is exposed.

Calipers

Outside calipers (Fig. 2-23) are used to test the diameters of round objects. They are especially useful in lathe work to establish critical or key diameters when turning spindles. Inside calipers (Fig. 2-24) are used to test the diameters of holes or other internal surfaces where a rule cannot easily be used.

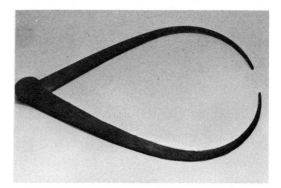

Fig. 2-23. Outside calipers

Fig. 2-24. Inside calipers

Contour Gauge

The contour gauge consists of a series of thin, flat metal reeds which fit snugly in a beam that keeps them pressed together in position. When the reeds are pressed against a surface, they adjust to the irregularities of that surface and duplicate its shape. The contour gauge is useful for transferring shapes (Fig. 2-25).

Fig. 2-25. Contour gauge

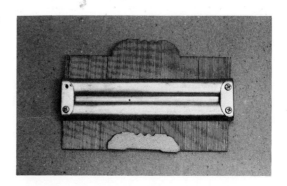

CUTTING TOOLS

Wedge

The wedge was one of the first tools discovered by man. Its edge functions only for an instant to start a split. Then the sides of the wedge continue to force the two portions of the wood apart (Fig. 2–26). In a true cutting operation, the cutting edge is in continuous contact with the material being cut. For this to happen, the material being cut away must be pliable enough to bend away from the surface of the cutter so that splitting does not occur (Fig. 2–27).

In general, as the angle between the sides of the cutting edge decreases, the amount of force required to make the cut is reduced. In practice, this angle must be limited because if it becomes too small, the edge will be easily damaged and may break (nick). Another factor affecting the smallness of this angle is the hardness of the material being cut (Fig. 2–28).

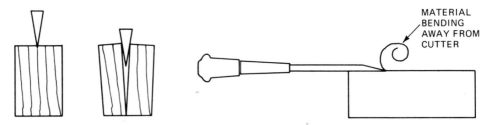

Fig. 2-26. Wedging action   Fig. 2-27. Cutting action

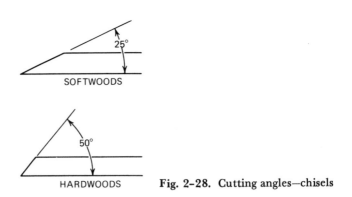

Fig. 2-28. Cutting angles—chisels

Knife

The knife is commonly used as a layout tool in woodworking. A cut line is more precise than one drawn with a pencil. Another advantage of the knife line is that it limits surface splitting which might be caused as a saw starts to cut or a chisel begins to remove material next to it (Fig. 2–29).

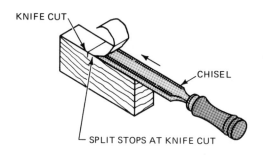

Fig. 2-29. Knife cut limits splitting

Fig. 2-30. "Slim-knife" disposable blade. (*Courtesy of Stanley Tools.*)

Short-bladed knives are useful for making layouts. Knives with disposable blades are also usable and available at relatively low cost (Fig. 2-30).

Chisels

The chisel consists of two basic parts, the handle and the blade. Chisels that are designed for use with a mallet usually have a handle that fits into a socket at the end of the chisel blade (Fig. 2-31). A second type of handle design utilizes a hole in the handle into which the tang, or pointed end of the chisel, fits. A metal ferrule fits around the end of the handle to help prevent splitting and to keep the chisel and handle together (Fig. 2-31). Chisels with plastic handles can be used with a mallet even though they are not of the socket variety.

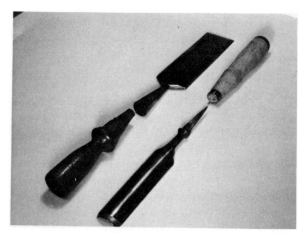

Fig. 2-31. (Left) Socket chisel; (Right) Tang in handle chisel

Fig. 2-32. Firmer chisel. (*Courtesy of Greenlee Tool Company.*)

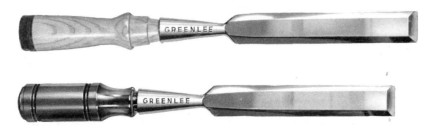

Fig. 2-33. Paring chisel. (*Courtesy of Greenlee Tool Company.*)

Fig. 2-34. Gouge. (*Courtesy of Greenlee Tool Company.*)

Chisel blades vary from 1/16 to 2 in. in width. The back of the chisel is kept absolutely flat, and the face has a bevel ground on its end.

Firmer chisel. The firmer chisel has a flat, relatively thick blade and is an all-purpose utility cutting tool (Fig. 2-32). Its name is said to have come from the fact that it is stiffer than the paring chisel.

Paring chisel. The paring chisel has a fairly long, thin blade which is chamfered along its edges to allow access to the work site when cutting rabbets and mortises (Fig. 2-33).

Gouge. A gouge is a curved chisel usually ground on its convex face (Fig. 2-34). It is used to cut round-bottomed grooves and to hollow-out objects, as in shaping the interior of a bowl.

General Safety Rules for the Chisel

1. Always keep both hands on the chisel. This will prevent you from cutting one hand while using it to hold the workpiece.
2. Always use a sharp chisel.
3. Clamp the workpiece securely before attempting to chisel it.
4. Never chisel toward any part of the body.
5. When not in use, keep the chisel well inside the work bench to prevent its rolling off the bench onto the floor or onto someone's foot.
6. Never use a chisel without a handle or with a broken handle that is likely to split and expose the tang.

Using the Chisel

The chisel is powered either by a mallet or by hand pressure. Hand pressure is the method which gives the craftsman the most control over the tool and should be used wherever a high degree of precision is required. The mallet is useful when roughing out a bowl or a mortise or when cutting very dense woods like maple.

Paring. When the chisel is used to cut with the grain, as along an edge, the operation is called *paring*. Maximum control in this type of cutting is obtained by using the chisel with the bevel held down against the work surface (Fig. 2-35). This position helps to prevent the chisel from cutting too deeply into the wood. For light precision cutting, as in joinery, the chisel is used flat face down (Fig. 2-36). In this position the chisel can be made to cut in a straight path, with the sides of the chisel parallel to the

Fig. 2-35. Using chisel with its bevel down

Fig. 2-36. Using chisel bevel up with wooden gauge guiding cut

Fig. 2-37. Chiseling across the grain

sides of the workpiece. It can also be used in a sliding cut with the chisel sides set at an angle to the sides of the workpiece (Fig. 2-36). In the sliding cut, a shearing action develops which makes cutting easier. The use of flat pieces of wood as gauges and guide surfaces (Fig. 2-36) helps in controlling the chisel. Vise lining blocks can also be used for this purpose.

Cross-grain chiseling. When chiseling across the grain, as in dado cutting, it is good practice to cut lines on either side of the area to be cut with a knife (Fig. 2-37).

Chiseling end grain. Chiseling end grain should be avoided when possible, because other tools such as the plane can often be used to accomplish this kind of cutting more efficiently. However, in certain operations like mortising or cutting an end rabbet, it must be done.

If possible, a shearing cut should be used when cutting end grain. This type of cutting will result in a smoother surface than can be obtained with a straight cut. If the chisel is held in the vertical position, as shown in Fig. 2-38, and the handle is rocked from side to side as downward pressure is applied, a smooth cut will result. In chiseling the ends of mortises, such a sliding cut is often impossible.

Fig. 2-38. Vertical chiseling of end grain

Saws

In effect, saws consist of a row of teeth which are chisellike in shape and in cutting action. In most cultures, saws were developed which utilized thin blades that were kept stiff by the action of a frame (Fig. 2-52). In most Western countries saws evolved that cut in compression. The stiffness of the blade was maintained by the blade width and thickness. The greatest advantage of this type of saw is the absence of a frame to interfere with the cutting action of the blade.

Handsaws (Fig. 2-39) consist of a blade and a handle. The toe of the blade is located at the front of the saw and is thinner than the heel, which is located under the handle. The blade thickness around the teeth is greater

Fig. 2-39. Handsaw. (*Courtesy of Stanley Tools.*)

than the blade thickness along the back. The toe is narrower than the blade at the heel. These tapers make the saw more rigid. In general, 24 or 26 inches is a typical length for handsaws. The fineness of cut is determined by the number of tooth points per inch. There is one more point per inch than teeth per inch (Fig. 2-40). Five to six points per inch is common for ripsaws, and seven to eight points is common for crosscut saws.

Crosscut saws. Crosscut saws have teeth that are shaped roughly like the bottom half of the letter X [Fig. 2-4(a) and (b)]. The teeth are bent alternately to the right and left. This sawtooth *set* causes the teeth to cut a *kerf*

Fig. 2-40. Saw points per inch. Ten points per inch—9 whole teeth per inch

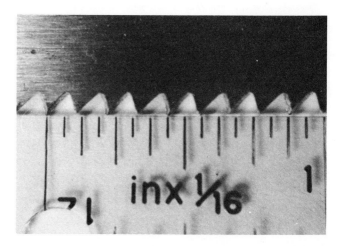

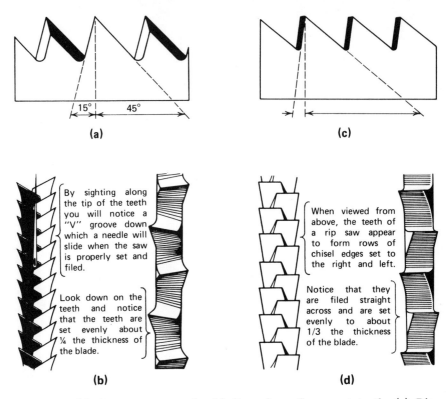

By sighting along the tip of the teeth you will notice a "V" groove down which a needle will slide when the saw is properly set and filed.

Look down on the teeth and notice that the teeth are set evenly about ¼ the thickness of the blade.

When viewed from above, the teeth of a rip saw appear to form rows of chisel edges set to the right and left.

Notice that they are filed straight across and are set evenly to about 1/3 the thickness of the blade.

15°   45°

(a)

(c)

(b)

(d)

Fig. 2-41. (a) Crosscut saw teeth; (b) Top view of crosscut teeth; (c) Ripsaw teeth; (d) Top view of ripsaw teeth

that is wider than the saw blade; thus the blade tends to bind less in the cut. As the crosscut saw teeth begin to cut, the knifelike points cut into the surface of the wood; as the teeth cut more deeply, the slanting cutting edges scoop out the wood between the knife cuts [Fig. 2-42(a) and (b)].

Using the Crosscut Saw

1. Lay out the line to be cut across the grain. Use a try square if the cut is to be at right angles to the edge of the workpiece.

2. Secure the workpiece in a vise or on sawhorses, with the layout line on the face of the workpiece facing up (Fig. 2-43). Position yourself so that your right shoulder is aligned with the layout line (Fig. 2-43).

3. Place the thumb of your left hand next to the layout line and place the saw blade against this thumb. Adjust the position of your thumb until the saw blade is on the layout line.

4. *Pull* the saw upward while applying downward pressure on the blade. This will make a starting notch in the workpiece.

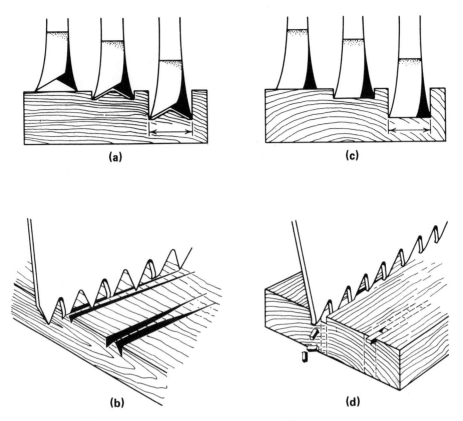

Fig. 2–42. (a) Cross section of crosscut teeth; (b) How a crosscut saw cuts; (c) Cross section of rip teeth; (d) How a ripsaw cuts

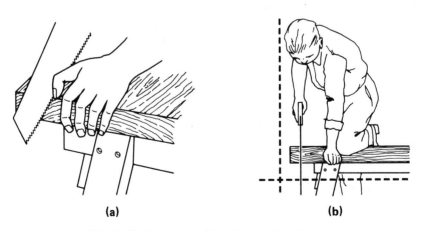

Fig. 2–43. Proper position for starting the cut

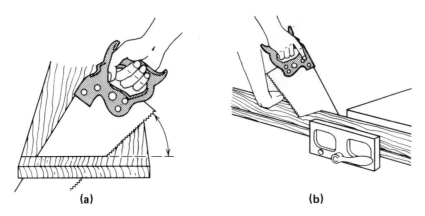

Fig. 2-44. (a) Cross cutting; (b) Cross cutting vise held work

5. *Remove your thumb* from the workpiece and begin sawing. If the saw binds or buckles, stop pushing, pull the saw back 2 or 3 in., and resume pushing (Fig. 2-44). If the saw cut begins to stray away from the line, bend the saw slightly in the direction you want it to go as you continue sawing. Complete the saw cut without starting a new cut from the other edge of the piece.

6. As the saw approaches within about an inch of the end of the cut, use your other hand to support the portion of the workpiece to be cut off. Slow the sawing rate and shorten the stroke. Complete the cut.

Ripsaws. Ripsaws have teeth that are shaped like the bottom of the letter R [Fig. 2-41(c) and (d)]. Their cutting edges act like a row of chisels during cutting [Fig. 2-42(c) and (d)]. Ripsaws have set teeth which cut a kerf that is wider than the saw blade and therefore reduces binding. More effort is required to rip with the crosscut saw than with the ripsaw. Ripsaws produce a very rough and ragged cut when used to cut across the grain and should not be used for this purpose.

Using Ripsaws

1. Lay out the line to be cut approximately parallel to the grain of the workpiece.

2. Secure the workpiece using one of the methods shown in (Fig. 2-45).

3. Saw the workpiece according to steps 2 through 6 above for the cross-cut saw (Fig. 2-45).

In long ripping cuts, it is advisable to insert a wedge in the saw kerf to reduce the tendency of the saw kerf to close and bind on the saw blade. In oblique ripping the saw cut should begin at the narrow end of the scrap piece (Fig. 2-46). In the event of splitting before the cut is complete, the split will then be in the scrap piece rather than in the workpiece.

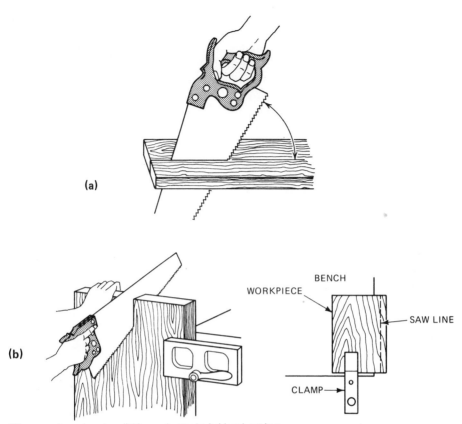

(a)

(b)

BENCH

WORKPIECE

SAW LINE

CLAMP

When a sawhorse is not available, work may be held and cut in a bench vise as illustrated. Note that the work should always be flat in the vise. If placed on edge, the cut cannot be made at a proper angle and cutting will be difficult.

Fig. 2-45. (a) Ripping; (b) Ripping vise held work

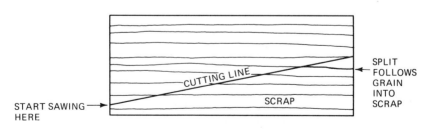

CUTTING LINE

SPLIT FOLLOWS GRAIN INTO SCRAP

SCRAP

START SAWING HERE

Fig. 2-46. Oblique ripping

Handtools **67**

Backsaw. The backsaw is a thin-bladed crosscut saw with a rectangular shape and a reinforced back. The reinforced back keeps the thin blade stiff. The thinness of the blade, together with its small teeth, enables this saw to produce a very fine and smooth cut with a small kerf. Backsaws generally have 12 to 15 points per inch and range in length from 12 to 30 in. The larger saws are used as miter saws in miter boxes. The smaller versions are used for fine cutting as in joinery. In general, the 12-in. backsaw can efficiently cut material up to about 3 in. in width and about 2 in. in thickness. If larger material is cut, the reinforced back will interfere with cutting [Fig. 2-47(b)].

Since this saw, like the dovetail saw described below, is used for precision work, the following suggestions will be helpful:

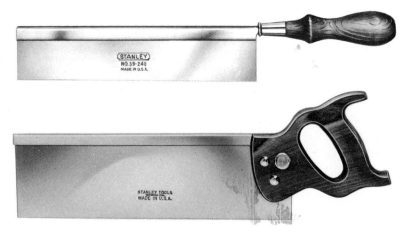

Fig. 2-47. (a) Dovetail saw; (b) Backsaw. (*Courtesy of Stanley Tools.*)

1. Make a starting notch for crosscuts by scoring a line across the grain with a knife drawn against a try square [Fig. 2-48(a)]. Chisel away material along the knife cut, working from the scrap side of the line [Fig. 2-48(b)]. This produces a notch for the saw to fit into.

2. When cutting with the backsaw in situations where a square cut is required (e.g., in dadoing or rabbeting), a guide block clamped to the surface of the workpiece is useful (Fig. 2-49).

3. Workpieces can be held in a vise or against a bench hook block (Fig. 2-50).

4. The angle between the saw and the surface of the work is 15°.

Dovetail saw. The dovetail saw is similar to the backsaw except that it is smaller and has a chisel-type handle. A typical dovetail saw is 10 in. long and 2 in. wide, with 16 points per inch. Its use is similar to that described for the backsaw [Fig. 2-47(a)].

Fig. 2-48. (a) Starting notch knife cut; (b) Starting notch chisel cut

Fig. 2-49. Block guiding saw during shoulder cutter of tenon

(a)

(b)

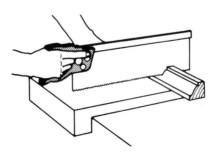

Fig. 2-50. Using saw with bench hook

Keyhole and compass saws. The keyhole and compass saws (Fig. 2-51) are designed for curved cutting. Blades for this type of saw are thick and pointed; they have wide-set teeth and range in size from about 10 to 16 in.

Coping saw or jigsaw. The coping saw is a narrow-bladed saw designed for curved cutting. The thin, flexible blade is kept rigid in a spring steel frame, which is put in tension by a threaded rod in the handle of the saw (Fig. 2-52). The blade has pins on it which fit into slots at the top of the frame and in the handle rod. Blades of various thicknesses and points per inch are available for use with the coping saw. A typical coping-saw blade is 6 1/2 in. long, 0.020 in. thick, 0.110 in. wide, and has between 10 (coarse) and 20 (fine) teeth per inch.

Blades can be installed with the teeth pointing toward or away from the handle. To install a blade in a coping saw, proceed as follows:

1. Unscrew the handle from the threaded chuck as far as possible without causing the handle to come free of the chuck.
2. If the saw is to be used on work held in a horizontal position, install the blade with its teeth pointing toward the handle. This will place the blade in tension when the saw is pulled down during vertical cutting of a horizontal piece. If this work is to be cut while in the vertical position, place the blade

Fig. 2-51. Compass saw. (*Courtesy of Stanley Tools.*)

Fig. 2-52. Coping saw. (*Courtesy of Stanley Tools.*)

Fig. 2-53. Blade pins in upper chuck of coping saw

in the frame with the teeth pointing away from the handle. Place the blade pin in the chuck at the top of the frame (Fig. 2-53).

3. Compress the frame until the lower end of the blade can be set into the lower chuck. Release the tension after installing the blade pin in the lower chuck.

4. Tighten the handle by holding the lower chuck pin with one hand while tightening the handle with the other.

Using the Coping Saw

1. Clamp the workpiece to a horizontal surface after laying out the line to be cut. Small workpieces can be held in position on a saddle (Fig. 2-54).

2. Squat down next to the workpiece and place the saw blade against the workpiece and in line with the layout line. Start the cut by pulling the saw down.

Fig. 2-54. Sawing on a saddle

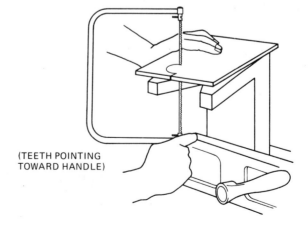

(TEETH POINTING TOWARD HANDLE)

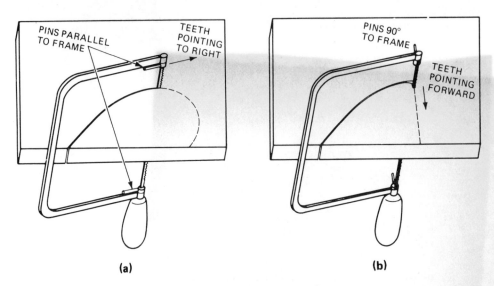

Fig. 2-55. Turning coping saw frame

3. Continue sawing by moving the saw up and down vertically. Keep both hands on the handle of the saw. *Do not place one hand at the frame top while sawing* because the saw blade may break and puncture your hand. While sawing, keep the blade in *vertical* motion at all times, especially while turning. If the saw binds, stop sawing and rotate the saw to the right or left until it frees itself; then resume sawing. Keep the saw vertical. Tilting it will result in an unsquare cut edge. Do not push the saw forward with excessive pressure or the blade will break. Be careful not to touch the blade while sawing, since friction causes the blade to become quite hot.

Cuts of very small radius can be made by stopping all forward movement of the blade while continuing the up and down motion as the saw is slowly rotated around its vertical axis. Internal cuts can be made by boring a hole inside the area to be cut out and then passing the blade through the hole and reinstalling it in the saw frame. The frame can be turned relative to the blade to accommodate cutting situations where the frame might interfere with cutting (Fig. 2-55).

Planes

The plane is basically a device for holding a chisellike blade at an angle to the workpiece as it shaves away a thin layer of material. Early planes were nothing more than a block of wood with a plane blade protruding through a rectangular hole in the bottom of the block. The blade was held in position by a wedge (Fig. 2-56).

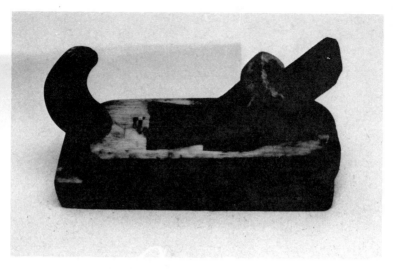

Fig. 2-56. Wooden plane

The modern iron plane consists of a machined metal casting which makes up the base, or sole, of the plane. The sides of the base are ground at right angles to the sole. The sole has a rectangular hole in it through which the plane blade protrudes. This is called the *throat* or *mouth* of the plane. The plane blade, or iron, rests on an inclined surface called the *frog.* The frog is attached to the plane base with screws and in many cases is adjustable forward and backward with respect to the throat.

The lateral position of the plane blade is adjusted by means of the lateral adjusting lever (Fig. 2-57). The blade is raised and lowered by means of an

Fig. 2-57. Metal plane. (*Courtesy of Stanley Tools.*)

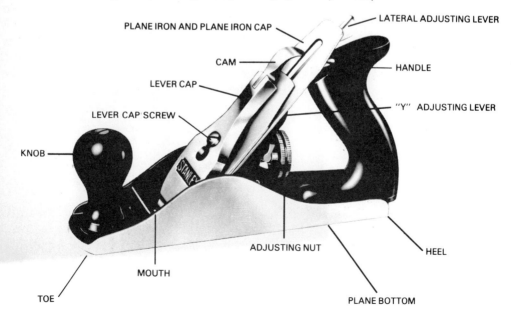

adjusting nut and "Y" adjusting lever, which protrudes up into a rectangular hole in the middle of the plane blade cap. The plane blade is clamped down to the frog by the action of a lever cap and the cap iron screw, which is threaded into the frog. A plane iron cap is attached to the plane blade and serves to stiffen it and to limit breaking caused by any splitting ahead of the plane blade. The "Y" adjusting lever fits into a rectangular hole in this cap. A wooden knob located over the toe of the plane is grasped with one hand while the other hand grasps a curved wooden handle located over the heel of the plane.

Planes are used for smoothing and straightening surfaces and for squaring surfaces to other surfaces. The most common use of the plane by the carpenter is to remove a small amount of material in a fitting operation such as installing a door. Most squaring operations are done on stationary or portable machines. However, when such equipment is not available or when its use is not practical, the plane becomes a valuable asset.

The basic plane is available in a variety of lengths. In general, a longer plane should be used to plane long surfaces (Fig. 2–58).

Fig. 2–58.

Block plane. A typical block plane is about 6 in. long and has a blade 1-3/8 in. wide (Fig. 2–59). The tool is designed to be used on small pieces (short surfaces such as ends) and to shape curved work. The block plane is used with one hand, and the blade is set at an angle of about 20° to the sole

Fig. 2–59. Block plane. (*Courtesy of Stanley Tools.*)

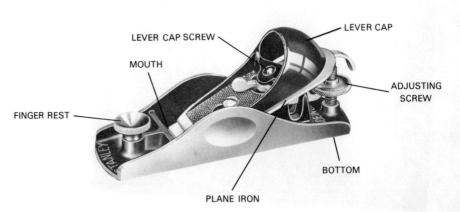

LEVER CAP SCREW

LEVER CAP

MOUTH

ADJUSTING SCREW

FINGER REST

BOTTOM

PLANE IRON

of the plane to make the plane easy to hold. This low angle makes it necessary to have the bevel up. In this position the angle between the wood and cutter is about the same as it is for other planes. The block plane is useful for squaring ends, using a bench hook to hold the workpiece (Fig. 3–11). In this position the bench hook becomes a shooting board. The machined 90° angle between the plane cheek and sole is utilized. In addition, if the end of the workpiece is kept close to the edge of the bench hook, splitting of the end will not take place.

Smooth plane. The smooth plane is typically 9 in. long, with a blade 1-3/4 in. wide. The unusual shape of the heel of the smooth plane makes it easy to recognize (Fig. 2–57). The smooth plane is used to plane short surfaces and is preferable to the block plane for that purpose when both hands can be used. Its name comes from its original purpose: smoothing a surface that was planed by a jack plane with a rounded plane iron. The crowned blade on the jack plane was used to facilitate rapid removal of material (Fig. 2–60). However, the surface produced, although straight, was concave (Fig. 2–61). The smooth plane was used to remove the high spots.

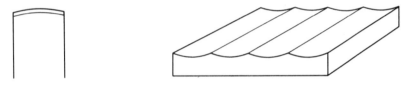

Fig. 2-60. Crowned plane iron   **Fig. 2-61.** Concave surface

Jack plane. The jack plane is an all-purpose tool which measures approximately 14 in. in length and has a blade 2 in. wide. This plane is the first choice of carpenters because of its versatility. A smaller version of this plane was designed for school use and is called the *junior jack*. It is about 11-1/2 in. long and has a blade 1-3/4 or 2 in. wide (Fig. 2–62).

Fig. 2-62. Jack plane. (*Courtesy of Stanley Tools.*)

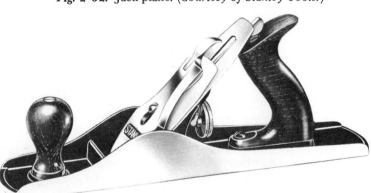

Fore plane. The fore plane is similar to the jack plane though larger in size. Typically, it is 18 in. long, with a blade about 2 in. wide. This plane is used for straightening longer workpieces.

Jointer plane. The jointer plane is at least 22 in. long, with a blade about 2-3/8 in. wide. This plane is used for straightening long surfaces. It is especially useful for large objects which cannot be easily brought to a powered machine like the jointer.

Adjusting and Using the Plane

The adjustment of the plane as described below applies to all of the planes discussed except the block plane.

1. Check the assembly of the plane and be sure that the bevel on the plane blade is facing down. The cap is set approximately 1/16 in. in from the edge of the blade, and the "Y" adjusting lever is seated in the slot of the cap. Check the tightness of the lever cap. It should resist moderate lateral pressure (side to side) applied with the hand. The pressure developed by the lever cap can be adjusted: turn the cap iron screw in to increase the pressure, or out to reduce the pressure. This adjustment is made with the lever cap removed.

2. Turn the adjusting nut until the cutting edge of the plane iron is visible as a black line above the sole when you sight along the sole (Fig. 2-63).

3. Using the lateral adjusting lever, adjust the blade until both corners of the blade are the same distance above the sole (Fig. 2-63).

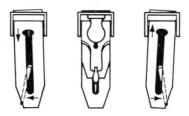

Fig. 2-63. Lateral adjustment of plane iron

4. Turn the adjusting nut to bring the blade back into the throat so that it will not cut.

5. Determine the grain direction of the surface to be planed (Fig. 2-64).

6. Place the sole of the plane down on the surface. With one hand on the knob, apply downward pressure to the toe of the plane. Hold the plane with its cheeks in line with the workpiece, and push the plane forward with the other hand on the plane handle. As the heel of the plane moves over the end of the workpiece, apply downward pressure to the handle, over the heel of

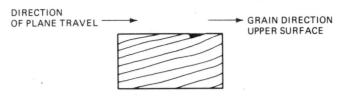

Fig. 2-64. Planing with the grain

the plane. When the toe of the plane moves past the forward end of the workpiece, stop downward pressure at the knob but continue to push the plane forward (Fig. 2-65).

7. At the end of the cut, lift the plane off the workpiece and repeat step 6. This time turn the adjusting nut clockwise a half-turn before pushing the plane across the workpiece surface. Repeat step 7 until the plane begins to cut; then turn the adjusting nut one more half-turn clockwise and leave it set at this position.

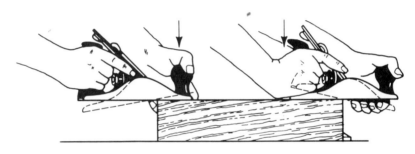

Fig. 2-65.

The procedure described in steps 6 and 7 is designed to overcome the most common error made by inexperienced woodworkers using the plane: not applying enough pressure during planing and adjusting the blade until it is out too far. When this happens, the plane gets clogged and is difficult to push. Pressure applied downward, first on the knob and then on the handle, prevents rounding of the surface being planed (Fig. 2-66). If this procedure is followed and practiced, the result will be very thin shavings and a very controlled removal of material from the surface.

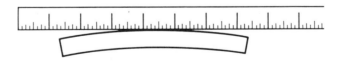

Fig. 2-66. Testing flatness with a rule

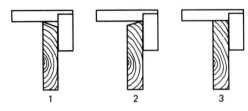

The drawing above shows a Try Square with its handle on a working face and its blade on an edge which we are trying to make square to the working face.

In #1 a high area is seen at the left. The plane must be held so that that area will be planed away.

In #2 a high area is shown at the right. That must be planed away.

In #3 no light is seen the edge is SQUARE TO THE WORKING FACE. No more planing is needed.

Fig. 2-67. Try square testing square surface

8. After *two* or *three* cuts have been made, remove the workpiece from the vise and check for squareness with the try square (Fig. 2-67). If the fit is not perfect, then a high area has developed (Fig. 2-67). Mark the high area with a pencil line. Place the workpiece back in the vise and plane the high area indicated by the pencil line by tilting the plane in the direction of the line slightly.

9. After one or two cuts, check for squareness again. Straightness is checked with a straightedge as shown (Fig. 2-66). If a high spot has developed, restrict planing to that high area. In general, the less the material removed, the more rapidly the surface will be made square and true. The complete squaring-up process is described in Chapter 3.

Special Planes

Rabbet plane. The Stanley No. 78 duplex rabbet plane is basically a one-piece casting. It has two frogs for securing and positioning the plane blade. One is located at the front of the body and is used for "bullnose" work, that is, work which requires planing into a corner (Fig. 2-68). The other frog is located approximately halfway between the toe and heel of the plane. The blade is 1-1/2 in. wide and extends across the sole from cheek to cheek. This allows the blade to cut into corners. The plane is fitted with a depth stop, which allows the depth of the rabbet to be controlled (Fig. 2-69). It has a fillister, or fence, which can be positioned on either side of the

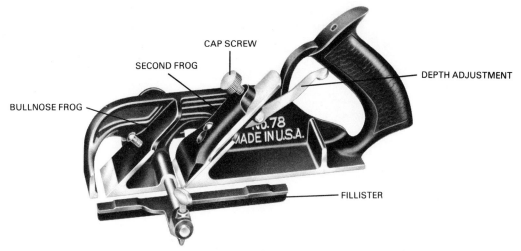

Fig. 2–68. Duplex rabbet plane. (*Courtesy of Stanley Tools.*)

Fig. 2–69. Depth stop on rabbet plane

plane. This fence controls the width of the rabbet (Fig. 2–68). A nib is set into the cheek of the plane and can be used to scribe a line ahead of the blade. It also reduces splitting when planing across the grain. The plane is adjusted and used in much the way way a jack plane is.

Router plane. The router plane is used to remove material inside an area determined by saw or knife cuts—a dado, for example. The blades are L shaped. The smaller model (Fig. 2–70) is useful for inlaying.

Fig. 2-70. Router plane

Scrapers

Scrapers are thin, flat pieces of steel of various sizes and shapes (Fig. 2-71) that are used to scrape away small amounts of material from a surface. They are particularly useful for smoothing cross-grained surfaces (e.g., around knots), removing glue, and old finishes. The cutting action of the scraper depends on a burr which is developed on its edge during the sharpening process (Fig. 2-72).

Hand scrapers. The hand scrapers are hand-held at approximately a 45° angle to the surface to be scraped and are generally pulled toward the operator. *Note:* When scraping glue, wear goggles; the particles removed sometimes fly about and may cause eye injury.

Cabinet scrapers. The cabinet scraper (Fig. 2-73) is a device which holds a flexible scraper blade and permits the operator to use both hands. The thumbscrew located on the front of the scraper between the two handles is used to flex the scraper blade out to increase the effective depth of cut produced (Fig. 2-73). The cabinet scraper can be used with either a pushing or pulling motion.

Fig. 2-71. Hand scraper.
(*Courtesy of Stanley Tools.*)

Fig. 2-72. Cross sectional view of typical scraper blade

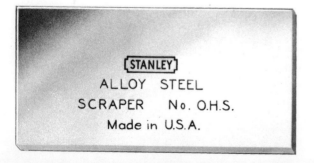

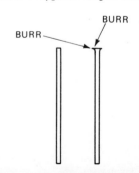

"CUT" DEPTH ADJUSTMENT

Fig. 2-73. Cabinet scraper. (*Courtesy of Stanley Tools.*)

Files

Files consist of flat or curved pieces of steel into which teeth have been cut. These teeth abrade the surface of the workpiece when pushed across it. The cabinet file and the rasp are two types of files specifically designed for use with wood. Other kinds of files tend to clog and become glazed. The craftsman rarely uses the file because they tend to round surfaces and leave a very rough, shredded surface that is difficult to finish. In coping-saw work and in wood sculpture, the file or rasp is often required because no other cutting tool can easily be used. When rasps are used, the rough surface produced may be improved by light refiling with a cabinet file.

Some of the common file types and shapes are shown in Fig. 2-74(a). The file card shown in Fig. 2-74(a) is used to clean wood particles out of the file teeth during use. Figure 2-74(b) shows a close-up of a cabinet file and rasp.

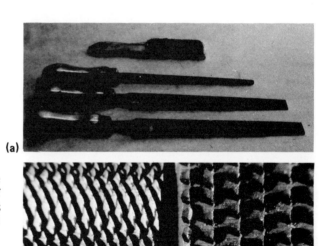

(a)

(b)

Fig. 2-74. (a) Shown, from the top, are: File card, Rat tail file, half round cabinet file, half-round rasp; (b) Right side– rasp teeth; Left side– cabinet file teeth

Fig. 2-75. "Surform" tool. (*Courtesy of Stanley Tools.*)

The Surform tool (Fig. 2-75) is a variety of rasp. Its cutting surface is replaceable and flexible and it works something like a cheese grater.

File use. Always use a file fitted with a handle; the unprotected tang can cause injury.

1. Place the workpiece in a vise so that the surface to be filed is approximately 1 in. above the vise jaws.
2. Place two hands on the file: one hand on the handle, the other on the front end of the tool.
3. Push the file forward while keeping it square to the face of the workpiece.
4. On curved surfaces, rotate the wrist of the hand on the handle as you push the file forward. This will enable you to follow the contour of the workpiece surface.
5. Use a flat file on flat or convex surfaces and a rounded file on concave surfaces.

Sharpening

All cutting tools require sharpening from time to time. The sharpening of chisels and plane blades is fairly simple and is frequently required. The sharpening of saws is more complex, and although it can be accomplished without specialized equipment, such equipment makes it much easier to do. This section deals with sharpening chisels and plane blades. Other similar cutting tools, like knives and axes, can be sharpened using a similar procedure.

Grinding. In some cases the tool to be sharpened requires grinding. This is necessary when the cutting edge is nicked (chipped), the bevel is rounded, the bevel angle is to be changed, or a double bevel develops during improper sharpening.

Low-speed tool grinders with integral cooling systems are ideal for grinding woodworking tools. If it becomes necessary to use a high-speed grinder, great care must be taken to prevent overheating the tool.

1. Set the grinder tool support to the required angle. If the existing angle on the tool is to be maintained, the tool itself can be used as a gauge in setting the tool support on the grinder (Fig. 2-76). Before grinding, put on an approved eye-protection device.

2. Turn the grinder on and place the flat side of the tool on the tool rest. Slowly move the tool forward until it contacts the surface of the grinding wheel. When using a high-speed wheel, quench the tool after every 10 or 12 seconds of grinding. During grinding, move the tool right and left to utilize the total wheel surface. Positioning the index finger of the right hand as shown in Fig. 2–76 is useful in controlling the position of the tool. Some grinders have a tool-holder accessory that keeps the position of the tool fixed with respect to the grinding wheel.

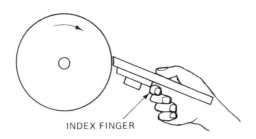

INDEX FINGER

Fig. 2–76. Tool being ground on grinding wheel

3. Continue grinding until the desired beveled surface is developed. For most tools, the wire burr that develops during grinding must be removed by the next step in the sharpening process—whetting.

Whetting. Whetting is done on an oilstone. These stones are available in a variety of types, materials, and degrees of coarseness. A medium-grade stone is commonly used for sharpening woodworking tools. If the tool to be sharpened does not require grinding, whetting on the oilstone will be the first step in the sharpening process. The stone used must be flat. Light machine oil serves as a lubricant and keeps metal particles from clogging the pores of the stone.

1. Oil the stone.
2. Place the tool's bevel on the surface of the stone and rock the tool until the bevel is felt to be in contact with the surface of the stone. Once this position is found, the angle formed by the blade and the stone's surface *must be kept constant* or a rounded bevel will result. A device such as that shown in Fig. 2–77 can be used to maintain this angle. Push the blade back and forth across the surface of the oilstone. Utilize the entire surface, or low spots will develop in the stone's surface. Continue until a smooth area on the bevel becomes noticeable (Fig. 2–78).
3. Turn the blade over and place the flat, unbeveled side of the blade on the surface of the stone (Fig. 2–79). *Do not lift the blade* or a double bevel will develop.

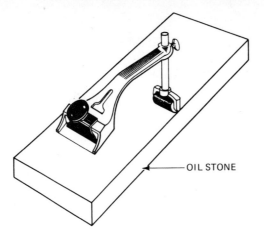

OIL STONE

Fig. 2-77. Chisel and plane iron sharpener

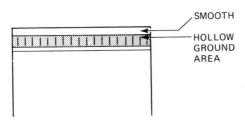

SMOOTH

HOLLOW GROUND AREA

Fig. 2-78. Plane iron after whetting on oil stone

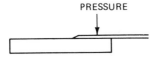

PRESSURE

Fig. 2-79. Whetting blade back

4. Repeat steps 2 and 3 until any wire edge or burr is removed from the cutting edge, or until the cutting edge no longer reflects light. This indicates that the edge is very thin and sharp.

Stropping. The final sharpening step is done on a leather strop or a flat piece of wood. The action of the strop is to remove any final remaining wire edge.

1. Hold the blade at a 45° angle to the surface of the strop and draw it across the strop two or three times (Fig. 2-80).
2. Reverse the blade so that it is tilted in the opposite direction and repeat step 1. Continue until the burr is completely removed.

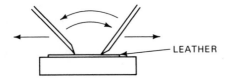

Fig. 2-80. Stropping

LEATHER

Fig. 2-81. Testing an edge

Test the sharpness of the tool by carefully drawing your thumb across the edge, as shown in Fig. 2-81. Note that your thumb travels at right angles to the surface of the cutting edge, *not with it.* The edge should feel slightly rough.

Slipstones. A variety of nonrectangular oilstones are available (Fig. 2-82). These shaped slipstones are used for sharpening tools like gouges and auger bits.

Fig. 2-82. Slip stones

CLAMPING AND HOLDING DEVICES

The Woodworker's Vise

The typical woodworker's vise is made of cast iron and has wooden liners attached to the inner surfaces of the vise jaws to protect the workpiece. The capacity of a woodworker's vise is determined by the jaw size and the maximum opening possible between them. The two most common sizes are 4 in. by 7 in. jaws with a 9-in. opening, and 4 in. by 10 in. jaws with a 12-in. opening.

Fig. 2–83. Holding workpiece between vise dog and bench stop

Fig. 2–84. Spacer block in vise

Many vises are fitted with an adjustable dog (Fig. 2–83) which can be raised and lowered. This dog, when used in conjunction with a bench stop (Fig. 2–83), can hold oversized pieces of material which are clamped between them. When holding work in the side of the vise (as when planing ends), a spacer block equal in thickness to the piece being held should be placed in the opposite end of the vise. This will equalize pressure and prevent the vise from being damaged. It also allows the vise to hold the workpiece more securely (Fig. 2–84).

Clamps

Hand-screw clamp. The hand-screw clamp consists of two hardwood jaws mounted on two wood-handled steel screws. The jaws can be set parallel or at an angle to each other. The wooden jaws provide a large clamping area and do not normally mar the wooden surface they are clamping (Fig. 2–85).

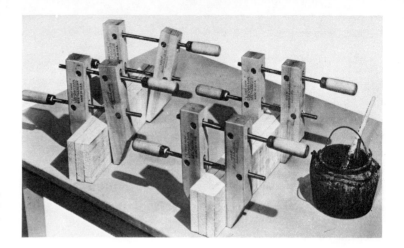

Fig. 2-85. Hand screw clamps. (Right side) correct; (Left side) incorrect. (*Courtesy of Adjustable Clamp Company.*)

Hand-screw clamps are stamped with a number ranging from 5/0 (4-in. jaws that open to a maximum of 2 in.) to 5 (18-in. jaws that open to a maximum of 14 in.).

Parallelness can be maintained during adjustment by holding the handle closest to the pointed end of the clamp stationary with one hand, while the other hand cranks the clamp around this stationary handle (Fig. 2-86). The jaws of the hand-screw clamp must be parallel when the clamp is tightened to obtain maximum clamping pressure. This is accomplished by tightening alternately with each handle.

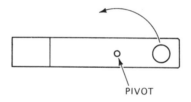

PIVOT

Fig. 2-86.

"C" clamp. The "C" clamp is an all-steel clamp which is usable in woodworking, though it is basically a metalworking device. Since the clamp is all metal, the workpiece must be protected from its jaws if marring is to be avoided (Fig. 2-87).

Bar clamp. Bar clamps (Fig. 2-88) are available in a variety of styles and sizes. A typical set includes clamps from 2 to 6 ft in length. One end of the clamp has a screw which allows pressure to be applied or removed, and the other end has a sliding stop which allows the clamp to be adjusted quickly to accommodate workpieces of various sizes (Fig. 2-88). The jaws tend to mar the workpiece unless a protective block is used. Bar clamps are useful in clamping wide, flat assemblies such as table tops.

Fig. 2-87. "C" clamps in use with scrap blocks protecting workpiece. (*Courtesy of Adjustable Clamp Company.*)

Fig. 2-88. Bar clamps. (*Courtesy of Adjustable Clamp Company.*)

Clamp fixtures are available which consist of a screwhead, which attaches to the threaded end of a standard 3/4-in. pipe, and a sliding foot stop, which also fits onto the pipe (Fig. 2-89).

Strap clamps. Strap, web, or band clamps are made of strong bands which can be drawn tight around an object to be clamped (Fig. 2-90).

Special clamps. Among the many special clamps are the following:

1. The miter-frame clamp (Fig. 2-91) which is used to clamp four-sided frames.
2. The corner clamp (Fig. 2-92) which is used to clamp two sides of a frame at the same time.

Fig. 2-89. Pipe fixture clamp

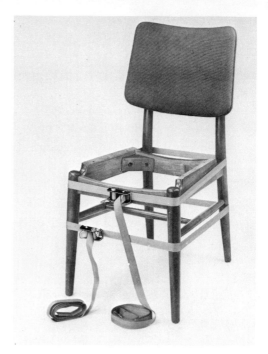

Fig. 2-90. Web clamp. (*Courtesy of Adjustable Clamp Company.*)

Fig. 2-91. Hargrave miter frame clamp. Clamps all four corners at one time. Quickly adjusted. Absolutely accurate. Aluminum alloy corner blocks. Screws and adjusting nuts are steel

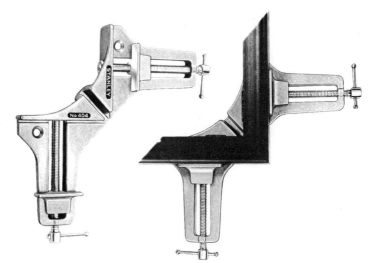

Fig. 2-92. Corner or miter clamp. (*Courtesy of Stanley Tools.*)

3. Hold-down clamps (Fig. 2-93) which are used to clamp materials down to a bench surface.

4. Rapid-action cabinet clamps (Fig. 2-94) which are used in place of "C" clamps.

5. The three-way edging clamp (Fig. 2-95) which can be used to clamp on edge bands when a bar clamp cannot be used.

6. The spring clamp (Fig. 2-96) which is useful for holding small pieces together under moderate pressure.

Fig. 2-93. Hold down clamp

Fig. 2-94. Rapid action cabinet clamps holding glue blocks. (*Courtesy of Adjustable Clamp Company.*)

Fig. 2-95. 3-way edging clamp

May Be Applied With Right Angle Screw "Off Center" | May Be Applied With Right Angle Screw "Centered" | May Be Applied To Clamp Around "Returns"

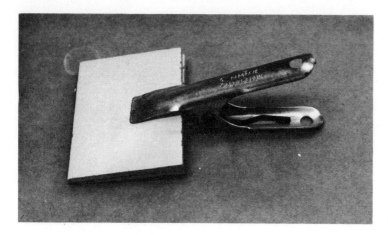

Fig. 2-96. Spring clamp

BORING AND DRILLING DEVICES

Boring Tools

The term *boring* is generally used by woodworkers to describe the making of circular holes with a rotating tool. The boring tool is called a *bit*. Holes are made in wood to accommodate screws, dowels, and tenons and to allow cables or pipes to pass through framing members.

Ratchet bitbrace. The rachet bitbrace is a crank-shaped tool designed to hold square-shanked boring tools (Fig. 2-97). The head of the brace provides a pivot for one end of the crank, and the handle produces the rotary motion which makes the accessories operate. The *sweep* of the handle is the diameter of the circle through which the handle travels. The *cam ring* is used to

Fig. 2-97. Ratchet bit brace. (*Courtesy of Stanley Tools.*)

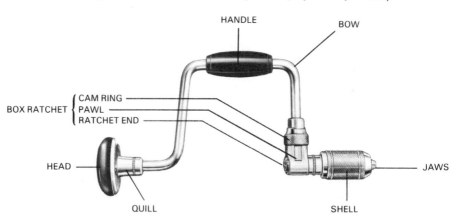

Fig. 2-98. Bit brace chuck

set the ratchet. The *ratchet* can be locked or set to ratchet right or left. The ratchet device allows the chuck to turn in one direction only, right or left. When the handle is swung in a direction opposite to the ratchet setting, the chuck remains stationary. This feature allows the brace to be used in situations which do not permit the handle to swing in a complete circle. The chuck has two jaws which have a 90° "V" groove milled into their inner surfaces. These grooves hold the square-shanked bits securely (Fig. 2-98).

To open the jaws of the chuck, the chuck shell is held with one hand while the handle is rotated counterclockwise. The bit is then inserted into the jaws as far as possible. To close the jaws, the chuck shell is held with one hand while the crank is turned clockwise.

Auger Bits

Auger bits (Fig. 2-99) are the primary hole-making tools used with the bitbrace. Two basic styles of auger bits are available—twist bits and solid-center bits. The solid-center bits are somewhat stronger than the twist bits and are preferable for heavy-duty use. Auger bits generally are available in diameters starting with 1/4 in. and going up to 1 in. by sixteenths. The bits are stamped with a fraction such as 12/16, or with the number 12, which indicates that the bit will bore a hole 12/16 in. or 3/4 in. in diameter.

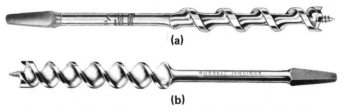

(a)

(b)

Fig. 2-99. (a) Solid center auger bit; (b) Twist bit. (*Courtesy of Stanley Tools.*)

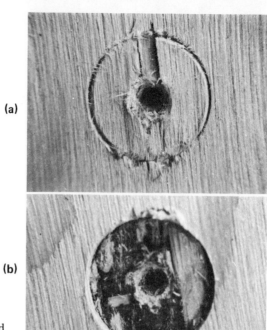

(a)

(b)

Fig. 2-100. (a) Auger bit screw and nib have penetrated wood; (b) Cutting edges have started removing material from inside nib circle

The cutting end of the bit consists of a screw, which pulls the bit into the wood and nibs, which cut a circle before the lips or cutting edges reach the wood and thus prevent splitting. The lips are the cutting edges of the bit that cut away the material inside the circle cut by the nibs (Fig. 2-100). A variety of screw pitches are used on auger bits. A fine pitch is used for hardwoods because it causes the bit to move forward more slowly. Medium- and steep-pitch screws are used for softwoods or in end grain, where the fine screw threads cut into the wood by the auger bit screw would be torn out during boring. When the medium-pitch screw (the most common type) is used, each complete turn of the bit pulls it 1/16 in. into the work.

When a bit is used to bore a through hole, the following procedure is recommended:

1. Select a bit of appropriate size and install it in a bitbrace.
2. Secure the workpiece in a vise so that the hole center is approximately at belt height. Have the workpiece vertical [Fig. 2-101(a)].
3. Place the auger bit screw on the center of the located hole.
4. Be sure the auger bit is at right angles to the face of the workpiece when viewed from the side and above [Fig. 2-101(a)].
5. Rotate the bitbrace clockwise while applying moderate pressure to the bit. It is important to rotate slowly or the screw will strip the threads it is cutting into the wood and it will no longer feed the bit into the piece.

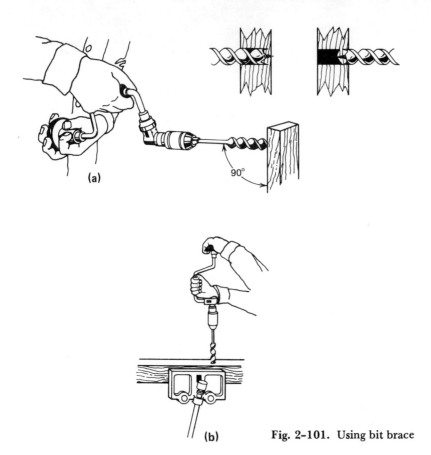

Fig. 2-101. Using bit brace

6. When the screw breaks through the opposite surface of the work-piece, remove it by rotating the brace counterclockwise while gently pulling outward away from the workpiece [Fig. 2-101(a)].

7. Remove the workpiece from the vise and reverse it so that the small hole made by the bit screw is visible.

8. Position the bit screw in this hole and finish boring. This reversal technique reduces the possibility of splitting the surface of the workpiece as the bit breaks through.

When boring into end grain, more pressure and a slower rate of rotation are required.

Bit gauges. When boring blind holes (holes that do not go through a piece from one surface to the opposite surface), care must be taken to prevent boring the hole too deep. The bit gauge is designed to limit hole depth.

A bit gauge can be made by boring a hole through a piece of wood of appropriate size with the bit to be used in boring the blind hole (Fig.

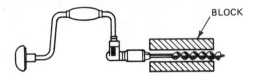

BLOCK

Fig. 2-102. Wooden bit gauge

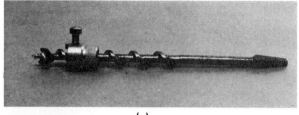

Fig. 2-103. (a) Screw on bit gauge; (b) Spring type bit gauge

(a)

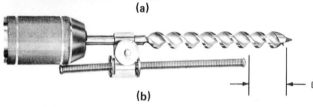

DEPTH

(b)

Fig. 2-104. 2-piece bit gauge

2-102). Commercially produced bit gauges are also available. These are made of metal and they clamp onto the bit itself [Figs. 2-103(a) and (b) and 2-104]. It is important to note that the effective hole depth is measured from the cutting edges of the auger bit to the base of the stop [Fig. 2-103(b)].

Doweling jigs. Doweling jigs perform two functions. They keep the auger bit straight and square to the work surface, and they position the bit at a fixed distance from a surface adjacent to that being bored (Fig. 2-109).

The *self-centering* type of doweling jig automatically centers the hole being bored (Fig. 2-106). For this type of jig, use the following procedure:

1. Lay out a line on the surface at the point where the hole is to be bored. Carry this line down the adjacent surface, as shown in Fig. 2-105.
2. Locate the hole in the jig which is equal in diameter to the hole to be bored. Align this hole with the layout lines on the workpiece. A witness line is cut into the side of the doweling jig under each hole. This line must be aligned with the layout line on the workpiece (Fig. 2-106).

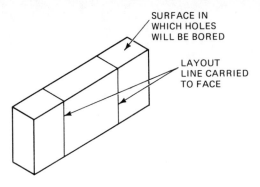

Fig. 2-105. Laying out hole center

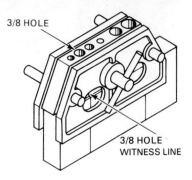

Fig. 2-106. Positioning jig on layout line

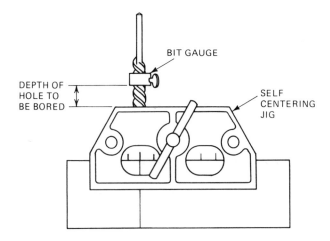

Fig. 2-107. Boring hole using self-centering doweling jig

3. Tighten the clamp screw on the jig and bore the hole to the desired depth (Fig. 2-107).

The Stanley doweling jig consists of a set of sleeves and a body fitted with a slide. The inside diameter of the sleeves matches various auger bit diameters. These sleeves are numbered in the same way that auger bits are (Fig. 2-108). The adjustable slide is used to accommodate workpieces of various thicknesses (Fig. 2-109).

| GUIDE SIZE | 3/16″ | 1/4″ | 5/16″ | 3/8″ | 7/16″ | 1/2″ |
| BIT SIZE | No. 3 | No. 4 | No. 5 | No. 6 | No. 7 | No. 8 |

Fig. 2-108. Stanley doweling jig sleeves

Fig. 2-109. Stanley doweling jig. (*Courtesy of Stanley Tools.*)

The adjustable Stanley doweling jig is used as follows:

1. Lay out lines as described in step 1 above.
2. Select a sleeve equal in size to the hole to be bored, and clamp it in the slide (Fig. 2-108).
3. Find the number on the slide under the words *bit size* equal to the bit sleeve and bit to be used. For example, if a hole of 3/8-in. diameter is to be bored, locate the number 6 (Fig. 2-110).
4. Align this number with a dimension on the fixed portion of the jig equal to half the thickness of the workpiece (Fig. 2-110). Thus, if the hole is to be bored on the edge of a piece 1-in. thick, use the 1/2-in. calibration because 1/2 in. is one-half the thickness of the workpiece.
5. Clamp the slide in place by turning the thumbscrew at the side of the jig.

Fig. 2-110. Number 6 on slide aligned with ½" calibration on jig

Fig. 2-111. Witness line aligned with layout line. Note: Slide has been removed for clarity

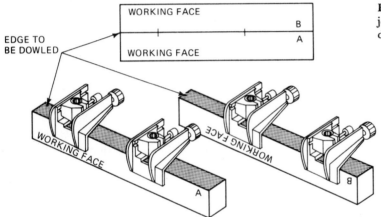

Fig. 2-112. Edge to edge dowel joint procedure using Stanley doweling jig

6. Place the jig on the workpiece and align the witness mark on the doweling jig with the layout line. Tighten the clamp (Fig. 2-111).

7. Bore the hole to the desired depth.

8. For all subsequent holes, be sure to position the witness end of the jig on the same face of the workpiece (Fig. 2-112). This will ensure that all of the holes will be the same distance from that face. Similarly, when matching holes are to be bored in adjacent pieces, as in an edge-to-edge joint, the same relative faces must be used in determining how to place the jig (Fig. 2-112).

Forstner bits. Forstner bits (Fig. 2-113) have no screw and can bore deeper into a piece without piercing the opposite surface. They are also useful for enlarging existing holes because they have no screw and therefore do not require wood for the screw to bite into. These bits range from 1/4 in. to 1 in. in diameter, in 1/16-in. increments.

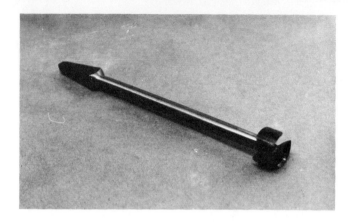

Fig. 2-113. Forstner bit

Fig. 2-114. Bitstock drill

Bitstock drills. The bitstock drill is, in essence, a metal drill with a square shank and can be used in wood or metal. Bitstock drills are useful for drilling through wood into metal or where holes less than 1/4 in. in diameter are required. These drills are available in sizes ranging from 1/8 in. to 3/8 in. in diameter (Fig. 2-114).

Expansive bits. Expansive bits are adjustable auger bits (Fig. 2-115). The blade provided is adjustable for a range of hole sizes. The adjustable blade is calibrated and locked in position by a screw. Most expansive bits are offered with two blades. A typical set allows holes to be bored ranging in size from 5/8 in. to 1-3/4 in. in diameter. With the second cutter, holes from 7/8 in. to 3 in. in diameter can be made. Expansive bits work well in relatively soft woods when fairly shallow holes are required.

Fig. 2-115. Expansive bit. (*Courtesy of Stanley Tools.*)

Countersinks. The countersink is used to make a cone-shaped depression in the surface of a piece of wood to receive the head of a flathead wood screw. In practice, this is done after the shank hole has been made (Fig. 2-116). The user determines when the countersinking is deep enough by placing the head of the screw in the countersunk hole (Fig. 2-116). Slow rotation tends to produce a smoother hole than fast rotation produces.

(a)   (b)

Fig. 2-116. (a) Countersink; (b) Testing depth of countersunk holes. (*Courtesy of Stanley Tools.*)

Screwdriver bit. The screwdriver bit converts the bitbrace into a screwdriver with tremendous leverage. For this reason it is advisable to use the screwdriver bit on relatively large-diameter screws, No. 12 and larger (Fig. 2-117).

Fig. 2-117. Screwdriver bit. (*Courtesy of Stanley Tools.*)

Drills

Many craftsmen consider drills to be metalworking tools. The high-speed drill bit is designed to drill holes in metal, but it can also be used in wood. The device which provides the rotary power for the drill bit is the hand drill or the hand electric drill. The hand electric drill and its accessories are considered in later sections on powered portable tools and the drill press. The hand drill is rapidly being displaced by relatively low cost electric hand drills. However, when complete control is required or where it is inconvenient to use an electrical device, the hand drill is still useful.

Hand drills. The hand drill is equipped with a three-jawed chuck (Fig. 2-118). To install a drill bit, proceed as follows:

1. To open, hold the chuck with one hand and turn the crank handle counterclockwise with the other hand (Fig. 2-119).
2. Insert the drill bit into the chuck. Then hold the drill bit and the

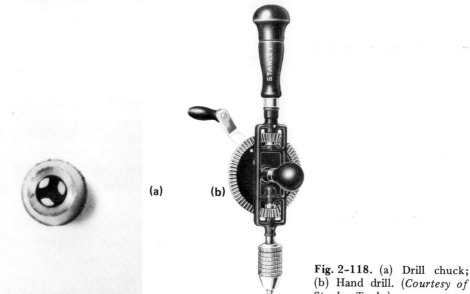

(a)　　(b)

Fig. 2-118. (a) Drill chuck; (b) Hand drill. (*Courtesy of Stanley Tools.*)

chuck with one hand and turn the crank handle clockwise with the other hand until the bit is securely held.

3. To drill a hole in wood, pierce the surface of the workpiece with an awl to locate and start the hole; then drill, holding the drill at right angles to the workpiece.

Small-diameter holes can be drilled in soft woods with nails whose heads have been removed. This technique is especially useful when drilling holes for nails to prevent splitting the wood. Most hand drills are fitted with a 1/4-in. maximum capacity chuck; however, 3/8-in. models are available.

Push drills. Push drills (Fig. 2–120) are similar to hand drills in function, that is, they are designed to drill small-diameter holes in wood. The rotary

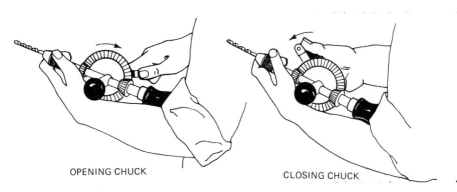

OPENING CHUCK   CLOSING CHUCK

Fig. 2-119.

Fig. 2-120. Push drill. (*Courtesy of Stanley Tools.*)

motion is developed when the handle is pushed. A spiral groove in the spindle of the tool converts the reciprocal motion of the handle into rotary motion. Thus this tool can be operated with one hand. This feature is useful when drilling holes while using a hinge or other piece of hardware as a template for the holes being made. Drill points are generally available in diameters ranging from 1/16 in. to 11/64 in.

Awls. An awl (Fig. 2-121) is a small pointed tool commonly used to start holes that are to be drilled. Awls are also used to make starting holes for small screws when they are to be driven into soft woods.

Fig. 2-121. Awl. (*Courtesy of Stanley Tools.*)

DRIVING TOOLS

Pounding tools and screwdrivers are discussed in this section.

Hammers

The claw hammer is a basic tool which has two primary functions, driving and drawing nails. A variety of handle types are available, including wood, fiberglass, and steel. The hammerhead consists of a face which strikes the nail, a pol, a neck, a cheek, an adze eye, and the claws. The standard curved claw, shown in Fig. 2-122, is the most common. Ripping hammers have straighter claws and are useful in framing work to pry materials apart.

Hammer faces are either flat or slightly convex, bell-faced. A convex face allows a nailhead to be driven flush to the surface of the workpiece without denting the surface. Hammers are available in a variety of weights; 13-, 16-, and 20-ounce hammers are the most common.

The following suggestions will enable you to use the hammer more efficiently:

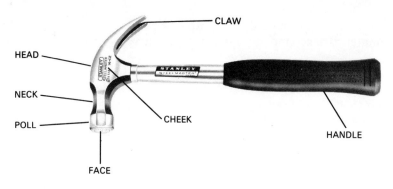

Fig. 2–122. Claw hammer. (*Courtesy of Stanley Tools.*)

1. Keep the face of the hammer clean. Gum or similar materials tend to cause the hammer to slip off the nailhead.

2. Use the face of the hammer to strike nails. Don't use the cheek because the metal is very thin at that point.

3. Grasp the hammer at the end of the handle. This will provide maximum driving power and control.

4. Avoid striking materials that are harder than the hammer face or else chipping may result.

5. Maintain a 90° angle between the hammer handle and the nail at the time of contact. This will reduce the tendency of the nail to bend (Fig. 2-123).

Fig. 2-123. Driving a nail

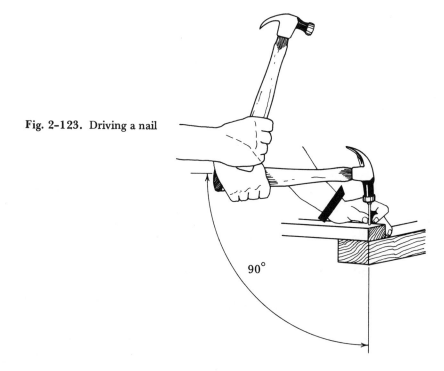

6. Start the nail by holding it with one hand while tapping it lightly with the hammer. Then remove your hand and drive the nail home with heavier blows.

7. When driving nails close to the end of a workpiece where splitting is likely, blunt the point of the nail by tapping it with the hammer before driving it in. This will reduce the wedge-like action of the nail.

8. When drawing nails, place the claws under the nailhead and pull the handle up until it is vertical; then place a block under the head and complete the draw (Fig. 2-124).

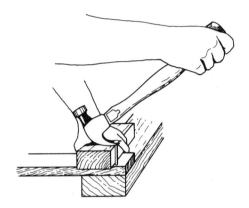

Fig. 2-124. Drawing a nail

Nail Set

A nail set is a steel punch with a cupped, pointed end into which the nailhead fits. It is used to set the head of a finishing nail or brad below the surface of the wood so that it can be covered with putty or plastic wood. Nail sets are available with tip sizes ranging from 1/32 in. to 1/8 in. in diameter (Fig. 2-125).

Fig. 2-125. Nail set. (*Courtesy of Stanley Tools.*)

Mallets

Mallets of wood or metal-faced plastic are used by the woodworker for a variety of purposes. These include driving socket chisels when making heavy cuts in hard wood and tapping two pieces together in joinery operations.

Brad Driver

The brad driver is a device for driving small brads, 1 in. in length and under. To use the brad driver (Fig. 2-126), the tube is first pushed up into the handle, exposing the magnetic ram. The brad head is touched to the ram, sticks to it, and is drawn into the tube as the tube is released. Then the pointed end of the tube is placed at the nailing location and the handle is struck with the palm of the hand.

Fig. 2-126. Brad driver

Magnetic Hammer

The magnetic hammer (Fig. 2-127) has a magnetized end and a driving end and is useful for driving tacks and other small-headed nails. To use the magnetic hammer, a nail is attached to the magnetic end and driven part way into the surface of the wood. Then the hammer is reversed and the rest of the driving is done with the nonmagnetic end of the hammer.

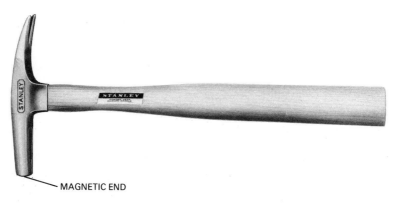

MAGNETIC END

Fig. 2-127. Magnetic tack hammer. (*Courtesy of Stanley Tools.*)

Screwdrivers

A screwdriver is designed to drive slotted screws. The length of a screwdriver is determined by the length of the blade (Fig. 2-128). As the length of the blade increases, the width and thickness of the tip also increase.

Two basic tip styles are available for slotted screws: standard and cabinet tip. The standard tip (Fig. 2-128) has slanted sides and is wider than the blade of the screwdriver. The cabinet tip has parallel sides and is equal in width to the blade. This enables the cabinet-tip screwdriver to be used for driving counterbored screws (Fig. 2-129). The handles of screwdrivers are made of a variety of materials, including wood and plastic.

Fig. 2-128. Screwdriver. (*Courtesy of Stanley Tools.*)

Fig. 2-129. Cabinet tip screwdriver. (*Courtesy of Stanley Tools.*)

Suggestions for selecting a screwdriver are as follows:

1. Select the longest screwdriver that is appropriate for the job intended. The longer the tool, the greater the leverage applied.
2. The tip of the screwdriver must fit the slot without wobbling. The width of the tip should be equal to the length of the screw slot.
3. The screwdriver tip should be square and sharp.

For driving screws, the following procedure is recommended:

1. Drill all of the required holes for the screw to be used.
2. If the workpiece is a hard wood like maple, apply soap to the threaded section of the screw.
3. Place the screw in the hole and place an appropriate screwdriver tip into the slot of the screw.
4. Steady the screw and screwdriver tip with one hand (Fig. 2-130) while pushing downward vertically on the handle with the other hand. Slowly rotate the screwdriver.

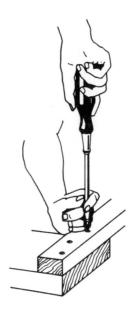

Fig. 2-130. Using a screwdriver

5. *Keep both hands on the screwdriver once the screw starts going into the work.*

Among the many special types of screwdrivers are the "close-quarter" or "stubby" and the Phillips. The stubby is used where space above the surface of the workpiece is limited. The Phillips is used for Phillips-head screws, which have a crossed slot [Fig. 2-131(a)]. Offset screwdrivers [Fig. 2-131(b)] are useful in close quarters.

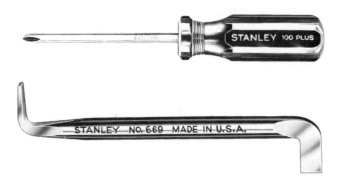

Fig. 2-131. (a) Phillips tip screwdriver. (b) Offset screwdriver. (*Courtesy of Stanley Tools.*)

PROJECT FABRICATION

The origin of a project design was discussed in Chapter 1. For a fairly complex project, the design may include a dimensioned, accurately made drawing. For a simple project, a free-hand, dimensioned sketch may suffice.

GENERAL PROJECT-MAKING SEQUENCE

1. Develop or obtain a project design, including a dimensioned drawing. In some cases a layout of each of the project's parts is made. A layout is a full-size drawing of each part as it would appear when transferred to the material from which the project is to be made (Fig. 3-1).
2. Make out a bill of material for the piece.
3. Select and rough-cut stock to size.
4. Square-up rectangular and square components completely. Partially square-up other parts, as required.
5. Lay out and fabricate joints.
6. Complete the fabrication of partially squared parts.
7. Bore holes for hardware if required.
8. Apply decorative materials (e.g., inlays).
9. Complete preliminary sanding (through No. 150 abrasive paper).
10. Complete a trial assembly.

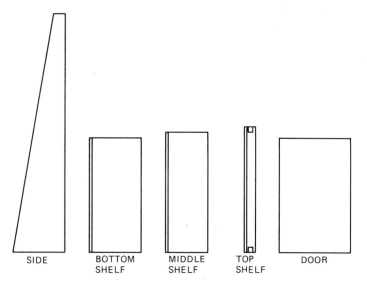

| SIDE | BOTTOM SHELF | MIDDLE SHELF | TOP SHELF | DOOR |

Fig. 3-1. Project layout

11. Apply adhesives and assemble project.
12. Complete final sanding.
13. Finish project.

These are the general steps in constructing a project such as an accessory or a furniture piece. Certain steps may be varied, depending on the individual piece. A craft is a highly individual enterprise and even the basic procedure should reflect the craftsman's experience and individual decisions.

GETTING STOCK OUT

The Bill of Material

Every craftsman, either formally or informally, makes a bill of material for each of his productions. The bill of material (Fig. 3-2) is simply a list of all the materials needed to make a project. The bill of material is a useful guide in getting out stock, especially when machines are being used. It can also be used to compute the cost of the materials required and is used for that purpose by cabinetmakers and other professional woodworkers.

The bill of material format shown in Fig. 3-2 is fairly typical. The sequence of the dimensions of the material required is conventionally listed as shown: thickness in inches first, width in inches next, and length in feet last. $T \times W \times L$ is read "thickness by width by length."

Student:

BILL OF MATERIAL

NAME OF PART	# PIECES	DIMENSIONS OF FINISHED PIECE Thickness × Width × Length	MATERIAL
Total MTL. Sides	1	1/2″ × 5 1/2″ × 31 1/8″*	Bass
Side	2	1/2″ × 4 1/4″ × 20″	Bass
Bottom Shelf	1	1/2″ × 4 1/4″ × 9 1/2″	Bass
Middle Shelf	1	1/2″ × 3 3/8″ × 10″	Bass
Top Shelf	1	1/2″ × 1″ × 10 1/2″	Bass
Door	1	1/2″ × 5″ × 9 1/2″	Bass
Dowels	4	1/4″ Diameter 1″ long	Birch

Hardware: Two hinges—butt 1″ × 3/4″, 1 brass knob 1/2 Diam., 1 magnetic catch

Finishing Material: Brushing Lacquer, oil stain

Non-Wood Materials: Masonite Back 1/8″ × 5 1/2″ × 10″

Fig. 3-2. Bill of material

Once a dimensioned drawing of the proposed project is available, the next step recommended is the completion of a bill of material. For illustrative purposes, the drawing in Fig. 3-3 is used as the sample project for the completion of the bill of material shown in Fig. 3-2.

The side of the project is listed first. It is a good practice to list the largest pieces first so that cutoffs produced in making larger pieces can be used for the smaller parts. The name of the part is listed in the first column. If identical parts are required, they are listed in the second column. In this case the number 2 is entered because the project has two identical sides. Dimensions are obtained from the drawing (Fig. 3-3). The note at the top of the drawing indicates that 1/2-in.-thick basswood will be used for all wooden parts, so 1/2 becomes the first dimension. At its widest point, the tapering side is 4-1/4 in. wide, so this figure is listed as its width. As shown in the drawing, the length of the side is 20 in. All of the other parts are listed as shown.

Material Selection

The quality of the materials used is directly related to the ease of fabrication. In general, the following guidelines are suggested for material selection:

1. Select well-seasoned wood to avoid warping problems later.

#1 = Through dowel one side, blind dowel on the second side.
#2 = Dado, #3 = Dovetail, #4 = Masonite back set in rabbet 1/8" material-
#5 = Door, fit into opening, hardware student choice

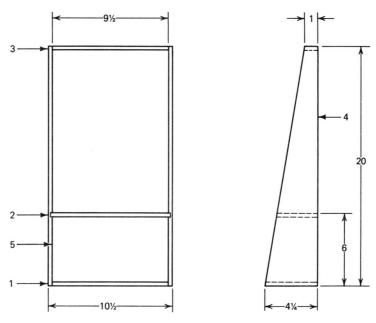

Fig. 3-3. Orthographic drawing

2. Select unwarped material. Warping makes most processing more difficult and complex.

3. Examine areas close to the ends of the pieces for checks. These splits are often present near end grain that has been exposed to the air for a long period of time.

4. Avoid pieces with knots. These areas are difficult to cut because of grain direction changes and hardness.

5. Check for processing defects such as unsurfaced areas and for edges with some bark remaining in place (wanes).

6. Examine the material closely for surface defects such as pike holes.

7. If possible, select straight-grained pieces (Fig. 3-4).

Cutting Stock to Rough Dimensions

In handtool processing, material should initially be cut oversized to allow for subsequent removal of material by the plane. A good rule of thumb is to add 1/2 in. to the length and width of the sizes listed in the bill of

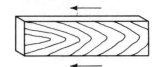

NO CHANGE OF GRAIN DIRECTION ON AN EDGE

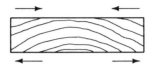

CHANGE OF GRAIN DIRECTION ON AN EDGE. AVOID SELECTING THIS TYPE OF MATERIAL

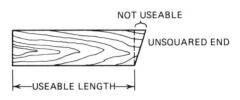

NOT USEABLE

UNSQUARED END

USEABLE LENGTH

Fig. 3–4.

material. The following steps are suggested for cutting the stock to rough dimensions:

1. Select a standard piece of material—in this case 1/2 in. by 6-in. wide basswood. The 6-in. width is a *nominal* dimension. In reality, it is approximately 5-1/2 in. wide.

2. Select the best edge of the piece and measure off 20-1/2 in. of length. Draw a line square to the edge of the piece with a try square [Fig. 3–5(a)].

3. Lay out the slanting edge of the piece on the board [Fig. 3–5(b)]. Note that the dimensions 4-1/4 and 1-1/2 are used here. Draw this line so that any usable extra width can be identified. In this case the two slanted side pieces can be "overlapped," as shown in Fig. 3–5(b).

4. Now that the longest pieces have been laid out, deal with the next longest and widest piece—the bottom shelf. Since it is to be 9-1/2 in. long, make a 10-in.-long layout [Fig. 3–5(c)]. Similarly, lay out its width as 4-3/4 in.

5. Next lay out the middle shelf [Fig. 3–5(d)]. Lay out its width as 3-7/8 in., which is 1/2 in. oversized. Its length is also 1/2 in. more than the length listed in the bill of material. Note that a piece 1-5/8 in. in width is left under the middle shelf piece. This can be used for the top shelf, which is to be 1 in. wide.

6. The door is the last piece to be laid out. Make it 10 in. long and 5-1/2 in. wide. The overall length of the piece required comes out to approximately 61-3/4 in.

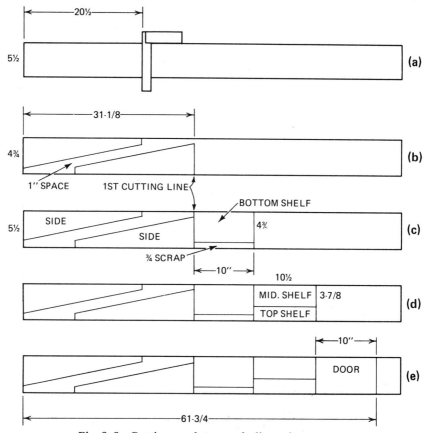

Fig. 3-5. Cutting stock to rough dimensions

Remember that the layout made on the piece of stock is a rough one and *is not to be used in actually reducing the pieces to final size and shape.*

7. When the layout is complete, label the parts and cut to length with a crosscut saw.

THE SQUARING PROCESS

Once the stock has been cut to rough size, the next step is *squaring-up the stock.* In the case of square or rectangular workpieces, this means reducing the material to finished size and shape while making all of the adjacent surfaces (those which meet to form a corner) square (90°) to each other.

Selecting a Working Face

1. Select and identify a *working face.* Most stock has some cup warping. If this is the case, select the concave face as the working face because it supports the try-square handle or the rule on two points (Fig. 3-6).

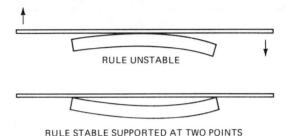

RULE UNSTABLE

RULE STABLE SUPPORTED AT TWO POINTS

Fig. 3-6. Cupped stock

In this instance the term *work surface* means reference surface. These surfaces will be used to make measurements from. For example, the length of the board will be measured from the *working end.* These working surfaces usually become part of the finished project (Fig. 3-7).

Planing a Working Edge

2. Determine the best edge on the piece. This is the edge that is most straight, most nearly square to the working face, and most smooth. Set the plane for a very light shaving (onion-skin thickness) and plane the working edge, going with the grain, until the edge is straight (Fig. 3-8), smooth, and square to the working face (Fig. 3-9). Identify the edge as the *working edge.*

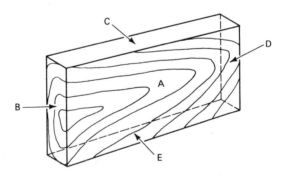

"A" is called the FACE (another face is located on the back of the piece opposite "A".) The face is usually the largest surface on a piece of wood.

"B" & "D" are called ends. The ends go across the grain and are usually the smallest and roughest surfaces on the piece. The distance from one end to the other is known as the LENGTH.

"C" & "E" are called edges. The edges run in the same direction as the grain and these surfaces are usually the second largest surfaces on the piece of wood. The distance from edge to edge is known as WIDTH.

Thus, every piece of wood has six surfaces. Two FACES, two ENDS and two EDGES.

Fig. 3-7.

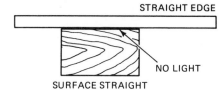

STRAIGHT EDGE

NO LIGHT

SURFACE STRAIGHT

Fig. 3-8. Testing for straightness

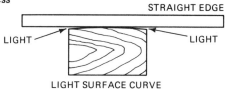

STRAIGHT EDGE

LIGHT   LIGHT

LIGHT SURFACE CURVE

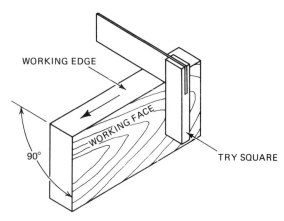

WORKING EDGE

WORKING FACE

90°

TRY SQUARE

Fig. 3-9. Use of try square

Above we see a board with a try square in position to check the squareness of an edge to the working face. Note that the handle of the try square is held against the working face.

The arrow shows the direction of the grain on the top edge. The plane will be pushed in that direction. Going the other way would produce a rough edge.

Note that the angle between the working edge and face is 90 degrees.

In most work the edge selected will be fairly square to the working face before any planing is done. It will also be quite straight. It is to the craftsman's advantage to *remove as little material as possible* during planing, because straightness is often lost during prolonged planing.

The whole squaring process should be approached thoughtfully and analytically. Frequent testing for squareness should be done with the workpiece removed from the vise (Fig. 3–10). High spots should be marked with a pencil, and only these high areas should be planed.

Shooting an edge is a process which takes advantage of the machined squareness of the cheek and sole of the plane. The setup shown in Fig. 3–11 can be adapted to end planing.

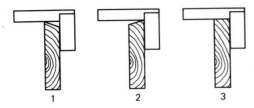

The drawing above shows a Try Square with its handle on a working face and its blade on an edge which we are trying to make square to the working face.

In #1 a high area is seen at the left. The plane must be held so that that area will be planed away.

In #2 a high area is shown at the right. That must be planed away.

In #3 no light is seen the edge is SQUARE TO THE WORKING FACE. No more planing is needed.

Fig. 3-10. Testing edge with try square

Planing a Working End

3. Select the best end. If the end is planed without any preparation, it may split during cutting [Fig. 3-12(a)] because the fibers closest to the edge are unsupported. Instead of being cut by the plane iron, they bend and break. If the planing is done so that the plane travels toward the working edge, the working edge could be damaged and may require replaning. Splitting can be avoided by cutting a chamfer on the corner formed by the scrap edge and the working end [Fig. 3-12(b)]. When planing the working end, the plane travels *toward* the chamfer. The chamfer prevents splitting because the fibers at the very end of the cut are not being touched by the plane iron [Fig. 3-12(b)]. If the workpiece width is too close to final size, a supporting scrap piece can sometimes be used instead of a chamfer to prevent splitting [Fig. 3-12(d)]. An alternate method is to plane in from the edges toward the middle of the working end [Fig. 3-12(c)].

Fig. 3-11. Shooting an edge

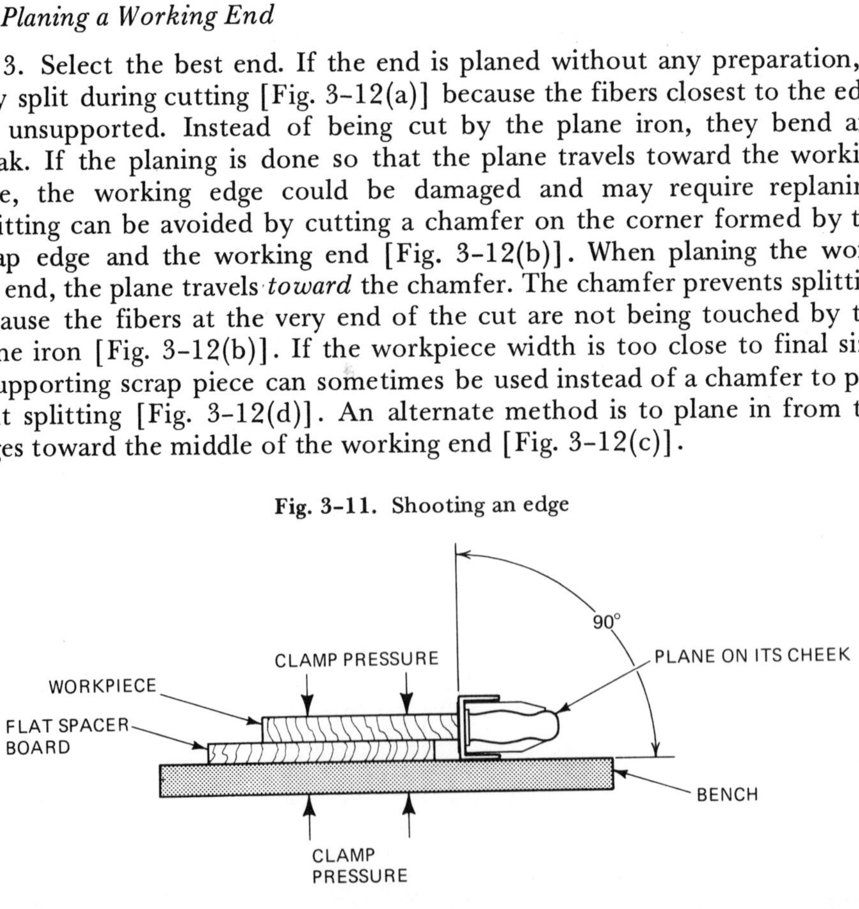

90°

CLAMP PRESSURE

PLANE ON ITS CHEEK

WORKPIECE

FLAT SPACER BOARD

BENCH

CLAMP PRESSURE

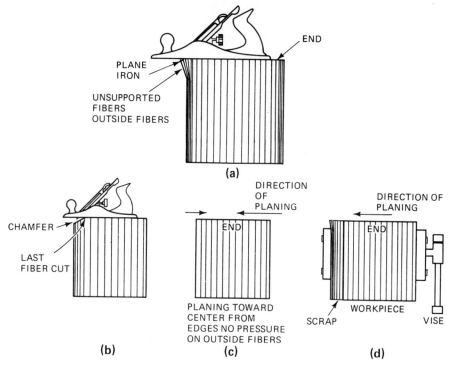

Fig. 3-12. Planing ends

For end planing, a very sharp plane is required. It should be set for a very light cut. Considerable downward pressure is necessary during cutting. One of the most common errors made during planing, especially of end grain, is to set the plane iron out too far. This is the direct result of inadequate downward pressure on the tool during use.

When the working end is square to the working face and the working edge, identify it (Fig. 3-13).

It is important to note that up to this point no attempt has been made to reduce the workpiece in size to any finished dimension.

Fig. 3-13. The working end

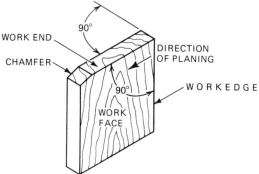

Cutting and Planing to Length

4. The next surface processed is the second end of the piece. If the finished length of the piece is to be 9-1/2 in., a 9-1/2-in. measurement is made along the working edge from the working end (Fig. 3–14). At this point, a line is laid out across both faces and edges with the try square, so that all lines are square to the working edge or the working face. This line represents the finished second end of the workpiece. It *cannot be removed* during processing. If it is, the piece will be *undersized* and may not be usable.

A second line is now laid out approximately 1/8 in. away from the line that represents the final finished length of the workpiece (Fig. 3–14). This broken line represents the cutting line. The extra 1/8 in. is left for removal during final squaring.

The piece is carefully cut along the broken line with a suitable cross-cut saw. A chamfer is cut on the corner formed by the second end and the *scrap edge* (Fig. 3–14). The second end is planed until it is square to the working face and the working edge, and is down to the layout line which represents the finished length of the piece.

Cutting and Planing to Width

5. The final surface to be processed is the second edge. The width measurement of the finished piece is used here. If the final width of the piece is to be 5 in., this measurement is made along the ends of the piece

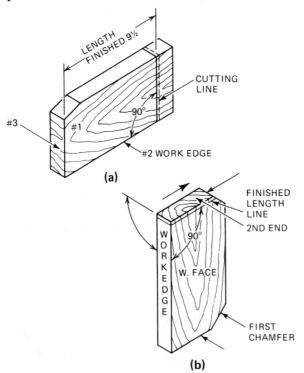

Fig. 3–14. Cutting to length

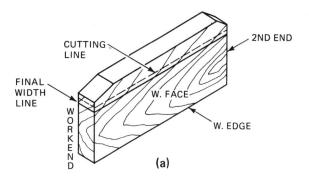

(a)

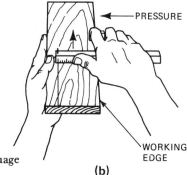

Fig. 3-15. Laying out lines with a marking guage

(b)

from the working edge [Fig. 3-15(a)]. An alternate method is to use a marking gauge to draw these lines. In this method the head of the gauge is kept in place against the working edge while the beam is tilted away from the operator [Fig. 3-15(b)]. This line represents the final finished second edge of the workpiece. A second broken line is drawn approximately 1/4 in. away from this line and parallel to it. This is the cutting line [Fig. 3-15(a)].

The piece is then ripped along the cutting line with a ripsaw, and the edge is planed until the final layout line is reached. At this point the edge should be straight, smooth, and square to the working face and parallel to the first edge (the working edge). Note that during this operation both chamfers are cut away. This is why the chamfers were cut on the scrap edge.

The squaring operation is now complete. If a complete squaring of the piece were done, the faces would also have been involved. This was not included in the squaring sequence because the operation is seldom required. Standard thicknesses of stock are available and this material is usually surfaced by machine at the mill so that the faces are parallel.

It is important to note that the complete squaring-up process (all five steps) is required only when the final shape of the workpiece requires four straight surfaces—two ends and two edges. In Fig. 3-16(a), only a working face and end are required, and in Fig. 3-16(b), only a working edge face and

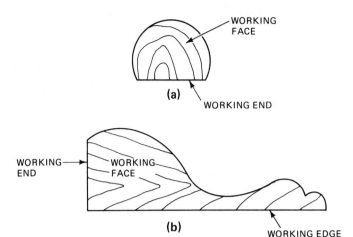

Fig. 3-16. Squaring requirements on pieces with curved surfaces

end are needed. For the cabinet in Fig. 3-3, the second edges of the shelves are planed at an angle other than 90° to the working face. This bevel is checked with a "T" bevel. The sides of this cabinet (Fig. 3-3) have a second edge that is not parallel to the working edge. This edge is laid out as required and processed in the same way the edge described in step 5 was processed.

When identical pieces are to be fashioned, such as the sides of the cabinet in Fig. 3-3, the pieces can be fastened together with small brads or rubber cement and processed as though they were a single piece, thereby cutting the processing time in half.

Curved Surfaces

If the project involves curved surfaces (Fig. 3-17), the necessary squaring operations are carried out first and then the curved cuts are made with the coping saw. Approximately 1/8 in. of extra material is left for final smoothing [Fig. 3-17(a)]. This final smoothing is carried out with a block plane, a spokeshave, or a file.

Fig. 3-17. Shaping curved surfaces

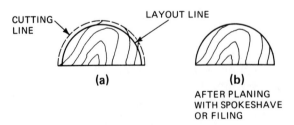

CUTTING STOCK TO SIZE AND SQUARING-UP USING MACHINES

In general practice, machines are used to process material to finished sizes. For clarity, let us consider getting out stock for the project described by the drawing in Fig. 3-3 and by the bill of material in Fig. 3-2.

1. The edge of the stock to be used for the project is made square to the working face using the jointer.
2. If the piece of stock is too long for convenient cutting to length on the table saw (over 4 ft), it should be cut to a manageable length using a handsaw or a radial arm saw.
3. One end of the material is cut square to the working edge using the table saw.
4. The first piece listed in the bill of material (Fig. 3-2) is 31-1/8 in. long. This distance is laid out on the stock *measuring from the squared end.* This squared end is the working end of the stock. A line square to the working edge of the stock is laid out at this point and the piece is cut to length on the circular saw. The working edge is held against the miter gauge, which is set at a 90° angle to the saw blade during cutting.

For most purposes, the surface produced by the circular saw blade on the end of the piece is smooth enough for finish sanding. If a smoother surface is required, the disk sander may be used. An alternate solution is to install a planer blade on the saw, which produces a smoother surface.

5. Each of the succeeding pieces on the bill of material is cut to length in a similar way.
6. At this point, each of the pieces cut has a working face (selected by the craftsman), a working edge (cut on the jointer), and two squared ends (cut on the circular saw). Note that it was *not* necessary to fully lay out any of the pieces. The next step is to lay out the two sides on the 31-1/8 in.-long piece (Fig. 3-18) and cut the two pieces apart along the cutting line using a taper jig on the table saw. Excess material should be removed from the slanting edges of the pieces on the jointer.
7. The bottom shelf (Fig. 3-3) is now ripped to width on the table saw, leaving 1/8 in. for removal on the jointer. To lay out the width, 4-1/4 in. is measured from the working edge and a line is drawn parallel to the working edge. Finally the jointer fence is tilted to the required angle and the piece is jointed until the layout line is reached.
8. A similar procedure may be followed for the middle and bottom shelves.

Fig. 3-18. Oblique cutting

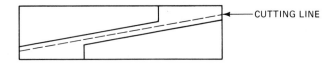

CUTTING LINE

All of the pieces of the cabinet, exclusive of the door and back, have been processed. Since the door and back fit into openings formed when the cabinet is assembled, it is suggested that these parts be cut to fit the actual openings after assembly. The joinery, with more detailed information on the use of machines, is discussed in the chapters on machine tools.

JOINERY

The term *joinery* describes the total process of selecting, designing, and fabricating joints when combining two or more pieces of wood.

All joinery has two goals: first, to improve the strength of the connection, usually by increasing the area of the surfaces in contact with each other; and second, to locate the pieces to be joined precisely with respect to each other. Increasing the surface area of joints was especially important before the development of modern adhesives. The second goal, location, is still very significant in production situations. For example, in a factory producing chairs, joining a rail to a leg could be accomplished with a simple butt joint; however, a dowel fitting into hole ensures fast and correct alignment during assembly. The craftsman uses joinery, which increases the surface area and guarantees alignment, for similar reasons.

General Rules of Joinery

The rules listed below are useful guidelines in joinery construction. They will be referred to in the section dealing with the design and construction of specific joints.

1. Wherever possible, make all measurements and layouts from a common surface or starting point.
2. Use superimposition in place of indirect measuring whenever possible.
3. Make all layouts with a sharp knife and marking gauge.
4. When laying out identical pieces, position them in such a way that layout lines can be made in one cut or pencil stroke.
5. Use pieces of wood as thickness gauge-rests for the flat side of your chisel while cuts are being made.
6. Make female joint components first; then fit male components to them. Final fitting should be accomplished by scraping rather than cutting.
7. In through-joint construction, leave male components oversized in length. Trim to final length after the joint is assembled.
8. For large pieces requiring many joints, work systematically, i.e., complete all dovetail joints before going ahead with other types. In gauging, the gauge should be left at one setting until the layout of all lines requiring this setting has been completed.

9. Allow for wood shrinkage and expansion.

10. Where possible, undercut joined surfaces slightly to provide clearance on the inside and to ensure a tight appearance. Surfaces to be glued should *not* be undercut.

11. The shoulders of tenons may be undercut to allow the edges of the two pieces to be pulled tight against each other. In blind mortise and tenon joints, the tenon should be chamfered slightly to permit easy assembly. Dowels should be pointed for the same reason.

Classification of Joints

All joints can be categorized under the following headings: spliced joints, butt joints, halved joints, mortise and tenon joints, dovetail joints, and beveled joints. In the following section, each category is discussed and one representative joint is described in detail.

Spliced joints. Spliced joints are used to increase the effective length of lumber. Lamination frequently requires the use of scarf joints, which are a variety of splice joint. The chapter on wood lamination describes the fabrication of scarf joints by hand and machine (Fig. 3-19).

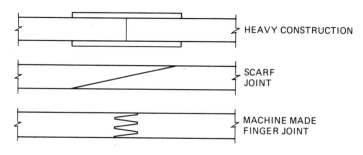

Fig. 3-19. Spliced joints

Butt joints. Figure 3-20 shows some common butt joints. These joints are the simplest; they are used widely in carpentry and are generally reinforced with nails, screws, metal plates, or gusset plates.

Nailed Butt Joint

1. After completing squaring operations, lay out the location of the joint on the face of the piece against which the end of the second member will rest [Fig. 3-21(a-I)].

2. Select three finishing nails of suitable length, and drive one nail through the member with the layout on it so that the nail just appears on the opposite face [Fig. 3-21(a-II)].

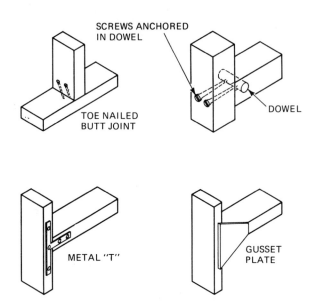

Fig. 3-20. Reinforced butt joints

3. Place the second member in a vise in a vertical position with its end flush with the jaws of the vise [Fig. 3-21(a-III)]. Apply glue to the end in the vise.

4. Place the member with the nail through it on the glued end of the piece in the vise so that the end in the vise is aligned with the layout on the second piece. Push the pieces together. The point of the nail will pierce the end of the piece in the vise and help to keep the two pieces from sliding during nailing. Drive the nail in vertically.

5. Check the position of the two pieces. Drive in two additional nails at the angles shown in Fig. 3-21(a-IV). This angle-driving increases the holding power of the nails. The heads of the nails may be set below the surface of the piece with a nail set.

Two screws, together with glue, can be used in a similar fashion for reinforcing a butt joint. The limited holding power of screws in end grain can be greatly improved by installing a dowel in the piece receiving the threaded portion of the screw (Fig. 3-20).

Screwed Butt Joint

1. Repeat step 1 above for nail-reinforced joints.

2. Place the member to hold the head of the screw in the vise as shown in Fig. 3-21(b-I).

3. Place a hand-screw clamp as shown in Fig. 3-21(b-I). Then position the second member against the clamp [Fig. 3-21(b-I)]. Now clamp this

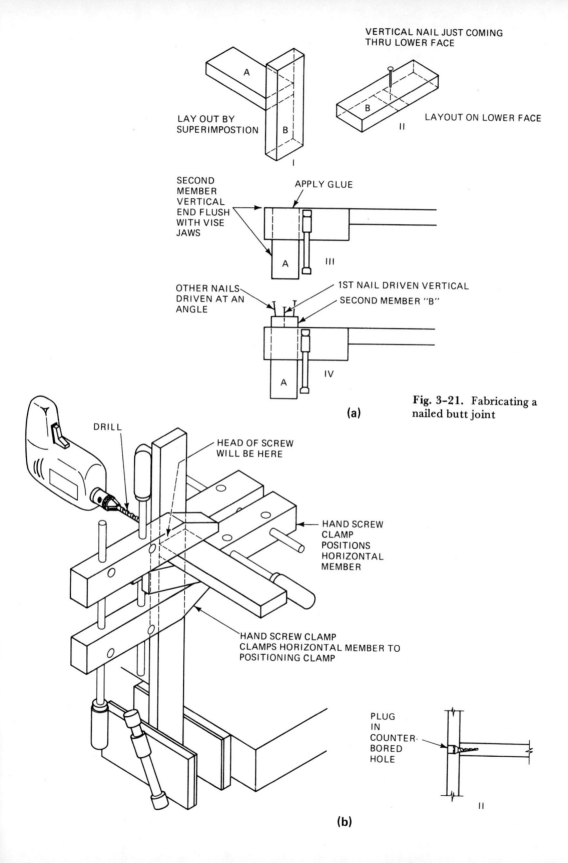

VERTICAL NAIL JUST COMING THRU LOWER FACE

LAY OUT BY SUPERIMPOSTION

LAYOUT ON LOWER FACE

A

B

I

B

II

SECOND MEMBER VERTICAL END FLUSH WITH VISE JAWS

APPLY GLUE

A

III

OTHER NAILS DRIVEN AT AN ANGLE

1ST NAIL DRIVEN VERTICAL

SECOND MEMBER "B"

A

IV

(a)

Fig. 3-21. Fabricating a nailed butt joint

DRILL

HEAD OF SCREW WILL BE HERE

HAND SCREW CLAMP POSITIONS HORIZONTAL MEMBER

HAND SCREW CLAMP CLAMPS HORIZONTAL MEMBER TO POSITIONING CLAMP

PLUG IN COUNTER- BORED HOLE

II

(b)

member to the first clamp as shown. This arrangement holds the two pieces to be joined in position during the drilling of the holes for the screws.

4. Locate the position of the screws on the outside face of the vertical piece [Fig. 3-21(b-I)]. Drill the root-diameter holes [Fig. 3-57(a)] through the first member into the second member. Repeat for each screw. Remove the clamp holding the horizontal member in position. Remove the horizontal member.

5. Drill the shank holes in the vertical member, using the already drilled root-diameter holes as starting holes.

6. Countersink the holes.

7. Apply glue to the end of the piece removed earlier and reposition it against the clamp and the other member [Fig. 3-21(b-I)]. Reinstall the clamp that was used earlier to hold the horizontal member to the first clamp.

8. Install the screws. By drilling the anchor holes all the way through one piece into the second piece, the position of the two, with respect to each other, is secured [Fig. 3-21(b-II)].

Dowel-reinforced butt joint. A good rule of thumb for determining the diameter of a dowel to be used in a given application is to select a dowel whose diameter is between one-half and one-third the thickness of the thinnest piece into whose edge or end the dowel will penetrate [Fig. 3-22(a)]. Penetration into each piece should be about 1-1/2 in., with a small air space left at the bottom of the hole for excess glue. Spiraled or striated dowels should be used to allow air and excess glue to escape [Fig. 3-22(a)].

End-to-face through dowel joint. This joint is made using a procedure similar to that described for the screwed butt joint above. Steps 1 through 3 are identical. In step 4, instead of drilling a root-diameter hole through the pieces, bore a hole equal in diameter to the dowel to be used. Then apply glue, insert the dowels, and clamp the pieces until the glue sets. This procedure utilizes *superimposition*—the second general rule of joinery.

Fig. 3-22. Dowel joint specifications

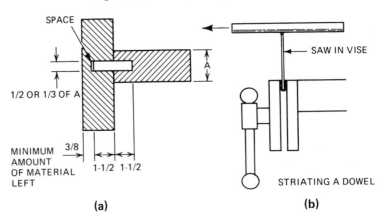

(a) (b)

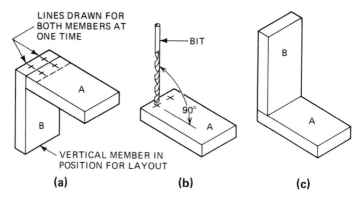

Fig. 3-23. Fabricating a blind dowel joint

End-to-Face Blind Dowel Joint—Precision Layout Method

1. After squaring-up the pieces to be joined, lay out the joint as shown in Fig. 3-23(a).
2. Bore the holes with care so that they are vertical (at right angles to the surfaces they penetrate) [Fig. 3-23(b)].
3. Insert dowels and check alignment and fit. If one dowel fails to align with its matching hole, plug each hole and lay out and bore a second set of matching holes. Do this in *new wood,* away from the plugged hole.
4. Reassemble pieces without glue to check alignment.
5. Apply glue, assemble, and clamp until glue sets.

End-to-Face Blind Dowel Joint—Dowel Center Alignment Method

1. Repeat step 1 above.
2. Bore holes into the end of one member using a dowel jig. This ensures the centering of the holes in the end of the piece [(Fig. 3-24(a)].

Fig. 3-24. Fabricating a blind dowel joint using dowel centers

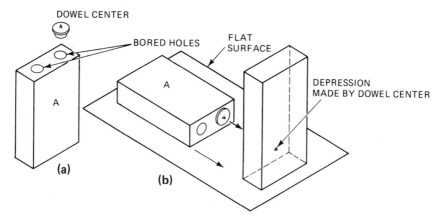

3. Insert a *dowel center* into one of the bored holes, align the two pieces to be joined on a flat surface, and push them together. This results in a depression in the face of the mating piece [Fig. 3–24(b)].

4. Bore a hole into the face of the second member, using the depression made by the dowel center as the center of the hole.

5. Remove the dowel center from the first hole and replace it with a dowel of suitable length and diameter. Install the dowel center in the second hole.

6. Reassemble the, two members on a flat surface, using the dowel as an alignment guide. Press the pieces together.

Edge-to-edge dowel joints. This variety of the reinforced butt joint is commonly used in cabinetmaking to combine several pieces to make a table-top or cabinet top of solid wood.

Precision Layout Method

1. After cutting pieces to length, arrange them so that the heartwood on alternate pieces faces up [Fig. 3–25(a)].

2. If the finished piece is to be surfaced [Fig. 3–25(a)], the grain of the faces on the same side of the finished piece must go in the same direction. Identify all upper faces [Fig. 3–25(a)].

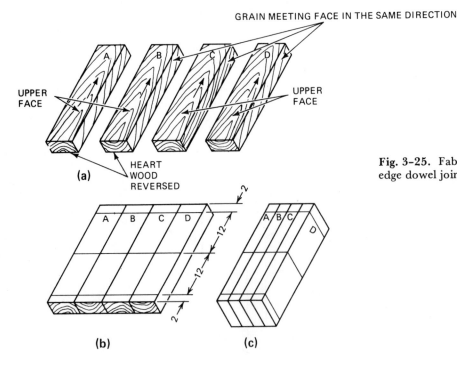

Fig. 3–25. Fabricating an edge to edge dowel joint

3. In edge-to-edge dowel joints the outermost dowels should be approximately 2 in. from the ends of the piece. Other dowels should be at approximately 12-in. intervals. With the pieces face down on the bench, lay out lines as shown in Fig. 3–25(b).

4. Carry these lines around to the adjacent edges after positioning mating pieces face-to-face with their mating edges up [Fig. 3–25(c)]. This is an example of general rule 4: When laying out identical pieces, position them in such a way that layout lines can be made in one cut or pencil stroke.

5. Lay out centerlines on these edges with a marking gauge.

6. Bore the holes with an appropriate bit.

7. Cut, striate, and install dowels and test joint fit. Glue and clamp.

Doweling Jig and Dowel Center Method

1. Repeat steps 1 through 4 above.

2. Position doweling jig over layout lines and bore required holes in one edge of a pair of pieces to be joined. Use the dowel centers to locate holes on the edges of the other pieces (Fig. 3–26).

Fig. 3–26(a).

DOWEL CENTER IN
FIRST HOLE BORED

EDGE PIECE #1

EDGE PIECE #2

PIECE #1

PUSHING PIECES
TOGETHER

PIECE #2

LAYOUT LOCATION
IMPRESSION MADE
BY DOWEL CENTER

EDGE PIECE #2

Fig. 3– 26(b).

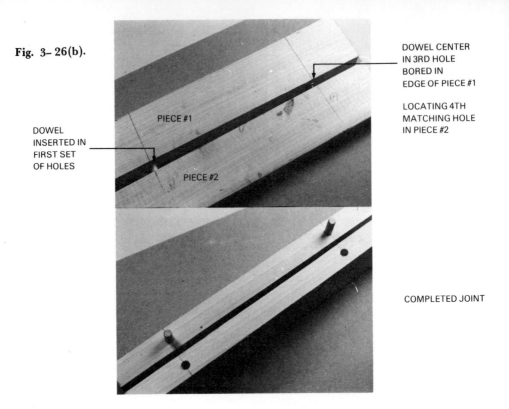

DOWEL CENTER
IN 3RD HOLE
BORED IN
EDGE OF PIECE #1

LOCATING 4TH
MATCHING HOLE
IN PIECE #2

PIECE #1

DOWEL
INSERTED IN
FIRST SET
OF HOLES

PIECE #2

COMPLETED JOINT

Glued and blocked reinforced butt joints. Glued and blocked joints are used where extra strength is required at a butt joint, where the blocks are not aesthetically objectionable, or where appropriate clamps are not available.

1. Position the pieces to be joined as shown in Fig. 3-27(a). The use of the cardboard shim leaves enough space between the block and the vertical member to allow the pieces to be drawn together.

2. Place a block of appropriate dimensions in position, secure it with a clamp, and drill anchor holes through the block into the member below. (The dimensions—width and thickness—of the block should be approximately twice the thickness of the smallest of the two pieces being joined. Its length should be equal to the width of these pieces.)

3. Remove the block and complete drilling it for screws.

4. Apply glue to the lower surface of the block and screw it to the bottom member.

5. Drill anchor holes through the block into the vertical member [Fig. 3-27(b)]. Complete drilling holes in the block for screws.

6. Remove the cardboard shim from between the vertical member and the block, and apply glue to the vertical edge of the block.

7. Reassemble the joint and drive screws in until the two components are drawn together.

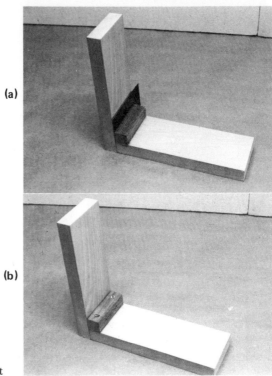

(a)

(b)

Fig. 3-27. Fabricating a blocked joint

Draw bolts. Draw bolts (Fig. 3–28) are often used in the construction of work benches and other heavy-use furniture. They are also useful in situations where clamping is difficult to accomplish. If desired, the bolt head hole and the nut hole can be plugged.

Lap joints. Lapped joints are among the simplest and strongest joints available to the woodworker (Fig. 3–29). Several varieties of the joint exist, including cross-lap, middle-lap, and end-lap. The basic procedure is similar for each.

The procedure for making an end-lap joint is as follows:

1. Square-up the pieces to be joined. Note that each member is full length because of the lapping of the pieces [Fig. 3–30(a)].

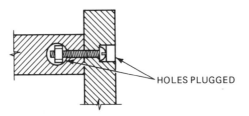

Fig. 3-28. Draw bolt joint

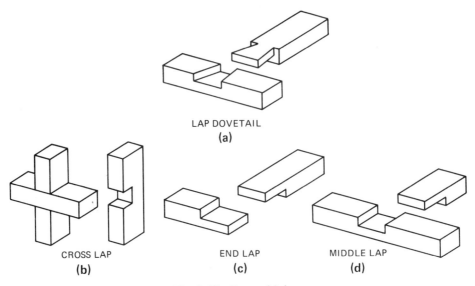

LAP DOVETAIL
(a)

CROSS LAP
(b)

END LAP
(c)

MIDDLE LAP
(d)

Fig. 3-29. Lapped joints

2. Lay out centerlines on the ends and edges of the pieces.

3. Complete the layout of each piece by superimposing the mating member on the second member [Fig. 3-30(b)].

4. Cut a starting notch for each of the cuts to be made on the faces of each member. Make these notched cuts with a backsaw, stopping 1/8 in. away from the layout line on the edge [Fig. 3-30(c)].

5. Place the work in a vise or clamp it down to the bench [Fig. 3-30(d)]. Chisel, bevel side down, toward the layout line saw cut until most of the material is removed between the saw cuts [Fig. 3-30(e)]. At this point approximately 1/8 in. of material remains to be removed.

6. With the chisel bevel side up, remove the balance of the material [Fig. 3-30(e)].

7. Repeat steps 4 through 6. As the layout line is approached, make trial fittings and pare until the desired fit is obtained.

Fig. 3-30. Fabricating an end lap joint: (a) End lap joint; (b) Laying out; (c) Saw cut next to layout line; (d) Rough chiseling between saw cuts; (e) Paring to final size using a guage block

(a)   (b)   (c)

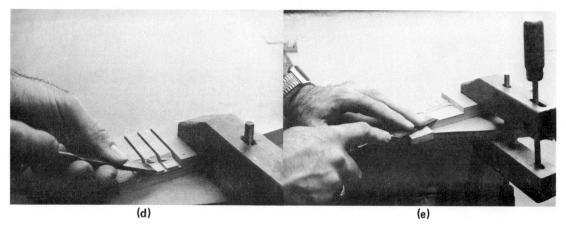

(d)   (e)

Fig. 3-30. Cont'd

In middle-lap joints, the recess or gain in the middle of one member should be cut out first. This procedure for cutting female portions of a joint first is common practice for all male-female-type joints.

Rabbet joints. A rabbet is a step cut into the end or edge of a piece. When this rabbet is cut to accept a second piece at right angles (Fig. 3-31), a rabbet joint is formed. This joint is commonly used for fitting the top shelf of a bookcase into position.

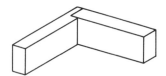

Fig. 3-31. A rabbet joint

The procedure for making rabbet joints is similar to that described for lapped joints. The length of the rabbet is equal to the thickness of the piece that mates with it. The depth of the rabbet is usually half the thickness of the piece into which it is cut.

Dado joints. A dado is a groove cut across the grain. This dado can be cut so that its width is equal to the thickness of a second member which fits into it [Fig. 3-32(a)]. When this is done, a dado joint has been fashioned. Such joints are commonly used for fitting shelves into cabinets and bookcases. The *stop dado* makes the joint appear to be a butt joint. In simple box or drawer construction, the dado is frequently combined with a rabbet to form a rabbet-dado joint [Fig. 3-32(b) and (c)].

The procedure for making a dado is as follows:

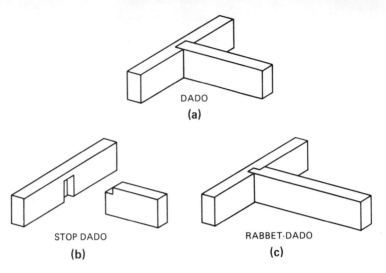

DADO

(a)

STOP DADO

(b)

RABBET-DADO

(c)

Fig. 3-32. Dado joints

1. After squaring-up the stock to be used, lay out the dado on the face of the workpiece [Fig. 3-33(a) and (b)]. The depth of the dado should not be more than half the thickness of the workpiece [Fig. 3-33(b)].

2. Make starting notches for the outside cuts of the dado.

3. Make one or more similar cuts between the first two cuts [Fig. 3-33(b)].

4. Remove the bulk of the material between the outside cuts with a chisel that is narrower than the dado [Fig. 3-33(c) and (d)].

5. Complete the bottom of the dado with a router plane. If a router plane is not available, use the chisel to complete the dado. Work with the bevel up, off a thickness block or the vise-liner edge [Fig. 3-33(d)].

Fig. 3-33. Fabricating a dado joint: (a) Knife line layout; (b) Saw cut next to line and saw cut stops short of depth line; (c) Rough chiseling; (d) Paring dado bottom; (e) Trimming sides of dado

(a)   **(b)**

Fig. 3-33. Cont'd

(c)

(d)

(e)

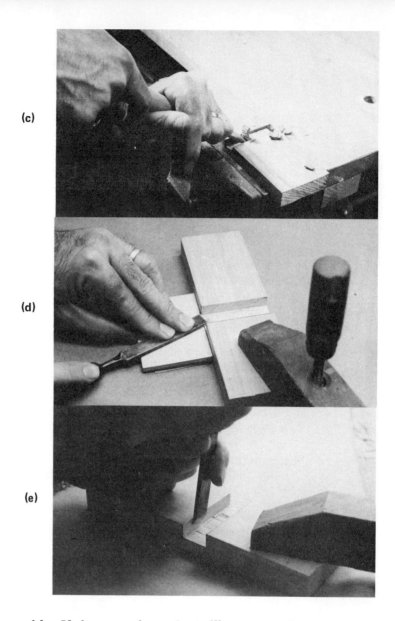

6. Make a trial assembly. If the second member will not enter the dado, scrape some material off one face of the piece and try again. The shoulders of the dado can be trimmed to fit with a chisel, as shown in Fig. 3-33(e).

Dovetail joints. The dovetail joint is a prime example of a lock-joint. Such a joint does not depend on glue for its strength. A number of variations of this joint are commonly used, including the lapped dovetail [Fig. 3-34(a)], the through dovetail [Fig. 3-34(b)], the blind dovetail [Fig. 3-34(c)], the multiple dovetail [Fig. 3-34(d)], and the half-slip dovetail [Fig. 3-34(e)].

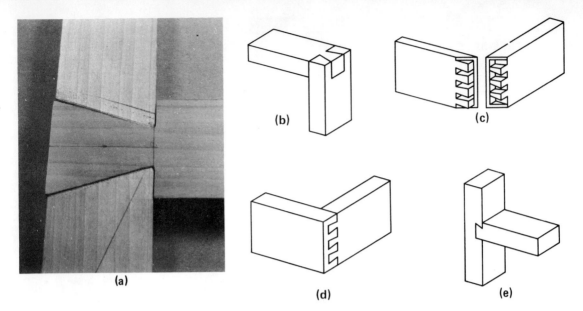

(a) (b) (c) (d) (e)

Fig. 3-34. Types of dovetail joints

Machine-made dovetails are made so that the male (pins) and female (sockets) are equally spaced and equal in width, with a slope of 20°. Hand-made dovetails can vary in design, with pins being wider than sockets (Fig. 3-35). The slope of these dovetails is usually one in six or one in eight [Fig. 3-37(g)]. If the slope numbers get too close, making the angle very acute, the corners of the dovetail pin will become subject to fracture along the grain lines [Fig. 3-37(h)].

For clarification, a procedure for making a single dovetail follows.

Fabricating a Single Dovetail Joint

1. Square-up the members to be joined.
2. Lay out the socket of the dovetail joint [Fig. 3-36(a)].
3. Cut *next to and inside* the layout lines with a dovetail saw.
4. Chisel out the material between the saw cuts [Fig. 3-36(b)]. Chisel

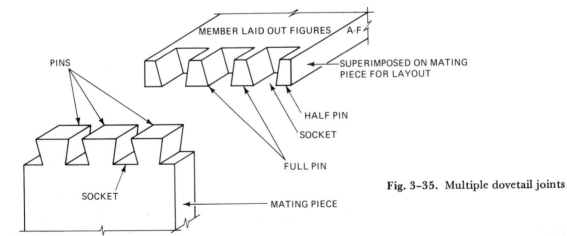

Fig. 3-35. Multiple dovetail joints

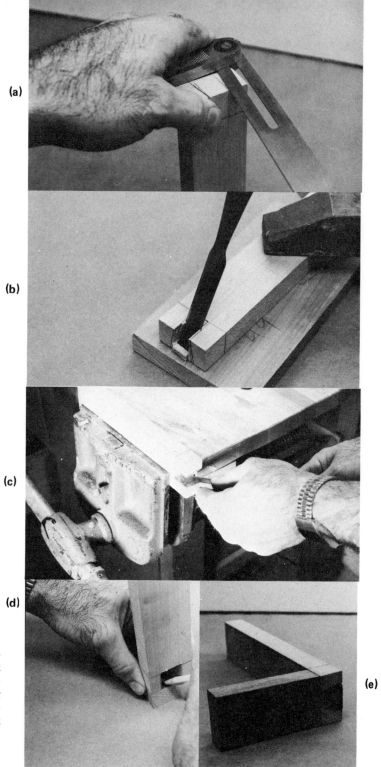

Fig. 3-36. Fabricating a dovetail joint: (a) Laying out dovetail socket; (b) Rough chiseling socket; (c) Paring socket; (d) Laying out dovetail using socket as a template; (e) Assembled joint

part way through the workpiece from one face, then reverse the piece and chisel in toward the opposite face. This will help to limit face-grain splitting.

5. Pare the sides of the socket as shown [Fig. 3-36(c)].

6. Complete the pin layout [Fig. 3-36(d)].

7. Go over the pin layout with a knife. Make the shoulder cuts with a dovetail saw.

8. Cut *outside* the layout lines, starting on the end of the pin. Pare away the remaining material with a chisel while frequently making test fittings to the socket. The final fit can be made by scraping with the chisel.

Multiple dovetails are commonly used in drawer construction. The following procedure can be used for laying out multiple dovetails for hand-tool fabrication.

Laying out Multiple Dovetails

1. After squaring-up the pieces to be joined, lay out the baselines of the dovetails on the pieces as shown in Fig. 3-37(a). Note that the distance from the end of the workpiece to the baseline is equal to the thickness of the mating piece.

2. A useful rule of thumb is to make the *wide end of the pin equal to the thickness of the thinner member* (approximate size). The width of the pin bases is approximately half the width of the wide ends. In the example shown in Fig. 3-35, each piece is 1/2 in. thick, so the wide end of the pin will be 1/2 in. in width.

3. Lay out half a pin width on each edge of the workpiece [Fig. 3-37(b)]. Draw in sloping lines, using a "T" bevel set to a one-in-six slope.

4. Make a trial pin layout [Fig. 3-37(c)] by measuring alternately one wide end of the pin (1/2 in. in this case) and then one base width (1/4 in. in this case). This trial layout indicates that three full pins will fit into the space between the half-pins on the ends.

5. Divide the space between the two half-pins into three equal parts [Fig. 3-37(d)]. These two lines represent the centerlines of the two full-size pins to be laid out.

6. Lay out a distance equal to half the width of the pin base on each side of the centerlines as in step 4 [Fig. 3-37(e)].

7. Lay out pins as shown in Fig. 3-37(f) using the "T" bevel set to a one-in-six slope. The spacing between the inner pins is equal.

To *fabricate a multiple dovetail joint (through version),* make the layout of the pins on one of the members, and cut these pins out using a dovetail saw and a chisel. Then use this set of pins to lay out the mating sockets and pins (Fig. 3-35).

Mortise and tenon joints. The mortise and tenon joint consists of a tongue or tenon which fits into a rectangular recess in the mating member, the mortise [Fig. 3-39(a)]. Mortise and tenon joints find their most com-

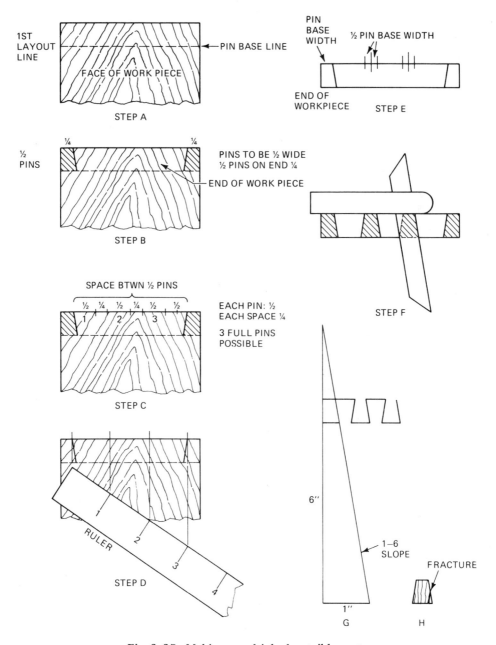

1ST LAYOUT LINE — **PIN BASE LINE**

FACE OF WORK PIECE

STEP A

PIN BASE WIDTH — ½ PIN BASE WIDTH

END OF WORKPIECE

STEP E

½ PINS

¼ ¼

END OF WORK PIECE

PINS TO BE ½ WIDE
½ PINS ON END ¼

STEP B

SPACE BTWN ½ PINS

½ ¼ ½ ¼ ½ ½

1 2 3

EACH PIN: ½
EACH SPACE ¼

3 FULL PINS
POSSIBLE

STEP C

STEP F

RULER

1
2
3
4

STEP D

6″

1-6 SLOPE

FRACTURE

1″

G

H

Fig. 3-37. Making a multiple dovetail layout

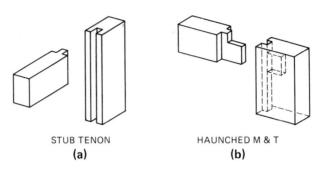

STUB TENON
(a)

HAUNCHED M & T
(b)

Fig. 3-38.

mon applications in mill work, in fashioning frames in frame and panel construction [Fig. 3-38(a) and (b)], and in furniture construction, where they are used to join rails and legs or aprons and legs. In many applications, the mortise and tenon joint has been replaced by the dowel butt joint because of their ease and simplicity of fabrication and the improvement of glues used with them.

Among the variations of the mortise and tenon joint are the *blind* [Fig. 3-39(a)], the *through* [Fig. 3-39(b)], the *housed* [Fig. 3-39(c)], the *bare-faced* [Fig. 3-39(d)], *splined* [Fig. 3-39(e)], *tusked* [Fig. 3-39(f)], *foxed* [Fig. 3-39(g)], the *open* [Fig. 3-39(h)], and the *stub* [Fig. 3-38(a)]. The blind mortise and tenon [Fig. 3-39(a)], is the variation most commonly used in leg-rail applications. The housed mortise, mortise and tenon joint [Fig. 3-39(e)], is a simplified version of the joint. The absence of shoulders reduces the stability and strength of the joint. The bare-faced version [Fig. 3-39(d)] is used where an apron's face is flush with the face or edge of a leg. If a standard centered tenon were used, the material left between the mortise and the face of the leg would be reduced to the point where the strength of the joint would be reduced.

The splined or loose tenon [Fig. 3-39(e)] is useful in situations where defects such as knots or cross grain occur at the point where a tenon would normally be formed. This variation is also useful in repair work when the original tenon has been damaged. The tusked tenon, mortise and tenon joint [Fig. 3-39(f)], was used in colonial furniture and is used in modern versions of such period furniture. Joints of this type were not glued, which allowed the pieces to be "knocked down" and disassembled.

The foxed tenon, mortise and tenon joint [Fig. 3-39(g)], is designed to expand the tenon's width during assembly, thereby making it almost a lock-joint. The open mortise and tenon joint [Fig. 3-39(h)] is used in light construction (e.g., screen frames) and is frequently used in contemporary furniture construction because of its decorative quality. The stub tenon is commonly used in frame and panel construction. The tenon is equal in thickness to the groove milled for the panel [Fig. 3-38(a)]. The haunched version [Fig. 3-38(b)] is used to reduce the possibility of splitting out the piece of wood directly above the tenon in the stile.

The guidelines listed below are intended for use with the standard blind mortise and tenon joint. However, these guidelines apply generally and should be used to the extent possible with other varieties of the joint.

Design Guidelines for the Mortise and Tenon Joint

1. The thickness of the tenon should be between one-third and one-half the thickness of the thinner member [Fig. 3-40(a)].

2. The width of the tenon should be fixed by making the shoulder of the tenon equal along the cheeks and the edges of the tenon [Fig. 3-40(a)]

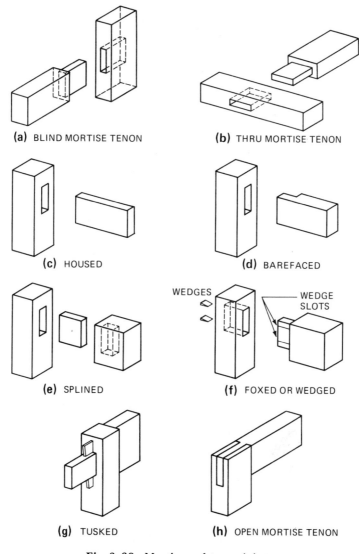

(a) BLIND MORTISE TENON

(b) THRU MORTISE TENON

(c) HOUSED

(d) BAREFACED

(e) SPLINED

WEDGES

WEDGE SLOTS

(f) FOXED OR WEDGED

(g) TUSKED

(h) OPEN MORTISE TENON

Fig. 3-39. Mortise and tenon joints

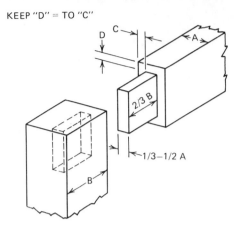

KEEP "D" = TO "C"

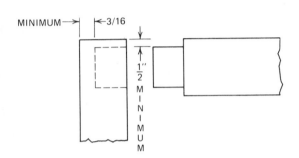

Fig. 3-40. Designing guidelines for a mortise and tenon joint

where practical. In extra-wide tenoned pieces, multiple tenons may be preferable.

3. The length of the tenon should provide a maximum penetration into the mortised piece equal to two-thirds of the width of the mortised piece [Fig. 3-40(a)].

For *laying out a mortise and tenon joint,* squared-up material is used [Fig. 3-41(a)]. First, lay out the mortises. Then make the tenon layout as shown in Fig. 3-41(b). Tenons are 1/16 in. shorter than mortise depth to allow space for excess glue during assembly.

Mortise Fabrication Procedure—Hand Tools

1. Draw a centerline through each of the mortise layouts [Fig. 3-41(b)].
2. Bore a series of holes along this centerline [Fig. 3-41(c)].
3. Remove the material between the bored holes with a chisel [Fig. 3-41(d) and (e)].

Tenon Fabrication—Hand Tools

1. Make cheek cuts *outside* the layout lines [Fig. 3-41(f)].
2. Make tenon edge cuts *outside* the layout lines [Fig. 3-41(f)].
3. Make shoulder cuts on the line, using a *starting notch* for the saw cut [Fig. 3-41(g)].

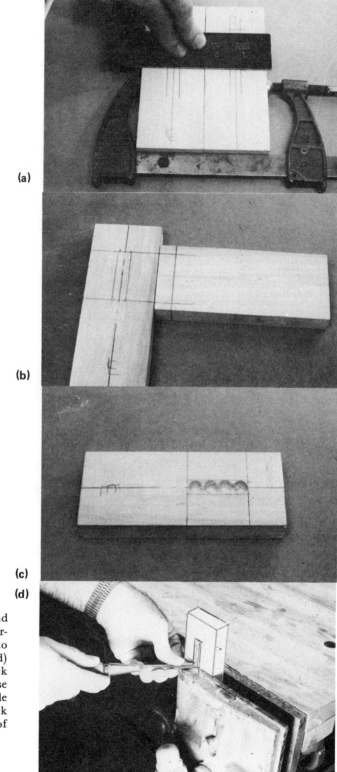

(a)

(b)

(c)

(d)

Fig. 3-41. Fabrication of a mortise and tenon joint. (a) Laying out identical mortises; (b) Transforming mortise layout to tenon; (c) Holes bored for mortise; (d) Chiseling mortise end using vise jaw block as a guide; (e) Chiseling sides of mortise using vise jaw; (f) Saw cuts made outside of layout lines for the tenon; (g) Block guiding saw during shoulder cutting of tenon.

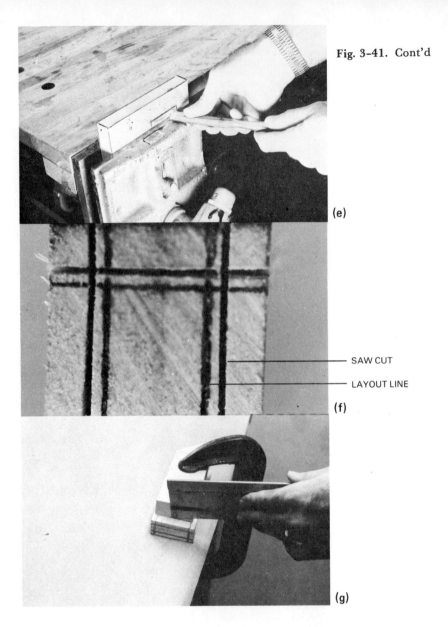

Fig. 3-41. Cont'd

(e)

SAW CUT

LAYOUT LINE

(f)

(g)

4. Pare and scrape the cheeks and edges of the tenon with a wide chisel until the tenon enters the mortise, fitting snugly. The ends of the tenons should be chamfered to facilitate final assembly.

Mitered joints. The most common miter joint is the one formed by two pieces cut to a 45° angle. These joints are inherently weak not only because they are a type of butt joint involving pieces with end grain, but also because effective clamping is difficult. Since the most common application of mitering is the making of picture frames, this topic is discussed in detail in this section.

Several variations of the miter joint are commonly used, including the
common butt miter [Fig. 3-42(a)], the slip feather miter [Fig. 3-42(b)],
[Fig. 3-42(c)], the doweled miter [Fig. 3-42(d)], and the
[Fig. 3-42(e)]. The butt miter is the most common and is
and nailed. The slip feather miter is a reinforced version which
ricate. The splined and the doweled miters provide added
cate the pieces with respect to each other. This makes clamp-
he half-lapped miter is really a composite consisting of a joint
mitered and half-lapped. It provides excellent strength, gives
of a miter on the face, but shows end grain.

ommon Butt Miter

rkpieces should be squared-up to width and left oversized in
both ends of the workpieces are to be cut, squaring ends is

re laid out on the workpieces with a try square and a miter
43(a)].

Fig. 3-42. Types of miter joints. (a) Butt miter; (b) Slip feather miter;
(c) Splined miter; (d) Doweled miter; (e) Half lap miter

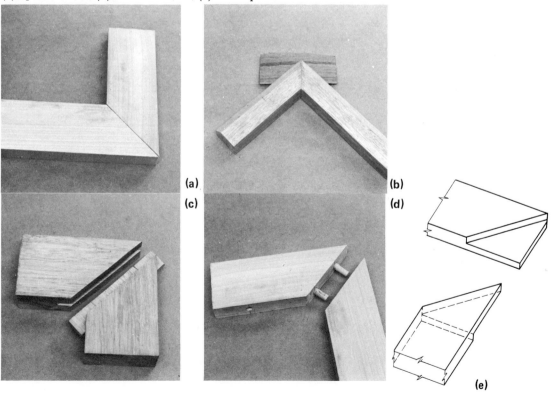

(a)   (b)

(c)   (d)

(e)

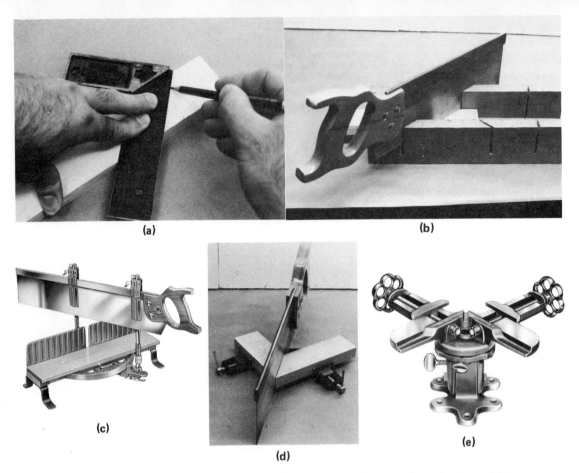

Fig. 3-43. (a) Laying out miter; (b) Cutting miter in a wooden miter box; (c) A steel miter box; (d) Resawing miter joint; (e) Miter vise

3. It is possible to cut miters with a backsaw and a guide block, and then to plane the mitered surfaces. In most instances the craftsman uses a miter box to facilitate the making of these cuts [Fig. 3-43(b) and (c)]. The ordinary wooden miter box is adequate for narrow pieces; however, the steel miter box is more reliable for wider workpieces. In any case, the workpiece is placed against the back fence of the miter box after the miter box has been set to the desired angle. It is held in place with one hand or a clamp while the saw is carefully lowered onto the workpiece. The cut is made *outside* or *scrap side* of the layout line.

4. After the mating pieces have been cut, a trial assembly is attempted. If the angle is incorrect, the pieces are placed in a miter vise and resawed with a backsaw. This process results in two new surfaces that are parallel to each other [Fig. 3-43(d)].

5. Glue is applied to the joint and the assembly is clamped in the miter vise or a miter clamp [Fig. 3-43(e)]. Nails may be driven while the piece is in the miter clamp.

Making a Picture Frame Having Butt Miters

1. Note that the essential requirements for a frame are to have the pieces opposite each other *equal in length* and to have the miter angles correct.

2. Lay out the miters on each of the four pieces to be used in the frame. Notice that the length of the pieces is determined by the inside measurements of the frame, which are made in the corner of the rabbet [Fig. 3-44(a)]. Approximately 1/8 in. should be added to the length of these measurements to allow extra material for later adjustment.

3. Cut the angles in a miter box as described in steps 2 and 3 above.

4. Assemble and glue the two pieces that make up the opposite corners of the frame [Fig. 3-44(b)].

5. Assemble the frame and recut if necessary. Glue the third corner [Fig. 3-44(c)].

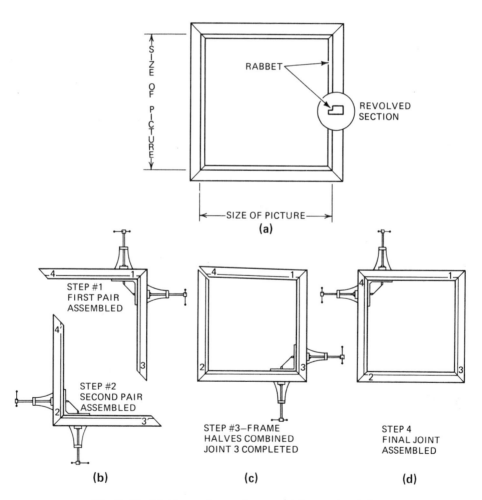

Fig. 3-44. Making a picture frame with butt miter joints

6. Repeat step 4 for the remaining corner of the frame after the glue has set on the other joints.

Making a Slip Feather Miter

1. Repeat steps 1 through 3 above for making a common butt miter, but leave the nails out of the joint.
2. After the glue in the joint sets, lay out a line on the edges of the joint as shown in Fig. 3-45(a).
3. Cut through the joint along the layout line, using a saw whose kerf is equal in thickness to a piece of cabinet veneer. Apply glue to the veneer and insert it into the saw cut with the grain of the veneer at right angles to the original miter cut. Clamp as shown in Fig. 3-45(b) and (c).

When the glue has set, trim away the excess veneer with a chisel.

Making a Splined Miter

1. Make the basic joint using the steps for making a common butt miter.
2. Lay out the groove for the spline on the face of the miter cut.
3. Cut the groove with a backsaw and chisel out any of the remaining material with a narrow chisel.
4. Cut an appropriate piece of stock for the spline to *length*. Note that the grain direction on the spline is at right angles to the miter cut [Fig. 3-42(c)].

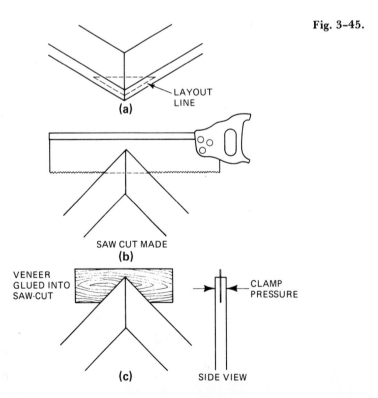

Fig. 3-45.

(a) LAYOUT LINE

(b) SAW CUT MADE

(c) VENEER GLUED INTO SAW-CUT — CLAMP PRESSURE — SIDE VIEW

5. Apply glue, assemble, and clamp the joint. The extra spline material may be cut away after the glue has set.

To *make a doweled miter joint*, first make the butt miter as described above under "Making a Common Butt Miter Joint." Then follow a procedure similar to that outlined for making an edge-to-edge dowel joint earlier in this chapter.

Making a Half-Lapped Miter

1. Square-up all workpieces *completely*, including the ends.
2. Lay out the joint [Fig. 3–42(e)].
3. Carefully make the miter cuts *halfway* into the face of each piece.
4. Make saw cuts parallel to the faces on the *scrap side* of the layout line.
5. Pare to the layout line on one piece with a chisel. Fit the second piece to the first piece by paring with a chisel and scraping until the desired fit is obtained.
6. Apply glue, assemble the joint, and clamp.

FASTENING DEVICES

Nails

Nails are the oldest and still the most commonly used metal fastening. In construction work, they are virtually the only fastening used. Nails develop their holding power by piercing and displacing wood fibers (Fig. 3–46). This holding power is affected by the density of the wood, the diameter of the nail, the depth of penetration of the nail, and the relationship between the nail direction and the grain of the wood.

Dense woods hold better because their cells contain less unfilled space; thus they deform less easily during nail penetration than soft woods do. A

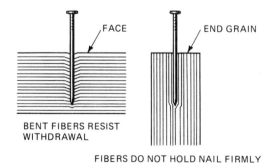

FACE   END GRAIN

BENT FIBERS RESIST
WITHDRAWAL

FIBERS DO NOT HOLD NAIL FIRMLY
SPLITTING POSSIBLE

Fig. 3–46. Nail holding power

larger-diameter nail forces fibers to displace to a greater degree than a thin nail, so the friction between the nail surface and these fibers is increased. Nail length determines nail surface area; so as the length increases, the skin resistance of the nail increases. The direction of driving is critical because of the way in which fibers are displaced as a nail penetrates a piece of wood (Fig. 3–46).

Selection and use of nails. Nails are sold by the pound. Select a nail which will provide the maximum holding power without causing the wood to split or the work to look unsightly (Fig. 3–47). In general, a nail's length

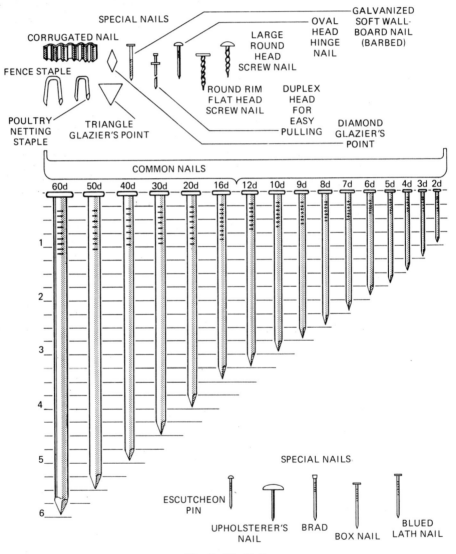

Fig. 3-47. Nails

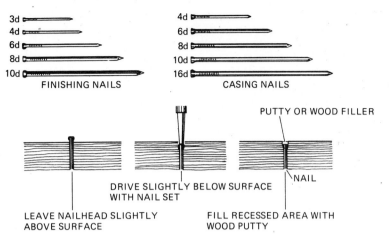

FINISHING NAILS

CASING NAILS

PUTTY OR WOOD FILLER

NAIL

DRIVE SLIGHTLY BELOW SURFACE
WITH NAIL SET

LEAVE NAILHEAD SLIGHTLY
ABOVE SURFACE

FILL RECESSED AREA WITH
WOOD PUTTY

HOW TO COUNTERSINK A NAIL

Fig. 3-47 Cont'd

should be three times the thickness of the piece it will go through first (Fig. 3-48).

In driving nails into relatively thin material, or in driving close to the end of a piece, splitting can be reduced by blunting the point of the nail slightly. This blunting causes the nail to crush fibers rather than to displace them (Fig. 3-49). It also results in some reduction in holding power.

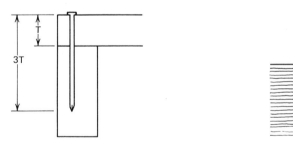

Fig. 3-48. Nail length

Fig. 3-49. Blunted nail

When driving a nail, use the following procedure:

1. Always check the hammer to determine whether or not the head is securely attached to the handle.

2. Begin by placing the face of the hammer on the head of the nail. This helps to establish the correct position for the hammer (Fig. 3-50).

3. Lift the head and give the nail a light tap; *use wrist action only.* (The fingers of the other hand are holding the nail in position.)

4. Once the nail is started, it can stand in the wood without support. Remove your hand from the nail and drive the nail in; *use forearm and wrist*

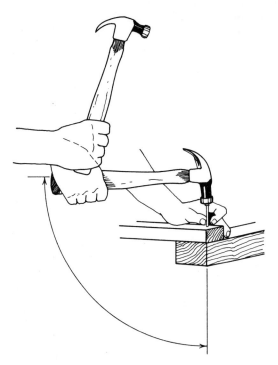

Fig. 3-50. Driving a nail

action. For very small nails, wrist action along may suffice. For medium-sized nails, wrist and forearm action are required. For heavy nailing, *wrist, forearm, and shoulder action are used.*

5. If the nail bends during driving and no obstruction such as a knot is found, the most likely cause of the bending is the failure to keep the face of the hammer parallel to the head of the nail.

Nail clinching. When maximum holding power is required in rough work, the nail can be clinched. This is accomplished by using a nail that will go through both pieces of wood. Then the piece is reversed and the point of the nail is bent over across the grain.

Drawing nails. The claws of the hammer are generally used to pull nails out (Fig. 3-51). For longer nails, a block is placed under the hammer after approximately 1 in. of the nail is exposed above the face of the workpiece. If the head of the nail is flush with the surface of the workpiece, a nail puller can be used (Fig. 3-52), but this will damage the surface of the piece. If possible, the two pieces can be pried apart and then pushed together again (Fig. 3-53). This sometimes results in the elevation of the nail. A small-headed nail can sometimes be driven through to the other surface of the piece with a pin punch and then pulled out with a pair of pliers.

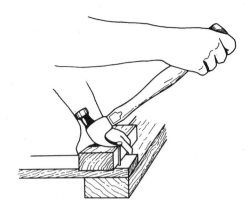

Fig. 3-51. Drawing nails

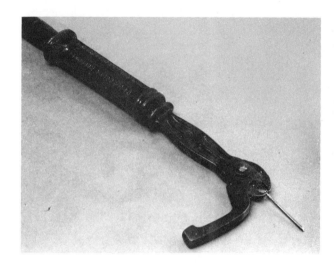

Fig. 3-52. Nail puller

Fig. 3-53. Prying pieces apart leaves nail head up above surface

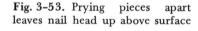 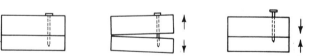

Wood Screws

Wood screws provide holding power that is superior to that of nails. They can be used to help clamp parts together while the glue sets, especially where the use of clamps is not practical or desirable. The holding or withdrawal resistance of wood screws is affected by the same factors which affect the holding power of the nail.

Wood screws are sold in boxes of one hundred. Each box is labeled to indicate screw length in inches, screw diameter by number (the larger the number, the larger the diameter), head type, the material the screws are

Fig. 3-54.

made from, and the finish on the screws. For example, the box may be labeled 1-1/2 in., No. 8, flathead, steel, blued, wood screws. In this case "blued" refers to the blue rust-resistant finish on the screws (Fig. 3-54).

Selection of wood screws by length. In general, wood screw length should be approximately three times the thickness of the piece the screw will go through first [Fig. 3-55(a)]. Where this is not possible, at least half of the threaded end of the screw should be embedded in the second piece [Fig. 3-55(a)].

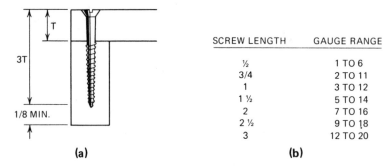

SCREW LENGTH	GAUGE RANGE
½	1 TO 6
3/4	2 TO 11
1	3 TO 12
1 ½	5 TO 14
2	7 TO 16
2 ½	9 TO 18
3	12 TO 20

(a)   (b)

Fig. 3-55. Determining screw length

Selection of wood screws by diameter. Hardwoods require larger-diameter screws to resist the tendency of the screw to twist apart while being driven because this type of wood resists displacement by the screw to a larger extent than softwoods do. The amount of holding power, or withdrawal resistance, increases with the diameter of the screw. In general, No. 8 through No. 10 screws are used most frequently [Fig. 3-55(b)].

Selection of wood screws by head type. Flathead screws are probably the most commonly used because their heads are flush with or below the surface (Fig. 3-56). The round head is often used in counterbored applications or in fastening metal to wood. The slots in round-head screws are surrounded with more metal for situations requiring large amounts of driving power.

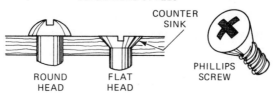

SCREW HEAD STYLES

ROUND HEAD   FLAT HEAD   COUNTER SINK   PHILLIPS SCREW

Fig. 3-56. Screw head types

The oval or button-type screws are a compromise between the flat and round heads. Various slot styles, such as the Phillips head, are often selected for their aesthetic appeal.

Material and finish. Material selection is determined by application requirements. For example, in marine applications, brass or stainless steel is the choice. For interior use, iron or steel will suffice.

Using wood screws. To prevent splitting, at least two holes of different diameters must be drilled for each wood screw driven. One of the holes provides space for the threaded portion of the screw and is known as the *root hole* or *pilot hole* (Fig. 3-57). The other hole provides room for the unthreaded shank of the screw and is called the *shank hole* (Fig. 3-57). In softwoods, the anchor hole should be about 1/8 in. shorter than the maximum penetration of the screw. In hardwoods, the anchor hole should be the full length of the threaded portion of the screw.

Suggested Procedure for Fastening with Wood Screws

1. Select the wood screw to suit application requirements.
2. Lay out screw hole locations on the workpiece which will receive the screw heads.
3. Clamp the two pieces in their mated positions.
4. If a drill is used to make both the anchor hole and the shank hole, drill the anchor hole through the top piece and to the required depth in the piece to receive the threaded portion of the screw [Fig. 3-58(a)]. If an auger bit is used for the larger hole, bore that hole first to the required depth. Then drill the anchor hole [Fig. 3-58(b)]. This procedure is suggested be-

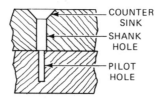

COUNTER SINK
SHANK HOLE
PILOT HOLE

Fig. 3-57(a). Holes required for a screw

Fig. 3-57(b).

BORING CHART FOR WOOD SCREWS

HOW TO USE THIS CHART

The table of wood screw specifications simplifies the selection of the bit or drill size best suited to your requirements. The fractional equivalents and undersize and oversize decimals indicate how close a bit of given fractional size will bore to the actual screw dimension and whether the fit will be snug or loose. In selecting a tool size for the pilot hole (for threaded portion of screw), note that root diameters are average dimensions measured at the middle of the threaded portion. On some screws the root diameter tapers slightly from the end of the screw, increasing toward the head. It is usually good practice to bore the pilot hole the same size as the root diameter in hardwoods, such as oak, and about 15% smaller for soft woods, such as pine and Douglas fir. In some cases, allowances can be made to advantage for moisture content and other varying factors. This same rule can be used for shank holes. The SHANK DIAMETERS shown below are standard specifications subject to tolerances of ±1/64. MAXIMUM HEAD DIAMETERS are also standard specifications which apply to flat and oval-head screws. Head sizes run from 5% to 10% smaller for round-head screws.

NO. OF SCREW	MAXIMUM HEAD DIAMETER	SHANK DIAMETER			ROOT DIAMETER			THREADS PER INCH	NO. OF SCREW
		BASIC DEC. SIZE	NEAREST FRACTIONAL EQUIVALENT		AVERAGE DEC. SIZE	NEAREST FRACTIONAL EQUIVALENT			
0	.119	.060	1/16	OVERSIZE .002	.040	3/64	OVERSIZE .007	32	0
1	.146	.073	5/64	OVERSIZE .005	.046	3/64	BASIC SIZE	28	1
2	.172	.086	3/32	OVERSIZE .007	.054	1/16	OVERSIZE .008	26	2
3	.199	.099	7/64	OVERSIZE .010	.065	1/16	UNDERSIZE .002	24	3
4	.225	.112	7/64	UNDERSIZE .003	.075	5/64	OVERSIZE .003	22	4
5	.252	.125	1/8	BASIC SIZE	.085	5/64	UNDERSIZE .007	20	5
6	.279	.138	9/64	OVERSIZE .002	.094	3/32	BASIC SIZE	18	6
7	.305	.151	5/32	OVERSIZE .005	.102	7/64	OVERSIZE .007	16	7
8	.332	.164	5/32	UNDERSIZE .007	.112	7/64	UNDERSIZE .003	15	8
9	.358	.177	11/64	UNDERSIZE .005	.122	1/8	OVERSIZE .003	14	9
10	.385	.190	3/16	UNDERSIZE .002	.130	1/8	UNDERSIZE .005	13	10
11	.411	.203	13/64	BASIC SIZE	.139	9/64	OVERSIZE .001	12	11
12	.438	.216	7/32	OVERSIZE .003	.148	9/64	UNDERSIZE .007	11	12
14	.491	.242	1/4	OVERSIZE .008	.165	5/32	UNDERSIZE .009	10	14
16	.544	.268	17/64	UNDERSIZE .002	.184	3/16	OVERSIZE .003	9	16
18	.597	.294	19/64	OVERSIZE .003	.204	13/64	UNDERSIZE .001	8	18
20	.650	.320	5/16	UNDERSIZE .007	.223	7/32	UNDERSIZE .004	8	20
24	.756	.372	3/8	OVERSIZE .003	.260	1/4	UNDERSIZE .010	7	24

GREENLEE TOOL CO

XLO Ex-Cell-O Corporation

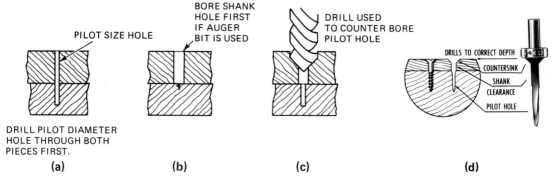

Fig. 3–58.

cause the auger bit screw requires material to enable it to pull the bit into the workpiece.

5. Redrill the hole with a drill equal in diameter to the screw shank.

6. If flathead screws are to be used, countersink the shank hole.

7. Repeat the process for all of the holes.

8. Unclamp the pieces, apply glue, reassemble, and drive the screws in.

If the holes are to be counterbored [Fig. 3–58(c)], bore the plug hole first; then follow steps 4 through 8 above.

Combination bits are available [Fig. 3–58(d)] that will drill the anchor and shank holes to the correct diameter and length and also countersink or counterbore all in one operation.

DECORATIVE TECHNIQUES

Decorative treatments of wooden surfaces should be carefully considered in terms of the total visual impact of the piece. Surface decoration can detract from the appearance of a piece if not carefully planned.

Edge Shaping—Chamfering

Edges are shaped to enhance their appearance and to render them less susceptible to damage. The simplest type of edge treatment is the chamfer.

1. Lay out lines parallel to the corner on the adjacent surfaces of the workpiece [Fig. 3–59(a)]. These lines are usually at the same distance from the corner.

2. Plane down to the lines with a plane held at a 45° angle to the faces on which the layout lines were made. The angle of the chamber may be checked with a combination square or a "T" bevel.

If the chamfering is to include the ends of the workpiece, complete

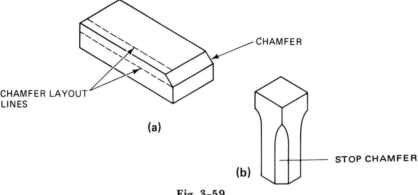

CHAMFER

CHAMFER LAYOUT
LINES

(a)

STOP CHAMFER

(b)

Fig. 3–59.

these first. Plane in from each edge toward the center of the end to avoid splitting. This will allow any split corners to be removed when the edges are chamfered.

For *stop chamfers* [Fig. 3–59(b)], the layout is similar to that of the chamfer described above. Cutting a stop chamfer usually involves the use of a chisel. A block plane can sometimes be used for the center portion of the chamfer.

Other Edge Shapes

Molding planes are available for forming other shapes on edges and ends. These planes have shaped plane irons to provide the required shaping. However, most edge shaping done by the craftsman today is accomplished with the power router, which is discussed in Chapter 5. In industry, edge and end shaping is done by processing the piece on the shaper.

Inlaying

Inlaying is a general term which means combining materials of different colors so that one or more pieces fit into areas surrounded by another material. Inlay work may involve the use of nonwood materials.

Intarsia. In intarsia work, a recess or gain is cut into the surface of an existing piece, and another shaped piece is fit into that recess. This is the easiest kind of inlaying; it will be discussed in detail below.

Marquetry. In marquetry, relatively thin materials such as veneers are assembled in a jigsaw-puzzle fashion and applied to an entire surface. This can be done with the scroll saw and layers of veneer.

Intarsia Procedure

1. After designing the intarsia, prepare a full-size layout of the piece(s) on tracing paper. Cut the shapes out and adhere the pattern to a piece of

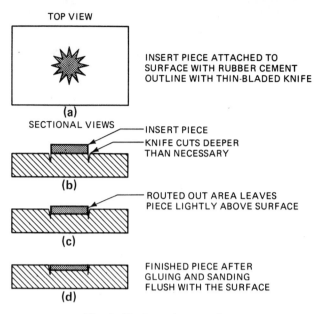

TOP VIEW

INSERT PIECE ATTACHED TO
SURFACE WITH RUBBER CEMENT
OUTLINE WITH THIN-BLADED KNIFE

(a)

SECTIONAL VIEWS

INSERT PIECE
KNIFE CUTS DEEPER
THAN NECESSARY

(b)

ROUTED OUT AREA LEAVES
PIECE LIGHTLY ABOVE SURFACE

(c)

FINISHED PIECE AFTER
GLUING AND SANDING
FLUSH WITH THE SURFACE

(d)

Fig. 3-60. Intarsia procedure

suitable wood approximately 1/16 in. thick. Rubber cement is recommended for this purpose.

2. Following the pattern lines, cut out the insert using a fine-tooth coping saw.

3. Apply rubber cement to the insert and place it in the desired position on the surface where it will be inset [Fig. 3-60(a)].

4. Outline the insert with a thin-bladed knife, such as an X-acto knife. Keep the knife blade at a 90° angle to the surface and make the cut depth slightly deeper than the thickness of the piece to be inset [Fig. 3-60(b)].

5. Remove the insert from the surface of the piece. Carefully remove the material from inside the knife-cut outlined area. A small hand router plane is ideal for this purpose. The depth of the routed-out area should be slightly less than the thickness of the piece to be inlaid [Fig. 3-60(c)].

6. Make a trial assembly of the insert to the gain. Adjust if necessary.

7. Apply glue to the gain. Place the insert into the gain and cover it with a piece of wax paper. Place a flat block over the wax paper and apply clamping pressure until the glue sets.

8. Remove the pressure block and wax paper. Sand the inlaid surface until the inlay is flush with the surrounding wood [Fig. 3-60(d)].

Regular shapes such as circles can easily be inlaid by boring a hole or series of holes in the piece and then gluing plugs or dowels into the holes. Commercial inlays, which are available in different shapes and bands, may be used according to the procedure outlined above for intarsia. In machine-tool work, saw cuts can be made parallel to edges and/or ends, and strips of contrasting woods can then be glued into these grooves (Fig. 3-61).

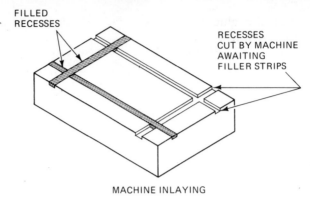

FILLED RECESSES

RECESSES CUT BY MACHINE AWAITING FILLER STRIPS

MACHINE INLAYING

Fig. 3-61.

Marquetry Checkerboard

Veneer checkerboard marquetry pieces are available from suppliers, but checkerboards can be fabricated easily if power tools are available.

1. Make a full-size layout of the checkerboard required.

2. Rip and joint five dark and four light strips so that the strips are *precisely the same width*. The length of the strips should be at least nine times their width [Fig. 3-62(a)].

3. Glue the strips together edge to edge [Fig. 3-62(a)].

4. After the glue sets, crosscut the piece into strips whose length is equal to the width of the original strips [Fig. 3-62(b)].

5. Reassemble as shown in Fig. 3-62(c).

6. Glue and clamp.

Fig. 3-62. Checkerboard fabrication

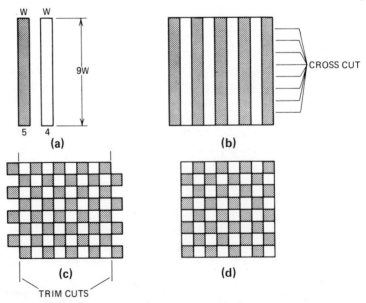

160

TRIM CUTS

7. When the glue has set, remove the clamps and trim the board. If desired, the thickness of the board can be reduced by surfacing.

ADHESIVES

A great variety of adhesives are available to the craftsman. A partial list and description are reproduced in Fig. 3–63. The selection of a particular adhesive is usually determined by:

1. The kind of wood involved.
2. The degree and type of stress to be applied to the joint.
3. The working properties of the adhesive and how they relate to the planned application (i.e., pot life and setting time).
4. The environmental conditions the joint is likely to be subjected to, and permanence of the joint.
5. The cost of the adhesive and, perhaps, its shelf life.

The species of wood involved is an important factor (Fig. 3–64). Certain woods, such as poplar and willow, glue easily; others, such as hard maple and birch, can present problems. If specific information is not available for a particular wood, a sample glue joint should be made and tested for strength.

The working properties of the adhesive are very important to the craftsman. A glue with a limited pot life may not be suitable for assemblies that are complex and require considerable application time, such as laminations.

Surface Conditions

Ideally, surfaces to be glued should be smooth and blemish-free. The practice of roughing-up surfaces prior to gluing does not improve glue joints. Newly exposed wood contains more moisture than the wood that was at the surface and when this moisture evaporates, deformation can occur. Processing of the material should take place as close as possible to gluing time.

Gluing Conditions for Strong Joints

Maximum joint strength is developed when the glue film wets the surfaces to be mated completely and uniformly, and is free of foreign matter. Under certain conditions, such as in end-grain gluing, excessive penetration of glue into the surface of the wood may result in starved joints. This can be reduced by sizing such surfaces with a thin glue mixture just prior to final glue application.

With dense woods (e.g., hard maple) that are difficult to glue, a more viscous (thicker) glue mixture is usually most effective. In more absorbent lighter woods, a thinner (less viscous) mixture works better because the glue is made more viscous as the wood absorbs moisture from the mixture.

Type Glue White Polyvinyl	Type Glue Plastic Resin	Type Glue Flake Animal
Brands include Elmers Titlebond.	*Brands include Weldwood, Cascamite.*	*Brands include Craftsman.*
Good for Paper, leather, small wood assemblies.	**Good for** Furniture, veneering, work exposed to dampness.	**Good for** Woodworking, furniture.
Not Good for Anything requiring resistance to water.	**Not Good for** Oily woods or poorly fitted unclamped joints.	**Not Good for** Anything that may be used or stored in damp places.
Advantages Fastsetting, ready to use at any temperature, colorless glue line.	**Advantages** Very strong, water resistant, leaves light-colored. Glue line and thickness can be varied.	**Advantages** Light-colored joints, fills cracks and gaps in joints.
Disadvantages Not water resistant.	**Disadvantages** Must be mixed for each use, needs heavy clamp pressure. Overnight clamping.	**Disadvantages** Inconvenient for quick or occasional use, must be kept hot.
Type Glue Liquid Animal and Fish Glue	Type Glue Powdered Casein	Type Glue Resorcinol
Brands include Le Page, Franklin.	*Brands include Casco.*	*Brands include Cascophen. Weldwood*
Good for Furniture and cabinetwork, general wood gluing.	**Good for** General woodworking, especially oily woods; teak, yew, lemon.	**Good for** Outdoor uses, boats, items that may be soaked.
Not Good for Work exposed to dampness.	**Not Good for** Acid woods unless staining is not important; outdoor furniture.	**Not Good for** Work done where temperature is below 70°.
Advantages Strong, easy to use, light color, resists heat, mold.	**Advantages** Strong, fairly water resistant, works in cool locations, fills poor joints.	**Advantages** Very strong, waterproof, works well with poor joints.
Disadvantages Not water resistant, must be warmed if used in cold location.	**Disadvantages** Must be mixed 15 min. before using, subject to mold, stains dark woods. Limited shelf life.	**Disadvantages** Powder and catalyst must be carefully mixed, has dark color.

Fig. 3-63.

FIGURE 3-64. CHARACTERISTICS, PREPARATION, AND USES OF THE ADHESIVES MOST COMMONLY USED FOR BONDING WOOD*

Class[1]	Form	Properties	Preparation and application	Typical Uses for Wood Bonding
Animal	Many grades sold in dry form; liquid glues available.	High dry strength; low resistance to moisture and damp conditions.	Dry form mixed with water, soaked, and melted; solution kept warm during application; liquid forms applied as received; both pressed at room temperatures; adjustments in gluing procedures must be made for even minor changes in temperature.	Furniture assembly, use is declining.
Blood protein[2]	Primarily, dry soluble whole blood. Commonly now handled and used like soybean glues.	Moderate resistance to water and damp atmospheres. Moderate resistance to intermediate temperatures and to microorganisms.	Mixed with cold water, lime, caustic soda, and other chemicals; applied at room temperature; and pressed either at room temperature or in hot presses at 240° F. or higher.	Primarily for interior-type soft-wood plywood. Sometimes in combination with soybean protein.
Casein	Several brands sold in dry powder form; may also be prepared from raw materials by user.	Moderately high dry strength; moderate resistance to water, damp atmospheres, and intermediate temperatures; not suitable for exterior uses.	Mixed with water; applied and generally pressed at room temperature.	Laminated timbers for interior use.
Vegetable protein[3] (mainly soybean).	Protein sold in dry powder form (generally with small amounts of dry chemicals added) to be prepared for use by user.	Moderate to low dry strength; moderate to low resistance to water and damp atmospheres; moderate resistance to intermediate temperatures.	Mixed with cold water, lime, caustic soda, and other chemicals; applied and pressed at room temperatures, but more frequently hot-pressed.	Bonding softwood plywood for interior use.

FIGURE 3-64. CONTINUED

Class[1]	Form	Properties	Preparation and application	Typical Uses for Wood Bonding
Urea resin	Many brands sold as dry powders, others as liquids; may be blended with melamine or other resins.	High in both wet and dry strength; moderately durable under damp conditions; moderate to low resistance to temperatures in excess of 120° F.; white or tan.	Dry form mixed with water; hardeners, fillers, and extenders may be added by user to either dry or liquid form; applied at room temperatures, some formulas cure at room temperatures, others require hot pressing at about 250° F.	Hardwood plywood for interior use and furniture; interior particleboard; flush doors.
Melamine resin	Comparatively few brands available; usually marketed as a powder with or without catalyst.	High in both wet and dry strength; very resistant to moisture and damp conditions depending on type and amount of catalyst; white to tan.	Mixed with water and applied at room temperatures; heat required to cure (250° to 300° F.).	Primarily as fortifier for urea resins for hardwood plywood, end-jointing and edge-gluing of lumber, and scarf jointing softwood plywood.
Phenol resin	Many brands available, some dry powders, others as liquids, and at least one as dry film. Most commonly sold as aqueous, alkaline dispersions.	High in both wet and dry strength; very resistant to moisture and damp conditions, more resistant than wood to high temperatures; dark red; often combined with neoprene, polyvinyl butyral, nitrile rubber, or epoxy resins for bonding metals.	Film form used as received; powder form mixed with solvent, often alcohol and water, at room temperature; with liquid forms, modifiers and fillers are added by users; most common types require hot pressing at about 260° to 300° F.[4]	Exterior softwood plywood and particleboard.
Resorcinol resin and phenol-resorcinol resins.	Several brands available in liquid form; hardener supplied separately; some brands are combinations of phenol and resorcinol resins.	High in both wet and dry strength; very resistant to moisture and damp conditions; more resistant than wood to high temperatures; dark red.	Mixed with hardener and applied at room temperatures; resorcinol glues cure at room temperatures on most species; phenol-resorcinols cure at temperatures from 70° F. to 150° F., depending on curing period and species.	Primarily for laminated timbers and assembly joints that must withstand severe service conditions.

Class[1]	Form	Properties	Preparation and application	Typical Uses for Wood Bonding
Polyvinyl acetate resin emulsions.	Several brands are available, varying to some extent in properties; marketed in liquid form ready to use.	Generally high in dry strength; low resistance to moisture and elevated temperatures; joints tend to yield under continued stress; white.	Marketed as a liquid ready to use; applied and pressed at room temperatures.[5]	Furniture assembly, flush doors, bonding plastic laminates. Assembly of panel systems (mobile homes).
Rubber-base adhesives A. Contact adhesives	Typically a neoprene rubber base in organic solvents or water emulsion. Other elastomer systems are also available.	Initial joint strength develops immediately upon pressing, increases slowly over a period of weeks; dry strengths generally lower than those of conventional woodworking glues; water resistance and resistance to severe conditions variable.	Used as received; both surfaces spread and partially dried before pressing. Commonly used in roller presses for instantaneous bonding.	For some nonstructural bonds, as on-the-job bonding of decorative tops to kitchen counters. Useful for low-strength metal and some plastic bonding.
B. Mastics (elastomeric construction adhesives).	Puttylike consistency. Synthetic or natural rubber base usually in organic solvents; others solvent-free.	Gap filling. Develop strength slowly over several weeks. Water resistance and resistance to severe conditions variable.	Used as received. Extruded by calking guns in beads and ribbons, with and without supplemental nailing.	Lumber and plywood to floor joist and wall studs; laminating gypsum board, styrene and other materials; assembly of panel systems.
Thermoplastic synthetic resins.	Solid chunks, pellets, ribbons, rods, or films; solvent-free.	Rapid bonding; gap filling; lower strength than conventional wood adhesives; minimal penetration; moisture resistant.	Melted for spreading; bond formation by cooling and solidification; requires special equipment for controlling bonding conditions.	Edge banding of panels; plastic lamination; patching; films and paper overlays.

*(Courtesy of U.S. Department of Agriculture Forest Products Laboratory)

Pressure applied to glue joints serves three primary purposes:

1. It forces the glue into a uniform and continuous film between the surfaces to be joined.
2. It forces air out from between the surfaces.
3. It forces the wood surfaces into intimate contact with the glue film.

Glues with a limited pot life can be used for a specific amount of time after mixing. Glues in liquid form are easier to use but their viscosity (thickness) cannot be altered. Fast-setting glues may be highly desirable for the craftsman who has limited clamping capability.

Environmental conditions can dictate adhesive selection. In marine applications, a truly waterproof glue may be required. Shelf life is also an important consideration because it determines the quantities of the adhesive that are economical for a given user. Another important factor is open assembly time. This is the maximum amount of time that can elapse between glue application and assembly and pressurization.

Preparations for Gluing

Moisture content of the wood at the time of gluing can be critical. Green wood which is very wet cannot generally be glued successfully. The basic reason for difficulties in gluing woods that contain too much moisture is that the dimensions change due to shrinkage when the wood dries out. These changes cause extreme stressing of the glue joints and failure often results. In addition, very high moisture content may interfere with glue film adhesion and penetration. In general, the moisture content of the wood should be such that the moisture added to the wood during gluing brings the moisture to a level suitable for the eventual use of the assembly. For most purposes, kiln-dried lumber is suitable for gluing.

Light pressure should be used with low-viscosity glues (e.g., polyvinyl resin emulsions—white glues); *heavy pressure should be used with high-viscosity glues* (e.g., plastic resin used on dense woods). The strongest joints are usually obtained when glue viscosity permits high gluing pressures (100 to 250 psi). Clamping times vary with glues and temperature conditions. The manufacturer's label directions should be followed for maximum strength.

Durability of Glue Joints

The durability of glued materials depends on:

1. Type of glue used.
2. Gluing technique.
3. Service conditions (e.g., exposure to moisture).
4. Finish or surface coating (protects against moisture).
5. Joint design and construction.

CLAMPING ASSEMBLIES

When fasteners are not used in assemblies, holding power is generally supplied by clamps. Adhesives, with the exception of contact-type cements, require pressurization while the adhesive is setting. Clamping procedures must meet two general requirements: they must supply adequate pressure, and they must hold the various components being joined in their correct final positions with a minimum of deformation.

Edge-to-Edge Clamping

1. Assemble all of the clamps required for the clamping job. At least three bar clamps should be used for edge-to-edge assemblies. Four 2-by-3 glue blocks of suitable length, plus four "C" clamps or hand-screw clamps for the glue blocks, are required. In addition, two 2-in.-wide caul blocks, equal in thickness to the pieces being clamped, are required. A supply of newspapers is needed to protect the bench from glue drips.

2. The first assembly is made *without glue*. This is done so that problems related to clamping can be discovered and solved before the time deadline imposed by glue application complicates the assembly process.

3. Spread newspapers over the area of the bench to be used for the clamping operation (if a bench is used).

4. Place half of the bar clamps (at least two) on the bench open side up (Fig. 3–65).

5. Place caul blocks against each of the clamp faces (Fig. 3–65).

6. Place the *unglued* assembly loosely inside the caul blocks (Fig. 3–65).

7. Slide the tail end of the clamp faces until they rest snugly against the caul blocks and the assembly. Then partially tighten the clamps.

8. Place the remaining bar clamps on the assembly and draw them up snugly against the caul blocks (Fig. 3–65).

9. Apply glue blocks (optional) and clamps as shown (Fig. 3–66).

10. Gradually tighten all of the clamps on a rotating basis.

If no problems arise (e.g., excessive deflection), remove clamps, apply glue to the assembly, and repeat steps 3 through 10 above. Place a strip of newspaper under each of the glue blocks to prevent the blocks from being glued to the workpiece. The clamps should be tightened until glue begins to seep out slightly at the joints.

When the clamps are tight, check the surface of the clamped workpiece with a straightedge to be sure that it is flat. If it is not flat, loosen the bar clamps slightly and adjust the glue block clamps.

Clamping Square or Rectangular Assemblies

1. Assemble all of the materials and clamps required for an *unglued trial assembly*.

Fig. 3-65. Edge-to-edge glue-up with bar clamps. (Courtesy of Adjustable Clamp Company)

2. Assemble the pieces on a flat surface protected with newspapers.

3. Apply bar clamps at the corners as shown in Fig. 3-67(a). If possible, also apply a bar clamp at a maximum interval of 6 in. Note the use of protective caul blocks at the corners.

4. Draw the clamps up and tighten each one gradually in a rotating pattern. During this tightening, look for any tendency for deformation and try to eliminate this by adjusting the clamps on adjacent sides of the piece.

5. When the clamps are tight, check all corners with a large square. If the amount of squareness is not acceptable, try to improve it by placing a bar clamp across the longest diagonal of the assembly [Fig. 3-67(b)]. Tighten this clamp until the corners become square. If the assembly is to have a back installed, this can be used to help keep the assembly square.

May Be Applied With Right Angle Screw "Off Center"

May Be Applied With Right Angle Screw "Centered"

May Be Applied To Clamp Around "Returns"

Fig. 3-66. Glue blocks help keep work flat

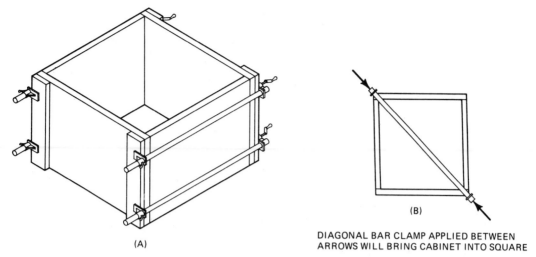

(A)

(B)

DIAGONAL BAR CLAMP APPLIED BETWEEN
ARROWS WILL BRING CABINET INTO SQUARE

Fig. 3-67. Clamping a cabinet

6. Check the clamped assembly to determine whether or not it has remained flat against the surface it was resting on during the clamping. If it has not, try clamping it to that surface.

7. Remove clamps, apply glue, and reassemble according to steps 2 through 6 above.

Figure 3-68 shows a frame clamped in a strap clamp.

Fig. 3-68. Frame clamped with a web clamp. (Courtesy of Adjustable Clamp Company)

MACHINE TOOLS

THE TABLE SAW

Principles of Operation and Nomenclature

The table saw consists of a table through which a circular blade projects (Fig. 4-1). The diameter of the blade is used to designate the saw's capacity. The blade is commonly set at a 90° angle to the table and is surrounded by a throat plate (Fig. 4-2). This plate is usually made of a soft die-cast metal so that accidental contact with the blade will not damage it. The throat plate can be removed to allow access to the arbor and arbor nut. The plate generally has leveling screws which make adjustments relative to the table surface possible.

Table saws are equipped with a movable rip fence which is used to guide work during ripping operations. For crosscutting operations, the workpiece is supported by a miter gauge, which travels in one of two table slots milled parallel to the blade.

Directly behind the blade, and in line with it, is the splitter guard (Fig. 4-3). In some machines the splitter guard is a separate piece that telescopes up through the table. With this type of guard, the antikickback fingers are also attached to the telescoping device (Fig. 4-4). Splitter guards are usually mounted on the tilting arbor mechanism so that the guard tilts with the blade and remains aligned with it. The function of the splitter is to keep the saw kerf open. This helps to prevent binding and reduces the possibility of kickback. Therefore, the splitter guard must be in position during all ripping operations in which a piece of material is cut free from the workpiece.

The saw guard is a metal or plastic cage which surrounds the blade. It permits the workpiece to pass under it during cutting operations and keeps the operator's fingers away from the blade. It also helps to stop small pieces of wood thrown back by the saw. In some of the illustrations in this book,

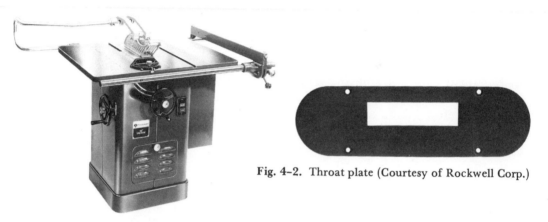

Fig. 4-2. Throat plate (Courtesy of Rockwell Corp.)

Fig. 4-1. Ten-inch table saw (Courtesy of Rockwell Corp.)

Fig. 4-3. Splitter guard (Courtesy of Rockwell Corp.)

Fig. 4-4. Anti-kickback guard (Courtesy of Rockwell Corp.)

the guard has been removed for improved visibility; however, *in actual use the guard should be used whenever possible.*

Antikickback fingers are usually mounted on the splitter guard. These fingers have teeth which allow the workpiece to slide through (under the teeth, toward the rear of the saw) during cutting. If there is binding between the workpiece and the saw blade, these fingers are designed to bind against the workpiece whenever the piece moves back toward the operator (Fig. 4-4).

Directly under the table, facing the operator, is the handwheel. This wheel permits the raising and lowering of the blade. It can be locked in place by means of a locking knob located at its hub (Fig. 4-1). A similar handwheel, located on the left side of the machine, is the tilt wheel. It is used to tilt the blade for miter cuts and to set the blade square to the tabletop for square cuts. This adjusting wheel also has a locking knob in its hub (Fig. 4-1).

The power switch is located on the front of the machine, facing the operator.

Table Saw Types

Tilt arbor saw. The tilt arbor saw is the most common machine found in nonmanufacturing facilities. It consists of a fixed table and a motor-arbor arrangement which allows tilting, raising, and lowering of the blade. One principal advantage of this type of unit is that it allows the workpiece to remain level at all times (Fig. 4-5).

Fig. 4-5. Table saw arbor tilting mechanism (Courtesy of Rockwell Corp.)

Fig. 4–6. Tilt table saw

   Tilt table saw. The tilt table saw is less frequently found in nonmanufacturing facilities. This machine has a tilting table and an arbor that remains fixed. The major disadvantage of this unit is found in the tendency of the workpiece to slide when the table is tilted for bevel cutting (Fig. 4-6).

   Variety saws. A saw with a single arbor is known as a variety saw.

   Universal saws. Universal saws have two arbors. One usually mounts a rip blade and the other mounts a crosscut blade.

   Belt-driven saws. Belt-driven saws are the most common type manufactured today. Small saws have a single belt and larger units have two or more matched driving belts (Fig. 4–7).

   Direct-drive saws. Direct-drive machines utilize the motor shaft as a saw arbor.

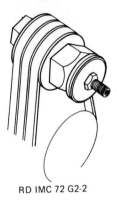

Fig. 4–7. Belt driven arbor

RD IMC 72 G2-2

Saw Blade Types

Set tooth blades. The blade with set teeth produces a saw kerf that is wider than the blade body because the teeth are bent, or set, alternately to the right and left when the blade is sharpened. The wide kerf produced reduces the tendency of the blade to bind in the workpiece. Binding can result in a dangerous "kickback" which can injure the operator. Dull blades lose some of their set and binding often results when they are used. Figure 4–8 illustrates some blade types.

Hollow-ground blades. In the hollow-ground blade, clearance is developed by grinding the face of the saw blade disk so that its thickness decreases as the arbor hole is approached. The teeth are at the thickest part

Fig. 4–8. Saw blade types

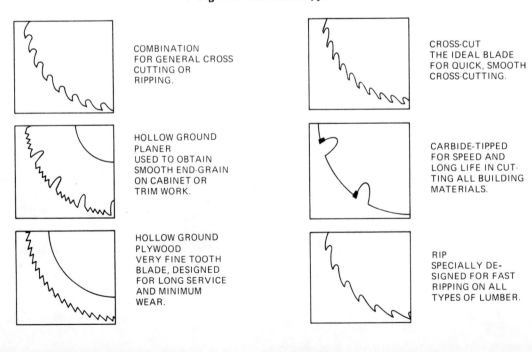

COMBINATION
FOR GENERAL CROSS
CUTTING OR
RIPPING.

CROSS-CUT
THE IDEAL BLADE
FOR QUICK, SMOOTH
CROSS-CUTTING.

HOLLOW GROUND
PLANER
USED TO OBTAIN
SMOOTH END-GRAIN
ON CABINET OR
TRIM WORK.

CARBIDE-TIPPED
FOR SPEED AND
LONG LIFE IN CUT-
TING ALL BUILDING
MATERIALS.

HOLLOW GROUND
PLYWOOD
VERY FINE TOOTH
BLADE, DESIGNED
FOR LONG SERVICE
AND MINIMUM
WEAR.

RIP
SPECIALLY DE-
SIGNED FOR FAST
RIPPING ON ALL
TYPES OF LUMBER.

of the blade disk. Hollow-ground blades can be identified by the ring of un-ground metal which surrounds the arbor hole (Fig. 4-9). This type of blade is more dangerous to use because it tends to bind unless the blade is operated at its maximum height above the workpiece. Hollow-ground blades are commonly used as miter saw blades or as planer blades because of their smooth cutting feature. They are not recommended for general use in the shop.

Crosscut blades. The crosscut blade is designed to cut across the grain efficiently. Since approximately 95 percent of all cutting is done across the grain, it is the most commonly used blade type.

Ripsaw blades. The ripsaw blade cuts with the grain efficiently. The chisel-shaped teeth have a large amount of back clearance to reduce any tendency to drag.

Combination blades. Combination blades are popular because they allow ripping and crosscutting without changing the blade. In one type of combination saw blade, some of the teeth are crosscut teeth and others are rip teeth (see hollow-ground blade in Fig. 4-9). In other types, a special combination tooth is used which looks similar to a rip tooth (see combination blade in Fig. 4-9).

Carbide-tipped blades. These blades are frequently combination saws. Each tooth is tipped with a piece of very hard carbide steel. This material requires one-tenth the sharpening of standard steel blades. Its special qualities permit its use with nonwood materials such as masonite, plastic laminate, and flake board. The carbide teeth are very brittle and can easily be damaged by careless use. Sharpening is more expensive than for a standard blade.

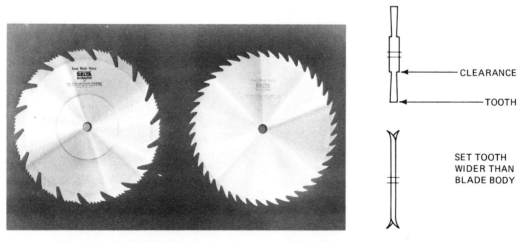

Fig. 4-9. Hollow ground and set tooth blade (Courtesy of Delta Div., Rockwell Corp.)

Plywood blades. These blades are hollow ground and have small teeth (Fig. 4-8). Plywood blades produce a very smooth cut surface, but they are limited to cuts of 1 in. or less in thickness.

General Safety Rules for the Table Saw

The most universal safety rule is to understand the operation of a machine fully and to operate it thoughtfully. More specific rules are listed below for the table saw.

1. Always wear approved eye protection when operating the table saw.
2. Check the blade for sharpness and secure fastening to the arbor before turning the machine on.
3. Always have the saw guards in place when using the machine.
4. Be sure to keep workpieces against either the rip fence or the miter gauge during cutting. Do not attempt to cut freehand.
5. Adjust the saw blades so that they project 1/4 in. above the surface of the workpiece.
6. Avoid standing directly in line with the saw blade when using the saw. This will help to prevent injury in the event of a kickback accident.
7. Never reach over the saw blade to support or catch a piece of work. Use an assistant or a support stand instead.
8. Use a push stick for ripping. Place the push stick on the end of the workpiece at a point halfway between the rip fence and the blade.
9. Do not attempt to crosscut oversize pieces on the table saw.
10. Secure loose clothing and hair before using the table saw.
11. Avoid cutting badly warped material.
12. Be sure that work to be ripped has a straight edge of sufficient length to ensure safe cutting.

Crosscutting Single Pieces to Length

1. Prepare the workpiece by jointing an edge square to the working face.
2. Check the blade for squareness to the table with a square (Fig. 4-10). Place the jointed edge of the workpiece against the face of the miter gauge and trim at least 1/4 in. off one end of the piece. A square cut is easier to make when the saw blade is surrounded with wood.
3. Check the cut surface for squareness to the edge.
4. Measuring from the end just trimmed, draw a layout line at the required distance from the working end.
5. Position the workpiece with the layout line aligned with the appropriate saw tooth (Fig. 4-11) and with its jointed edge against the face of the miter gauge.
6. Start the saw and move the miter gauge and workpiece up to the blade (as a unit) until the saw blade scores the workpiece lightly. Check the

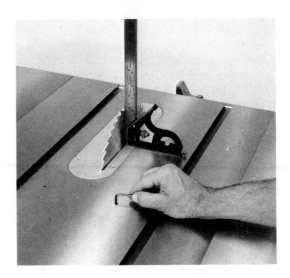

Fig. 4–10. Checking squareness of blade to the table (Courtesy of Delta Div., Rockwell Corp.)

cut for alignment with the layout line. Adjust the position of the workpiece if necessary and complete the cut.

This *partial sawing* technique permits the operator to check the location of a cut to be made before the piece is fully cut and possibly spoiled.

Possible problems. The cut end is not square to the working edge of the workpiece.

Possible cause and remedy. If the working edge was placed against the miter gauge and the gauge was square to the saw blade, the most likely cause of this problem is slippage. This is frequently caused by the vibration produced during cutting. A piece of fine sandpaper, folded in two with the coated sides out, can be inserted between the workpiece and the face of the miter gauge to reduce this tendency for slippage.

Fig. 4–11. Crosscutting single pieces to length

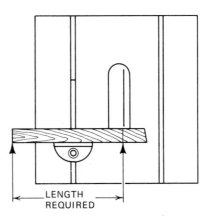

LENGTH
REQUIRED

Crosscutting Oversize Wide Pieces to Size

In fabricating large pieces (e.g., tabletops) which require crosscutting, special problems arise because of the excessive width of the workpiece. The following crosscutting procedures are useful in such a situation.

1. Use a framing square to lay out a line on the workpiece square to a jointed edge. Locate the line so that the saw blade is surrounded with a minimum of 1/4 in. of wood throughout the length of the cut.

2. Place the miter gauge in one of the table slots in a reversed position so that the head of the gauge is away from the operator (Fig. 4–12).

3. Place the jointed edge of the workpiece against the face of the miter gauge and align the layout line with the appropriate saw tooth.

4. Turn on the machine and make a *partial cut.* If the alignment is satisfactory complete the cut.

5. Lay out the second line at the required distance from the cut just made, and repeat steps 2 through 5.

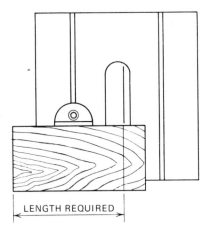

LENGTH REQUIRED

Fig. 4–12. Cutting oversized wide pieces

If the width of the workpiece makes the method described above awkward, proceed as follows:

1. Cut a strip of wood to fit the table slot in width and thickness.

2. Lay out the first line as described in step 1 above.

3. Place the wooden strip in the table slot. Then place the workpiece on the table saw, with the layout line aligned properly with the saw blade teeth and parallel to the table slots, and cut to size (Fig. 4–13).

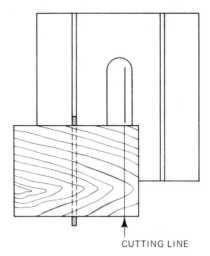

Fig. 4-13. Crosscutting using a strip inserted in table slot fastened to workpiece

CUTTING LINE

Crosscutting Duplicate Pieces to Length

Woodworking projects often require several pieces of identical length in their construction. Table legs are an example of such pieces.

Miter gauge and stop rod method.

1. Joint an edge of each workpiece square to each piece's working face. Trim an end of each piece square to the working edge and the working face.

2. Measuring from the working end of one of the pieces, lay out a line on the face and edge of the piece, representing the desired length of the piece to be cut.

3. With the miter gauge in the left table slot, insert the straight section of the stop rod attachment into the hole in the left side of the miter gauge (see Fig. 4-14). Secure the rod with the screw provided.

Fig. 4-14. Miter gauge with stop rod (Courtesy of Delta Div., Rockwell Corp.)

4. Place the working edge of the workpiece against the face of the miter gauge, with the working end to the left and the layout line aligned with the saw blade.

5. Loosen the stop rod thumbscrews, and position the L-shaped rod against the left end of the workpiece. Tighten the thumbscrews.

6. Before turning the machine on, travel the miter gauge and stop rods past the blade to test for clearance between the blade and the stop rods. This step is important because it is possible to position the stop rods in such a way that the blade will engage the rods during cutting.

7. Replace the workpiece and make a scoring cut to test the accuracy of the stop rod setting.

8. If the setting is satisfactory, complete the cut.

9. With the same setting on the stop rods, complete cutting all of the pieces required.

Miter gauge auxiliary fence method.

1. Prepare a straight piece of wood approximately 12 in. longer than the piece required. This material should be at least 2 in. wide.

2. Fasten this auxiliary fence to the face of the miter gauge using wood screws of appropriate length.

3. Repeat steps 1 through 4 of the stop rod method described above.

4. Position a wooden block against the left end of the workpiece and clamp it to the auxiliary miter gauge fence (Fig. 4–15).

Rip fence—clearance-block method. This variation is useful if a single long piece is to be cut into several identical shorter pieces.

1. Prepare a clearance block. Any flat piece of wood measuring approximately 3/4 in. by 2 in. by 2 in. may be used for this purpose.

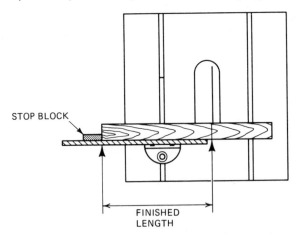

STOP BLOCK

FINISHED
LENGTH

Fig. 4–15. Crosscutting using auxiliary fence attached to miter gauge

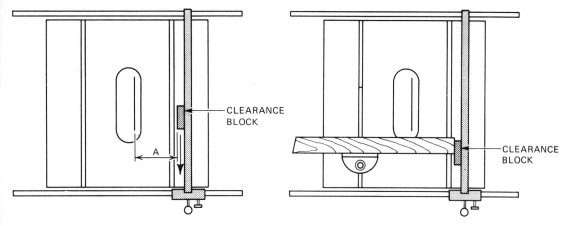

Fig. 4–16. Using rip fence and clearance block for crosscutting

2. Temporarily position the clearance block against the rip fence, opposite the saw blade.

3. Travel the rip fence and the clearance block until the distance between the block and a sawtooth set toward the block is equal to the length of the pieces to be cut (Fig. 4–16).

4. Lock the fence.

5. *Slide the clearance block back away from the blade until it is about 4 in. from the infeed end of the table,* and clamp it to the rip fence. This repositioning step is essential if binding of the cut-off piece between the block and the saw blade is to be avoided. It is good practice to leave approximately 1/2 in. of space under the clearance block to prevent sawdust buildup . Cut the piece to length (Fig. 4–16).

Mitering

Miter cuts are made on the table saw with the miter gauge. These cuts range from an angle of 30° to an angle of 90°.

1. Set the miter gauge to the required angle by loosening the miter gauge lock knob and rotating the miter gauge head until the indicator is aligned with the desired angle. Most miter gauges have several positive stops for common angles such as 45°.

2. After the gauge has been set to the desired angle, in the closed position (Fig. 4–17), make a test cut on scrap material. Check the angle of the cut for accuracy against a layout of the angle or with a T bevel set to the desired angle.

3. The tendency for mitered pieces to slide along the face of the miter gauge during cutting can be reduced if a clamp miter fence is used (Fig. 4–18).

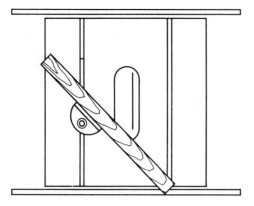

Fig. 4-17. Closed miter cut

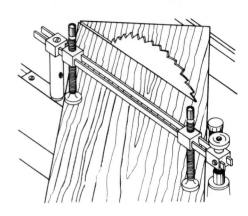

Fig. 4-18. Clamp miter gauge

Compound miters. Compound miters are produced when both the miter gauge and the saw blade are set at angles other than 90°. Hopper-joint fabrication requires such joinery. See Fig. 4-19 for compound miter setup.

Dado Cutting

A dado is any groove cut across the grain. Such a groove can be produced by making a series of cuts side by side on the table saw, or by using a dado cutter. A standard dado set [Fig. 4-20(a)] consists of two outside cutters and a number of inside cutters or chippers. For narrow dadoes, one or two outside cutters are mounted side by side on the saw arbor. For wider dadoes, one or more inside cutters are positioned between the outside cutters on the saw arbor.

Fig. 4-19. Compound miter cutting with miter gauge and blade set at an angle other than 90° (Courtesy of Delta Div., Rockwell Corp.)

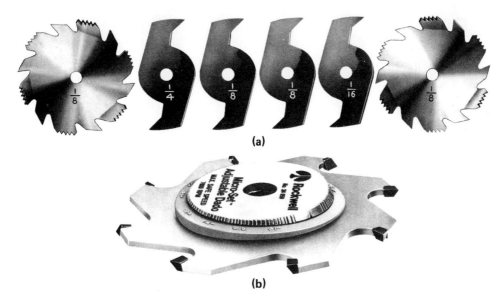

(a)

(b)

Fig. 4–20. Set of dado cutters (Courtesy of Delta Div., Rockwell Corp.)

The following procedure may be used to produce a dado:

1. Lay out the desired dado on squared-up material.
2. Select a combination of cutters, including two outside cutters, that will produce a cut equal in width to the dado.
3. After removing the saw blade from the circular saw arbor, place the first outside cutter on the arbor. Its teeth must point toward the infeed end of the saw.
4. Place the inside cutters on the arbor against the first outside cutter. Make certain that the teeth of the inside cutters are positioned in the gullets of the outside cutters (Fig. 4–21).
5. Place the other outside cutter on the arbor with its gullets aligned with the teeth of the chipper next to it. Replace the washer and nut and tighten the nut.
6. Install a dado throat plate of appropriate size in the table (see Fig. 4-2).

Fig. 4–21. Dado inside cutters aligned with gullets of outside cutters

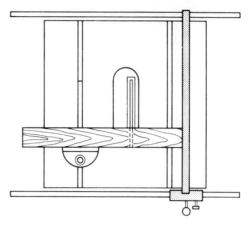

Fig. 4–22. Using flip fence as a stop in positioning piece during dado cutting

7. Replace the saw guard if possible. Raise the arbor until the dado cutter is elevated to the required height, and check the clearance between the cutter and the saw guard.

8. Place the workpiece against the face of the miter gauge and make a test cut on scrap material. Small increases in the width of the dado can be made by inserting paper or cardboard "washers" between the dado cutters.

8. In cutting identical dadoes on several pieces, the rip fence may be used as a stop. No clearance block is required, since no material is being cut off the workpiece (Fig. 4–22).

Possible problems. The edge of the workpiece splits around the dado as the cutter breaks through the edge during the cut.

Cause and remedy. The splitting is caused by a lack of support for the wood fibers on the edge surface. If the dadoes are cut into a workpiece that is oversize in width, the split edges can be removed when the workpiece is reduced to final width. If the workpiece is supported by an auxiliary wooden fence attached to the miter gauge, the splitting is less likely to occur. A knife-line layout of the dado cut extra deep into the edges also helps to prevent splitting.

Other dado cutters and applications. Various types of dado sets are available which depend on cutters that are tilted with respect to the arbor on which they are mounted [Fig. 4–20(b)]. These are known as wobble-action dado cutters.

Dado cutters can also be used to produce rabbets and tenons if the correct procedure is followed. In cutting operations going with the grain, the slot produced by the dado cutters is called a *groove.*

Ripping and Cutting with the Workpiece against the Rip Fence

Ripping cuts are generally made with the workpiece positioned against the rip fence. The common procedure for ripping stock to width is described below.

Ripping stock to width.

1. Examine the workpiece to determine the quality of its best edge. If necessary, joint an edge square to the working face on the jointer.

2. If the saw is equipped with a telescoping splitter, make sure that it is in operating position.

3. Adjust the blade height so that the blade is elevated to a point 1/4 in. above the face of the piece to be cut.

4. Adjust the position of the rip fence until the distance between the fence and a tooth set toward the fence is equal to the desired width of the piece to be cut (Fig. 4–23). If the edge of the workpiece is to be jointed after being ripped, leave approximately 1/8 in. of material for this purpose.

5. Lock the rip fence, place the saw guard in position, and place working edge against the rip fence.

6. Turn the machine on and make a scoring cut while moving the workpiece against the rip fence. Adjust if necessary.

7. Place the working edge against the fence and push the end of the workpiece into the revolving saw blade. Apply pressure to the edge of the workpiece to keep it in position against the rip fence.

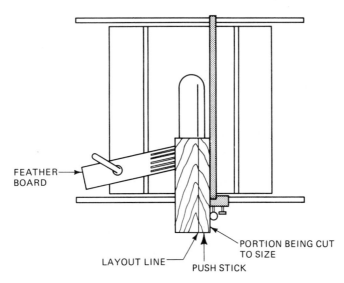

Fig. 4–23. Ripping using a feather board

Pushing force should be applied to the near end of the workpiece at a point approximately halfway between the edges of the workpiece (Fig. 4-23). Pressure can be applied to the edge of the workpiece with a feather board (Fig. 4-23).

Resawing wide material. If the workpiece is too wide or too thick to be cut all the way through by the saw in a single pass, resawing can be used to accomplish this operation.

1. Lay out a cutting line on the workpiece.
2. Adjust and lock the fence.
3. Raise the blade until it is elevated above the table approximately one-third of its maximum height.
4. Remove the saw guard and the splitter.
5. Turn the machine on and make a scoring test cut. Adjust if necessary.
6. Make the first cut through the edge of the workpiece using a push stick and a feather board. Turn the machine off.
7. Reverse the workpiece, *keeping the same face* against the rip fence. Turn the machine on and make the second cut into the edge of the workpiece. Turn the machine off.
8. Raise the blade an additional third of its maximum height above the table.
9. Repeat steps 6, 7, and 8 until the piece is cut all the way through. If the piece is not cut through when the blade is at its maximum height, the remaining material can be cut through using the band saw (see Fig. 4-69).

Reverse sawing. At times it becomes necessary to rip a narrow workpiece into two equal thinner pieces. Ripping such a piece safely is difficult because the saw blade is very close to the rip fence. The procedure outlined below is suggested as a solution.

1. Set the rip fence for the required cut. Lock the fence.
2. Adjust the blade height.
3. Remove the saw guard but leave the splitter in place.
4. Turn the machine on and rip halfway through the length of the workpiece (Fig. 4-24).
5. Stop the movement of the piece, and turn the machine off.
6. Reverse the workpiece, *keeping the same face against the rip fence,* and repeat steps 4, 5, and 6.

Cutting an edge bevel. A bevel is an angular cut made through a piece from one surface to the opposite surface (Fig. 4-25). This is accomplished by tilting the table saw blade to the desired angle and then ripping the piece in the usual manner.

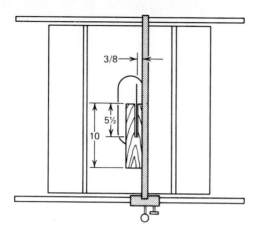

Fig. 4–24. Reverse resawing

Cutting an edge rabbet.

1. Lay out the required rabbet on the edge and face of a squared-up workpiece.

2. Set the fence so that the first cut into the face of the piece will be made just inside the material to be removed, next to the layout line (Fig. 4–26).

3. Adjust the blade height so that the saw blade will cut to the required depth (Fig. 4–26).

4. Start the machine. Place the edge of the workpiece against the rip

Fig. 4–25. Bevel ripping

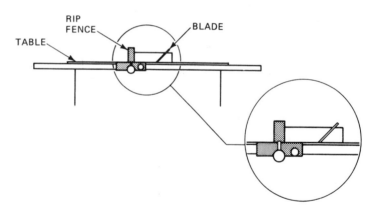

Fig. 4–26. Cutting a rabbet on the table saw

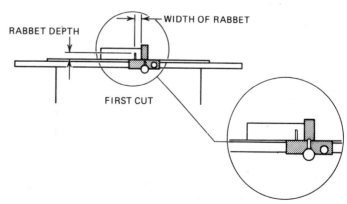

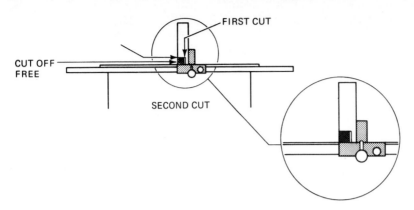

Fig. 4-27. Cutting a rabbet on the table saw

fence and make a scoring test cut. Adjust the fence if necessary. Complete the first ripping cut.

5. Readjust the blade height and fence position for the second cut into the face of the workpiece. Position the workpiece so that the material *being cut free* is positioned outside of the blade, and not between the blade and the rip fence (Fig. 4-27). This will prevent kickback.

Cutting a straight edge on an irregular piece. If a badly "crooked" piece or an irregular piece such as a circle is to be processed into one with a straight edge or squared-up completely, then cutting a straight edge is the first essential step (Fig. 4-28).

Cutting grooves or ploughing. Grooves are recesses (like dadoes) cut into the face or edge of a piece parallel to the grain. Such grooves can be cut by making a series of side-by-side cuts with the workpiece positioned against the rip fence. A second method involves the use of a dado cutter and generally requires a single cut.

Tapers. A tapering cut is an oblique cut that is commonly at an acute angle to an edge. Since such a cut is almost parallel to the grain, it is usually made in a holding device or jig that is moved along the rip fence. It is helpful to realize that the cutting line of the taper is *parallel to the rip fence.*

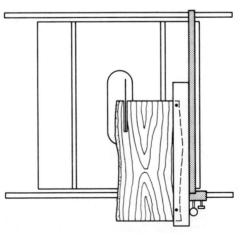

Fig. 4-28. Cutting a straight edge on an irregular piece attached to a straight edge piece

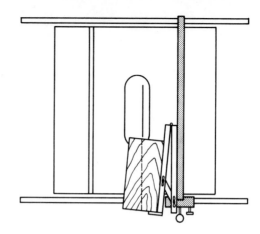

Fig. 4-29. Taper cutting with an adjusting jig

Among the several types of positioning devices or jigs used in taper cutting are the fixed and adjustable types. The following procedure is used with an adjustable taper jig:

1. Prepare the workpiece by squaring it to final length. Leave it oversize in width.
2. Lay out the taper on the workpiece so that the working edge of the workpiece remains on the completed piece.
3. Place the adjustable taper jig in position against the rip fence with its hinged end facing the outfeed end of the table (Fig. 4-29).
4. Place the working edge of the workpiece against the taper jig with the layout facing up.
5. Adjust the taper jig until the *layout line is parallel to the rip fence* (Fig. 4-29).
6. Slide the workpiece along the jig arm until it comes into contact with the stop.
7. Moving the rip fence, taper jig, and the workpiece as a unit, align the layout line on the workpiece with a saw blade tooth set toward the rip fence (Fig. 4-29).
8. Check the position of the layout line to make certain that when the line is cut, the stop on the taper jig *will not be cut*. Adjust the position of the stop if necessary.
9. Replace the saw guard and turn on the machine.
10. During cutting, move the taper jig and the workpiece as a unit. *Do not slide the workpiece along the taper jig.* Be sure that adequate clearance exists for safe holding during the cutting operation.

It is also possible to cut a taper with the adjustable tapering jig by calculating the desired taper in inches per foot. Once this is done, the arms of the tapering jig are moved apart so that at a point 12 in. from the hinge, the distance is equal to the taper per inch.

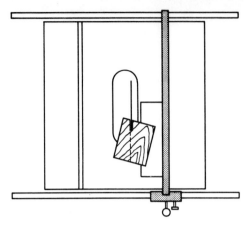

Fig. 4–30. Taper cutting with a fixed jig. Workpiece fits jig snugly

Making and using a fixed taper jig.

1. Square-up the piece to be tapered, leaving it oversize in width.
2. Lay out the desired taper on the workpiece.
3. Superimpose the workpiece on another squared-up piece of stock which is larger than the workpiece (Fig. 4–30). Trace around the workpiece with a sharp pencil or knife.
4. Cut along the lines made in step 3 using a band saw with a wide blade.
5. The workpiece must fit snugly into the cut-out area. Cut as shown in Fig. 4–30.

Making duplicate irregular straight-sided pieces. It is sometimes necessary to fabricate several identical irregularly shaped pieces which have straight sides. The following procedure can be used:

1. Fabricate a full-size pattern piece using a band saw and a stationary belt sander.
2. Clamp a raised auxiliary fence to the table saw rip fence (Fig. 4–31).
3. Prepare enough workpieces to satisfy the requirements of the project. These pieces should be approximately 1 in. longer and wider than the finished piece.
4. Clamp the auxiliary fence to the rip fence. Move the rip fence until the edge of the auxiliary fence is aligned with a sawtooth set away from the fence. Elevate the blade until it just touches the underside of the auxiliary fence (Fig. 4–31).

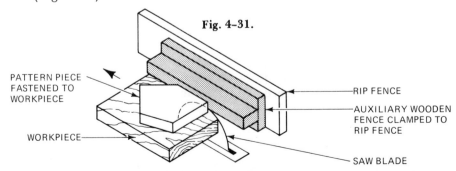

Fig. 4–31.

PATTERN PIECE FASTENED TO WORKPIECE

WORKPIECE

RIP FENCE

AUXILIARY WOODEN FENCE CLAMPED TO RIP FENCE

SAW BLADE

5. Fasten the pattern piece to the workpiece using small brads or rubber cement. Place the workpiece on the table saw with the pattern piece on top.

6. Position the edge of the pattern piece against the edge of the auxiliary fence. Turn the saw on and cut through the workpiece (Fig. 4-31).

7. Examine the cut to make sure the pattern piece has not been cut. If it has, adjust the rip fence to eliminate this problem.

8. Repeat step 6 while positioning each of the sides of the pattern piece against the auxiliary rip fence.

9. Repeat steps 5, 6, and 8 for each of the workpieces.

Do not attempt to use this procedure on any workpiece which requires a side less than 3 in. long. Such a piece will be unstable during cutting.

JOINERY

Joinery was discussed in detail in Chapter 2. Information on joint design and selection can be found there. This section focuses on the use of the table saw in joint fabrication.

End lap joint. The end lap joint consists of two rabbets. When the rabbets are matched, their combined thickness is equal to the thickness of each piece before cutting. The procedure for making an end lap joint is as follows:

1. Lay out each rabbet on squared-up stock.

2. Install a set of dado cutters on the table saw arbor. If possible, have the width of the dado cutters equal to the width of the rabbet to be cut.

3. After installing a suitable dado throat plate, raise the dado cutters above the table an amount equal to half the thickness of the workpiece.

4. Lock the table saw handwheel, and make a test cut on the ends of two scrap pieces whose combined thickness equals the workpiece thickness. Slide the two pieces together and mate the rabbets (Fig. 4-32). If the cuts are

Fig. 4-32. Testing cut depth on a lap joint

correct, complete each end rabbet using the setup shown in Figs. 4-33 and 4-34.

Cross lap joint. The procedure for making an end lap joint may be used for making a cross lap joint. If more than one dado cut is required in the fabrication of each piece, a set of stop rods can be used to locate the second shoulder of the joint (Fig. 4-34).

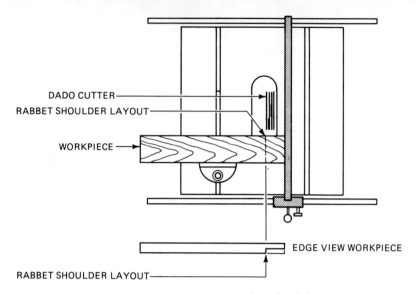

DADO CUTTER

RABBET SHOULDER LAYOUT

WORKPIECE

EDGE VIEW WORKPIECE

RABBET SHOULDER LAYOUT

Fig. 4-33. Cutting a rabbet for a lap joint

Fig. 4-34. Using rip fence and stop rods to locate the gain for a crosslap joint

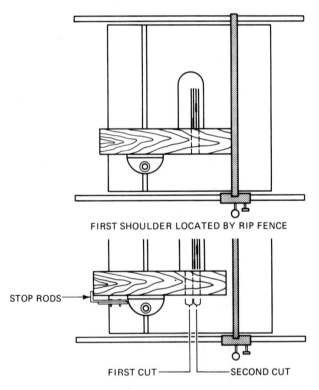

FIRST SHOULDER LOCATED BY RIP FENCE

STOP RODS

FIRST CUT — SECOND CUT

SECOND SHOULDER LOCATED BY STOP RODS

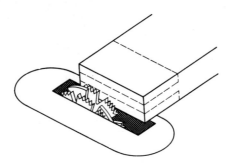

Fig. 4–35. Cutting a tenon using a dado cutter head

Tenons. The procedures described here are useful in the fabrication of the most common type of tenon which is centered on the end of the workpiece and whose shoulders are equal in width. Other types of tenons can be made using the same basic procedures with minor variations.

The mortise into which the tenon fits should be made first. Then the mortise may serve as a gauge for checking the tenon for fit.

Dado Cutter Method for Making Tenons

1. Square-up the workpiece to be used in making a tenon. If possible, leave the piece oversize in length. This will permit more than one attempt at cutting a tenon to fit the mortise.

2. Lay out the tenon on the end of the workpiece.

3. Install a set of dado cutters and adjust as shown in Fig. 4–35.

4. Place the edge of the workpiece against the face of the miter gauge, with the piece positioned so that the first cut will remove approximately 1/8 in. of material from the end of the workpiece (Fig. 4–36). Cut the material off the face of the piece.

Fig. 4–36. Testing partial short tenon fit in mortise

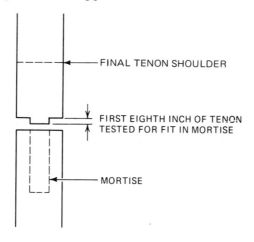

5. Reverse the workpiece and repeat step 4. Check the fit of the small portion of the tenon against the mortise into which the tenon will fit. If the tenon is too tight, raise the dado cutters slightly. If the tenon is too loose, lower the dado cutters slightly. Recut the workpiece and retest the fit. Complete cutting the tenon faces.

6. If more than one identical tenon is to be produced, cut them at this point.

7. Cut the tenon edges using a similar procedure.

Tenoning Jig Method

1. Lay out the tenon on the end of a squared-up workpiece.

2. Elevate the blade until it is aligned with the shoulder depth layout on the end of the workpiece (Fig. 4-35). (A single saw blade is used here; see Fig. 4-33.)

3. Align the shoulder layout line with the saw blade while keeping the edge of the workpiece against the face of the miter gauge (see Fig. 4-33). Move the rip fence up until it makes contact with the end of the workpiece. Lock the rip fence.

4. Make the shoulder cuts into the faces of the workpiece while keeping the workpiece in contact with the miter gauge and the rip fence. The same procedure can be used to make the edge shoulder cuts. An adjustment of the blade height may be necessary for these cuts.

5. Place the tenoning attachment or jig in the left table slot.

6. Elevate the saw blade until it is aligned with the shoulder of the laid-out tenon (Fig. 4-37).

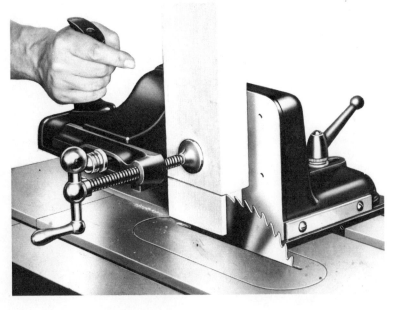

Fig. 4-37. Table saw tenoning jig (Courtesy of Delta Div., Rockwell Corp.)

7. Place the workpiece in the tenoning jig and clamp it in position. The end of the workpiece is in contact with the table (Fig. 4–37).

8. Unclamp the tenoning jig slide and move the upper portion of the jig sideways until the layout line on the edge of the workpiece is aligned with a sawtooth set toward the scrap material to be cut away. Lock the slide in position.

9. Turn the machine on and make the cut. Turn the machine off.

10. Reverse the piece, turn the machine on, and make the second cheek cut.

11. Cut tenon edges by repeating steps 8, 9, and 10.

Rabbet dado joint. The rabbet dado joint is useful for connecting the corners of boxes. In furniture manufacturing this joint is frequently used for the rear corners of a drawer (Figs. 4–38, 4–39, and 4–40).

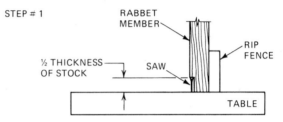

Fig. 4–38. Making a rabbet dado joint–step #1

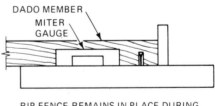

Fig. 4–39. Making a rabbet dado joint–step #2

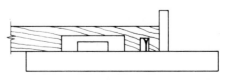

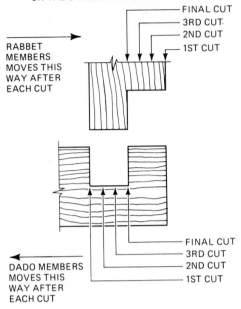

CUTTING THE RABBET—DADO JOINT
ON THE CIRCULAR SAW

FINAL CUT
3RD CUT
2ND CUT
1ST CUT

RABBET
MEMBERS
MOVES THIS
WAY AFTER
EACH CUT

FINAL CUT
3RD CUT
2ND CUT
1ST CUT

DADO MEMBERS
MOVES THIS
WAY AFTER
EACH CUT

Fig. 4-40. Making a rabbet
dado joint–step #3

Finger joint. The finger joint provides a secure method of joining two pieces together at right angles. It is commonly used in the construction of small boxes.

1. Fasten a straight, flat piece of wood to the face of the miter gauge with a clamp.
2. Install a dado cutter whose width is equal to the width of the fingers to be cut.
3. Raise the dado cutter above the table until its height is equal to the workpiece thickness.
4. Turn on the saw and make a cut through the auxiliary fence clamped to the miter gauge.
5. Fashion a square pin of wood equal in width to the dado cutter. Insert it into the cut made in step 4. It should extend out approximately 1/4 in. (Fig. 4-41).

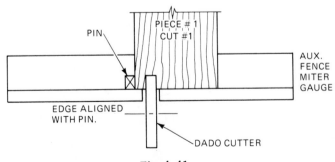

PIN

PIECE # 1
CUT #1

AUX.
FENCE
MITER
GAUGE

EDGE ALIGNED
WITH PIN.

DADO CUTTER

Fig. 4-41.

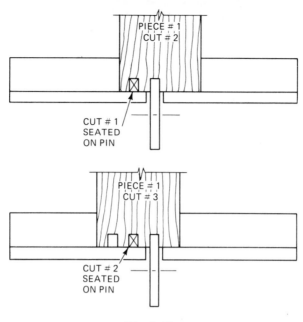

Fig. 4-42.

6. Unclamp the auxiliary miter fence. Move it to the right a distance equal to the width of the dado cutter. An extra piece of the pin made in step 5 can be used as a gauge for this adjustment. Place it against the pin installed in step 5 to gauge the movement to the right. Fasten the auxiliary fence to the miter gauge with screws (Fig. 4-41).

7. Make a second cut through the fence. The finger between the two cuts must equal the width of each cut. Adjust if necessary.

8. Place the edge of the workpiece against the pin, with its face against the miter gauge and its end down on the saw table. Make a cut through it using the miter gauge for support (Fig. 4-41).

9. Place the dado cut made in step 8 over the fence pin. Make a second cut through the workpiece with the dado cutter (Fig. 4-42).

10. Repeat step 9 until the whole end of the workpiece is processed. Follow the same procedure for the opposite end of the workpiece.

11. Take the workpiece, which will mate with the one processed in steps 8 through 10, and position it with its face against the auxiliary miter fence and with its edge *aligned with the dado cut next to the pin* in the auxiliary miter fence (Fig. 4-43).

12. Make a cut through the workpiece with the dado cutter.

13. Slide the workpiece to the right until the cut made in step 12 is against the fence pin and then make the second cut in the workpiece.

14. Position the workpiece so that the cut made in step 13 fits over the fence pin, and then make the third cut. Repeat this step until the end of the workpiece is completely processed.

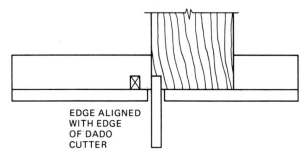

EDGE ALIGNED
WITH EDGE
OF DADO
CUTTER

Fig. 4–43.

Adjustments and Basic Maintenance

Although complex maintenance operations are beyond the scope of this book, simple, common adjustments are described.

Changing a blade on the table saw.

1. Turn off the power supply to the machine and attach a note to the switch box indicating that machine maintenance is being performed.

2. Bring the blade down to its lowest position.

3. Place an open-end wrench—not an adjustable wrench which can damage the arbor—on the arbor flats, and place a second open-end wrench on the arbor nut. Since the arbor has a left-hand thread, loosen its nut by turning it clockwise. If the arbor flats are not accessible (which often occurs when dado cutters are installed), wedge a wooden block of appropriate size between the blade and the throat of the machine (Fig. 4–44).

4. Remove the nut, washer, and blade, and replace the blade with the new one. Reinstall the washer and nut, and tighten the arbor nut using two open-end wrenches.

5. Replace the throat plate and restore power to the machine.

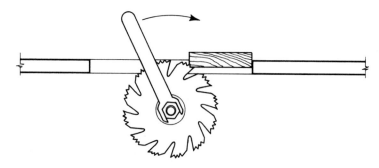

Fig. 4–44. Loosening arbor nut on the table saw with a wood block as a blade stop

Fig. 4–45. Realigning rip fence (Courtesy of Delta Div., Rockwell Corp.)

Rip fence adjustment. The rip fence should be set to lock parallel to the saw blade, or it should lock so that the far end of the fence is 1/16 in. further from the back edge of the blade than from its front edge. This can be checked by positioning the fence adjacent to one of the table slots and then locking it. When locked, the fence should be parallel to the table slot. If it is not, loosen the two bolts located at the infeed end of the fence (Fig 4-45). Then unlock the fence and adjust it until it is parallel to the table slot. Re-lock the fence and tighten the two bolts.

THE JOINTER

Principles of Operation and Nomenclature

The jointer is the mechanical equivalent of the plane. Cutting is accomplished by a cutterhead (Fig. 4-46) which usually has three knives. The length of the knives determines the machine capacity. The cutterhead rotates at a high speed, usually between 3500 and 6000 revolutions per minute (rpm). As the work passes over the cutterhead, a series of small ridges is produced on the workpiece as material is cut away. The interval between the ridges varies directly with the rate at which the workpiece is pushed over the cutterhead.

Fig. 4-46. Jointer cutter head (Courtesy of Delta Div., Rockwell Corp.)

Fig. 4-47. Six inch jointer (Courtesy of Delta Div., Rockwell Corp.)

The jointer has two tables whose heights relative to the cutterhead can be adjusted (Fig. 4-47). If the infeed table is set 1/4 in. below the cutting circle of the cutterhead, 1/4 in. of material will be removed. A depth indicator on the machine indicates the depth of cut. This depth ranges from zero to 1/2 in. on most units. The outfeed table is aligned with the cutterhead cutting circle (Figs. 4-48 and 4-49). It provides support for the newly cut surface as the workpiece moves away from the cutterhead. The tables are raised and lowered by means of a clamp and a handwheel located directly below the table (Fig. 4-50).

An adjustable fence is provided with the jointer. This fence can be tilted to the right or left for beveling (Fig. 4-51). It can also be moved from side to side.

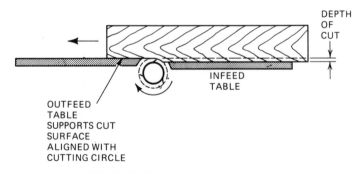

Fig. 4-48. Piece being cut on jointer

Fig. 4–49.

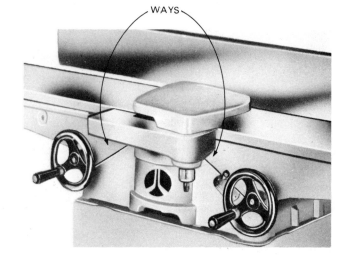

Fig. 4-50. Tables travel on inclined ways (Courtesy of Delta
Div., Rockwell Corp.)

WAYS

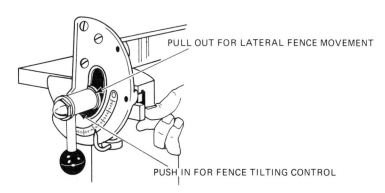

PULL OUT FOR LATERAL FENCE MOVEMENT

PUSH IN FOR FENCE TILTING CONTROL

Fig. 4-51. Jointer fence adjustments

General Safety Rules for the Jointer

1. Always wear approved eye-protection devices.
2. Be sure guards are in position and operative before starting the machine.
3. Do not attempt to joint any surface less than 8 in. long on a jointer.
4. Use a push stick whenever the size of the piece or the operation being performed brings your fingers closer than 4 in. to the cutterhead.
5. Be sure the cutterhead knives are sharp.
6. Keep the jointer tables free of all objects when the machine is in use.
7. Be sure all loose clothing and hair is secured before turning the machine on.

Jointing an Edge

After checking the depth of cut setting and the fence for squareness to the table, determine the grain direction of the workpiece (see Fig. 4–48). Place the face of the workpiece against the fence and have the edge to be jointed resting on the infeed table (Fig. 4–52). Turn the machine on and push the workpiece across the cutterhead. Maintain pressure against the fence and on the infeed table.

Jointing an End

Safe end jointing requires that the workpiece be at least 8 in. wide and short enough to manage during jointing. Since the second edge of the workpiece to pass over the cutterhead almost always splits, ends should be jointed before edges. Many craftsmen avoid jointing ends. Instead, they square and smooth the ends using sanding equipment such as the disk sander.

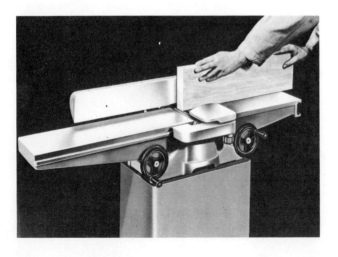

Fig. 4–52. Edge joining on a long bed jointer (Courtesy of Delta Div., Rockwell Corp.)

1. After checking the width of the workpiece for conformity to minimum safe size, adjust the cut depth to 1/32 in.

2. Place the face of the workpiece against the fence, and place its end on the infeed table. If a working edge has been established, this edge should pass over the cutterhead first.

3. Turn the machine on and slowly feed the workpiece over the cutterhead while maintaining pressure against the fence and the infeed table.

4. Repeat steps 2 and 3 for the second end.

Jointing a Face

If a surfacer is not available, narrow pieces can be surfaced on the jointer. Pieces with cup warp can also be flattened on the jointer using this process.

1. Set the cut depth to 1/32 in.

2. Check the grain direction on the face to be jointed.

3. Place the face of the workpiece on the infeed table with the grain pointing toward the infeed end of the machine.

4. Turn the machine on and push the workpiece over the cutterhead using a pusher (Fig. 4-53).

5. Repeat steps 3 and 4 if necessary.

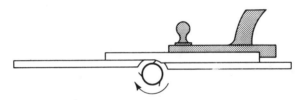

Fig. 4-53. Face jointing using a wooden pusher

Beveling and Chamfering

1. Unclamp the fence and tilt it to the left until the desired angle is formed between the fence face and the infeed table. Check the angle with a T bevel. Note that a pocket is formed between the fence and the infeed table (Fig. 4-54).

2. Set the depth of cut to 1/16 in.

3. Place the face of the workpiece against the fence, and place its corner on the infeed table. Start the machine and feed the piece over the cutterhead. Maintain pressure against the fence and the table.

4. Repeat step 3 until the required chamfer or bevel is cut.

If the ends of a workpiece require beveling or chamfering they should be processed first.

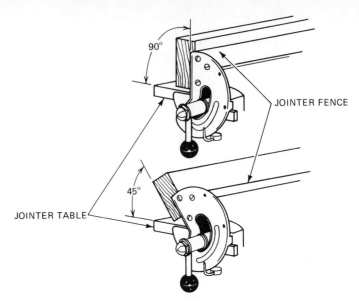

Fig. 4-54. Beveling—chamfering on the jointer

Rabbeting

1. Turn off the power supply and remove the guard on the left side of the fence.

2. Adjust the fence until its distance from the end of one of the knives in the cutterhead is equal to the width of the rabbet to be cut (Fig. 4-55).

3. Lock the fence and set the depth of cut equal to the depth of the rabbet to be made.

4. Turn on the power supply, start the machine, and feed the workpiece over the cutterhead. Check the size of the rabbet and make any adjustments necessary.

Setting the Outfeed Table

Several problems can develop if the outfeed table is misaligned. If the table is too high, the workpiece will appear to be passing over the cutterhead in the normal fashion until the midpoint of the workpiece is passed. Then the front of the workpiece will tip down and the last section of the

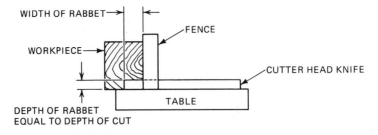

Fig. 4-55. Cutting a rabbet on the jointer

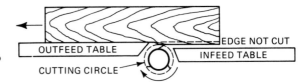

Fig. 4-56. Outfeed table too high

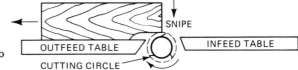

Fig. 4-57. Outfeed table too low.

edge of the piece will not be touched by the cutterhead (Fig. 4-56). If the outfeed table is too low, the rear portion of the edge being joined will drop at the end of the cut and a snipe will develop (Fig. 4-57).

The outfeed table must be aligned with the cutting circle of the cutterhead. This can be accomplished in the following way:

1. Lower the outfeed table to a point where it is obviously too low.
2. Set the infeed table for a cut 1/4-in. deep. Turn the machine on.
3. Take a scrap piece with an existing straight edge and feed it over the cutterhead until approximately one-third of its length is cut (see Fig. 4-48).
4. Raise the outfeed table until it just touches the cut surface of the workpiece (see Fig. 4-48).
5. Clamp the outfeed table in position and complete the cut on the scrap piece.

BAND SAW

Principles of Operation and Nomenclature

The band saw consists of an endless saw blade or band that travels over two wheels and passes through a slot in a table (Fig. 4-58). The workpiece is supported by the table and pushed into the blade as the blade passes through the slot in the table.

Blades range in width from 1/16 in. to 3/4 in. A variety of blades types are available for different kinds of work (Fig. 4-59). The width of the blade determines the minimum radius which the blade can cut (Fig. 4-60). Saw capacity is determined by wheel diameter (Fig. 4-61).

The lower wheel is driven by direct connection to a motor shaft or through a system of belts and pulleys. Each wheel is rimmed with a rubber tire which prevents the blade teeth and the metal wheel from damaging each other. The rim of each wheel is crowned (Fig. 4-62). This crowning helps to

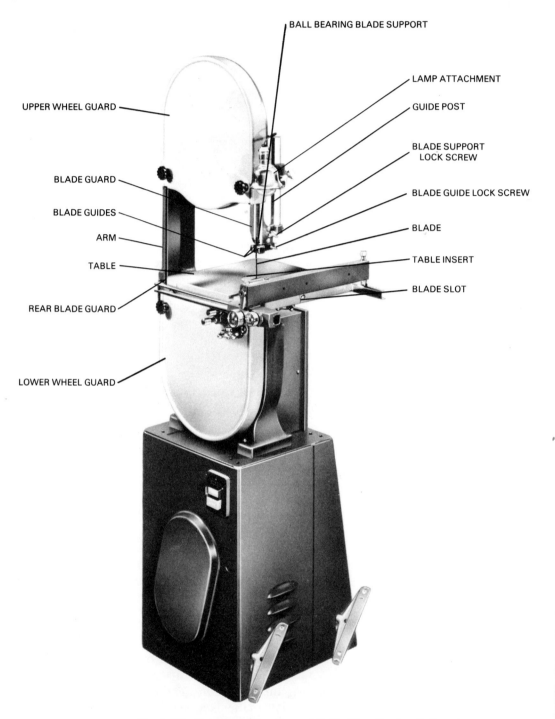

BALL BEARING BLADE SUPPORT

LAMP ATTACHMENT

UPPER WHEEL GUARD

GUIDE POST

BLADE SUPPORT
LOCK SCREW

BLADE GUARD

BLADE GUIDE LOCK SCREW

BLADE GUIDES

ARM

BLADE

TABLE

TABLE INSERT

REAR BLADE GUARD

BLADE SLOT

LOWER WHEEL GUARD

Fig. 4-58. Band saw (Courtesy of Delta Div., Rockwell Corp.)

(A)   6 TEETH PER INCH = 6 PITCH

(B)   4 TEETH PER INCH = 4 PITCH

Fig. 4-59.

BLADE WIDTH	MINIMUM RADIUS OF CUT
1/8″	1/8″
3/16″	5/16″
1/4″	5/8″
3/8″	1 7/16″
1/2″	2 1/2″
5/8″	3 3/4″
3/4″	5 7/16″

Fig. 4-60.

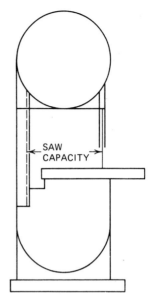

SAW CAPACITY

Fig. 4-61. Band saw capacity

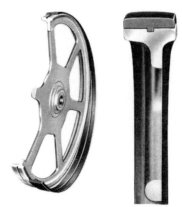

Fig. 4-62. Crowned rubber tired band saw wheels (Courtesy of Delta Div., Rockwell Corp.)

keep the blade tracked on the wheels during operation of the machine. The upper wheel can be raised, lowered, and tilted. The ability to raise and lower the upper wheel makes tensioning and untensioning the blade possible. The tilting feature permits the saw blade to be tracked or moved into a fixed position on the wheels. The upper wheel mounting includes a spring which acts as a shock absorber during the operation of the band saw (Fig. 4-63).

The saw table has a slot in it to allow the saw blade to pass through it during blade changing operations (Fig. 4-64). This slot terminates in a

Fig. 4-63. Blade tensioning knob (lower); blade tracking knob (upper) (Courtesy of Delta Div., Rockwell Corp.)

circular hole in the center of the table. The hole accepts a soft metal insert or throat plate. The two sides of the table on either side of the table slot are kept in alignment by a tapered pin that fits into a tapered hole bored into the slot on the edge of the table (Fig. 4-64). The table is mounted on trunions and can be tilted up to 45° to the right and 10° to the left (Fig. 4-64).

The saw blade passes through two similar sets of blade guides and supports. One set of guides is mounted on the adjustable guidepost and is positioned above the table. The guidepost can be raised or lowered to accommodate workpieces of varying thicknesses. The guides are located on either side of the saw blade and keep the blade from moving sideways during cutting operations (Fig. 4-65). A clearance of approximately 1/64 in. is left between the guides and the smooth surface of the blade. The blade teeth are on the portion of the blade that remains outside of the guides.

Fig. 4-64. Blade support and blade guides under the bandsaw table (Courtesy of Delta Div., Rockwell Corp.)

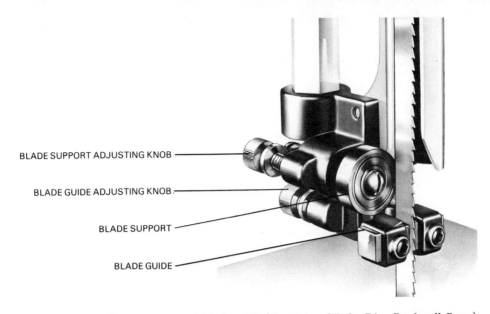

BLADE SUPPORT ADJUSTING KNOB

BLADE GUIDE ADJUSTING KNOB

BLADE SUPPORT

BLADE GUIDE

Fig. 4-65. Upper blade support and blade guide (Courtesy of Delta Div., Rockwell Corp.)

Fig. 4-66. Blade support and blade guide knobs under the table (Courtesy of Delta Div., Rockwell Corp.)

Directly behind the guides and the saw blade is the blade support. This is a ball bearing which supports the back edge of the saw blade during cutting. This blade support is set approximately 1/64 in. behind the edge of the saw blade.

A similar set of guides is located under the table (Fig. 4-66).

The band saw has several guards to provide protection for the operator. Each of the wheels is covered by a door or cover during operation. The saw blade is shielded by a blade guard as it passes along the arm which supports the upper wheel. The section of the blade passing off the upper wheel into the table is protected by a metal guard attached to the guidepost. The band saw should never be operated with any of these guards out of position or open.

Many floor-mounted units are provided with a friction brake which enables the operator to stop the machine quickly after the power has been shut off.

Safety Rules for the Band Saw

1. Be sure the blade is sharp and positioned correctly with respect to blade supports and guides.
2. Have all guards and other safety devices in position.
3. Wear approved eye protection.
4. Keep the right side of the machine clear. If the blade breaks, it can whip out to the right side of the machine.
5. Adjust the guidepost so that it is not more than 1/8 in. above the workpiece.
6. Use a push stick when making through cuts on small pieces.
7. Stop the machine before attempting to pull a workpiece out of an incomplete cut.
8. Use a blade width appropriate for the minimum radius of the cut to be made. Avoid excessive twisting of the blade, which causes friction between the blade and the blade guides.
9. Be sure that round or irregularly shaped pieces are firmly supported by the table during cutting to avoid possible blade kinking and breakage.

Curved Cutting

The band saw is the ideal machine for heavy-duty curved cutting. Larger units can cut through material up to 6 or 7 in. in thickness.

1. Lay out the curve to be cut.
2. Adjust the guidepost so that the blade guides are positioned approximately 1/8 in. above the surface of the workpiece.

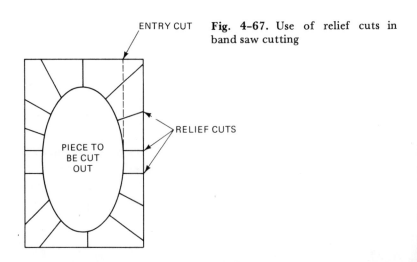

ENTRY CUT

Fig. 4-67. Use of relief cuts in band saw cutting

RELIEF CUTS

PIECE TO
BE CUT
OUT

3. Turn on the machine and make relief cuts at right angles to the curve at approximately 1-in. intervals (Fig. 4–67).

4. Guide the workpiece into the saw blade so that the saw kerf is made about 1/16 in. to the scrap side of the layout line. This allows sanding of the cut surface to remove saw blade marks.

5. Use a push stick to avoid moving fingers close to the saw blade during cutting.

6. If it becomes necessary to back the workpiece away from the saw blade before a cut is completed, *stop the machine* before doing so.

Straight Cutting

The band saw can be used to make relatively straight cuts if a wide blade is used.

Ripping

1. Use the widest blade available on the machine.

2. Set the rip fence (Fig. 4–68) so that its distance from a blade tooth set toward the fence is equal to the width of the piece to be made in the cutting operation. If a standard rip fence is not available, a straight-edged board can be clamped to the tabletop in its place.

3. Set the guidepost to a position appropriate for the workpiece to be cut.

4. Make the cut.

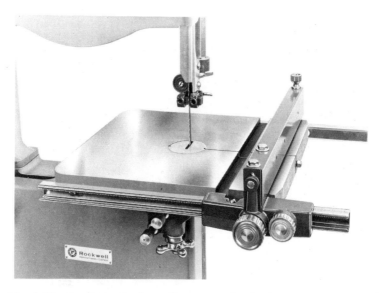

Fig. 4–68. Band saw rip fence (Courtesy of Delta Div., Rockwell Corp.)

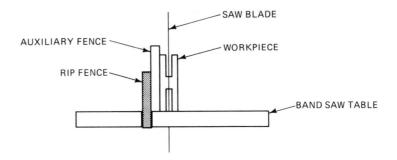

Fig. 4-69. Resawing on the band saw

In resawing operations, an extra wide rip fence should be used to provide adequate stability for the workpiece during the cut (Fig. 4-69).

Crosscutting

Crosscutting can be accomplished with a degree of precision if the miter gauge is used.

1. Place the miter gauge in the slot in the saw table.
2. Place the working edge of the workpiece against the face of the miter gauge and align the layout line with the saw blade.
3. Turn the machine on and push the work into the blade with the miter gauge supporting it.

Multiple Cutting

The stacking method is illustrated in Fig. 4-70.

1. Stack the pieces to be cut one on another and secure them together with brads driven into the scrap portion of the piece.
2. Lay out the shape to be cut on the face of the top piece.
3. Cut the stack of pieces as though a single piece is being cut.

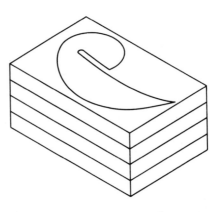

Fig. 4-70. Multiple cutting stacking method

The slicing method is illustrated in Fig. 4-71.

1. Lay out the shape to be cut on the end of the workpiece.
2. Cut out the shape using a band saw.
3. Position the workpiece on its widest edge and slice off the required number of pieces using the miter gauge for support.

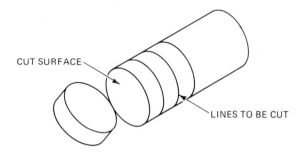

CUT SURFACE

LINES TO BE CUT

Fig. 4-71. Multiple cutting - slicing method

Compound Sawing

Compound sawing involves making at least two cuts at right angles to each other through the workpiece. The following procedure for making a cabriole leg illustrates the technique:

1. Prepare the workpiece by squaring it to finished size.
2. Lay out the leg using a template on one face of the workpiece.
3. Lay out the leg again using the same template on an adjacent edge (Fig. 4-72).
4. Cut along one of the layout lines. *Caution:* relief cuts may not be used.

Fig. 4-72. Compound sawing

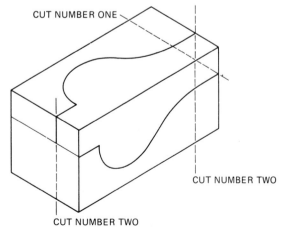

CUT NUMBER ONE

CUT NUMBER TWO

CUT NUMBER TWO

5. Stop the saw and reassemble the cutaway material and the workpiece. Tape the pieces together.

6. Rotate the workpiece so that the uncut layout line is facing upward.

7. Start the machine and cut the second layout line.

Cutting Circular Disks and Segments of Disks

In most cases it is necessary to construct a simple circle-cutting jig to use on the band saw for this purpose. The simplest jig consists of a piece of plywood 1/2-in. thick which is clamped to the table after a single saw cut is made into it as shown in Fig. 4–73.

1. Draw a line at right angles to the saw blade and in line with its teeth.

2. Measure along the line on the jig base, from a sawtooth set toward the right, a distance equal to the radius of the disk or segment to be cut.

3. Drive a 1-in. brad into the jig base at this point. Trim the nail to 3/8 in. in length with a pair of nippers.

4. Make a pocket cut in the workpiece as shown in Fig. 4–73.

5. Make a hole in the center of the disk or segment to be cut. An awl can be used for this purpose.

6. Turn the workpiece over and position the hole (located at the center of the segment or disk to be cut) over the brad protruding from the jig.

7. Press the workpiece down on the brad until it is flush with the jig (Fig. 4–73).

8. Turn on the machine and cut the circle or segment by feeding the workpiece into the saw blade while pivoting it around the brad in the jig base.

Fig. 4–73. Circle cutting on the band saw

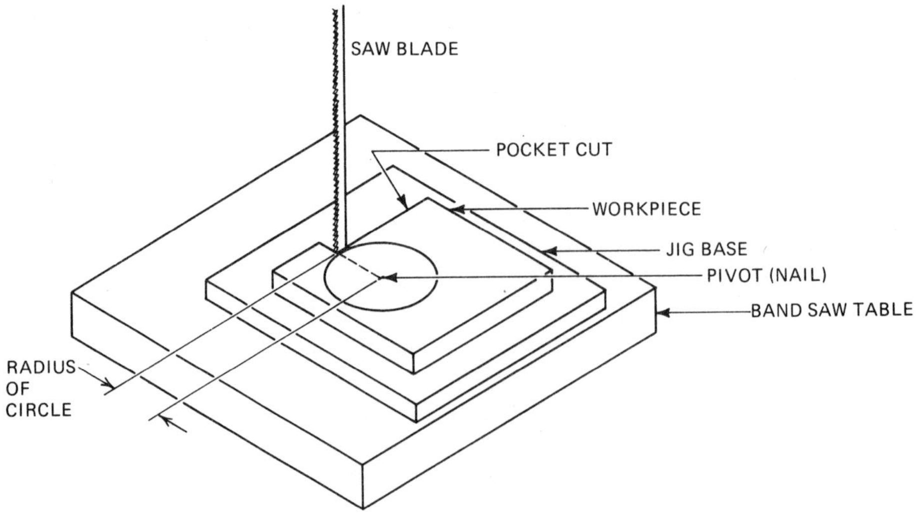

SAW BLADE

POCKET CUT

WORKPIECE

JIG BASE

PIVOT (NAIL)

BAND SAW TABLE

RADIUS OF CIRCLE

Circular cuts can be accomplished with the table set for a beveling cut if desired.

Blade Installation

1. Turn off the power supply to the machine.
2. Remove the table insert and aligning pin.
3. Release tension on the blade by turning the blade tensioning wheel counterclockwise.
4. Lift the blade off the wheels and guide it through the table slot.
5. Coil the blade as shown in Fig. 4-74.
6. Adjust the upper and lower guides and blade supports so that they are as far toward the rear of the machine as possible.
7. Uncoil the blade to be installed, and guide it through the blade slot in the table.
8. Hang the blade over the upper wheel and position it around the lower wheel with the saw teeth pointing toward the table.
9. Tension the blade by turning the tensioning wheel clockwise. Some machines have an indicator which registers the tension on the blade. If such a device is not available, tension the blade until a moderate amount of force (5 pounds) is needed to move the blade sideways 1/4 in.
10. Turn the upper wheel by hand until the blade stops moving on the wheel. At this point it is stabilized. The objective is to center the blade on the tires. If the blade is not centered, adjust the tilt wheel while turning the upper wheel by hand until the blade is centered. The blade is now tracked.
11. Adjust the upper and lower blade supports so that about 1/64 in. of clearance remains between the blade support and the rear edge of the blade.
12. Adjust the blade guides so that the teeth are just outside the front edge of the blade guides (see Fig. 4-65).
13. Turn the machine over by hand to check the travel of the blade through the blade guides and the blade support.
14. Close or replace the wheel guards. Replace the aligning pin and the table insert. Turn the power supply on.
15. Jog the machine to check the blade travel. Then make a test cut with the band saw.

SURFACE PLANER

Principles of Operation and Nomenclature

The planer is essentially an oversize jointer with an automatic feeding mechanism. One of the more common-size planers can accommodate a workpiece up to 6 in. thick and 18 in. wide. Thus the capacity of such a unit is 6 by 18. Most small planers remove material from the uppermost surface of

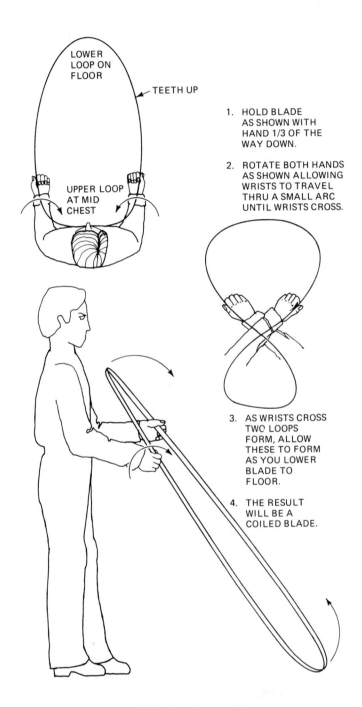

LOWER LOOP ON FLOOR

TEETH UP

UPPER LOOP AT MID CHEST

1. HOLD BLADE AS SHOWN WITH HAND 1/3 OF THE WAY DOWN.

2. ROTATE BOTH HANDS AS SHOWN ALLOWING WRISTS TO TRAVEL THRU A SMALL ARC UNTIL WRISTS CROSS.

3. AS WRISTS CROSS TWO LOOPS FORM, ALLOW THESE TO FORM AS YOU LOWER BLADE TO FLOOR.

4. THE RESULT WILL BE A COILED BLADE.

Fig. 4–74. Band saw coiling

Fig. 4-75. Surface planer (Courtesy of Delta Div., Rockwell Corp.)

the workpiece and in so doing generate a new face which is parallel to the opposite face.

The machine consists of a base which supports a table bed (Figs. 4-75 and 4-76). The bed can be raised and lowered to vary the depth of the cut. The thickness of the workpiece, after passing through the planer, is indicated on a depth indicator which is usually located on the front of the machine (Fig. 4-77). The table is raised and lowered by means of a handwheel which is generally mounted on the front of the unit under the table.

The table has two idler rollers set into its surface on either side of the cutterhead (Fig. 4-78). Directly above the infeed table idler roller is a powered grooved feed roller. This feed roller is mounted in bearing blocks which allow it to lift to accommodate workpieces with irregular faces. Both

Fig. 4-76. Surface planer bed construction

Fig. 4-77. Surfacer planer depth indicator
(Courtesy of Delta Div., Rockwell Corp.)

ends of the infeed roller can move up and down independently of each other. When the machine is in operation, the workpiece is inserted between the grooved feed roller and the smooth idler roller located directly below it in the table.

Directly behind the infeed roller is a heavy curved casting called the *chip breaker* (Fig. 4-78). The chip breaker holds the workpiece down against the table of the machine so that the rotating cutterhead does not lift it. It also acts as a split breaker in much the same way that a cap in a plane iron assembly does.

Directly behind the chip breaker is the cutterhead. This component rotates at 3500 to 5000 revolutions per minute (rpm). The cutterhead has three or more knives mounted on it which do the actual cutting of the workpiece. The cutterhead is located above the workpiece and rotates counterclockwise.

Directly behind the cutterhead is the pressure bar (Fig. 4-78). Like the chip breaker, this pressure bar presses the workpiece down against the table

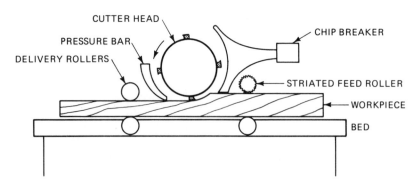

Fig. 4-78. Cross sectional view of surface planer

of the machine. To the rear of the pressure bar is the powered delivery roller. This roller, together with the idler roller located below it, keeps the workpiece moving through the machine once its end passes through the infeed rollers.

Planners have a speed control which enables the operator to change the speed at which the workpiece travels through the machine. This device varies the feed rate from 25 to 125 ft per minute. The slower speeds are generally used for hardwoods or in situations where the smoothest possible surface is required (Fig. 4-79).

General Safety Rules for the Surface Planer

1. Always wear approved eye-protection devices.

2. Be sure that the workpiece meets the minimum length requirements of the machine. This length is equal to the distance from the infeed rollers to the delivery rollers, plus 2 in.

3. Never allow any part of your body to pass beyond the front edge of the table bed when the machine is in operation or the power supply is turned on. Use a push bar, if necessary, to help a stalled piece pass into the delivery rollers.

4. Stand to one side of the machine when the unit is in operation to avoid being struck by objects thrown back.

5. Be sure that the workpiece is free of nonwood objects such as nails or screws before attempting to process it in the machine.

6. Check the grain direction on the face of the material to be surfaced to be sure that it points toward you.

Fig. 4-79. Rate of feed control on surface planer (Courtesy of Delta Div., Rockwell Corp.)

7. Set the initial depth of cut by measuring the maximum thickness of the workpiece and then setting the table to a depth thickness 1/16 to 1/8 in. less than this thickness.

Surfacing Material to Thickness

1. Check the workpiece for defects which might interfere with the safe operation of the machine. Buried nails, screws, or other nonwood materials should be avoided.
2. Measure the workpiece to determine whether or not its length is sufficient for processing. The piece should be 2 in. longer than the space measured between the infeed and the delivery rollers.
3. Determine the grain direction on each face to be surfaced. Indicate this grain direction with an arrow drawn on one edge. When feeding the workpiece into the planer, the grain on the surface being cut should point toward the *infeed end* of the machine.
4. Determine the greatest thickness of the workpiece. Set the table in a position where the depth indicator reads 1/8 in. less than the greatest thickness of the workpiece.
5. Check the position of the feed-rate selector and adjust if necessary.
6. Start the machine and feed the workpiece into the infeed end of the machine.
7. Stand to one side of the machine to avoid being struck by any material thrown back. If the workpiece stalls, push it with a wooden push bar.
8. Move to the delivery end of the machine and support the workpiece as it exists the delivery rollers. Failure to provide this support may result in sniping at the end of the cut.
9. Repeat steps 4 through 8 until the desired thickness is obtained.

When more than two cuts are to be made during processing, equal amounts of material should be removed from each face of the workpiece. This reduces the tendency of the workpiece to warp because of unequal drying and helps to maintain the stability of the workpiece by exposing equal amounts of "new wood."

If more than one workpiece is to be surfaced to the same thickness, each piece should be machined in turn, at each setting of the depth of cut. This ensures that the final thicknesses of the workpieces will be identical.

Warped Material

In general, warped stock is flattened by the feed rollers and the chip breaker as it passes into the planer. However, the warp will return (via spring-back) as soon as the workpiece passes out of the delivery rollers. Narrow pieces more than an inch or so in thickness may resist this temporary flattening, and may have a cup warp planed flat. One way to flatten stock with a

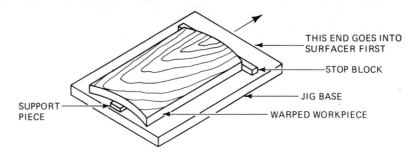

THIS END GOES INTO
SURFACER FIRST

STOP BLOCK

JIG BASE

SUPPORT
PIECE

WARPED WORKPIECE

Fig. 4-80. Cup warp jig

cup warp is to surface the convex face in a jointer until a flat face is developed. Then the material can be surfaced in the planer, with the flat face down and the opposite face planed parallel to it.

A second method permits the total process to be accomplished by the planer:

1. Construct the surfacing jig shown in Fig. 4-80.
2. Place the workpiece on the jig with its end against the stop and with the convex face uppermost.
3. Surface a piece of scrap until its thickness is equal to the space between the underface of the workpiece and the surface of the jig (Fig. 4-80).
4. Insert this strip into the space formed by the workpiece and the surface of the jig.
5. Determine the combined thickness of the jig and the workpiece. Set the depth indicator to this measurement minus 1/8 in.
6. Turn the machine on and feed the jig and the workpiece into the machine, with the stop end of the jig going in first.
7. Repeat steps 5 and 6 until a flat face is developed.
8. Remove the workpiece from the jig, and surface the opposite face until the warp is cut away.

This process removes the warp effectively; however, a significant reduction in workpiece thickness results.

Reducing Square Stock to Octagonal Cross-sectional Shape

1. Fabricate the jig shown in Fig. 4-81 by making two 45° ripping cuts on the table saw.
2. Select a workpiece whose cross-sectional shape is a square. Lay out an octagon on the end of the workpiece.
3. Place the workpiece in the jig as shown in Fig. 4-81. Determine the combined thickness of the workpiece and the jig.
4. Set the depth indicator to a position that indicates a measurement 1/8 in. less than the combined thickness of the workpiece and the jig.

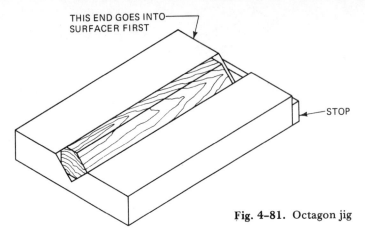

THIS END GOES INTO
SURFACER FIRST

STOP

Fig. 4-81. Octagon jig

5. Start the machine and feed the workpiece and jig into the machine with the stop end of the jig going in first.

6. Rotate the workpiece 90° and repeat step 5.

7. Repeat step 6 two more times. *Note:* The depth setting has not been changed.

8. Raise the table 1/8 in. and repeat step 6 four times.

9. Repeat step 8 until the octagon is completed and matches the layout on the end of the workpiece.

Common Problems and Remedies

1. The workpiece is delivered from the machine with a raised bead running from end to end on the processed face (Fig. 4-82). This condition is probably the most common surfacing defect and it is usually caused by a blade nick. The remedy is to have a newly sharpened set of knives installed in the machine.

2. The rear end of the workpiece is sniped from edge to edge. This condition usually results from failure to support a fairly long workpiece as

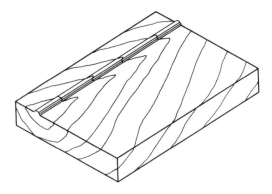

Fig. 4-82.

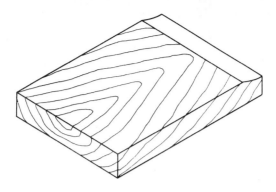

Fig. 4–83.

it exits the planer. The weight of the piece thrusts the rear end of the work-piece up into the cutterhead as the end passes out of the infeed rollers and the chipper (Fig. 4–83).

3. "Torn-up" surface. A pitted face is caused by feeding the workpiece into the planer with the grain going against the direction of the cutterhead's rotation. Resurface the face with the grain on the uppermost face pointing toward you.

4. Ridge (depressed) across the face from edge to edge. This situation frequently develops if the workpiece stops while the machine is running. The pause allows the cutterhead to cut a little more deeply at the point of stoppage. Continuous pressure with a feed pushbar can eliminate this prob-lem. (Fig. 4–84).

5. Ridge (depressed) across the workpiece from edge to edge at the rear end of the piece (Fig. 4–85). This ridge develops even if the workpiece is supported, and so it is unlike the snipe discussed above. It often develops in cup-warped stock. As the end of the piece passes out of the infeed rollers and the chipper, it partially springs back into its cup warp and the cutter-head cuts into the end.

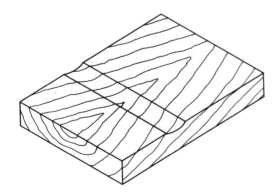

Fig. 4–84.

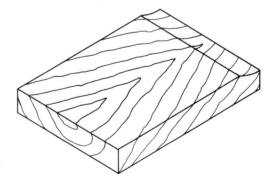

Fig. 4–85.

THE SCROLL SAW

Principles of Operation and Nomenclature

The scroll saw or jigsaw is essentially a powered version of the common coping saw. Like the coping saw, its relatively narrow blade makes it the ideal machine for intricate, small-radius, curved cuts. The narrow blade is kept in tension so that it remains rigid during operation. The up-and-down or reciprocating motion of the blade is developed by a mechanical device, very much like a crank and piston in an automobile engine. The machine cuts on the downstroke because the saw teeth point down and because this method of cutting tends to keep the thin flexible blade rigid during cutting.

The machine (Fig. 4–86) consists of a fairly long, narrow, base casting which houses the driven pulley and the mechanical drive that converts the rotary motion of the pulley into the reciprocating motion of the lower plunger and its chuck. The motor is mounted either on the base, as shown in Fig. 4–86, or directly below the driven pulley on a shelf which is part of the machine stand. Each of the pulleys has several steps which allow speed variation. In some machines, a variable pulley on the motor allows speed changes while the machine is in motion. This is accomplished by adjusting a speed-control handle mounted on the machine.

Directly above the lower plunger is a table that is mounted on trunions and can be tilted 45° to the right or left. This table is equipped with a throat plate which provides access to the lower plunger and chuck. Attached to the rear of the base, or as an integral part of the base casting, is an overarm. This overarm extends toward the front of the machine and positions the upper

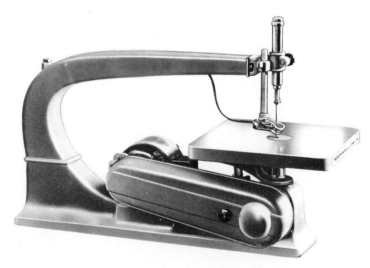

Fig. 4–86. (Courtesy of Delta Div., Rockwell Corp.)

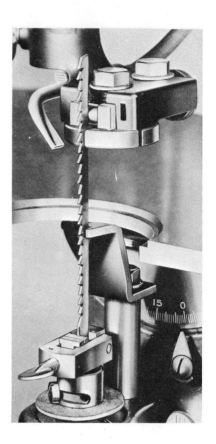

Fig. 4-87. Saber saw in position in scroll saw show guides (Courtesy of Delta Div., Rockwell Corp.)

head and the guidepost over the lower plunger and chuck. The guidepost can be raised and lowered to accommodate workpieces of various thicknesses. The guide assembly is attached to its lower end (Fig. 4-87). This assembly provides blade support and guidance in very much the same way the blade supports and guides on the band saw do. The sideways or lateral motion of the blade is controlled by a guide disk. This disk has slots of various widths to accommodate a variety of saw blades, and it can be rotated so that the slot required can be aligned with the blade.

Directly below the guide disk is a steel roller which supports the blade during cutting operations. The blade support can be moved forward or backward to match the width of the blade being used. A spring foot or hold-down is positioned under the guide disk. This foot holds the workpiece down on the table as the blade moves up and out of the piece. The foot can be tilted to match the table angle (Fig. 4-88).

Some machines have a hole drilled into the base behind the lower plunger (Fig. 4-89). This hole is designed to receive a lower blade guide which can be used with a saber saw blade. Many machines are equipped with a blower which keeps the cutting site free of sawdust.

Fig. 4–88. Tilt table sawing with hold down tilted (Courtesy of Delta Div., Rockwell Corp.)

Fig. 4–89. Under the table auxiliary blade guide (Courtesy of Delta Div., Rockwell Corp.)

The tension sleeve, located directly above the lower chuck and plunger (Fig. 4-90), has a coil spring inside of it which provides tension for the saw blade. The sleeve can be raised or lowered inside the upper head which is fastened to the overarm. The sleeve clamp locks the sleeve in position in the upper head. This tension sleeve has two positions in the upper head. In the normal position, its chuck positions the saw teeth so that they face the front of the machine. In the secondary position, its chuck is rotated 90° to the left and the saw teeth point toward the left side of the machine.

General Safety Rules for the Scroll Saw or Jigsaw

1. Always wear approved eye protection when operating the jigsaw.
2. Be sure the power supply is shut off when installing blades.
3. Always turn the machine over by hand, before turning the power on, to check blade tension and correct installation.
4. Adjust the hold-down so that it provides adequate pressure on the workpiece.

Fig. 4-90. Scroll saw tension sleeve (Courtesy of Delta Div., Rockwell Corp.)

5. Use a push block in making through cuts on small pieces of work.

6. When saber sawing, be sure that the lower guide is correctly positioned to provide adequate support.

7. In saber sawing, be sure that the guide assembly is raised high enough for the blade end to run free during operation. Make certain that the guidepost is locked securely in place so that machine vibration will not cause it to move down into the range of the saber saw.

Cutting Curves

The scroll saw is best suited for making small-radius curved cuts. The following procedure is recommended for external curved cutting:

1. Lay out the lines to be cut on the workpiece.
2. Adjust the hold-down foot to pressurize the workpiece.
3. Start the machine and feed the workpiece into the blade. Follow the line by rotating the workpiece as it travels forward toward the rear of the machine.
4. Small-radius turns can be made by slowly rotating the workpiece, with the blade as the center of the rotation. This type of cutting requires a very thin blade (Fig. 4–91).

Piercing

Piercing involves making internal cuts without cutting into the internal area from the outside of the piece.

1. Lay out the lines to be cut on the workpiece.
2. Drill a small hole inside the area to be cut out. This hole should be large enough to permit the saw blade to pass through it.
3. Install a saw blade through the drilled hole with its teeth pointing down. Fasten the lower end of the blade in the lower chuck.
4. Raise the lower chuck to its highest point and attach the upper chuck to the upper end of the saw blade. Tension the blade.
5. Bring the hold-down foot down on the workpiece and lock it in position.
6. Start the machine and cut along the layout line.
7. Stop the machine. Unfasten the upper chuck from the blade and remove the workpiece.

Coped Joint

The coped joint is shown in Fig. 4–92. In this joint, less space is developed between the two pieces when shrinkage takes place because the shrinking of only one piece is visible at the joint. In a miter joint, the shrink-

MATERIAL CUT	WIDTH IN.	TEETH PER INCH	BLADE FULL SIZE
STEEL ■ IRON LEAD ■ COPPER ALUMINUM	.070	32	
PEWTER ASBESTOS PAPER ■ FELT	.070	20	
STEEL ■ IRON LEAD ■ COPPER BRASS	.070	15	
ALUMINUM PEWTER ASBESTOS	.085	15	
WOOD	.110	20	
ASBESTOS ■ BRAKE LINING ■ MICA STEEL ■ IRON LEAD ■ COPPER BRASS ALUMINUM PEWTER	.250	20	
WOOD VENEER PLUS PLASTICS CELLULOID HARD RUBBER BAKELITE IVORY EXTREMELY THIN MATERIALS	.035	20	
PLASTICS CELLULOID	.050	15	
BAKELITE	.070	7	
IVORY ■ WOOD	.110	7	
WALL BOARD PRESSED WOOD WOOD ■ LEAD BONE ■ FELT PAPER ■ COPPER IVORY ALUMINUM	.110	15	
HARD AND SOFT WOOD	.110	10	
	.187	10	
	.250	7	
PEARL ■ PEWTER MICA	.054	30	
PRESSED WOOD SEA SHELLS	.054	20	
HARD LEATHER	.085	12	

Fig. 4–91. Scroll saw blade chart

AS A GENERAL RULE, ALWAYS SELECT THE NARROWEST BLADES RECOMMENDED FOR INTRICATE CURVE CUTTING AND WIDEST BLADES FOR STRAIGHT AND LARGE CURVE CUTTING OPERATIONS.

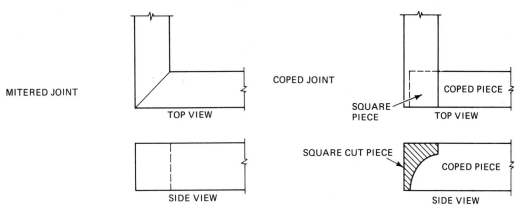

Fig. 4-92. Coped joint

age of each piece adds to the space that develops between the pieces at the joint. The coped joint is commonly used for joining molding used as trim in rooms.

1. Cut the first piece to be joined so that its end is square to its face. Cut the second piece so that its end is at a 45° angle to its face.

2. Place the face of the mitered piece on the table of the scroll saw with its beveled 45° surface facing up (Fig. 4-93).

3. Follow the line formed by the intersection of the bevel and the face of the workpiece with the scroll saw blade (Fig. 4-93).

4. The surface produced by this cut should fit against the shaped face of the second piece with the square-cut end (Fig. 4-92).

Angle Sawing and Marquetry

If two workpieces are cut at the same time, one on top of the other, while the table is tilted, one of the cut-out pieces will start into the hole in

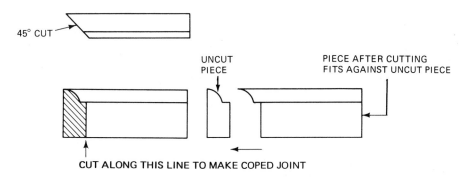

Fig. 4-93. Fabricating a coped joint

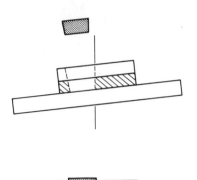

Fig. 4-94. Angle Sawing — marquetry

the second piece, but will not seat in it (Fig. 4-94). This procedure can be used to produce raised surfaces.

1. Lay out the cut to be made on one workpiece.
2. Fasten the two workpieces together with tape or with brads driven into the scrap area.
3. Tilt the table approximately 5° to the left.
4. Adjust the hold-down foot angle to conform to the table tilt.
5. Pressurize the workpiece with the hold-down foot.
6. Start the machine and feed the workpiece into the blade. *Keep the area around which the saw cut is being made on the left side of the blade.* (Fig. 4-94).
7. Stop the machine and remove the pieces. The piece cut out of the top piece should start to fit into the bottom piece. If you want the top piece to be raised higher, adjust the table to a greater angle. If you want the top piece to be raised less, make the table angle smaller. When the angle is correct, the top piece should fit into the bottom piece so that the pieces are flush with no visible saw kerf. When this occurs, the combined workpieces are known as *marquetry*. This decorative effect is often used to advantage on the surfaces of projects such as jewelry boxes.

Saber Sawing

Saber sawing involves the use of a thick blade that requires no tensioning. This leaves the upper end of the blade free. Therefore, in making piercing cuts, the workpiece is slid over the unattached upper end of the saber saw blade before cutting begins. Other kinds of cutting are also possible with saber saw blades. The extra width and thickness of these blades increases the minimum radius which can be cut on the scroll saw. Saber saw blades generally have large teeth; therefore, they cut rapidly but leave a rough saw kerf. The blades can be used with or without the hold-down foot.

Blade Installation

Installing blades on the jigsaw is a common requirement for efficient operation. Blades break, become dull, or must be changed for various types of cutting. Their installation is simple, provided a few basic steps are followed. The suggested procedure for such an installation is as follows:

1. Turn off the power supply to the machine.
2. Turn the machine over by hand until the lower chuck is raised to its highest point of travel above the machine base.
3. Remove the table insert (throat plate).
4. Open the jaws of the lower chuck and place the lower end of the blade into the space between the flat jaws. Tighten the lower jaws with the thumbscrew.
5. Check the back edge of the blade for squareness to the table top with a try square or a small square block (Fig. 4-95). Repeat step 4 if necessary to achieve squareness.

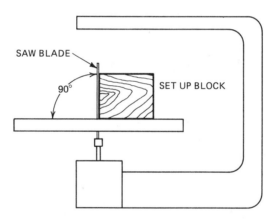

Fig. 4-95. Checking of scroll blade's squareness to table

6. Loosen the tension sleeve clamp and lower the tension sleeve and its upper plunger and chuck as a unit until the upper end of the jigsaw blade passes into the upper chuck (Fig. 4-96).
7. Tighten the upper chuck around the blade and pull the tension sleeve upward until the desired blade tension is developed. Thinner blades generally require more tension than thicker ones.
8. Replace the table insert and lower the guidepost and its blade supporting assembly until they are positioned correctly for the work to be cut.

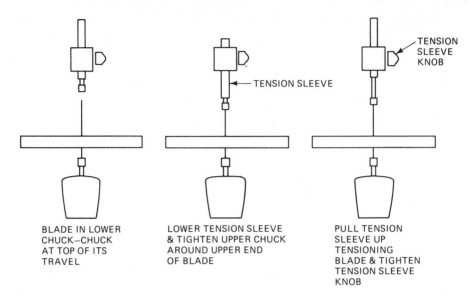

BLADE IN LOWER
CHUCK—CHUCK
AT TOP OF ITS
TRAVEL

LOWER TENSION SLEEVE
& TIGHTEN UPPER CHUCK
AROUND UPPER END
OF BLADE

PULL TENSION
SLEEVE UP
TENSIONING
BLADE & TIGHTEN
TENSION SLEEVE
KNOB

Fig. 4-96. Tensioning scroll saw blade

9. Adjust the blade disk so that the slot aligned with the blade is wide enough for the blade being used. The edge of the disk slot should be set just to the rear of the blades' teeth (Fig. 4-87).

10. Adjust the blade support roller so that it just touches the rear edge of the blade.

11. Turn the machine over by hand to check the operation of the blade.

12. Repeat steps 2 through 11 if necessary. Turn power supply on.

Saber Saw Blade Installation

1. Turn off the power supply to the machine.

2. Turn the machine over by hand until the chuck reaches its highest point of travel.

Fig. 4-97. Lower chuck can be rotated (Courtesy of Delta Div., Rockwell Corp.)

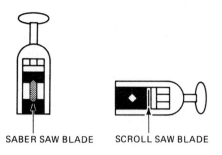

SABER SAW BLADE   SCROLL SAW BLADE

Fig. 4–98. Saber saw blade and scroll saw blade

3. Loosen the screw which holds the lower chuck in position, and rotate the lower chuck 90° to the left (clockwise) (Fig. 4–97).

4. Install the saber saw blade guide in the hole provided directly behind the lower chuck.

5. Install a saber saw blade in the V notch in the jaws of the lower chuck (Fig. 4–98).

6. Position the saber saw guide against the blade and reinstall the throat plate.

7. Turn the machine over by hand to make sure the blade guide located above the table is free of the upper end of the saber saw blade at its highest point of travel.

8. Turn on the power and commence cutting.

SECONDARY AND PORTABLE POWER TOOLS

DRILL PRESS

Principles of Operation and Nomenclature

The drill press consists of a base, a machined steel column, a head, and a table. The head and table can be traveled vertically on the column. The head includes a motor that provides power to the spindle, a feed lever that raises and lowers the spindle, and a chuck that holds the various accessories used in the machine (Fig. 5–1).

The drill press can be thought of as a kind of vertical lathe. The column is similar to the ways of the lathe, and the head is very much like the lathe headstock. The capacity of this machine is determined in two ways. The first is the distance from the center of the chuck to the column. The second is the maximum travel of the spindle vertically. Thus a 15-in. drill press with a 6-in. stroke is one that measures 7-1/2 in. from chuck center to column and has a spindle that can travel vertically 6 in. The 15-in. designation indicates that the machine can drill a hole in the center of a 15-in. circle.

The base is provided with holes that enable the machine to be fastened to the floor or, in the case of a bench model, to the bench top. The upper surface of the base is usually slotted and can be used in place of the table to support large workpieces.

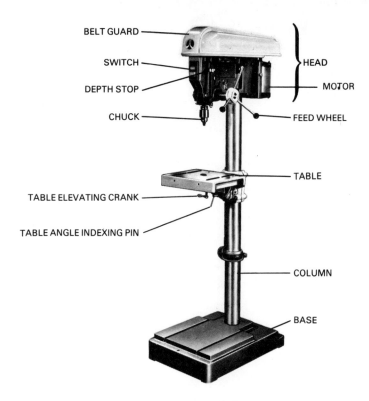

BELT GUARD

SWITCH

DEPTH STOP

CHUCK

TABLE ELEVATING CRANK

TABLE ANGLE INDEXING PIN

HEAD

MOTOR

FEED WHEEL

TABLE

COLUMN

BASE

Fig. 5–1. Drill Press. (Courtesy of Rockwell Manufacturing Co., Delta Power Tools Div.)

The table is clamped to the column and can be traveled vertically to accommodate workpieces of various sizes. On many units, the table can be tilted for angle boring. The head is also clamped to the column. Although the head can be repositioned on the column, it is generally fixed in position during installation and seldom adjusted. *Caution:* The head is extremely heavy and should never be unclamped by a person working alone.

Spindle speeds vary from approximately 300 rpm to 3000 rpm, depending on the motor speed and the power transmission system. The chucks on most woodworking drill presses have a 1/2-in. capacity and are usually geared. The spindle is raised and lowered by means of a feed wheel or lever (Fig. 5-1). Most units have an adjustable stop which can be used to limit the travel of the spindle (Fig. 5-2). The amount of travel can be determined by means of a pointer which indicates the distance along a calibrated spindle housing. The spindle lock is a clamping device which enables the operator to lock the spindle after traveling it to a desired point. The driving system, usually stepped pulleys and a V belt, is covered by removable guards (Fig. 5-3).

ADJUSTABLE STOP

Fig. 5-2. (Courtesy of Rockwell Manufacturing Co., Delta Power Tools Div.)

Fig. 5-3. (Courtesy of Rockwell Manufacturing Co., Delta Power Tools Div.)

General Safety Rules for the Drill Press

1. Always wear approved eye protection.
2. Secure clothing that might become engaged by the drill press spindle.
3. Secure all accessories in the chuck with the chuck key.
4. Always remove the chuck key from the chuck immediately after tightening. *Never leave the chuck key in the chuck even for a moment.* If the key is left in the chuck, it will fly out when the machine is turned on.
5. Be sure the workpiece is clamped securely to the table. Never hold the workpiece with your hands while drilling or boring.
6. Keep your feet off the base of floor units to prevent injury in the event the table slides down the column.
7. Before unclamping the table, be sure that it is adequately supported. Keep your feet clear of the base of the drill press.

8. Check the pulleys, or speed-setting mechanism, to determine whether or not the machine is set to operate at the correct speed for the operation to be performed.

9. Turn the spindle by hand before turning on the power to check the free swing of the accessory to be used.

Boring Operations

The most common use of the drill press is to bore holes in wood. The great advantage of the machine over hand-held tools is the degree of precision that the drill press can provide. The chart in Fig. 5–4 lists the more common hole-making accessories and their capabilities. The following steps are general in nature and can be altered to fit most hole-making operations.

Boring through-holes.

1. Locate the hole to be made on the workpiece and lay out its center.

2. Select the appropriate boring tool for the operation and install it in the chuck. Tighten with the chuck key. Make certain that the tool is centered in the three jaws of the chuck.

3. Adjust the speed of the machine to suit the operation to be performed. In general, boring operations which produce a hole of 1/2 in. or less in diameter should use a speed of approximately 2500 rpm. For holes of larger diameter, lower speeds should be used.

4. Position the workpiece on a flat piece of wood under the chuck on the table.

5. Travel the spindle down until the center of the boring tool is touching the layout of the center of the hole to be bored. Clamp the spindle in position with the spindle clamp. Clamp the workpiece to the drill press table (Fig. 5–5).

6. Unclamp the spindle and return it to the top of its travel.

7. Turn the spindle by hand to check the security of the boring tool and its free swing.

8. Turn the power on and bore the hole using moderate pressure.

Boring blind holes. Most boring tools have a point which leads the tool into the workpiece and makes alignment of the tool simple. The common exception is the Forstner bit (Fig. 5–4). The useful, or functional, depth of the hole is that portion which is generated by the cutters of the tool. Thus, in setting the depth of cut for a blind hole, the cutting edge of the tool is used, not the point (Fig. 5–6).

Boring identical holes in several pieces. In production work or in project work where identical pieces are required, it often becomes necessary to bore identically located holes in several pieces. One simple way to accomplish this is to fasten several pieces together temporarily with masking tape

ACCESSORY DIAGRAM & NAME	CHARACTERISTICS USE	SIZE RANGE	DIRECTIONS FOR USE
Twist Drills 	Small Holes in Wood and Metal	1/16–1/2	Use in metal with center punched hole. Gives rough finish. In wood use only when other wood bits are not available.
Spur Bit Machine Spur Bits— Production type. 	All purpose smooth BORING	1/4–1"	Use in normal fashion. For through holes support piece with scrap material to prevent splitting
Multi-spur Bit	Large Holes in all woods smooth boring	1/2–2"	Used as above for spur bit
Forstner Bit 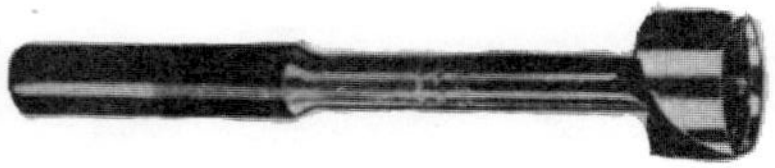	Used for maximum depth blind holes. Used to enlarge existing holes. Smooth bore	1/4–1"	Difficult to match to center lines
Spade Bits 	Used for rough work like holes for cable in construction	1/4–1 1/2	Use as above for spur bit. Extension rod available for less accessible work as in construction. Often used in hand drill
Hole Saw Set 	Holes in material approximately one inch thick maximum	In sets 7/8" 3 1/2"	Use slowest speed. Saw halfway one surface—reverse and saw through from opposite surface.
Fly Cutter 	Holes in material up to 3/4" thick	1"–6"	Use lowest speed. Secure work Keep Hands clear of work. Use with great care on soft materials. Most other accessories preferable to fly cutter.
Plug Cutter 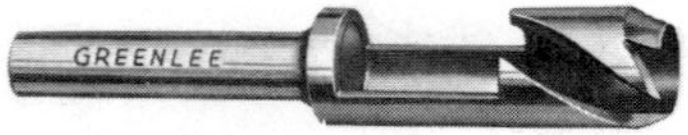 Plug Cutters—Used for making wood plugs and dowels.	Cuts Wooden Plugs for Filling Holes Made for Screws	1/4"–1"	Bore Straight through piece. Stop machine and remove plug. If bored in face plug can be matched to grain around hole to be plugged.

Fig. 5-4. (Courtesy of Greenlee Tools)

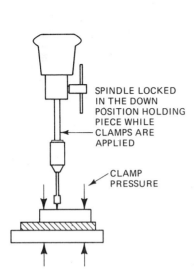

SPINDLE LOCKED IN THE DOWN POSITION HOLDING PIECE WHILE CLAMPS ARE APPLIED

CLAMP PRESSURE

Fig. 5-5. Clamping work to the drill press table

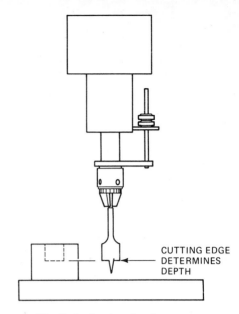

CUTTING EDGE DETERMINES DEPTH

Fig. 5-6. Setting depth stop

and then follow the procedure for boring through-holes. If this method is not practical, the jig shown in Fig. 5-7 can be used. Each succeeding piece is positioned in the pocket formed by the strips and bored. Blind holes can also be located in this manner.

Boring holes through extra-long workpieces. For certain operations the length of a boring tool is inadequate for the depth of hole required. This is often the case with a lamp base. Special, extra-long bits are used for this purpose (electrician's augers), but they may not be available. The procedure shown in Fig. 5-8(a-d) can be used to approximately double the depth of a hole which a bit can bore.

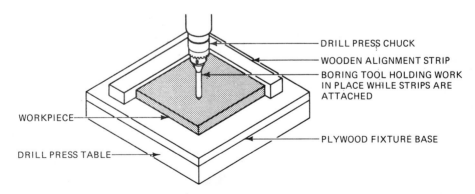

DRILL PRESS CHUCK

WOODEN ALIGNMENT STRIP

BORING TOOL HOLDING WORK IN PLACE WHILE STRIPS ARE ATTACHED

WORKPIECE

DRILL PRESS TABLE

PLYWOOD FIXTURE BASE

Fig. 5-7. Drill press fixture

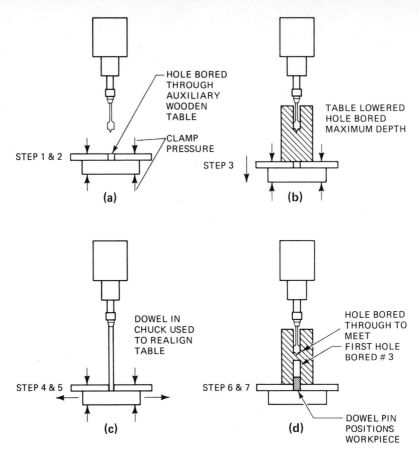

Fig. 5-8. Boring holes whose depth exceeds bit length

Angle boring. Many drill presses are equipped with tiltable tables. Such adjustable tables are secured in position by a nut located under the table and next to the column (Fig. 5-9). To tilt the table, loosen the nut, remove the indexing pin, and rotate the table to the required angle. To obtain a 45° angle, rotate the table until the alignment hole lines up with the matching hole in the casting attached to the column. Reinsert the indexing pin and tighten the nut. For other angles, see Fig. 5-9.

Pocket holes. Pocket holes are used to fasten rails to tabletops by means of screws. The diagram in Fig. 5-10 shows the setup.

Nonboring Accessories

Drum sanders. Commercially made drum sanders and sleeves are available for use on the drill press. These consist of a metal shaft threaded at one end and equipped with a rubber sleeve. The sanding sleeve fits over the drum when the nut on the threaded end is loose. After the sleeve is in place, the

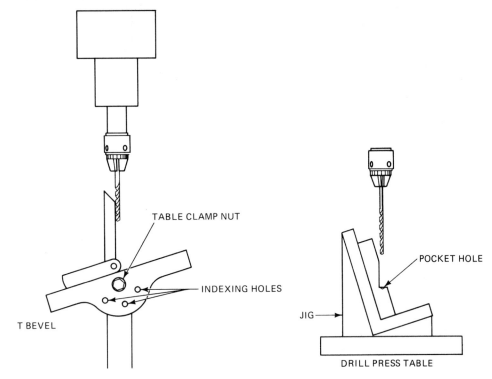

Fig. 5-9. Angle boring

TABLE CLAMP NUT

INDEXING HOLES

T BEVEL

POCKET HOLE

JIG

DRILL PRESS TABLE

Fig. 5-10.

nut is tightened, and it compresses the rubber drum which expands and secures the sanding sleeve (Fig. 5-11). The sanding drum is mounted in the drill press chuck, and the workpiece is held against the abrasive surface as the drum revolves. An auxiliary table can be fabricated for use with drum sanders (Fig. 5-12).

 Rotary files. Rotary files of various diameters and shapes are available for use in the drill press and can be used to rough-shape softwoods. These files must be used carefully because they are very rough and can abrade the operator's skin very rapidly (Fig. 5-13).

Fig. 5-11. Drum sander. (Courtesy of Rockwell Manufacturing Co., Delta Power Tools Div.)

Fig. 5-12.

AUXILIARY WOODEN TABLE FITS OVER DRILL PRESS TABLE

Fig. 5-13. (Courtesy of Stanley Tools Co.)

Router bits. Router bits of various types can be used in the drill press, converting the drill press into an overarm router. However, most drill presses cannot approach the high speeds (25,000 rpm) of the router. Therefore, the finish provided is not as smooth as might be expected of a standard router.

Using Piloted Bits with an Auxiliary Fence and Table

1. Set the speed of the drill press to its highest rate.
2. Install a piloted router bit in the chuck so that approximately 1/4 in. of the shank remains outside the chuck jaws.
3. Position the auxiliary table on the drill press table [Fig. 5-14(a)].
4. Travel the drill press table up to within 1 in. of the bottom of the bit.
5. Position the auxiliary table fence and the workpiece as shown in Fig. 5-14(a). The near edge of the workpiece is against the pilot.
6. Bring the spindle and router bit down next to the workpiece so that the desired cut will be made by the bit. Lock the spindle clamp, with the hold-down block in position [Fig. 5-14(b)].
7. With the workpiece to the left of the router bit and against the fence with the grain pointing left, start the drill press. Feed the workpiece into the revolving bit slowly. The workpiece must be straight-grained, free of knots and other defects, and at least 12 in. long. *Stop the machine and check the chuck tightness frequently* because the vibration may cause the chuck or clamps to loosen.

Following a Template

One of the commercial methods of duplicate routing involves the use of a template attached to the underside of the workpiece. A pin fastened to the table of an overarm router follows the template. This operation can be performed on the drill press if the following procedure is followed:

1. Prepare a template from 1/4-in. masonite, and fasten it to the underside of the workpiece with small brads.
2. Fasten a 1/2-in.-thick piece of plywood to the drill press table.

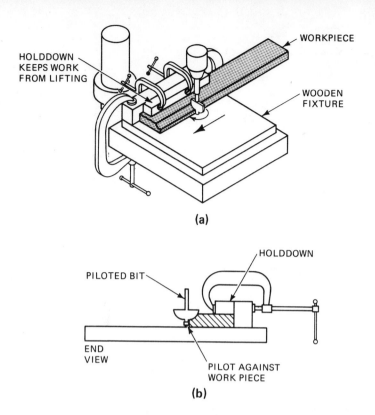

HOLDDOWN KEEPS WORK FROM LIFTING

WORKPIECE

WOODEN FIXTURE

(a)

PILOTED BIT

HOLDDOWN

END VIEW

PILOT AGAINST WORK PIECE

(b)

Fig. 5-14. Routing on the drill press

3. Install a straight router bit in the drill press chuck. Bore a hole 3/8 in. deep into the plywood attached to the table.

4. Insert a dowel into the hole so that 3/16 in. of the dowel extends above the surface of the plywood [Fig. 5-15(a)].

5. Place the template attached to the workpiece over the dowel [Fig. 5-15(b)].

6. Temporarily clamp the workpiece to the table and turn the machine on.

7. Travel the router bit down into the workpiece to the desired depth, and lock the spindle in position with the spindle clamp. Turn the machine off. (The depth of cut that can easily and safely be made depends on the hardness of the workpiece. Softwoods such as pine can be cut to about 1/4 in. in depth at each pass. Harder woods should be limited to about 1/8 in. per pass. Do not attempt to cut through knots or other defects, and do not force the piece.)

8. Remove the clamp. Hold the workpiece with one hand while turning the machine on. Place both hands on the workpiece and move it into the revolving router bit while following the template with the dowel inserted in the table. *For safe operation, a minimum distance of 4 in. should remain between the edge of the workpiece and the area to be routed.*

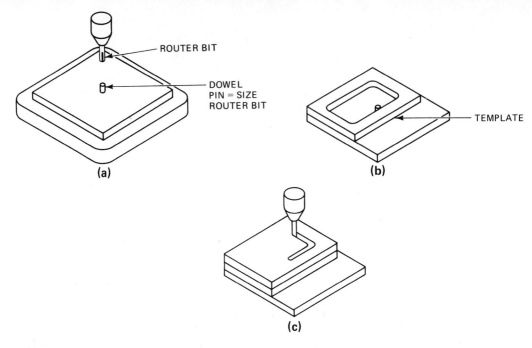

Fig. 5-15. Routing on drill press using a template

Changing Spindle Speeds

Most 14- and 15-in. drill presses are equipped with stepped pulleys which are used to vary spindle speeds. The maximum spindle speed is obtained when the largest motor pulley is driving the smallest spindle pulley (Fig. 5-16). Conversely, the slowest spindle speed is obtained when the smallest motor pulley is driving the largest spindle pulley. Most small drill presses are not equipped with a belt tension release; so the following changing procedure should be used:

1. Shut off the power supply to the machine and leave a note on the supply switch indicating that the machine is being worked on.
2. Remove the belt guard from the machine.
3. Place a hand on the center of the belt and pull away from the larger pulley as you slowly pull the belt toward the front of the machine (Fig. 5-17). This should cause the belt to move onto the next smaller pulley, thereby releasing the tension. If this does not happen, repeat step 3.
4. Now that the belt is loose, move it to the smaller pulley of the pair desired.
5. Place a hand on the center of the belt and push it toward the larger pulley as you slowly travel the belt toward the front of the machine. The belt should ride into the pulley and, in so doing, regain tension.
6. Turn the power supply back on after replacing the machine guard.

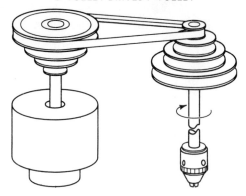

5″ PULLEY DRIVES 1″ PULLEY

Fig. 5-16. Varying speed on the drill press

1 TURN MOTOR SHAFT = 5 TURNS SPINDLE

1750 RPM × 5 = 8750 RPM
MOTOR   SPINDLE

Fig. 5-17. Changing belt position in drill press pulleys. (Courtesy of Rockwell Manufacturing Co., Delta Power Tools Div.)

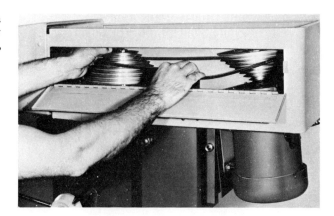

HOLLOW CHISEL MORTISER

Principles of Operation and Nomenclature

In essence, the mortiser is a special kind of drill press. Many manufacturers have drill press attachments which can be used to convert a standard drill press into a hollow chisel mortiser. The mortiser mounts an auger, which revolves inside of a square, hollow chisel. The auger and chisel are lowered onto the workpiece. The auger, which protrudes out of the end of the hollow chisel, bores a hole. The chisel squares up the hole as it moves into the workpiece. A series of these holes in a row produces a rectangular mortise.

The machine is mounted on a heavy base. Rising from the base is a vertical column whose forward machined surface makes up the ways of the machine. Just above the base, and protruding from it, is the treadle. This device is used to lower the ram under spring tension. When pressure is released, the treadle rises, allowing the ram to rise with it (Fig. 5-18).

The table is located on the ways above the treadle. It has a vise mounted on it to hold the workpiece. The table and vise can be traveled longitudinally (forward and back) by means of the longitudinal feed wheel located below the table. This longitudinal feed enables the operator to position the workpiece under the chisel and auger for mortising. The table can also be traveled laterally (from side to side) by means of the lateral feed wheel. This is located below the table, above and to the right of the longitudinal feed wheel. The lateral travel of the table is limited by adjustable table stops located at either end of the underside of the table (Fig. 5-18). A hold-down device is mounted on the table fence. In practice, this hold-down is needed only when fairly deep mortises are being made in hardwoods.

The ram is mounted on the ways above the table. Two basic components comprise the ram: the motor and the chisel bracket. The motor is the uppermost part of the ram (Fig. 5-18). Attached to the motor shaft is a keyed chuck which holds the auger.

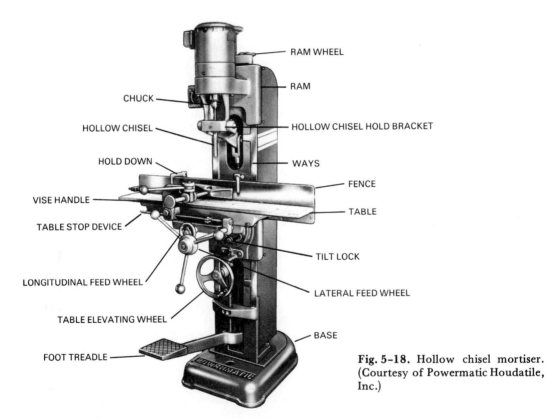

RAM WHEEL

RAM

CHUCK

HOLLOW CHISEL

HOLLOW CHISEL HOLD BRACKET

HOLD DOWN

WAYS

VISE HANDLE

FENCE

TABLE

TABLE STOP DEVICE

LONGITUDINAL FEED WHEEL

TILT LOCK

TABLE ELEVATING WHEEL

LATERAL FEED WHEEL

FOOT TREADLE

BASE

Fig. 5-18. Hollow chisel mortiser. (Courtesy of Powermatic Houdatile, Inc.)

The chisel bracket is below the motor. This bracket, together with its bushing, holds the hollow chisel. Because the motor and bracket are fastened to the ram, they maintain their positions relative to each other as the ram moves up or down. As described earlier, the ram is moved by the action of the treadle located near the base of the machine. Fine adjustments in the position of the ram are made by means of the ram wheel, which is located above and to the rear of the motor on the ram (Fig. 5-18). This wheel is secured by a clamp located directly in front of the wheel itself (Fig. 5-18).

General Safety Rules for the Hollow Chisel Mortiser

1. Wear approved eye protection when operating this machine.
2. Check the security of the chisel and auger before turning power on.
3. When cutting mortises over 1/2 in. deep in hardwoods, use the hold-down device.
4. Be sure to check all locking clamps before turning the mortiser on.
5. Turn the machine over by hand before turning the power on.
6. A small amount of noise and smoke is normally produced when the mortiser is in operation; however, if either becomes excessive, stop the machine and check the condition and clearance of the chisel and auger. Adjust or replace as required.

Installing a Bit and Chisel in the Mortiser

1. Select a chisel and its matching bit. The width of the chisel should equal the width of the mortise to be made. Mortise and tenon joints are usually designed to match one of the sets of chisels and bits available.
2. Turn off the power supply to the machine.
3. Raise the ram to its highest point by unlocking the ram wheel and turning it counterclockwise.
4. Place the auger into the hollow chisel and insert the chisel into its bushing with the auger inside of it [Fig. 5-19(a)].
5. Adjust the chisel so that it is square to the ways of the machine. Use a try square to check [Fig. 5-19(b)].
6. Tighten the screw that holds the chisel in position [Fig. 5-19(b)].
7. Open the chuck with the chuck key provided, and push the auger up into the chisel and chuck as far as it will go. Lower the auger until the correct clearance develops between the auger and chisel. This clearance is approximately 1/32 in. for chisels up to 3/8 in., and 1/16 in. for larger sizes. Tighten the chuck while holding the auger in the slightly lowered position. This gives clearance between the bit and the inside of the chisel [Fig. 5-19(a)]. A thin piece of wood of suitable thickness can be inserted between the chisel and auger to act as a gauge in setting the spacing between them.

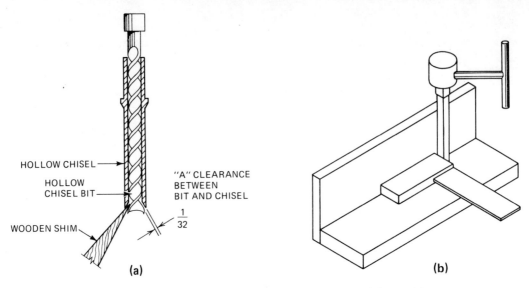

HOLLOW CHISEL
HOLLOW CHISEL BIT
"A" CLEARANCE BETWEEN BIT AND CHISEL
$\frac{1}{32}$
WOODEN SHIM

(a)　　　　　　　　　　　(b)

Fig. 5-19. (a) Clearance between chisel and bit. (b) Checking squareness of hollow chisel to the fence

Setting up the Mortiser

After the chisel and auger have been installed, set up the mortiser by adjusting the depth of cut of the chisel, positioning the workpiece under the chisel, and setting the stops to limit the travel of the workpiece in the vise.

Adjusting Chisel Depth

1. Lay out the mortise on the workpiece. Include a depth indication on the side of the workpiece [Fig. 5-20(a)].
2. Place the workpiece on the table of the machine with the layout facing up. Depress the treadle and hold it in its lowest position.
3. Move the workpiece against the chisel and auger, which are now at the bottom of their travel. Unlock the ram wheel. Adjust the vertical position of the chisel and auger, using the ram wheel, until the lowest corner of the chisel matches the depth layout line [Fig. 5-20(b)].
4. Lock the ram wheel and release the treadle.

Positioning the Workpiece under the Chisel

5. Secure the workpiece in the vise on the mortiser table. Align the mortiser chisel with the layout on the surface of the workpiece by turning the longitudinal feed wheel right or left until alignment is obtained. If necessary, move the chisel and auger down, closer to the layout, with the foot treadle. Relock the table with the tilt-table clamp.

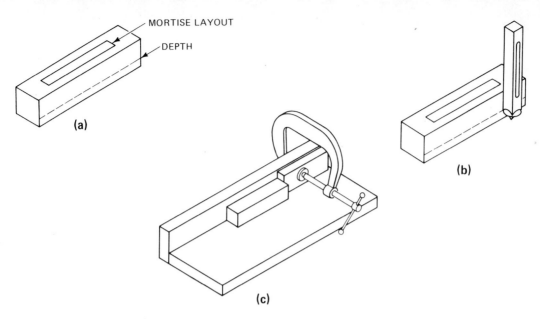

Fig. 5-20. Hollow chisel mortiser set-up with stop block for positioning identical workpieces on mortiser table

6. Adjust the right and left stops so that the travel of the table and workpiece matches the layout of the mortise

7. If identical mortises are to be made in other pieces, clamp a stopblock to the vise so that subsequent workpieces will automatically be positioned correctly in the vise [Fig. 5-20(c)].

Making a Mortise

1. Place the workpiece in the vise on the table against the positioning stopblock. Position the hold-down clamp if required.

2. Travel the table to the left stop and hold the table in that position with the lateral feed wheel.

3. Turn the power on and slowly depress the treadle. Allow the ram to move upward after each 1/4 in. of depth is cut. Continue until the first hole is complete. Then turn the machine off and raise the treadle [Fig. 5-21(a)].

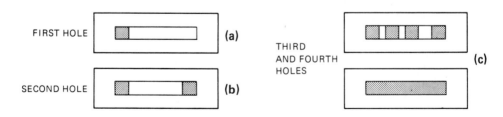

Fig. 5-21. Hole-making sequence mortiser

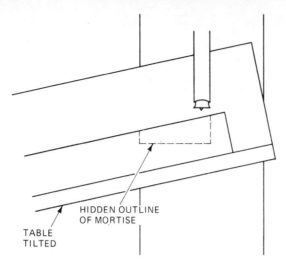

HIDDEN OUTLINE
OF MORTISE

TABLE
TILTED

Fig. 5-22. Angle mortising

4. Travel the table to the right table stop and repeat step 3 [Fig. 5-21(b)].

5. Complete the removal of the material between the first two holes [Fig. 5-21(c)].

Caution: Allowing the table to shift during cutting, or permitting the chisel to deflect when completing a mortise, can cause the chisel to break.

Angle Mortising

Most mortises are cut at a 90° angle to the layout surface. In some pieces such as chairs, mortises are cut at other angles. Such mortises should be laid out on two surfaces: one on the surface which shows the rectangular outline of the mortise, and the other on the surface which shows the depth and angle of the mortise (Fig. 5-22). This second layout (the hidden outline drawing) is used to set the angle of the workpiece. If the machine has a tiltable table, the workpiece is placed on the table with the chisel in position against it, and the table is tilted until the chisel is aligned with the mortise layout (Fig. 5-22). If the table does not tilt, a suitable jig must be made to position the piece. Once positioning is complete, the usual procedure for completing the setup can be used.

WOOD LATHE

Principles of Operation and Nomenclature

Unlike any other machine commonly found in noncommercial shops, the lathe can produce a completely finished product. In most woodworking machines, the cutting tool's cutting edges travel at a high rate of speed while

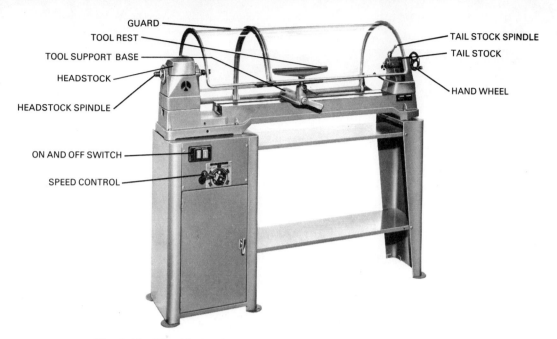

GUARD
TOOL REST
TOOL SUPPORT BASE
HEADSTOCK
HEADSTOCK SPINDLE
ON AND OFF SWITCH
SPEED CONTROL
TAIL STOCK SPINDLE
TAIL STOCK
HAND WHEEL

Fig. 5-23. Wood lathe. (Courtesy of Rockwell Manufacturing Co., Delta Power Tools Div.)

the workpiece moves slowly into and through the rotating cutting edges. In the lathe, the cutting tool remains relatively stationary while the workpiece rotates rapidly past it. In normal operation the lathe produces pieces of circular cross-section, such as leg spindles and bowls. Figure 5-23 shows a typical wood lathe.

The foundation of the machine is the *bed*. The upper machined surfaces of the bed are called the *ways*. These railroad track-like surfaces support the essential functioning parts of the machine (Fig. 5-24).

Attached to the left end of the ways is the *headstock* which provides the driving power to rotate the workpiece. It is generally composed of a hollow

Fig. 5-24. Lathe ways. (Courtesy of Rockwell Manufacturing Co., Delta Power Tools Div.)

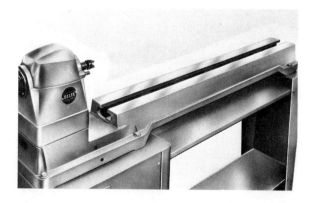

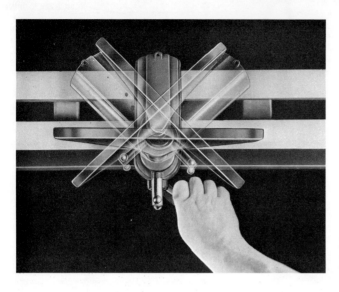

Fig. 5-25. Adjustable tool rest. (Courtesy of Rockwell Manufacturing Co., Delta Power Tools Div.)

spindle threaded on both ends. The outboard end (outside) of the spindle usually has a handwheel mounted on it which can double as a faceplate for outboard turning. The inboard end (inside) of the spindle is threaded to accept a faceplate which can be used for faceplate turning. The spindle is internally tapered (No. 2 Morse) to receive a variety of accessories. On most units the headstock spindle can be locked to facilitate faceplate removal. The headstock spindle is usually belt driven. Speed changes are accomplished by shifting a belt from step to step on pulleys on the shaft and the driving motor. With such a step-cone pulley system, speed ranges run from approximately 900 to 3000 rpm. Other machines have variable speed-control settings. On such units speeds range from approximately 340 to 3600 rpm.

The tailstock (Fig. 5-23) is mounted on the machine ways and can be clamped to them. Like the headstock, it has a hollow spindle with an internal taper for accessories. The spindle can be fed toward the headstock or away from it by means of a handwheel located at the right end of the tailstock (Fig. 5-23). This spindle can be clamped in position by the tailstock spindle clamp.

The *tool support base* (Fig. 5-25) is usually mounted on the ways between the tailstock and the headstock. Its function is to hold the *tool rest,* which, in turn, supports the various tools which are brought into play against the revolving workpiece. A useful accessory is the *floor-stand tool-rest holder* [Fig. 5-26(a)]. This stand supports the tool rest during outboard turning.

The tool rest, or T rest, is a T-shaped casting available in various sizes and shapes. This T rest supports the tool during cutting operations. It can be angled to more efficiently conform to the contour of the workpiece. The rest is mounted in the tool support base (Fig. 5-25). Its vertical position can be adjusted in the base. The *steady rest* is an accessory that is used to

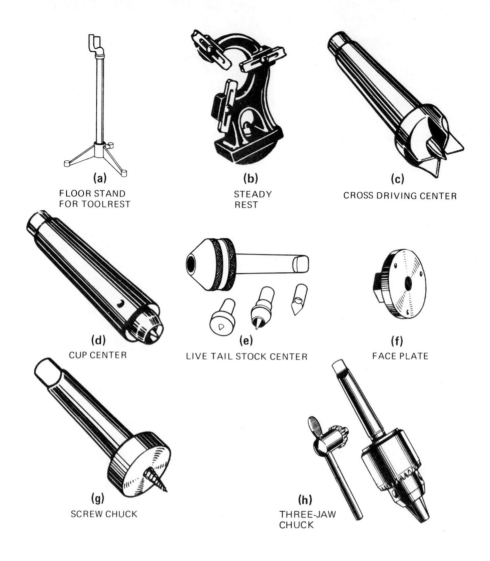

(a)
FLOOR STAND
FOR TOOLREST

(b)
STEADY
REST

(c)
CROSS DRIVING CENTER

(d)
CUP CENTER

(e)
LIVE TAIL STOCK CENTER

(f)
FACE PLATE

(g)
SCREW CHUCK

(h)
THREE-JAW
CHUCK

Fig. 5-26. Lathe accessories. (Courtesy of Rockwell Manufacturing Co., Delta Power Tools Div.)

provide support for long spindles during turning. It is mounted on the bed of the lathe close to the T rest [Fig. 5-26(b)].

The *cross center* is a live center, which is inserted in the headstock. Its function is to transmit power from the headstock spindle to the workpiece; it also supports the workpiece [Fig. 5-26(c)]. The *cup center* is a dead center, which is inserted into the hollow tailstock spindle. This center does not rotate, so its end must be lubricated with wax or oil. It supports the end of the workpiece during spindle turning [Fig. 5-26(d)]. The *live tailstock center* rotates with the workpiece and therefore does not require lubrication [Fig. 5-26(e)].

The *faceplate* mounts on the headstock spindle and is provided with holes which can be used to fasten stock to it for faceplate turning [Fig. 5-26(f)]. The *screw chuck* is a small faceplate with a wood screw protruding from its center. The workpiece screws directly onto this screw, facilitating removal and remounting of workpieces. This faceplate is used for turning small-diameter, short knobs and similar shapes [Fig. 5-26(g)]. The *three-jaw chuck* has a shaft that is tapered to fit into the headstock spindles. In position on the headstock spindle, it can be used to hold workpieces during turning [Fig. 5-26(h)].

Lathe Capacity

Lathe capacity is determined by the largest diameter workpiece which can be turned over the lathe bed. Another capacity factor is the length of the bed. A 12-in. unit usually has a usable bed (maximum distance from center to center) of about 36 in.

General Safety Rules for the Wood Lathe

1. Always wear a face shield when operating the lathe.
2. Sleeves should be rolled up and secured, and all hand jewelry should be removed.
3. Secure or remove any loose clothing which might become entangled in the lathe.
4. Always operate the machine at the slowest possible speed when beginning work.
5. When work on the lathe is complete for an individual operation, return the speed setting to its low-speed position.
6. Turn the machine over by hand before turning the power on. This allows the clearance between the workpiece and the tool rest to be checked. It is also a test of the secureness of the workpiece.
7. Be sure that glued material is correctly glued and cured before attempting to turn it.
8. Whenever possible, preshape workpieces before attempting to turn them.
9. Avoid high spindle speeds for large diameter workpieces.
10. At the first sign of any unusual vibration, step toward the headstock and turn the lathe off. Determine the cause of the vibration.
11. Use dust-collecting equipment when operating the lathe, or wear a suitable dust-filtering face mask.
12. Always keep the tool rest within 1/8 in. of the surface of the workpiece being cut.
13. Stop the machine completely before making any adjustments.
14. Check the tool rest and the tailstock clamps frequently during operation, because vibration can cause these clamps to loosen.

15. Always support the turning tool with the tool rest and keep the cutting edge of the tool as close to the tool rest as possible.

16. Select turning stock that is straight-grained and free from defects such as knots and checks.

17. Do not leave tools on the lathe bed during turning operations. Vibration may cause them to "walk off" the bed and fall to the floor, with the possible result of injury to the operator.

Cutting Methods

Two cutting methods are generally used in lathe work. One is known as *cutting;* the other is called *scraping.*

Cutting method. In this method the cutting tool is held tangent to the workpiece. The cutting edge should be razor sharp and carefully whetted. The resulting surface is smooth, and the material cut away comes off in the form of shavings (Fig. 5-27). This method requires a relatively high level of skill and experience. Though the surface produced is relatively smooth, a high degree of precision is difficult to obtain using the cutting method. This method is easier to use when the workpiece has a small diameter. The novice will find that the cutting tool tends to catch on the workpiece.

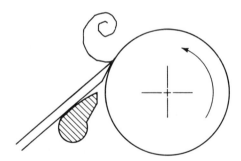

Fig. 5-27. Cutting—Method of material removal on the lathe

Scraping method. In the scraping method, the cutting tool is held at a 90° angle to the surface of the workpiece (Fig. 5-28). The cutting edge is approximately in line with the centerline of the workpiece. The material cut away comes off as sawdust rather than shavings. The surface generated is relatively rough and requires considerable sanding. Since the tool is easy to control, less skill is required and greater precision can be obtained than in the cutting method. The cutting tool works well when it has a wire edge. Grinding alone can produce a cutting edge of this type.

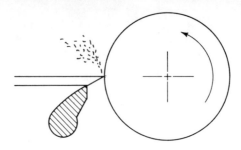

Fig. 5-28. Scraping—Method of material removal on the lathe

Mounting Material between Centers

Spindles, such as chair and table legs, are mounted between centers inserted in the headstock and tailstock spindles (Fig. 5-29).

1. Prepare a drawing of the piece to be made. Divide the drawing, as shown in Fig. 5-30(a), so that key diameters are located along the axis of the piece.
2. Prepare turning stock as follows:

a. Square-up the material to be used so that it is approximately 1 in. longer than required, and 1/2 in. wider and thicker than the largest diameter of the piece. At this point the workpiece has a square cross-section [Fig. 5-31(a)].

b. Draw diagonals on each end of the workpiece to locate the centers [Fig. 5-31(a)].

c. If the workpiece is more than 2 in. wide and thick, reduce it to an octagon. The procedure for laying out an octagon on the end of the workpiece is shown in Fig. 5-31. The piece can be shaped using the surfacer or the jointer.

Fig. 5-29. Turning between centers

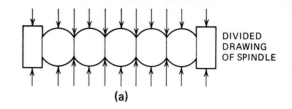

DIVIDED
DRAWING
OF SPINDLE

(a)

KEY DIAMETERS LAID OUT ON STOCK ON THE LATHE WITH PENCIL

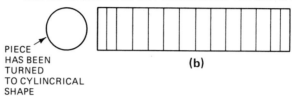

PIECE
HAS BEEN
TURNED
TO CYLINCRICAL
SHAPE

(b)

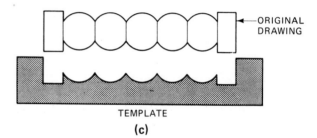

ORIGINAL
DRAWING

TEMPLATE

(c)

Fig. 5-30.

Fig. 5-31. Laying out an octagon on a square

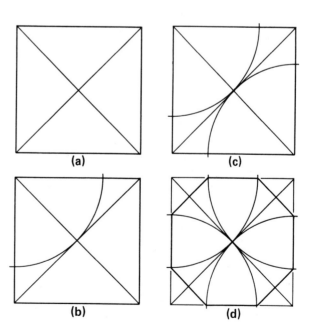

(a)

(c)

(b)

(d)

d. With a backsaw, deepen the diagonals made in step b to 1/8 in.

3. Mount the workpiece as follows:

a. Place a cross center on one end, align it with the diagonals, and drive it into place with light taps, using a mallet. The edges of the center should penetrate approximately 1/8 in. into the end of the workpiece.

b. Place the cross center and its attached workpiece into the headstock spindle. Provide adequate support or the piece will fall free of the center.

c. While supporting the workpiece with the left hand, use the right hand to move the tailstock, fitted with a cup center, up to the free end of the workpiece. Align the centerpin with the diagonals and move the pin approximately 1/8 in. into the end.

d. Clamp the tailstock to the lathe ways with the tailstock clamp.

e. Apply a lubricant to the cup center lip. Advance the center into the end of the workpiece, using the handwheel on the tailstock, until the cup lip is 1/16 in. into the end of the workpiece. Lock the tailstock spindle.

Turning between Centers (Scraping Method)

1. Place a tool rest in the tool support base so that the tool is in line with the centerline of the workpiece and approximately 1/8 in. away from it (Fig. 5–28).

2. Turn the machine over by hand to check clearance and workpiece stability. Put face shield and dusk mask on.

3. Set the machine for its slowest speed. Turn the machine on.

4. Holding the roundnose turning tool bevel side down (Fig. 5–28), reduce the workpiece to the largest diameter possible. Cut toward the headstock to keep pressure on the cup center to a minimum.

5. Transfer the key diameter locations from the drawing to the surface of the cylindrical workpiece [Fig. 5–30(b)].

6. Set a pair of outside calipers to the first key diameter.

7. Using a parting tool, make a recess in the workpiece at the location of the first key diameter. This should be approximately 1/8 in. deep. At this point, the machine should be set approximately in the middle of the speed range.

8. Using the left hand, carefully place the outside calipers in the groove made in step 7 (the machine is running).

9. With the right hand, deepen the groove with the parting tool until the calipers slip over the newly cut diameter. Turn the machine off. *Note:* The parting tool will cut more efficiently if pressure is applied and released at about 1-second intervals during cutting.

10. Repeat steps 6 through 9 for each of the key diameters until the entire spindle is grooved.

11. Using the drawing or a template made from the drawing as a guide [Fig. 5-30(c)], shape the segments between each of the grooves with the appropriate tools (Fig. 5-32, tool-use table). Most of the roughing out should be accomplished with a narrow roundnose tool.

13. Sand the spindle to final shape and finish, starting with coarse (No. 80) sandpaper and working down through the finer abrasives to very fine (No. 220). Continue sanding with No. 80 sandpaper until all tool marks are removed. Use the finer grades for removing sanding scratches.

Faceplate Turning

Faceplate turning is best suited for turning wide, flat objects such as bowls. Several mounting procedures are available for processing the stock into the finished product. The basic steps for each are similar. In this section the procedure for faceplate turning, using a temporary chuck block, is described in detail. The other methods are described in Fig. 5-33.

1. Prepare a full-size drawing of the piece to be turned. Top and front views are required (Fig. 5-34).

2. Prepare the stock to be used by laying out and cutting a circle from the material on the bandsaw. The circle should be approximately 1/2 in. larger in diameter than the finished piece.

3. From 1-in.-thick stock, lay out and cut a circle whose diameter is equal to the diameter of the faceplate to be used. This is the *chuck block*.

4. Glue the chuck block to the center of the workpiece. Be sure to provide adequate clamping pressure, and leave the clamps on for at least 24 hours. It is possible to insert a piece of heavy paper between the chuck block and the turning stock during gluing. This facilitates separation later. However, for pieces over 6 in. in diameter, this procedure frequently results in premature separation during turning. The procedure described here is safer.

5. Attach the glued assembly to the center of a suitable faceplate, using at least four of the thickest and longest screws possible. The screws should provide approximately 1/8 in. of clearance between their points and the workpiece (Fig. 5-35).

6. Mount the faceplate on the headstock spindle with a paper washer inserted between the faceplate and the spindle flange (Fig. 5-35). This washer makes loosening the faceplate easier.

7. Repeat steps 1 through 5 in Turning between Centers (above).

8. Cut the outside shape of the piece, using the drawing or a template made from the drawing as a guide. *Note:* If the project cannot be completed in one session, leave the workpiece mounted on the faceplate. Repositioning it in exactly the same position after removal is almost impossible.

9. Reposition the tool rest so that it is at an angle of 90° to the axis of the machine (Fig. 5-36).

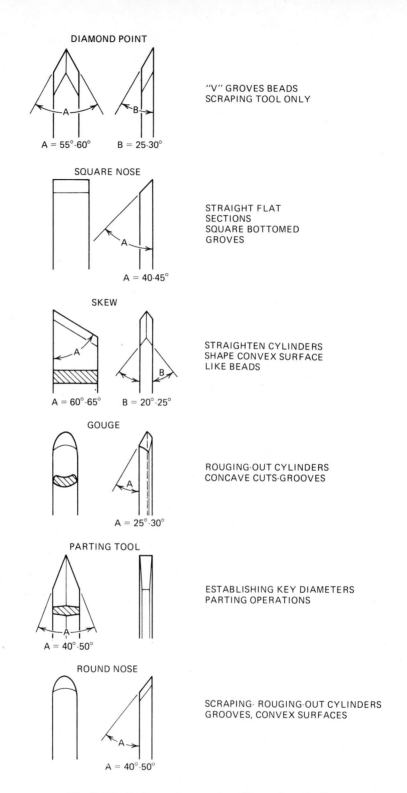

DIAMOND POINT

"V" GROVES BEADS
SCRAPING TOOL ONLY

A = 55°-60°   B = 25-30°

SQUARE NOSE

STRAIGHT FLAT
SECTIONS
SQUARE BOTTOMED
GROVES

A = 40-45°

SKEW

STRAIGHTEN CYLINDERS
SHAPE CONVEX SURFACE
LIKE BEADS

A = 60°-65°   B = 20°-25°

GOUGE

ROUGING-OUT CYLINDERS
CONCAVE CUTS-GROOVES

A = 25°-30°

PARTING TOOL

ESTABLISHING KEY DIAMETERS
PARTING OPERATIONS

A = 40°-50°

ROUND NOSE

SCRAPING- ROUGING-OUT CYLINDERS
GROOVES, CONVEX SURFACES

A = 40°-50°

Fig. 5-32. Lathe tool use and geometry for grinding

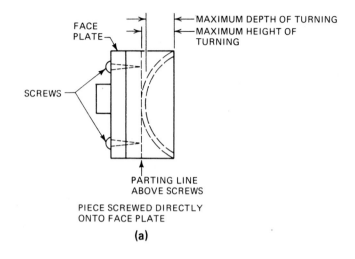

FACE PLATE

SCREWS

MAXIMUM DEPTH OF TURNING
MAXIMUM HEIGHT OF TURNING

PARTING LINE
ABOVE SCREWS

PIECE SCREWED DIRECTLY
ONTO FACE PLATE

(a)

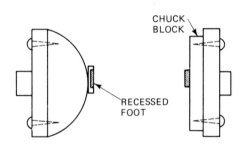

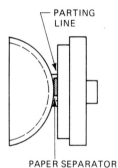

CHUCK BLOCK

PARTING LINE

RECESSED FOOT

PAPER SEPARATOR

#1A. WORKPIECE FASTENED
DIRECTLY TO FACEPLATE
B. OUTSIDE SHAPED
WITH RECESSED FOOT*

#2. CHUCK
BLOCK
SHAPED TO
FIT RECESSED
FOOT

#3A. WORKPIECE
GLUED &
CLAMPED TO
CHUCK BLOCK
WITH PAPER
SEPARATOR IN
PLACE
B. INSIDE SHAPED
C. AFTER PARTING
REMAINING BLOCK
CHISELED OUT OF RECESS

TWO STEP METHOD OF FACE PLATE TURNING

(b)

Fig. 5-33. Face plate turning methods

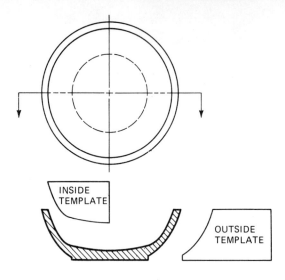

Fig. 5-34. Use of templates in face plate turning

10. Face off the workpiece. This is usually accomplished with a square-nose tool.

11. Rough out the inside of the piece with a roundnose tool.

12. Sand smooth.

Removing the Workpiece from the Chuck Block

1. Set up the small tool rest as for spindle turning, and position it close to the chuck block.

2. With the machine running at low speed, cut a groove with the parting tool into the chuck block as shown in Fig. 5-36.

3. When approximately a 1-in. section of the block remains, *stop the lathe* and carefully cut through the remaining material with a handsaw. Be sure to provide support for the workpiece during sawing.

4. The base of the workpiece can be smoothed and trued by sanding. If the paper separator is used, the pieces can be parted by carefully inserting a chisel between the chuck block and the workpiece.

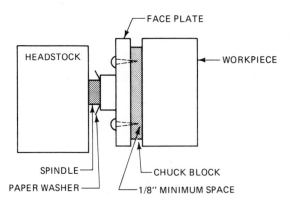

Fig. 5-35. Chuck block method of face plate turning

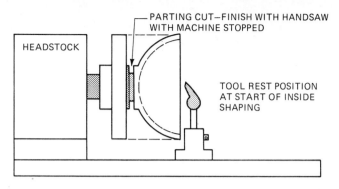

Fig. 5-36. Removing workpiece from chuck block

SANDING MACHINES

Stationary Disc Sanders

The disc sander consists of a metal disc to which a circular sheet of coated abrasive is attached. The disc is either directly mounted on a motor shaft or, as in most combination units, mounted on a belt-driven spindle [Fig. 5-37(a)]. A tiltable table is attached to the front of the machine to support the workpiece. The table is usually provided with a slot which receives a miter gauge [Fig. 5-37(b)]. The sanding disc is surrounded with a housing which doubles as a guard for the protection of the operator and as part of the dust-collecting system. Dust-producing equipment of this type should always be provided with a dust-collecting vacuum system.

Fig. 5-37. 6″ belt and 12″ disc finishing machine. Table tilted for angle finish. (Courtesy of Rockwell Manufacturing Co., Delta Power Tools Div.)

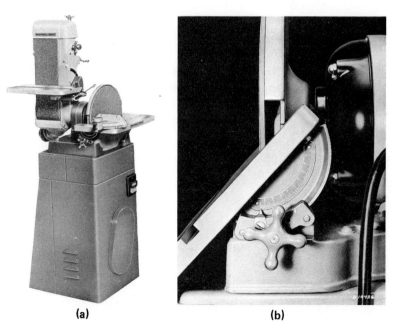

(a)　　　　　　　　(b)

General Safety Rules for the Disc Sander

1. Always wear approved eye protection while operating this machine.
2. Only sand work that provides adequate clearance (at least 3 in.) for the fingers.
3. Use only the upper left quadrant of the disc for sanding. The right quadrant tends to lift the workpiece and force sawdust up into the air.
4. Keep the machine table free of objects which might "walk off" the table during operation because of vibration.
5. Check the disc before operation to be sure it is securely adhered.
6. After adhering an abrasive to the disc, jog the machine before turning it on completely, to test the adherence of the disc.

Basic Operations on the Disc Sander

Squaring an end. One of the principal uses of the disc sander is the squaring of workpiece ends.

1. Place a miter gauge set at 90° in the table slot.
2. Place the working edge of the workpiece against the face of the miter gauge, with the working face down on the table surface.
3. Travel the miter gauge and the workpiece to the left quadrant of the machine.
4. Turn the machine and its dust-collecting system on.
5. Slide the workpiece end up to the rotating disc until it touches, and then slowly move the workpiece and the miter gauge to the right and left so that the left half of the disc is fully utilized (Fig. 5-38). *Caution:* The cutting speed of the abrasive particles on the disc increases as the workpiece moves from the center to the periphery (outer edge) of the disc. Therefore, cutting will occur more rapidly on the left half of the surface being sanded.

Rounding corners, beveling, and chamfering. Corners can be rounded by placing the face of the workpiece on the table and rotating it as the corner is brought into contact with the left quadrant of the disc (Fig. 5-38). Chamfers and bevels can be developed by tilting the table during sanding operations [Fig. 5-37(b)].

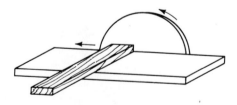

Fig. 5-38. Sanding disc use

Basic Adjustments on the Disc Sander

Table Tilting or Adjustment

1. Turn off the power supply to the machine.
2. Loosen the table clamps [Fig. 5-37(b)].
3. Adjust the table to the desired angle. Some machines have a protractor scale [Fig. 5-37(b)].
4. Retighten the clamps.
5. Restore the power, and the machine is ready for use.

Stationary Belt Sanders

Although separate disc sanders are fairly common, belt sanders are often part of the disc-belt combination machines. In combination units, both the disc and the belt are driven by a single motor via belts and pulleys.

The belt portion of the machine consists of an abrasive-coated cloth belt traveling over two drums and a platen (Fig. 5-39). One drum is fixed in position and is driven by a belt connected to a motor. The other drum is movable and can be traveled toward or away from the driven fixed drum. This feature makes belt tensioning and removal possible. In addition, the drum can be tilted to facilitate tracking, i.e., adjusting the position of the belt on the drum [Fig. 5-40(a)]. The belt width determines the capacity of the machine. Therefore, a 6-in.-wide belt is used on a 6-in. stationary belt

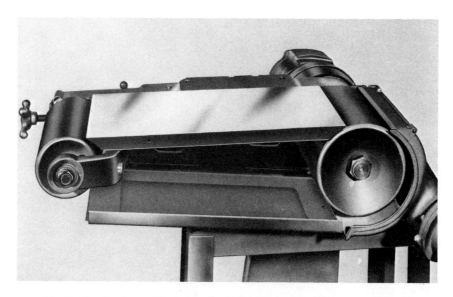

Fig. 5-39. Stationary belt sander (belt removed). (Courtesy of Rockwell Manufacturing Co., Delta Power Tools Div.)

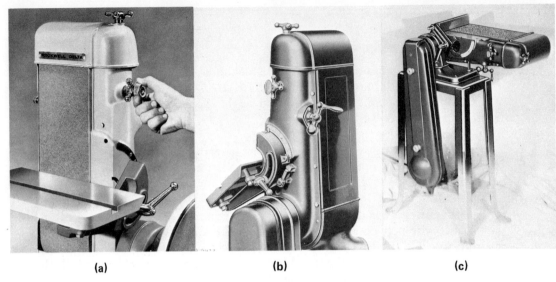

(a)   (b)   (c)

Fig. 5-40. (Courtesy of Rockwell Manufacturing Co., Delta Power Tools Div.)

sander. The length of the 6-in.-wide belt is usually about 48 inches. The exposed area of the belt is approximately 6 in. by 14 in.

The sander is fitted with a tiltable table [Fig. 5-40(b)]. Most units can be operated in the vertical or horizontal position. A table slot is available for use with a miter gauge [Fig. 5-40(a)].

General Safety Rules for the Stationary Belt Sander

1. Always wear approved eye-protection devices while operating this machine.

2. Maintain at least 3 in. between fingers and the abrasive belt.

3. Keep the table free of objects which might "walk off" during operation.

4. When tracking the belt, jog the machine to provide movement. Do not turn the unit on fully until tracking has been completed.

5. Always check to see that the unit is locked when in the vertical position. Tighten locknut if necessary.

6. Use a push stick when doing face sanding on the machine.

Basic Operations on the Stationary Belt Sander

Workpiece ends and other fairly short surfaces are sanded in much the same fashion as they would be on the disc sander. Longer surfaces are commonly sanded with the unit in a horizontal position.

Face sanding. Faces can be sanded on the belt sander if the material is thick enough to permit the fingers to be safely out of the way of the abrasive belt. With the table removed, oversize pieces can easily be sanded on this unit [Fig. 5-40(c)].

Drum sanding. Concave surfaces can be sanded on the drums when the drum guard is removed (Fig. 5-39).

Basic Adjustments on the Stationary Belt Sander

Belt Installation

1. Turn off the power supply to the machine.
2. Remove drum and belt guards from the machine (Fig. 5-39).
3. Unlock the tensioning knob and release the tension on the belt.
4. Slip the belt off the drums. Slide the replacement belt into position with the arrow printed inside the belt pointing in the direction of machine rotation.
5. Retension the machine and lock the tensioning knob.
6. Turn the machine over by hand while tracking the belt with the tracking knob.
7. Replace the guards. Jog the machine to check tracking. Adjust if necessary.
8. Lock the tracking knob.

For *table tilting and miter gauge use,* refer to the procedures in the preceding section, Stationary Disc Sanders.

Repositioning the Belt Sander from the Vertical to the Horizontal Position

1. Loosen the clamp or bolts which hold the sander head in position.
2. Rotate the sander head into the new position.
3. Reclamp or bolt the head in the new position.

Portable Belt Sanders

A variety of portable belt sanders are available on the market. They have a cloth abrasive belt which travels over two drums. The rear drum is rubber covered and fixed in position. It delivers power to the sanding belt from the motor. The front drum is crowned, can be moved forward or backward, and is tiltable. The longitudinal movement of this drum allows tension to be adjusted, and its tilting capability allows the belt to be tracked.

The capacity of the unit is determined by the width and length of the belt. Therefore, a 4 in. by 27 in. sander has a belt 4 in. wide and 27 in. long, with a usable sanding area of approximately 4 in. by 6 in.

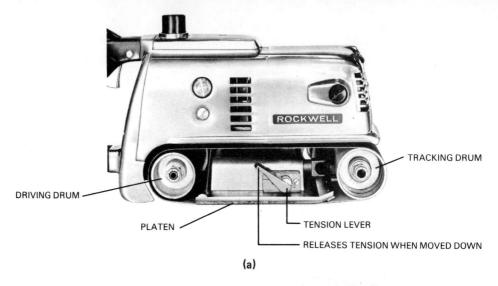

DRIVING DRUM

TRACKING DRUM

PLATEN

TENSION LEVER

RELEASES TENSION WHEN MOVED DOWN

(a)

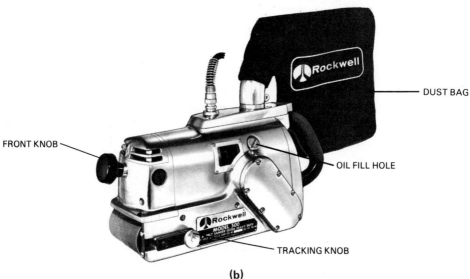

DUST BAG

FRONT KNOB

OIL FILL HOLE

TRACKING KNOB

(b)

Fig. 5-41. (Courtesy of Rockwell Manufacturing Co., Delta Power Tools Div.)

Various types of switches and switch positions are used. Most models have a "dead man" type of switch which can be locked in the ON position [Fig. 5-41(a)]. Portable belt sanders are useful on large surfaces and workpieces which cannot be easily sanded on a stationary unit.

General Safety Rules for the Portable Belt Sander

1. Always wear approved eye protection when operating this machine.
2. Ensure that the motor switch is in the OFF position *before plugging*

in the machine. If this is not done, the machine will begin to run as soon as the plug is in and it may run off the bench.

3. Position the belt sander on its side when not in use. This will prevent machine runaway if it is plugged in with the switch in the ON position.

4. Avoid sanding over nails and other obstructions.

5. Check the belt tracking before attempting to use the machine. Failure to do so may result in the belt running off the drums or cutting into the machine housing.

6. Adjust the position of the cable so that it is not in contact with the edge of the belt during sanding. This situation will result in abrasion of the insulation which protects against electric shock.

7. Carefully secure workpieces before sanding to prevent the moving belt from propelling the workpiece off the work surface.

Sanding with the Portable Belt Sander

The portable belt sander is generally traveled with the grain when sanding edges and faces. A good beginning grit to use for general sanding is No. 60. Once blemishes are removed, switch to No. 80, and finally to No. 100. At this point it is advisable to begin sanding with a straight-line finishing sander.

General Procedure

1. Secure the workpiece to a suitable working surface so that sanding with the grain can be accomplished.

2. Check the abrasive belt to be sure the grit is suitable for the operation. Check the tracking.

3. Hold the sander just above the surface to be sanded; turn the power switch on and lower the sander onto the workpiece.

4. Travel the sander forward until the edge of the platen under the abrasive belt [Fig. 5-42(a)] reaches the edge of the surface being sanded.

5. Travel the sander backward (toward you) until the back edge of the platen reaches the edge of the surface being sanded.

6. With each forward and backward stroke, work the sander to the left until the left edge of the workpiece is reached. Continue backward and forward travel while working to the right [Fig. 5-42(b)]. This pattern of travel will prevent deep grooves from being cut into the work surface.

Adjusting the Portable Belt Sander

Lubrication. Belt sanders require regular lubrication. Check the operating manual provided with the machine to determine the lubricant and its interval of use.

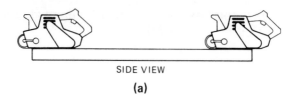

SIDE VIEW

(a)

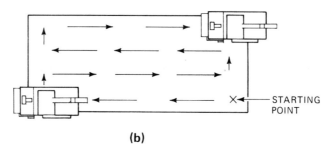

STARTING
POINT

(b)

Fig. 5-42. Side and top views of portable belt sander travel

Belt installation.

1. Unplug the machine and release the tension on the tracking wheel [Fig. 5-41(b)].

2. Check the arrow on the belt to be installed for direction of travel. Slip the belt over the drums with the arrow pointing in the correct direction.

3. Retension the tracking drum. Place the machine on its side and plug it in.

4. Tilt the sander back on its rear housing so that the belt can run free (Fig. 5-43).

5. With one hand on the tracking knob, support the rear of the unit with the other hand and turn the power on with the thumb of this hand.

6. Immediately rotate the tracking knob and track the belt.

7. Begin sanding. *Note:* If the belt untracks appreciably during sanding, this may be an indication of a worn belt.

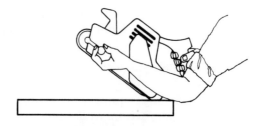

Fig. 5-43. Tracking belt

To sand a large surface, use the following technique to ensure uniformity of sanding: Draw pencil lines on the surface of the workpiece. During sanding, all of these lines should be removed. Any lines remaining indicate that that area has not been sanded.

Finishing Sanders

Finishing sanders are designed primarily for finishing operations in which small imperfections, such as scratches left by other sanding equipment, are removed. The uppermost part of the sander consists of a motor housing and a handle assembly. On most units, the switch is built into the rear handle of the machine (Fig. 5-44). The base of the sander includes a pad and a clamping system which permits abrasive paper to be fastened to the pad.

Orbital sander. The orbital sander has a pad which moves in an elliptical path. This mode of operation produces small curved scratches on the surface being sanded. In the case of two pieces meeting at right angles, as in a frame, an orbital sander represents a compromise in sanding with the grain of each piece.

Straight-line sander. The straight line sander's pad produces scratches that parallel the sides of the sanding pad.

Combination units are available which have a switching feature that allows the selection of either straight-line or orbital operation.

Fig. 5-44. Installing sandpaper on finishing sander. (Courtesy of Rockwell Manufacturing Co., Delta Power Tools Div.)

Sanding with the Finishing Sander

1. Secure the workpiece to a suitable surface. Attach a piece of No. 100 grit paper to the pad of the machine.
2. Plug the sander in and systematically sand the entire surface. If a straight-line sander is used, work with the grain.
3. Sand until the surface is uniformly smooth.
4. Replace the No. 100 paper with a finer type (e.g., No. 150) and resand. Repeat until No. 220 or No. 250 paper has been used.

Caution: If the surface being sanded has "hard spots" like dowels, these areas will sand away more slowly. The soft backing pad on the finishing sander causes this uneven sanding Although this is difficult to avoid, minimizing the amount of sanding done with the finishing sander will reduce this problem.

Adjusting the Finishing Sander

The most common adjustment required on a finishing sander is the replacement of the sandpaper. Generally, an abrasive with a heavy paper backing is used.

1. Unplug the unit. Release the sandpaper clamps.
2. Select a piece of sandpaper of suitable size and grit and limber it up. (Run it across the corner of a table with the abrasive side up. This breaks the glue coating up into small pieces and prolongs the life of the paper.)
3. Slip the paper under one of the clamps and clamp it. Pull the paper tightly around the pad and close the second clamp (Fig. 5–44).
4. The machine is ready for use.

RADIAL ARM SAW

Principles of Operation and Nomenclature

The radial arm saw is primarily a crosscutting machine that developed from the cut off saws frequently found in lumber yards and mills. It consists of a column mounted in a base, which forms the table of the machine. Attached to the top end of the column is an overarm, which has a track on its underside. The column and its attached track can be raised and lowered. The arm can be swung to the right or left for mitering cuts. The motor is mounted in a yoke, which travels on the overarm track. This yoke is similar to an oversize bicycle fork. The motor shaft forms the arbor of the machine. The yoke can be swiveled around its vertical axis like a bicycle fork. This allows the motor and the saw blade to be set so that the blade is parallel to the track and arm, or at right angles to the track and arm [Fig. 5–45(b)].

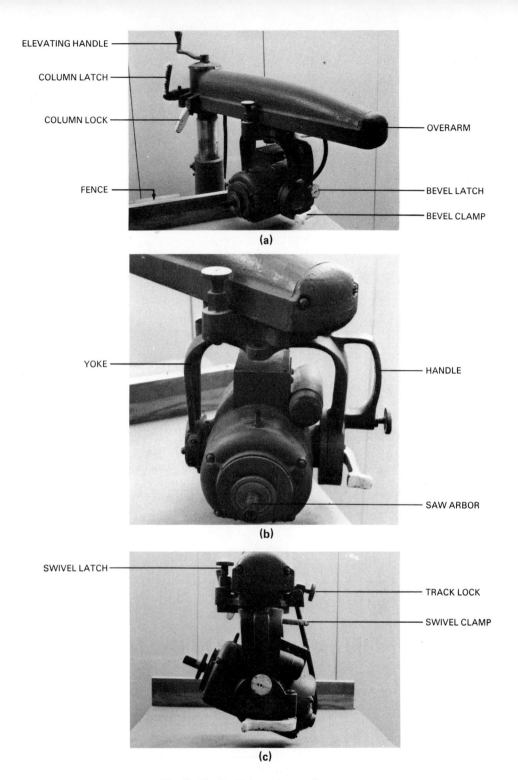

ELEVATING HANDLE

COLUMN LATCH

COLUMN LOCK

FENCE

OVERARM

BEVEL LATCH

BEVEL CLAMP

(a)

YOKE

HANDLE

SAW ARBOR

(b)

SWIVEL LATCH

TRACK LOCK

SWIVEL CLAMP

(c)

Fig. 5-45. Radial arm saw adjustments

The motor can also be tilted in the yoke, around its horizontal axis, for bevel cutting.

Each of the basic movable components of the radial arm saw is locked in position by a clamp and an indexing pin or device. The overarm is clamped to the column by means of a column clamp and locked by means of a column lock. It can be indexed to 45° or 90° [Fig. 5-45(a)]. A protractor scale on the column allows the arm to be set at other angles. This clamp and lock are used to set the overarm for making square and miter cuts. The yoke is secured by the swivel clamp and the swivel lock. The lockpin allows the yoke to be indexed into one of three positions.

The motor is mounted between the prongs of an oversize fork or yoke [Fig. 5-45 (b) and (c)]. It can rotate on its axis in the fork and is controlled by the bevel clamp and the bevel pin.

The capacity of the radial arm saw is determined by the diameter of the saw blade. Crosscutting and ripping capacity is limited by the length of the overarm. Crosscutting capacity ranges from approximately 15 in. on the smaller models to approximately 24 in. on the larger models.

Safety Rules for the Radial Arm Saw

Several important differences between the table saw and the radial arm saw are closely related to safe use. First, the workpiece is fixed (in crosscutting operations) and the saw blade and arbor move across the workpiece at right angles to the grain of the piece. This means that the saw blade can move toward the operator under its own power under certain conditions. Second, the whole saw blade is above the table at all times. Finally, the location of the blade above the table causes the blade to tend to lift the workpiece during cutting.

1. Always wear approved eye protection when operating the machine.
2. Adjust the saw guard so that a minimum number of blade teeth are exposed for each cut.
3. Check all clamps and locks to make sure that all clamps are tight and, wherever possible, all locks are engaged.
4. When crosscutting, be sure the workpiece is firmly in place against the table fence.
5. Long workpieces must be properly supported during crosscutting so that they will not drop and bind on the blade before the cut is completed.
6. Keep your left hand against the workpiece during crosscutting to hold it in place against the table fence. Keep the holding hand at least 8 in. to the left of the path to be followed by the saw blade.
7. Be sure the saw blade is free of the workpiece when starting the motor. Pull the motor and blade from the rear of the machine toward the front. *Caution:* During crosscutting, the blade tends to pull into the work-

piece. You may have to hold the cutting rate down by applying pressure to the motor handle during cutting.

8. If the machine is equipped with a brake, use it to stop blade rotation before removing your right hand from the motor handle. If no break is available, keep your right hand in place on the motor handle until the blade stops rotating.

9. When adjusting the guard or changing the blade, turn off the power supply to the machine.

10. When ripping, be sure the yoke is locked to the track.

11. In setting up for ripping, adjust the blade guard as far forward as possible [Fig. 5-46(a)]. Be sure the antikickback fingers are adjusted and operative [Fig. 5-46(a)].

12. When ripping thin material, use a hold-down device set in position opposite the blade [Fig. 5-46(b)].

13. During ripping, always feed into the blade rotation from the front of the arbor [Fig. 5-46(a)].

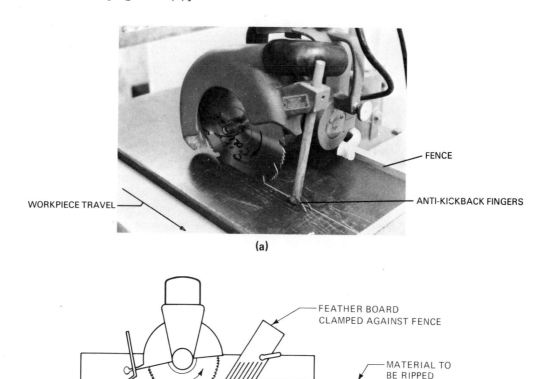

(a)

(b)

Fig. 5-46. (a) Ripping on the radial arm saw. (b) Ripping thin material on radial arm saw

1. Lay out a line on the face of the workpiece with a try square and a pencil.

2. Place the working edge of the workpiece against the table fence and align the layout line with the saw blade. See crosscutting operations on the table saw in Chapter 4.

3. Hold the workpiece against the table fence with the left hand; be sure your hand is at least 8 in. to the left of the path to be followed by the saw blade [Fig. 5-47(b)].

4. Start the saw and slowly pull it into the workpiece.

5. When the cut is finished, return the saw to its original position behind the table fence, and turn the machine off.

6. Do not release the motor handle until the blade stops rotating.

Bevel crosscutting.

1. Raise the column so that the blade is 4 or 5 in. above the table.

2. Unclamp the bevel clamp and pull out the bevel lockpin [Fig. 5-45(c)]. Tilt the blade to the desired angle (it locks at 45°), release the lockpin, and tighten the bevel clamp.

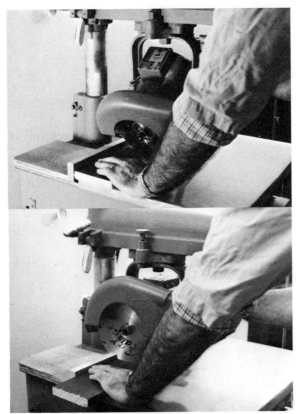

Fig. 5-47. Bevel crosscutting and crosscutting on the radial arm saw

(a)

(b)

3. Lower the blade to a position which will permit it to cut through the workpiece.

4. Cut as described in steps 1 through 6 above [Fig. 5-47(b)].

Other crosscutting operations. Cutting dadoes, rabbets, etc., is accomplished in much the same way as described for the table saw (Chapter 4).

Mitering cuts.

1. Raise the column so that the blade is approximately 1/2 in. above the table surface.

2. Unlock the column.

3. Swing the overarm to the required angle (it locks at 45°), using the built-in protractor. Relock the overarm [Fig. 5-45(a)].

4. Follow the steps described for crosscutting operations.

Compound miter cutting. Follow the steps under bevel crosscutting and mitering cuts and cut as in standard crosscutting.

Ripping on the Radial Arm Saw

In the ripping mode, the radial arm saw cuts in very much the same way the table saw does. The saw arbor is fixed in position and the workpiece is pushed through the revolving saw blade. To set up the radial arm saw for ripping, proceed as follows:

1. Raise the blade until it is approximately 1/2 in. above the table.

2. Unclamp the swivel clamp. Unlock the yoke by pulling the swivel lock out. Rotate the yoke until the saw blade is parallel to the table fence [Fig. 5-46(a)].

3. Relock the yoke (the swivel lockpin will slip into an indexing hole in this position). Reclamp the swivel clamp.

4. Travel the yoke along the overarm track until the space between the saw blade and the table fence is equal to the width of the workpiece to be ripped off.

5. Clamp the yoke to the track, using the track clamp.

6. Lower the blade until it reaches a position which will permit it to cut through the workpiece.

7. Set the antikickback fingers so that they will prevent kickback.

8. Set the saw guard as far forward as possible [Fig. 5-46(a)].

9. Rip as usual, using a push stick where necessary.

Other ripping operations like grooving, edge beveling, chamfering, and rabbeting can be accomplished similar to the way they would be on the table saw.

Caution: When ripping thin, flexible pieces (3/8 in. or less), install a hold-down opposite the blade [Fig. 5-46(b)] to prevent the rotation of the saw blade from lifting the piece during cutting. This is especially important when cutting a groove in a thin piece using a dado cutter, because lifting can cause the workpiece to shatter.

THE SHAPER

Principles of Operation and Nomenclature

The shaper consists of a spindle which protrudes through a hole in a table and rotates at a high speed (5000 to 10,000 rpm). The spindle is threaded and a variety of cutters can be mounted on it. It can be raised and lowered (or the table can be raised and lowered), and its direction can be reversed. The table is fitted with a removable, two-piece fence, which can be used to support the workpiece. The opening around the spindle accepts table inserts that can be used to control cut depth. The table is provided with a milled table slot, which can be used to guide a sliding fence similar to a clamp miter gauge [Fig. 5-48(c)].

The high speed of the shaper makes clean cutting possible. The machine is most commonly used for edge and end shaping, though some face shaping is possible. In operation, the workpiece is fed into the revolving cutter, while the depth of cut is limited by one of several devices. The unit is motor-driven, with the motor connected to the spindle by means of pulleys and belts.

This machine is, without question, potentially the most dangerous in the woodshop. It must be used with great care and intelligence.

Cutters

The safest cutter to use is the solid-head cutter, which consists of three wings or blades milled from a single piece of steel. A great variety of cutter designs are available, including matched cutters such as the tongue-and-groove set [Fig. 5-49(b)].

Flat-knife cutters are made from two flat pieces of cutting steel which are mounted in grooved collars. This type of knife can be ground to the required shape and is therefore commonly used in commercial work. The knives must be perfectly matched and balanced. The danger in using flat-knife cutters arises from the possibility that the knives may loosen or break during cutting. The use of this type of cutter is not recommended for the nonprofessional [Fig. 5-49(a)].

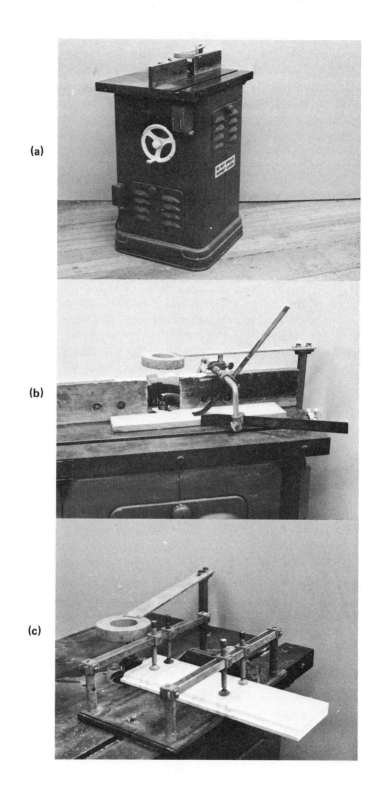

(a)

(b)

(c)

Fig. 5-48. (a) Shaper. (b) Shaper fence ring guard and hold downs. (c) Sliding fence holding workpiece as end is shaped

FLAT KNIFE

GROOVED SHAPER COLLAR

(a)

THREE-WING SOLID CUTTER

(b)

3-LIP SHAPER CUTTERS

ALL HAVE 1/2″ SPINDLE HOLE. INVOLUTE
RELIEF DESIGN PERMITS HONING OF THE
FACE WITHOUT CHANGING THE SHAPE.
CUTTERS 09-128 AND 09-137 ARE COUNTER-
BORED TO FIT STUB SPINDLE NO. 43-345
(OLD 1345). CUTTERS ARE SHOWN 3/8 SIZE.
1/2 LB. EACH.

3-LIP SHAPER CUTTERS

ALL HAVE 1/2″ SPINDLE HOLE. INVOLUTE
RELIEF DESIGN PERMITS HONING OF THE
FACE WITHOUT CHANGING THE SHAPE.
CUTTERS ARE SHOWN 3/8 SIZE. 1/2 LB. EACH.

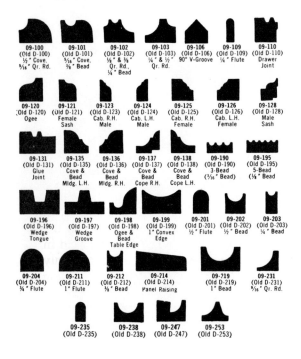

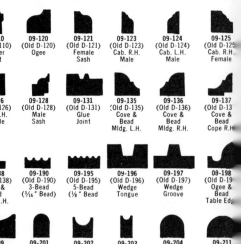

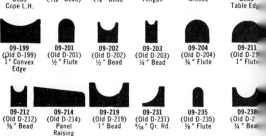

Fig. 5–49.

(c)

General Safety Rules for the Shaper

1. Always wear approved eye protection when using this machine.
2. Disconnect the power supply before attempting to install or remove cutters. Also, set the direction-of-rotation switch in the neutral position.
3. Select straight-grained, defect-free material for use on the shaper.
4. Always have the workpiece supported by one of the cut-limiting devices during shaping.
5. Operations and workpieces which permit the operator's hands to remain at least 8 in. from the cutter head should be used.
6. Whenever possible, use hold-downs to keep the workpiece in position during cutting [Fig. 5–48(b)].
7. When shaping the ends of workpieces, make sure the ends are held in the sliding fence [Fig. 5–48(c)].
8. Whenever possible, use the fence provided with the machine to support the workpiece.
9. Do not use the machine unless the ring guard is in place [Fig. 5–48(a)].
10. Place the keyed washer under the spindle nut when installing the cutter [Fig. 5–50(a)]. This washer helps to prevent the nut from loosening during clockwise rotation.
11. Be sure the cutters are sharp. Do not attempt to use dull cutters.
12. When making a cut in a workpiece for the first time, set the machine for a light cut (not more than 1/8 in.) to test the cutting characteristics of the setup.
13. Keep the machine table free of everything but the workpiece.

Basic Operations on the Shaper

Cutting against the fence—partial-edge shaping. The safest mode of cutting is against the fence. The fence consists of two identical sections which can be aligned or offset with respect to each other [Fig. 5–50(c)]. In addition, the fence is provided with a hold-down device which keeps the workpiece against the fence and table during cutting. The fence is held in position by two table studs (which are removable) and fence nuts. Only straight surfaces can be shaped while using the fence as the depth-controlling unit.

1. Disconnect the shaper from its power supply and set the rotation switch in the neutral position.
2. Select a cutter to be used for shaping and install it on the ·shaper spindle with a suitable number of collars under and above it. A good rule of thumb is to have two collars under the cutter and one above. This will position the cutter far enough above the spindle flange to allow its full employment during cutting [Fig. 5–50(a)].

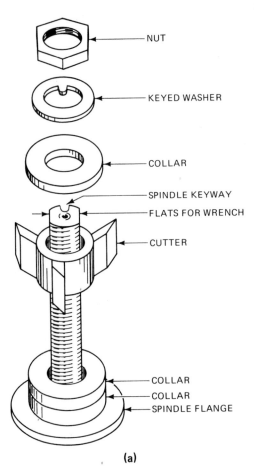

NUT

KEYED WASHER

COLLAR

SPINDLE KEYWAY

FLATS FOR WRENCH

CUTTER

COLLAR

COLLAR

SPINDLE FLANGE

(a)

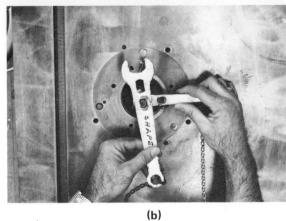

(b)

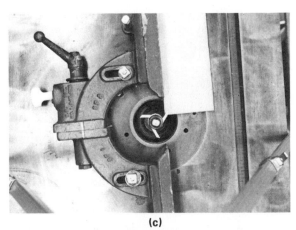

(c)

(d)

Fig. 5-50. (a) Partially exploded view—shaper cutter head assembly. (b) Tightening spindle nut. (c) Shaping against the fence. (d) Partially shaped piece

3. Tighten the spindle nut using two wrenches, one on the spindle and one on the nut [Fig. 5–50(b)].

4. Place the workpiece on the shaper table and raise or lower the spindle and cutter to the desired position; use the workpiece as a guide.

5. Loosen the fence nuts and reposition the fence so that it limits the depth of cut the cutter can make [Fig. 5–50(d)].

6. Tighten the fence nuts and attach and adjust the hold-down device.

7. Install the ring guard.

8. Set the rotation switch to the appropriate position (from neutral to clockwise or counterclockwise).

9. Check the ON/OFF switch on the machine to be sure it is in the OFF position. Turn the power supply to the machine on.

10. Make sure the table is free of any tools or other loose objects. Put on eye-protection devices, and turn the machine on.

11. Feed the workpiece into the hold-down device and the cutter, making sure that the cutter is cutting with the grain.

12. Shape approximately 1 in. of the surface. Turn the machine off and wait until the cutter stops revolving. Then remove the workpiece. Check the cut made on the workpiece and reposition the fence or change the spindle elevation if necessary.

13. Complete the shaping operation.

Whole-edge shaping. The procedure described above is suitable for partial-edge shaping, where the width of the workpiece is not reduced. Some cutters, like the tongue-and-groove set, shape the whole edge and reduce the width of the piece. The following procedure should be used for such operations:

1. Repeat steps 1 through 12 above.

2. Shape approximately 4 in. of the workpiece. Turn the power off and wait until the spindle stops rotating. Disconnect the shaper from its power supply [Fig. 5–51(a)].

3. Loosen the fence nut which holds the left half of the fence down to the table. Loosen the fence clamp. Turn the fence adjusting knob so that the left half of the fence moves toward the cut surface of the workpiece [Fig. 5–51(b)].

4. Travel the fence until it touches the cut surface of the workpiece. Retighten the fence clamp and the wing nut which holds the left half of the fence down against the table. Reconnect the power supply.

5. Complete shaping the edge. *Note:* The left half of the fence now supports the cut surface of the workpiece just as the outfeed table on the jointer supports the cut surface of the workpiece being jointed.

End shaping. The ends of workpieces 10 in. or more in width can be shaped in the same way that edges are shaped, against the fence. In most

Fig. 5-51. Whole edge shaping. (a) Fence halves aligned (note witness line). Cut started. (b) Fence (left half) moved up against cut surface (note witness line)

cases only the upper portion of the hold-down can be used. If the width of the workpiece is less than 10 in., the sliding fence should be used to secure it during shaping (Fig. 5-52).

Note: The steel baseplate of the sliding fence raises the workpiece 1/4 in. above the table. The spindle must be raised by that amount to shape the edge of the same workpiece (Fig. 5-52).

If the edges and ends of a workpiece are to be shaped, the ends should be done first because the edges are usually split during end shaping. Thus, when the edges are shaped, the split material is removed.

Fig. 5-52. End shaping

Shaping a curved surface against a collar. In shaping curved surfaces, the fence cannot be used to control the depth of cut. In such instances, a collar is placed under or over the cutter to limit the depth of cut [Fig. 5-53(a)]. The edge of the workpiece is supported by the collar during cutting.

1. Turn off the power supply to the shaper.
2. Remove the fence and the fence studs from the table.
3. Install a pivot pin in one of the holes to the right of the spindle [Fig. 5-53(a)].

Fig. 5-53. (a) Collar on top of cutter limits cut depth. Pin in table stabilizes work as cutting begins. First half of cut complete (b) Collar under reversed cutter. Cutter height being adjusted to cut made in (A). Second half of the cut will be started at the end of the piece closest to the pin. (c) Completed cut

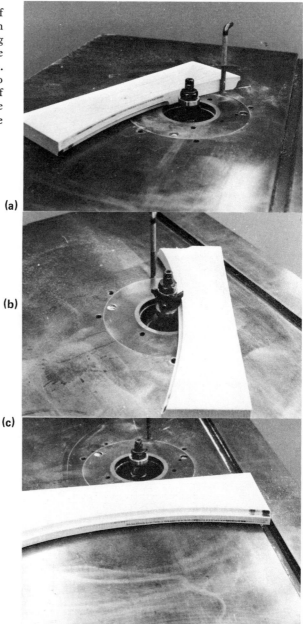

(a)

(b)

(c)

4. Place the cutter selected and a collar of suitable diameter on the shaper spindle in the usual fashion. Install the keyed washer, additional collars, and the spindle nut, and tighten.

5. Place the ring guard in position over the cutterhead.

6. Adjust the elevation of the cutter to the desired position.

7. Turn the power supply on and set the spindle rotation for *counterclockwise rotation*.

8. Place the workpiece against the pivot pin, turn the machine on, and feed the workpiece into the cutter until the collar touches the edge of the

Fig. 5-54. Shaping against a table insert. (a) Table insert. (b) Table insert in position-workpiece pivoted off pin to start cut. (c) Edge of workpiece against table insert which controls cut depth

(a)

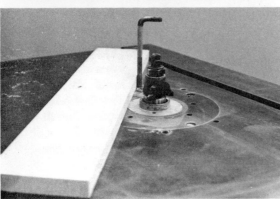

(b)

(c)

piece. Complete the cut *until the point is reached where the cutter is no longer cutting with the grain* [Fig. 5-53(a)].

At this point the cutter must be removed and reversed on the spindle, as shown in Fig. 5-53(b). Steps 1 through 6 are then repeated with the pivot pin on the left side of the spindle. The collar is positioned below the cutter. The direction of rotation is *clockwise,* and the workpiece is turned over with its face down on the table. This makes cutting with the grain possible for the remainder of the cut [Fig. 5-53(b) and (c)].

Shaping against table inserts. Shaping against table inserts is similar to shaping against a collar. However, the burning which sometimes results from shaping against a collar is eliminated [Fig. 53(a)]. Figure 5-54 illustrates the procedure.

ELECTRONIC GLUE WELDER

Using Heat to Accelerate Glue Setting

A radio-frequency generator produces a rapidly oscillating magnetic field (about 40 million cycles per second) which agitates the molecules of materials close to it. Certain materials, such as wood, are nonconductors and are not heated appreciably. Other materials, such as a glue-water mixture, are fairly good conductors and are heated by the friction created as their molecules react to the radio-frequency field passing through them. The energy in the field can pass through wood, so no direct contact between the electrodes and the glue line is necessary.

The wood welding unit consists of a radio-frequency generator, a coaxial cable to transmit the energy from the generator to the workpiece, and a gun, with various electrodes, which carries radio-frequency current to the workpiece [Fig. 5-55(a)]. Various types of heat-setting glues are used, including melamine resin, resorcinol, and urea resin.

General Safety Rules for Using the Glue Welder

1. Use wooden clamps wherever possible. If metal clamps must be used, avoid touching them when the gun is in use, since they may be heated.
2. Position the welding gun so that if arcing occurs, you will not be in its path.
3. If arcing occurs, release the trigger immediately and adjust the control on the gun.
4. Remove all pencil marks in the glue-welding area. Such lines sometimes cause arcing because graphite provides a path for current flow.
5. Keep the coaxial cable that connects the gun to the generator off the floor and out of traffic lanes where it can easily be damaged.

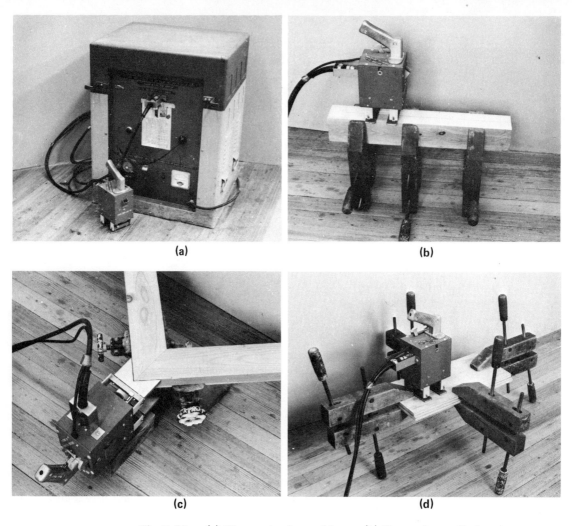

Fig. 5-55. (a) Electronic glue welder. (b) Electrodes applied across glue line. (c) Glue welding a miter joint with special miter electrodes. (d) Glue welding pieces positioned face to face. Field goes through wood to excite glue molecules

Basic Operations Using the Glue Welder

1. Prepare the workpiece in the same way that you would if the glue welder were not to be used (clamp as usual, but avoid metal clamps).

2. Attach the handgun to the generator by connecting the coaxial cable to the connector on the generator.

3. Select suitable electrodes for the application, and install these on the gun.

4. Set the gun control lever to the middle position.

5. Turn the generator on and allow it to warm up for 5 minutes.

6. Apply the gun electrodes to the glue line [Fig. 5-55(b)] and press the trigger on the gun. If arcing occurs, release the trigger and move the gun control lever toward the handle. Press the trigger again, and if arcing still occurs, reset the gun lever away from the handle.

7. Leave the trigger depressed for approximately15 seconds or until the glue bubbling stops.

8. Move the gun approximately 10 in. away from the first welding site and repeat steps 6 and 7.

Two indicators can be used to determine the relative flow of current through the glue. One is the meter on the generator. The higher this meter reads, the more current is flowing. The other indicator is the neon lamp on the gun. The brighter this lamp glows, the more current is flowing. Figure 5-55(c) and (d) illustrates how various types of electrodes can be used for various types of work.

PORTABLE POWER TOOLS

Portable power tools should not be thought of as substitutes for stationary machines. They are highly useful portable devices which can be brought to the workpiece when the size or location of the workpiece makes it impractical to bring it to the shop and the stationary units. With the exception of the power router, the portable tools discussed below are less precise in terms of the results they produce.

Power Router

The router is essentially a high-speed rotary cutting device. It is capable of a great variety of operations, including edge shaping, dadoing, grooving, rabbeting, template following, dovetailing, and gain cutting.

Principals of Operation and Nomenclature

The router consists of two essential major components; the motor and the base. The motor is a universal unit whose power rating ranges from 1/2 to 3 horsepower. It operates at approximately 25,000 rpm. Its shaft is fitted with a chuck, which accepts 1/4-in. or 1/2-in. router cutters. The base supports the motor and is usually provided with a calibrated device, which permits the motor to be raised and lowered vertically (Fig. 5-56). Some routers have a spindle-locking device as an integral part of the machine. Others employ a second wrench to hold the spindle while the chuck is adjusted.

MOTOR

DEPTH CONTROL RING

CHUCK

BASE

Fig. 5–56. Power router

General Safety Rules for the Power Router

1. Always wear approved eye protection when operating the power router.

2. Ensure that the switch is in the OFF position before plugging the unit in.

3. Make all adjustments with the router unplugged.

4. Hold the router securely when turning the motor on. The high starting torque will cause the router to twist when it is turned on.

5. Keep the cable free of the cutting area when the router is in use.

6. Wait until the router spindle stops rotating before putting it down on the work surface.

7. Be sure that workpieces are securely anchored during routing.

8. Be sure the router is properly grounded electrically before attempting to use it.

Basic Operations Using the Power Router

Edge shaping with a piloted router bit. One of the simplest operations with the router is edge shaping with a piloted router bit [Fig. 5-57(a)]. This bit follows an edge, straight or curved, and shapes it uniformly. The edge must be smooth because the bit reproduces any irregularity it passes over.

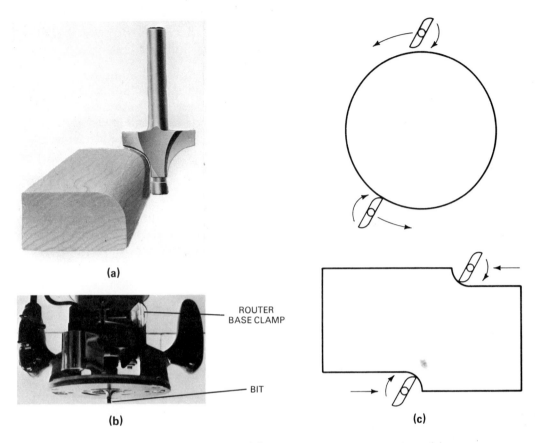

(a)

ROUTER
BASE CLAMP

BIT

(b)

(c)

Fig. 5-57. (a) Piloted router bit. (b) Setting bit below router base. (c) Direction of travel

1. Select a suitable piloted router bit.

2. Install the bit in the router chuck so that approximately 1/4 in. of the shank remains outside of the chuck.

3. Adjust the motor position (in the base) so that the desired portion of the router bit extends below the base [Fig. 5-57(b)].

4. Lock the base and motor together with the base clamp [Fig. 5-57(b)].

5. Secure the workpiece to the work surface, hold the router steady, plug the unit in, and turn the router on.

6. Holding the router base with both hands, place the router base on the face of the workpiece. Travel the router into the edge of the workpiece until the pilot's movement is stopped by the edge of the workpiece.

7. Make a short test-cut traveling the router to the right [Fig. 5-57(c)]. Examine the cut. Adjust the router if necessary.

8. Complete the cut.

Note: If ends are to be shaped, these should be done first so that any edge splitting can be cut away when the edges are shaped. If the pilot is pressed into the edge too hard, it will burn a recess into the edge and the piece will be damaged.

Setting the depth of cut. In all grooving operations the depth of cut is critical. A depth-of-cut device is built into the router for this purpose, or a trial-and-error setting can be attempted. The simple method described below is useful for routing gains for hinges. The same method can be used for any grooving operation.

1. Install a suitable router bit in the router chuck.
2. Place the router base on a flat surface and adjust the position of the motor until the bottom cutting edges of the router bit touch the flat surface [Fig. 5–58(a)].
3. Place two strips of wood of equal thickness or two hinge leaves under the router base as shown in Fig. 5–58(b).
4. Lower the router motor until the bottom edges of the router bit again touch the flat surface as shown in Fig. 5–58(b).
5. Lock the base. The depth of cut produced by the router will be equal to the thickness of the strips inserted under the base in step 3.

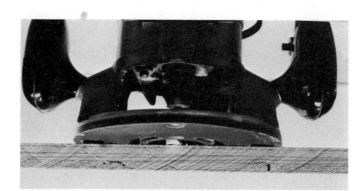

(a)

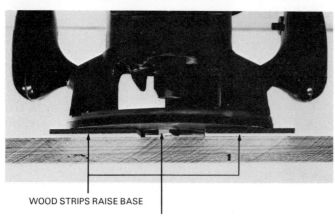

(b)

WOOD STRIPS RAISE BASE

BIT LOWER THAN BASE

Fig. 5–58. (a) Router bit touching flat surface—flush with router base. (b) Router base raised by wood strips—bit lowered to surface

Fig. 5-59. (a) Standard router bit with cutting edges on sides and bottom. (b) Router guided by two base guides. (c) Router guided by fence accessory. (d) Router guided in circular cut by trammel accessory

Rabbets, dadoes, and grooving operations. Rabbets, dadoes, and other similar cuts are made with router bits which have cutting edges along their bottom and side edges [Fig. 5-59(a)]. The movement of the router is most precise when it is controlled by a guide.

The simplest guide is a straight piece of wood fastened to the workpiece against which the router base travels [Fig. 5-59(b)]. A modified try square-shaped guide is a useful accessory which can be fabricated. A curved guide can be used for making curved grooves. The easiest and most foolproof guide consists of two parallel guide strips which allow the router base to travel between them [Fig. 5-59(b)].

The straight guide is an accessory which attaches to the router base. It acts as a traveling fence which can be used to keep the router at a fixed distance from a surface [Fig. 5-59(c)]. Some straight guides have a trammel attachment which permits the router to be used to cut circular grooves or to cut out large-diameter circles [Fig. 5-59(d)].

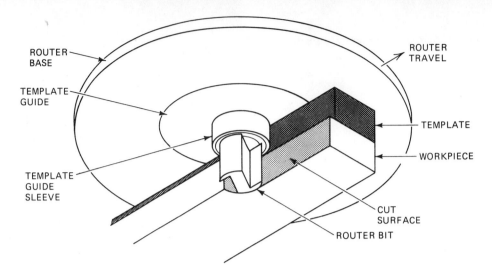

Fig. 5-60. Router guided by template guide

Template guides and the use of templates. The template guide consists of a plate which has a hollow sleeve at its center (Fig. 5-60). The template guide sleeve limits the cutting area of the router bit to that portion of the bit which extends out beyond the sleeve. This template guide follows a template and allows the router bit to reproduce the shape of the template (Fig. 5-60). The area routed will be slightly smaller than the template because of the distance between the cutting edge of the router bit and the outer surface of the sleeve. In Fig. 5-61(a) and (b), note that the template guide follows the "fingers" of the template shown at the top of the multiple-dovetail fixture.

Fig. 5-61. (a) Dovetail fixture. (b) Dovetail router bit and template guide

(a)

(b)

PORTABLE ELECTRIC DRILL

Principles of Operation and Nomenclature

Portable electric drills consist of a motor, a housing, a handgrip switch, and a chuck (Fig. 5-62). Most electric drills operate at approximately 2000 rpm in the 1/4-in. chuck capacity and proportionately slower in the larger chuck sizes (700 rpm is a common speed for 1/2-in.-capacity models). Many drills are available with reversing switches and speed controls which give the drill a range of speeds from zero to 2000 rpm (Fig. 5-62). In woodworking operations, units with low-speed capability are desirable.

General Safety Rules for the Portable Electric Drill

1. Always wear approved eye protection when operating the portable electric drill.
2. Be sure the drill is unplugged when making any adjustments on it or when installing or removing bits.
3. Be sure the switch on the drill is in the OFF position before plugging the machine in.
4. Check for proper installation of any accessories in the chuck before turning the machine on.
5. Always remove the chuck key from the chuck immediately.

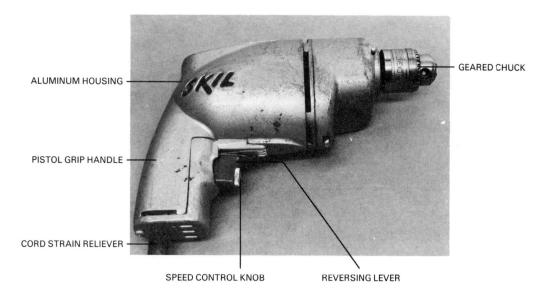

ALUMINUM HOUSING

GEARED CHUCK

PISTOL GRIP HANDLE

CORD STRAIN RELIEVER

SPEED CONTROL KNOB

REVERSING LEVER

Fig. 5-62. Variable speed reversible hand drill

6. Be sure the workpiece is secure before attempting to work on it.

7. When using the drill in places where hidden utilities may exist under the surface being drilled, proceed slowly and examine the hole to determine whether or not utility lines are present.

Basic Operations Using the Portable Electric Drill

Many of the accessories described in the section on the drill press can be used in the portable drill.

PORTABLE JIG SAW

Principles of Operation and Nomenclature

The portable jigsaw consists of a motor, enclosed in a housing, which is used to drive a narrow blade in a vertical reciprocating action. In operation, the saw is supported by a tiltable base. The blade is secured to the machine by means of a setscrew [Fig. 5-63(a)]. The capacity of the portable jig saw is usually expressed in terms of its maximum cutting depth. A 2-in. capacity in wood is common.

Fig. 5-63. (a) Portable jig saw. (b) Shaping edge with jig saw. (c) Plunge cutting

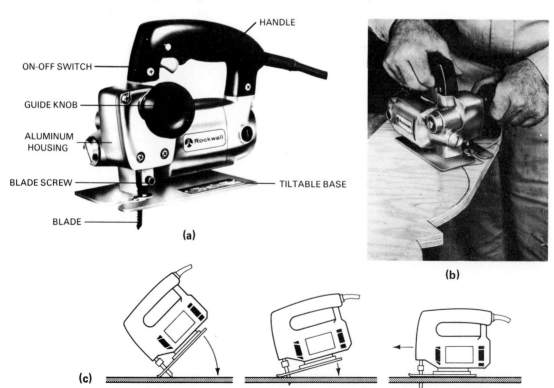

HANDLE

ON-OFF SWITCH

GUIDE KNOB

ALUMINUM HOUSING

BLADE SCREW

TILTABLE BASE

BLADE

(a)

(b)

(c)

The saw blade is installed in the chuck with its teeth pointed upward toward the base of the machine [Fig. 5-63(a)]. The blade cuts during the upward stroke, and this cutting action tends to keep the material in contact with the underside of the machine's base.

A variety of blades are available for various materials, including metals. If the machine is to be used on nonwood materials, a speed-varying device is a necessary feature. For woodcutting, a speed of 3200 strokes per minute is usually satisfactory; for nonwood materials, a lower speed of 2600 strokes per minute is desirable.

Most models are equipped with a wing screw or similar device which makes the use of a ripping fence possible. The machine is most suitable for curved cutting because of the narrowness of most of the blades available. The tiltable base makes bevel cutting possible.

General Safety Rules for the Portable Jig Saw

1. Always wear approved eye protection when operating the jigsaw.
2. Unplug the machine before attempting to make any adjustments on it, including blade installation or removal.
3. Be sure the machine switch is in the OFF position before plugging the machine into the power supply.
4. Be sure the blade is suitable for the work to be performed.
5. Ensure that the blade is tightly attached to the chuck before operating the unit.
6. Be sure the workpiece is properly secured before attempting to cut it.
7. When starting the machine, have the blade clear of the workpiece.
8. When stopping the machine in a cut, wait until all blade motion stops before removing the saw from the cut.

Basic Operations Using the Jigsaw

Curved cutting.

1. Lay out the line to be cut on the workpiece.
2. Place the front end of the base on the workpiece, with the saw blade opposite the layout line and clear of the workpiece.
3. Turn the machine on and slowly move the blade into the workpiece. Keep pressure on the machine so that the base remains down on the surface being cut [Fig. 5-63(b)].
4. If the saw must be stopped before the cut is completed, wait until the saw blade motion stops before removing the blade from the cut.
5. To restart cutting in an unfinished cut, place the saw blade in the cut with the blade approximately 1/4 in. away from the point where cutting was stopped. Restart the saw and resume cutting.

Plunge cutting. When internal cutouts are required, plunge cutting can be employed. Plunge cutting eliminates the need for boring a starting hole in the workpiece. The following procedure may be used:

1. Lay out the line to be followed during cutting.
2. Position the saw on the scrap side of the layout line.
3. Tilt the saw up on the front edge of the base, with the blade point above the surface of the workpiece [Fig. 5–63(c)].
4. Turn the saw on and slowly pivot it so that the saw blade point touches the surface of the workpiece. Considerable pressure must be applied to the saw to keep the front edge of the saw base in a fixed position. The pivoting takes place around the front edge of the saw base [Fig. 5–63(c)].
5. As the saw blade pierces the workpiece, slowly lower the base of the machine down onto the surface of the workpiece.
6. Complete the saw cut in the normal fashion.

PORTABLE CIRCULAR SAW

Principles of Operation and Nonmenclature

The portable circular saw consists of a motor mounted in a housing. The motor is connected to an arbor through a gear train. The arbor mounts a circular saw blade which usually ranges from 6-1/2 in. to 10-1/4 in. in diameter. The cutting depth ranges from 2-1/4 in. to 3-7/8 in. The saw has a handle and power switch, a telescoping saw guard, and a base which can be tilted for bevel cutting. The portable circular saw is also provided with a variable depth-of-cut capability (Fig. 5–64).

Portable circular saws are most frequently used in on-site carpentry projects. Precision cutting is difficult with this machine, so it is used primarily for rough cutting.

No-load speeds average approximately 5500 rpm. These machines are among the largest consumers of electricity and frequently draw 10 to 15 amperes during operation. Therefore, an adequate power supply is essential.

General Safety Rules for the Portable Circular Saw

1. Always wear approved eye protection when operating this machine.
2. Be sure to unplug the machine before making any adjustments. Adjust the depth of cut so that it is equal to the thickness of the workpiece plus 1/2 in.
3. Be sure the power switch on the machine is in the OFF position before plugging the machine into the power supply.
4. Workpieces must be securely supported and anchored in place during cutting. Support must also be provided for portions of the workpiece

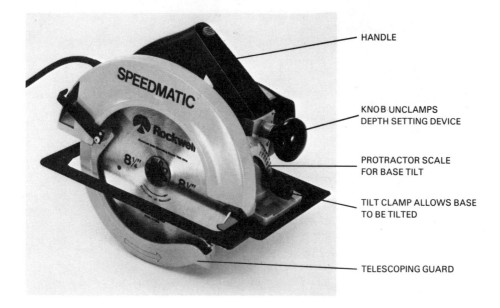

HANDLE

KNOB UNCLAMPS
DEPTH SETTING DEVICE

PROTRACTOR SCALE
FOR BASE TILT

TILT CLAMP ALLOWS BASE
TO BE TILTED

TELESCOPING GUARD

Fig. 5-64. Portable circular saw

to be cut off. Unsupported cutoffs will bind on the blade and may cause dangerous kickback.

5. Keep the saw blade free of the workpiece when starting the machine, and wait until the machine reaches operating speed before attempting to cut with it.

6. When stopping the saw in an incomplete cut, wait until the blade stops revolving before removing the saw from the cut.

7. When restarting an incomplete cut, place the saw blade in the cut in a position that will not result in binding and will allow the saw to reach operating speed before cutting is resumed.

8. When a cut is complete, turn the machine off and wait until the saw blade stops before lifting the saw off the workpiece.

9. Keep the power cable clear of the cutting site.

10. Sharp saws are safe and efficient. Never attempt to use a portable circular saw with a dull blade.

Using the Portable Circular Saw to Make Straight Cuts

1. Lay out the line to be followed during cutting. Adjust the saw blade so that it protrudes past the underside of the base, a distance equal to the thickness of the workpiece plus 1/2 in.

2. Place the front edge of the saw base on the surface of the workpiece, with the blade clear of the work surface.

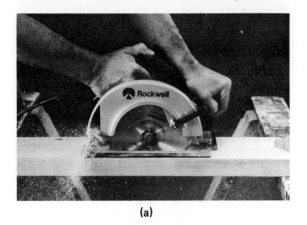

(a)

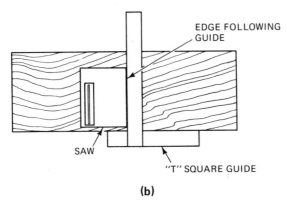

EDGE FOLLOWING
GUIDE

SAW

"T" SQUARE GUIDE

(b)

Fig. 5-65. (a) Ripping with a portable circular saw. (b) Edge of sawblade and edge of workpiece aligned for straight cut

3. Turn the saw on. After it has reached operating speed, advance it into the workpiece.

4. When the cut is complete, turn the power off. Wait for the saw blade to stop, and lift the saw off the workpiece.

If desired, a straight edge, straight guide, or right-angle cutting guide may be used to assist in cutting [Fig. 5-65(a) and (b)].

6

CABINETMAKING

A cabinet is a boxlike unit which can be refined to suit a variety of functions. With drawers inserted, it may be a dresser. With a pair of doors attached, it can be a storage unit. Although this use of the term is precise and, in many instances accurate, it does not go far enough in describing the work of the cabinetmaker. Actually, any fine woodworking is within the domain of the cabinetmaker. Many carpenters who specialize in renovation, especially when kitchens are involved, build simple cabinets. The distinction—and it is an arbitrary one—between fine woodworking and carpentry is to be found in the amount of precision joinery and the quality of the finishing involved in making the piece. The cabinetmaker usually produces pieces that are made of hardwoods, involve fairly complex joinery, and usually have transparent finishes applied to them. The carpenter who builds cabinets more commonly works with softwood plywood, uses glued and nailed butt joinery, and applies opaque finishes, such as paint, to the pieces.

Most fine furniture is made in factories which produce numerous replicas of a given design. Where possible, these manufacturers utilize automatic or semiautomatic machinery to accomplish operations that would require the skill of a cabinetmaker if handtools or basic machines were employed. The modern cabinetmaker is usually involved in custom work, where mass-produced pieces would not be suitable. Craftsmen produce individual pieces for a limited, appreciative market. These pieces include basic furniture such as tables, chairs, and chests, but they are usually unique, one-of-a-kind

Fig. 6-1. Craftsman made piece

creations (Fig. 6-1). Novices tend to look for rules of construction in wood-working. They are anxious to produce work of quality and assume that there is a "right" way to accomplish any operation or construction in cabinet-making. A more useful approach is to learn enough to select a method from several alternatives.

The beginner is well advised to study examples of early Colonial furniture because these pieces are highly functional. Very little time was spent on decorative work. Every joint was essential. It is also helpful to examine well-made commercial work, but keep in mind that such work is produced with the use of specialized equipment not available to the craftsman.

Finally, a study of the work of contemporary craftsmen in wood is useful. Here, pieces in which the limitations of wood as a material were stretched and explored can be seen. This kind of study, together with experience, will enable the novice to design pieces that are well constructed and reasonable, in terms of ability and the limitations imposed by the equipment and materials available.

This chapter examines some of the problems involved in the fabrication of fine furniture.

LEG-RAIL CONSTRUCTION

Legs are used to support horizontal surfaces at a convenient height. In a sense, they are a means of economizing on the amount of material. The problem the cabinetmaker, or really the designer, faces when attempting to attach legs to a piece is very closely related to leverage. Levers increase force by spreading the effort applied over a long motion path (Fig. 6-2). Levers can also be used in the opposite way to increase motion, in which case the force is reduced. Although table legs are not designed to operate as levers, they do, every time the table is pushed (Fig. 6-3). When the table is pushed, the force applied to the ends of the legs is multiplied several times by leverage.

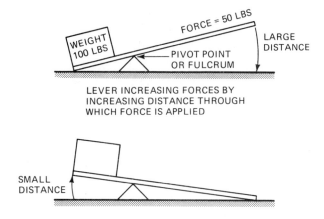

Fig. 6-2. Force increasing lever

Though some simple constructions use metal hardware to tie the end of the leg to the tabletop, most designs involve the use of an apron rail, and sometimes a secondary rail further down the leg (Fig. 6-4). The apron rail serves several functions: It allows the leg to be attached to a secondary component, the rail, without utilizing an inherently weak end-grain joint. It also allows the fastening of the rail to the tabletop. Finally, the effective length of the lever, the leg in this case, is reduced by the width of the apron rail. If a second rail is used further down the leg (Fig. 6-4), the effective length of the lever is further reduced. Rails have another function when they are located under wide, flat surfaces such as tabletops and chair seats. They add support to the surface and they help to keep it flat.

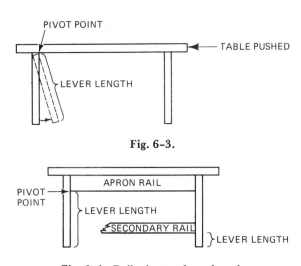

Fig. 6-3.

Fig. 6-4. Rails shorten lever length

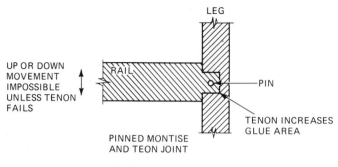

UP OR DOWN
MOVEMENT
IMPOSSIBLE
UNLESS TENON
FAILS

LEG

RAIL

PIN

TENON INCREASES
GLUE AREA

PINNED MONTISE
AND TEON JOINT

CROSS SECTIONAL VIEW

Fig. 6–5. Pinned mortise and tenon

Leg-Rail Joinery

Mortise and tenon leg-rail joint. The mortise and tenon leg-rail joint is commonly used in chair construction (Fig. 6–5). This joint is almost an ideal solution to the leg-rail fastening problem; however, it does have some disadvantages, especially from a commercial point of view. First, it is a complex joint to produce in a production operation. Although the mortise can be cut in one operation with a chain mortiser, there are certain limitations imposed by this machine. The leg must be sufficiently thick for the chain mortiser to penetrate deeply enough to develop a full mortise (Fig. 6–6). For pieces where the ability to remove the legs easily for compact packaging and shipping is important, this joint is not suitable because it cannot be knocked-down easily.

Open-stub tenon, mortise and tenon joint. The open-stub tenon, mortise and tenon joint is used in commercial work because it is simpler to fabricate than the standard mortise and tenon joint. This joint is not as strong as the standard mortise and tenon joint for several reasons. First, it has less glue area. Second, when the leg is loaded, the absence of material above the tenon

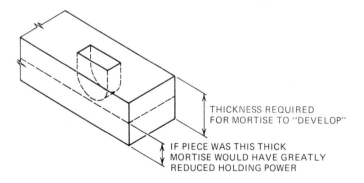

THICKNESS REQUIRED
FOR MORTISE TO "DEVELOP"

IF PIECE WAS THIS THICK
MORTISE WOULD HAVE GREATLY
REDUCED HOLDING POWER

Fig. 6–6. Mortise made by chain mortiser

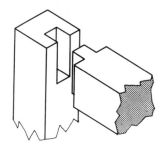

Fig. 6–7. Open stub mortise and tenon

makes the joint more likely to fail than would be the case in a standard mortise and tenon joint (Fig. 6–7).

Dovetail tenon. The dovetail tenon or dovetail dado is also commonly used in commercial furniture construction (Fig. 6–8). The advantage of this joint over the open-stub tenon, mortise and tenon is its resistance to pulling apart (Fig. 6–8). In extreme tension, the single dovetail with its short grain will fail.

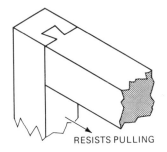

RESISTS PULLING

Fig. 6–8. Dovetail mortise and tenon

Dowel joint. The dowel joint has replaced the mortise and tenon joint in many applications because it is very easy to fabricate. The use of reinforcing corner blocks (Fig. 6–9), together with modern adhesives, makes the dowel joint adequate for many leg-rail applications. The weakness of this joinery method is related to the excessive amount of end-grain gluing involved (Fig. 6–10).

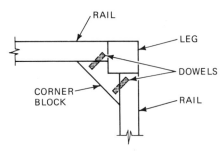

RAIL

LEG

DOWELS

CORNER BLOCK

RAIL

Fig. 6–9. Blocked dowel leg-rail joint

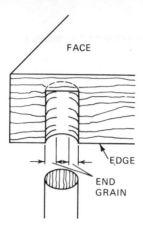

Fig. 6-10. End grain problem in dowel joints

Stretcher dowel joints. When stretchers or secondary rails are used, as in chair construction (Fig. 6–11), the end of the stretcher itself is frequently shaped into a cylinder. This fits into a hole bored into the leg.

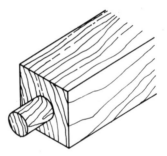

Fig. 6-11. Stretcher dowel joint

Corner plate leg-rail fastening. The corner plate leg-rail fastening system is widely used in table construction because of its relative strength and its simplicity of fabrication. The rails are dadoed to receive the plate, and the stud is pressed into the leg. Then the bolt is fitted to the plate, and a nut pulls the leg and the rails together (Fig. 6–12). The bonus, from the manufacturer's point of view, is that the legs can be quickly removed for compact packaging and shipping.

Fig. 6-12. Corner plate fastening

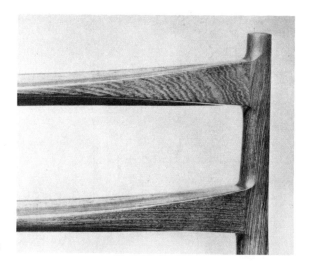

Fig. 6-13. Sculptured chair components

Sculptured leg-rail joints. Many contemporary designs required sculptured leg-rail components (Fig 6-13). In designing and fabricating such pieces, care must be taken to avoid the production of short-grain areas (Fig. 6-14) which are easily fractured during processing. This portion of the joint, including the radii, should be made on the leg, using material added to the leg (Fig. 6-15). The final shaping of such joined pieces should be done after the pieces are assembled.

Drawbolt joints. Drawbolts (Fig. 6-16) are used in the construction of pieces which are likely to be subjected to heavy use. Workbenches and school equipment are examples of such furniture. In designing a drawbolt joint, special consideration must be given to the amount of material left between the nut and the end of the rail (Fig. 6-16). A minimum of 1 in. of

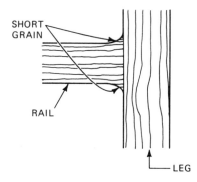

Fig. 6-14. Short grain problem in sculptured joint

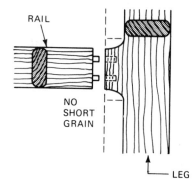

Fig. 6-15. No short grain problem in sculptured joint

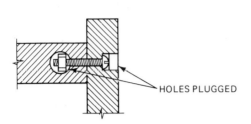

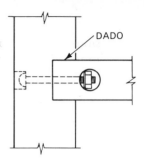

Fig. 6-16. Leg-rail drawbolts

Fig. 6-17. Dado drawbolt joint

material should be left in this area. When glue is used, clamps are unnecessary because the bolts provide adequate pressure for glue setting. In some applications, dadoes are made in the leg units to facilitate assembly through positive location of the pieces with respect to each other (Fig. 6-17).

TABLE AND COUNTER TOPS

Large-Panel Fabrication

In modern practice, when solid wood panels and tabletops are constructed, the pieces are made of relatively thin strips joined edge to edge, with the heart face of the boards reversed (Fig. 6-18). This process tends to reduce the total effect of the warping.

Lumber-core plywood. A variation of the method described above is the production of lumber-core plywood. This material is made of very narrow strips and often utilizes scrap material. A smooth, continuous surface is produced by gluing veneer to the faces of the core. This results in a dimensionally stable and uninterrupted surface on the tabletop. The edges and ends of the top must be treated to hide the core. The top itself can otherwise be handled as though it were solid wood [Fig. 1-56(b)].

Veneer-core plywood. Veneer-core plywood [Fig. 1-56(a)] is very commonly used where wide material is required. Its advantages are dimen-

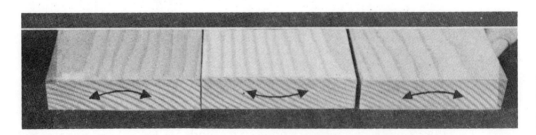

Fig. 6-18. Reversing the heartwood in edge to edge glue-up

sional stability, resistance to warping, and relatively high strength-to-weight ratio. Like lumber-core plywood, its edges must be masked in some way. When used for tabletops, the panel presents no special problems in terms of fabrication. In other applications where edge fastenings are required, holding problems can develop. Plywood tends to split when screws are driven into its edges.

Particle or flake board. Particle board is widely used in medium- and low-priced furniture (Fig. 1–61). Its primary attraction is its low cost— roughly half the price of softwood plywood. Although the material is adequately strong and has superior dimensional stability, several problems are related to its use. First, all exposed surfaces must be covered. In most table- or dresser-top application, this covering is accomplished with a plastic laminate. Although such material is suitable for surfaces intended for heavy use, some questions concerning its aesthetic suitability can be raised when it is disguised to look like wood. In other applications, fastening becomes a problem. The material is difficult to glue successfully and, because particle board crumbles easily, lock joints can not be used.

Lumber-core and hardwood plywood. Lumber-core and hardwood plywood usually have banded or framed edges which mask the unsightly edges of the material under them. When banded, the edges are usually left square [Fig. 6–19(a)]; when framed, the edges can be shaped as if they were solid wood [Fig. 6–19(b)].

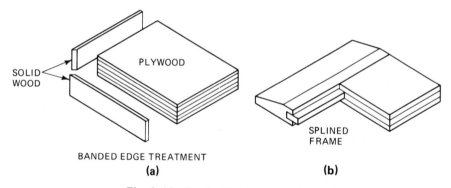

Fig. 6–19. Banded lumber core plywood

Softwood plywood. The edges of softwood plywood can be veneered or banded. If the plywood is covered with plastic laminate, the edges can also be covered with the same material (Fig. 6–20). For rough work, various metal and plastic edges are available (Fig. 6–20).

Table Leaves

Inserts. Among the most common methods for increasing table size is the use of separate insertable leaves (Fig. 6–21) of the same width and thickness

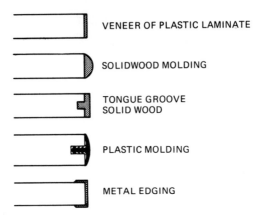

VENEER OF PLASTIC LAMINATE

SOLIDWOOD MOLDING

TONGUE GROOVE
SOLID WOOD

PLASTIC MOLDING

METAL EDGING

Fig. 6–20. Plywood edge treatment

as the tabletop. They are provided with holes and dowel pins which mate with the holes and pins in the edges of the table (Fig. 6–21).

Drop leaves. Drop leaves are hinged to tabletops by means of various types of hardware (Fig. 6–22). The rule joint is commonly used to provide an interlocking joint for a drop leaf.

Draw-leaf table. One contemporary solution to the expandable-tabletop problem is shown in Fig. 6–23. In this Scandinavian piece, the top floats, that is, it can be raised vertically. Two leaves are positioned under the top. Either or both of these leaves can be pulled out to add to the usable area of the top (Fig. 6–23).

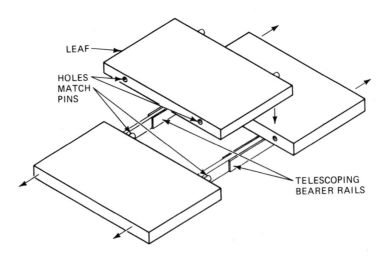

LEAF

HOLES
MATCH
PINS

TELESCOPING
BEARER RAILS

Fig. 6–21. Table leaves

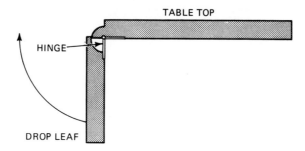

Fig. 6-22. Drop leaves

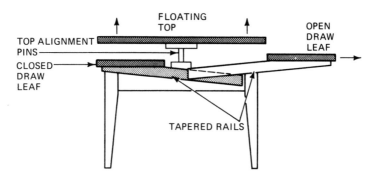

Fig. 6-23. Draw-leaf table

Fastening Tabletops to Leg-Rail Assemblies

Screws. A variety of methods are used to fasten tabletops to rails. The simplest is to screw the top directly to the rails. This method is suitable only for tops that are dimensionally stable, e.g., plywood or particle board tops [Fig. 6-24(a) and (f)]. If such a fastening method were used on solid wood tabletops, the necessary expansion of the top across the grain could not take place. As a result, the top would buckle or the leg-rail joints would fail. The pocket hole [Fig. 6-24(b)] allows shorter screws to be used, and it weakens the rail less than counterboring the screws would.

Corner blocks and angle irons. Corner blocks screwed to the rail faces and the tabletop are an effective way to fasten tops to rails. The blocks are attached to the rails first, with a paper spacer between the block and the tabletop [Fig. 6-24(a)]. Screws driven into the top pull it down tightly against the blocks. Angle irons can be used in the same way [Fig. 6-24(c)].

Step blocks and S plates. Step blocks, Fig. 6-24(d) and (e), are fastened to the table top with wood screws. The rabbet on the block fits into a groove cut into the inner face of the rail as shown. Steel S plates function in much the same way as step blocks do.

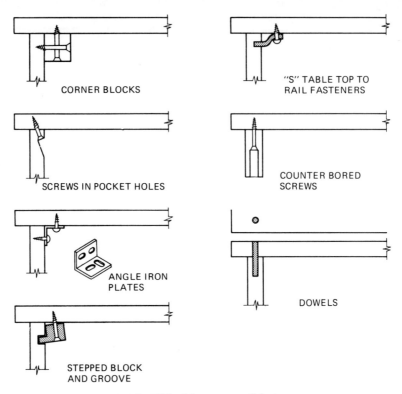

CORNER BLOCKS

"S" TABLE TOP TO RAIL FASTENERS

SCREWS IN POCKET HOLES

COUNTER BORED SCREWS

ANGLE IRON PLATES

DOWELS

STEPPED BLOCK AND GROOVE

Fig. 6-24. "S" table top to rail fasteners

Dowels. When special effects are required, as in some contemporary pieces [Fig. 6-24(g)], dowels may be used to fasten tabletops. Though dowels do not provide the holding power of some of the other devices described, when properly used they can perform satisfactorily.

CARCASE CONSTRUCTION

A carcase is basically a box or boxlike unit which is used for dressers, storage cabinets, and similar pieces of furniture. The six-sided box without openings is a very strong construction and is fairly easy to build of materials such as plywood. To make it useful, one or more sides must be removed (Fig. 6-25) so that access to the interior space is possible. However, when the box

Fig. 6-25. Basic carcase

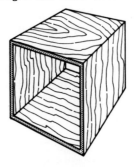

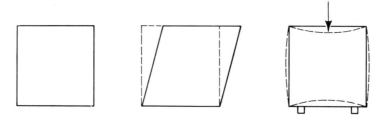

Fig. 6–26. Deformed carcase

is opened up in this fashion, it loses some of its inherent structural stability and strength.

In practice, a cabinet such as the one shown in Fig. 6-26 consists of four basic components which are securely fastened to each other: the top, two sides, and a bottom. This frame is inherently weak, and when it is loaded, it tends to collapse into a parallelogram or to sag (Fig. 6-26). Cabinetmakers strengthen this form in a variety of ways:

1. The addition of a back will strengthen and square a cabinet.

2. If the open end of the box is divided into compartments so that drawers can be inserted, the basic open box will be reinforced [Fig. 6-33(a)].

3. The installation of shelves or vertical dividers will also stiffen this basic cabinet.

4. The use of stiffer materials in the sides and bottom of the carcase will provide added reinforcement [Fig. 6-27(b) and (f)].

5. The addition of a base unit, or plinth, will support the bottom and reduce the tendency for the bottom to sag [Fig. 6-27(c)].

6. The installation of heavy frames in the opening, to support doors, will make the frame more rigid [Fig. 6-27(d)].

7. Posts which double as legs are sometimes used to stiffen the vertical components of the cabinet [Fig. 6-27(e)].

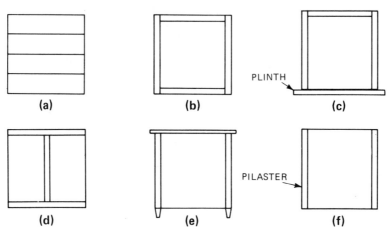

Fig. 6–27. Reinforcing the carcase

Fig. 6-28. Grain direction on carcase

Materials Used to Construct the Carcase

Veneered hardwood plywood is one of the materials used in constructing contemporary-styled carcases. This material allows simple butt-joint construction and provides an unbroken exterior surface Particle board can be combined with plywood because both are dimensionally stable. Cabinet tops are often made of particle board. Solid or glued wood should not be combined with plywood or nonwood materials because it expands and contracts across the grain significantly.

The grain direction of face veneers on plywood is usually arranged as shown in Fig. 6-28. The vertical grain direction in vertical surfaces (e.g., doors and sides) looks "right" because that is the grain direction which would be seen if solid wood were used. For drawer fronts, the grain should be horizontal for the same reason (Fig. 6-28).

Carcase Tops

Carcases with integral tops. The simplest type of carcase has a top which is one of the four basic parts of the box. Figure 6-29 shows a carcase made of hardwood veneered plywood, with the top covered with a plastic laminate or veneer. The sides, top, and bottom are jointed with a rabbet dado. In Fig. 6-30 the top is positioned above the sides. Its edges are recessed to allow for the thickness of a solid wood band which covers the edges of the

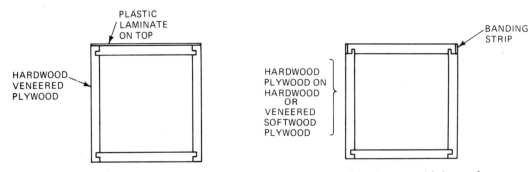

Fig. 6-29. Carcase with integral top   Fig. 6-30. Carcase with integral top

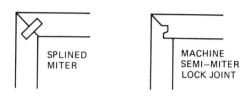

SPLINED
MITER

MACHINE
SEMI—MITER
LOCK JOINT

Fig. 6-31. Carcase with integral top

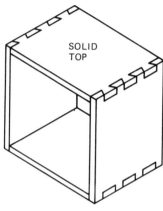

SOLID
TOP

Fig. 6-32. Carcase with integral top

DOVETAILED CONSTRUCTION

plywood. Figure 6-31 shows other types of joinery. In Fig. 6-32 solid wood top and sides are dovetailed together.

Carcases with separate tops. Manufactured period pieces generally utilize separate tops which are fastened to the carcase base. When nonwood tops are used (especially particle board), the problems of joinery are reduced by using this method of fabrication.

Figure 6-33 shows a solid undertop fastened to the sides of the carcase. In quality pieces these parts would be joined by means of a machine-made

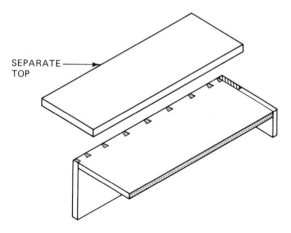

SEPARATE
TOP

Fig. 6-33. Separate top

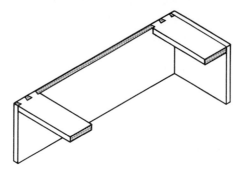

Fig. 6-34. Bearer rail top support

multiple dovetail. A solid top of this type would provide maximum rigidity for the carcase and good support for the top. Construction of this type might be used to provide extra support in a piece which is to have a marble top.

A more common arrangement is shown in Fig. 6-34, where front and rear *bearer rails* are used to connect the sides together and to support the top. Sometimes a third center rail is added. These strips should ideally be dovetailed into the side for maximum strength. Other variations, including corner-blocked butt joints, are used in medium- and low-quality pieces.

One common method for fabricating framed carcases is shown in Fig. 6-35. This method allows thin sheet material to be used for the sides of the carcase. In lower-priced pieces this might be plastic-coated hardboard. The solid posts are used to give style and strength to the cabinet. The bottom section of the post is usually turned and functions as a leg for the piece. The use of the horizontal cleat eliminates the need for more complex joinery.

Carcase Bottoms

Bottoms are fastened by methods similar to those employed for fastening tops. If a plinth is to be attached to the carcase, an open-framed bottom may be used.

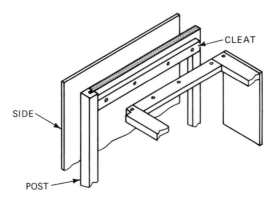

Fig. 6-35. Flush panel cleated framed carcase

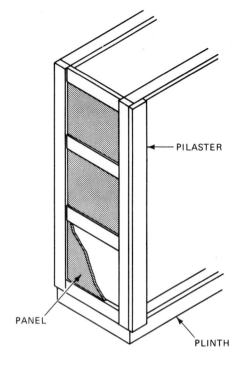

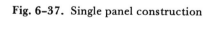

Fig. 6-36. 3-panel framed carcase

Framed Construction

Framed construction (modern) is used to save materials and to reduce weight. Figure 6-36 shows a three-panel unit in which the two intermediate rails strengthen the unit while adding stylistic elements.

In open, undivided pieces a *pilaster* (Fig. 6-36), fastened to the front edge of the carcase, stiffens the sides and provides a place to attach doors. Since the pilaster laps the top front rails (Fig. 6-36), it also makes the total carcase more rigid and keeps the top and sides square with respect to each other.

Figure 6-37 shows single-panel construction, which is simple and inexpensive to fabricate. Figure 6-38 illustrates typical construction in medium-

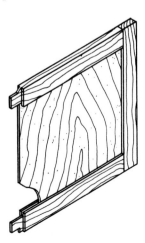

Fig. 6-37. Single panel construction

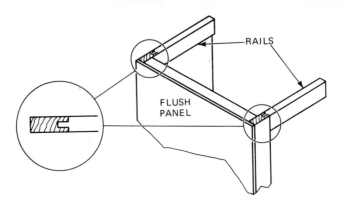

Fig. 6-38. Flush panel construction

priced pieces. The rail position allows tongue-and-groove joints to be used in tying the top rails to the side frame components. The flush panel arrangement allows the framing to be almost completely covered. When hardboard panels veneered with vinyl are used, finishing is simplified and reduced in cost.

Horizontal and Vertical Dividers

Drawer rails (Fig. 6-39) can be stub-tenoned into solid sides. These rails provide part of the supporting structure for drawers. If a fixed shelf is required, a stop dado can be cut to receive the piece (Fig. 6-39).

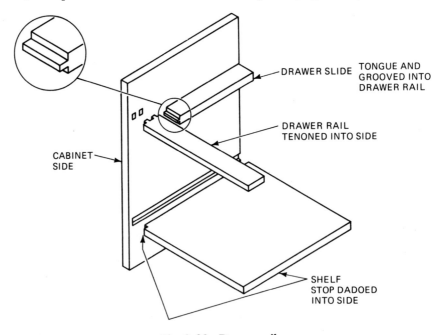

DRAWER SLIDE TONGUE AND GROOVED INTO DRAWER RAIL

DRAWER RAIL TENONED INTO SIDE

CABINET SIDE

SHELF STOP DADOED INTO SIDE

Fig. 6-39. Drawer rails

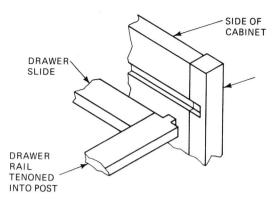

Fig. 6–40. Rails tenoned into posts

In framed construction, drawer rails can be tenoned into posts (Fig. 6–40) or stop-dadoed into posts. In some types of construction, drawer rails are not used—the entire face of the piece is covered by drawer fronts [Fig. 6–69(b)].

Drawer rails are generally jointed to drawer slides, which stiffen the side panel frames (Fig. 6–39). Slides can be tongue-and-grooved into the drawer rails (Fig. 6–39). Vertical dividers can be dadoed into drawer rails and top rails (Fig. 6–41).

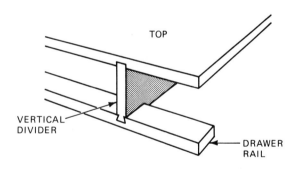

Fig. 6–41. Vertical dividers

Web Frames

Web frames are horizontal separators which serve as drawer supports and dust barriers (Fig. 6–42), and also to reinforce the cabinet. They were once commonly used in framed carcases, and a version of these frames is still used, even in some nonframed carcases, to provide support for the drawers and for dust protection.

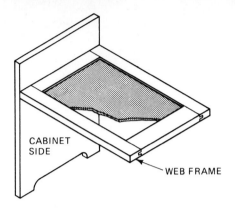

Fig. 6-42. Web frame construction

CABINET
SIDE

WEB FRAME

Carcase Backs

The primary functions of a carcase back are to close the opening and add rigidity to the structure. In most manufactured furniture, hardboard is used for this purpose. The back usually fits into a recess created by rabbets cut into the top, sides, and bottom (Fig. 6-43).

Fig. 6-43. Carcase backs

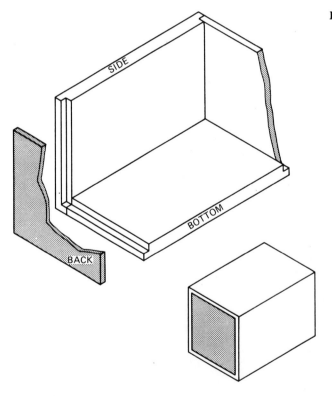

SIDE

BOTTOM

BACK

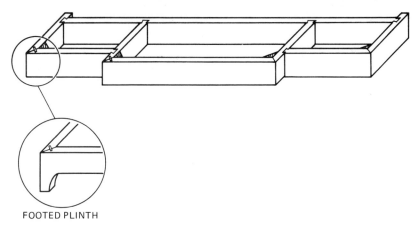

FOOTED PLINTH

Fig. 6–44. Plinths

Plinths

A plinth is a base upon which a carcase rests. In some cases the plinth is larger than the piece and provides a visual and functional foundation (Fig. 6–44). In other instances the plinth is recessed to provide toe room for someone standing and working at the cabinet. This toe room makes working on the top of the cabinet much more comfortable. Kitchen cabinets have such recessed plinths.

In quality pieces the plinth is fabricated separately and fastened to the carcase. Short feet are frequently an integral part of the construction of the plinth (Fig. 6–44). Feet provide several advantages for the furniture user. For example, cleaning under the piece is made easier. The footed unit tends to be more stable on surfaces that are not true and flat. Where unfooted plinths are used, metal guides are attached at the corners to add stability. Where mobility of the piece is required, hidden casters can be installed inside the plinth corners (Fig. 6–45).

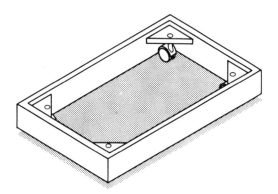

Fig. 6–45. Hidden casters

Door Construction Types

Frame and panel. Before the advent of large-dimension sheet materials, the cabinetmaker was faced with problems of expansion and contraction in large panels. One common solution, in large units made of solid wood, was the invention of the frame and panel. In such constructions the panel floated in the frame and could expand and contract as required [Fig. 6–46 (a) and (d)]. Although frame and panel doors are made today for the same reasons, most are made to satisfy style requirements.

The nomenclature of the frame and panel door is given in Fig. 6–46(e), and the various combinations and types of framing and paneling are shown in Fig. 6–46(a), (b), (c) and (d). Similar types of frame-and-panel construction are used in the fabrication of carcase sides and backs in some styles of furniture.

Solid, glued stock. Although solid wood doors are used, problems arising from the expansion and contraction of the wood across the grain often limit their use to doors which fit over openings and not into them (Fig. 6–53).

Plywood. Plywood is ideally suited for doors because of its dimensional stability. However, problems arise when veneer core plywood is used, because hardware can be fastened successfully only to the faces of veneer core plywood (Fig. 6–47).

Particle board. Particle board can be used for doors, but limitations exist in attaching fastenings to this material. In addition, the faces of particle board are not generally acceptable for use on exposed doors unless covered with material such as plastic laminate or veneer.

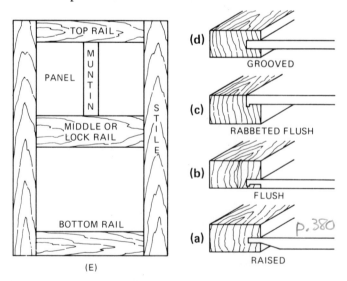

Fig. 6–46. Frame and panel construction

Fig. 6–47. Lipped door hinge

Hardboard. Hardboard can be used for rough work and is suitable for sliding doors. Like particle board, it suffers from some limitations relative to fastenings. Kitchen cabinet doors are sometimes made of hardboard because the smooth finish makes it suitable for painting.

Hollow doors. Hollow, flush doors (Fig. 6–48) are relatively inexpensive and light in weight. They are usually constructed of two sheets of 1/8-in.-thick plywood mounted on a wooden or plastic flush frame. The space between the plywood sheets is fitted with corrugated cardboard or plastic strips which help to support the plywood surfaces. The solid wood edges of the doors allow hardware to be attached securely.

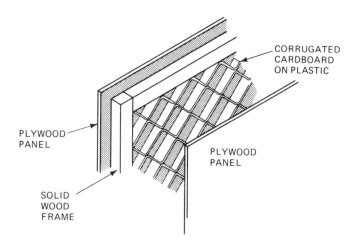

Fig. 6–48. Hollow door construction

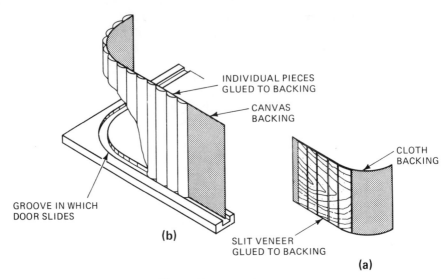

Fig. 6–49. Flexible doors

Flexible doors. Flexible doors are similar in construction to rolltop desk covers. A sheet of veneer is cut into narrow strips and glued to a flexible canvas backing material [Fig. 6–49(a)]. When the door is flat, the joints in the veneer are almost invisible. The canvas backing provides flexibility which allows the door to be slid away through curved grooves into the side of the piece [Fig. 6–49(b)]. This type of door does not interfere with access to the cabinet's interior. An alternate method involves the use of strips of wood in place of the continuous veneer surface [Fig. 6–49(b)].

Door Mountings

Sliding doors. Sliding doors are the simplest type of doors to fabricate and fit. They usually consist of two sheets of thin material, such as plywood or hardboard, which fit into grooves on all four sides of the cabinet (Fig. 6–50). These grooves can be cut into the sides, top, and bottom, or milled wooden or metal strips can be installed in the opening. The doors are designed to overlap each other when they are in the closed position. Installation is accomplished by inserting the back door into the top slot and then allowing the door to drop into the bottom slot. Then the forward door is installed in the front track.

Though installation is simple, sliding doors have several disadvantages. First, only 50 percent of the cabinet can be opened at any one time unless the doors are removed. Second, the tracks or grooves at the bottom tend to become fouled with dust, dirt, and small objects. Finally, the cabinet is not completely sealed because a small space between the doors remains when the doors are in the closed position (Fig. 6–50).

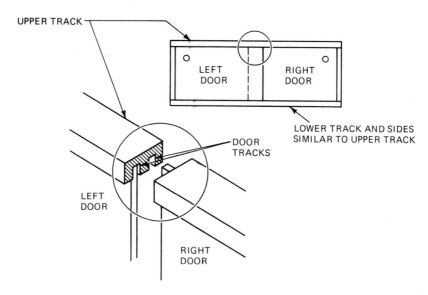

UPPER TRACK

LEFT DOOR

RIGHT DOOR

LOWER TRACK AND SIDES
SIMILAR TO UPPER TRACK

DOOR TRACKS

LEFT DOOR

RIGHT DOOR

Fig. 6-50. Sliding doors

Various types of rollers and tracks are available for larger and heavier doors that require them. An alternate installation, often used in pocket doors and in wardrobe units, utilizes a top track from which the doors are suspended on roller units (Fig. 6-51). In such units the lower track acts as a guide.

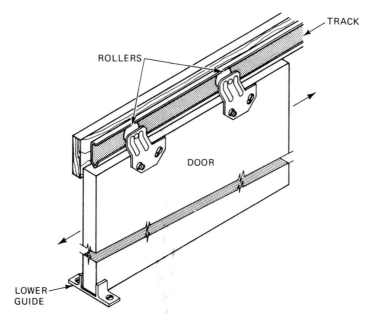

TRACK

ROLLERS

DOOR

LOWER GUIDE

Fig. 6-51. Top track rolling doors

Hinged doors.

Meeting-Edge Treatments for Hinged Doors

1. Butt meeting. This requires a good parallel match and leaves the interior of the cabinet exposed to a slight extent (Fig. 6-52).
2. Rabbeted edges. This method, like all lapping methods, requires the doors to be closed in a fixed sequence.
3. Front surface strip. This simple method of sealing off the cabinet interior reduces the precision needed when fitting the doors. The space between the doors can vary because it is hidden from view.
4. Rear surface strip. This strip is simple to install and gives the doors a butt-meeting appearance. Space must be left behind the doors for the strip (Fig. 6-52).

Flush doors fitting over an opening. This type of installation [Fig. 6-53(a)] is among the least complicated utilizing hinged doors. The doors cover the side and bottom edges of the cabinet. The cabinet top is made wide enough to cover the top edges of the doors when they are closed. If a plinth is used which extends out beyond the edges of the cabinet [Fig. 6-53(b)], the doors are fitted between the plinth and top.

Flush doors fitting into the opening. This type of flush installation [Fig. 6-54(a)] requires a good deal of care in fitting the doors to the opening. Problems arise if the opening is not close to being perfectly square. The doors can be made as a single unit and then cut in half vertically after fitting to the opening.

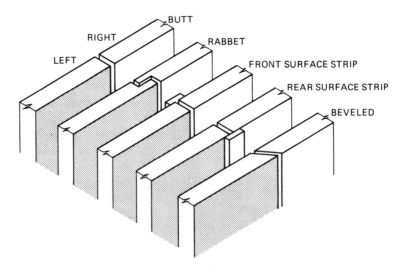

Fig. 6-52. Double door meeting

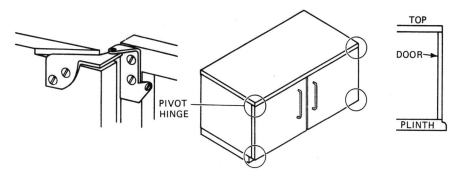

Fig. 6-53. Flush doors fit over opening. Top covers door edge

A useful approach is to fit the top and bottom edges of the door to the opening first. This is usually less difficult because the top and bottom of the carcase are usually parallel [Fig. 6-54(b)]. The door is then placed on the cabinet front, using spacers under the door to position it. With the door clamped in place, the sides of the doors are located by tracing around the inside of the opening from the inside of the carcase. The door is removed, trimmed along the lines, and refitted. Finally, the doors are cut apart. If two separate doors are to be fitted, they can be fastened together temporarily and fitted in the same way.

Lipped doors. Lipped doors are commonly used on kitchen cabinets. The lipped portion of the door covers the opening, so the actual fit of the door to the opening is not critical. Special hinges are required; the H type is shown in Fig. 6-55.

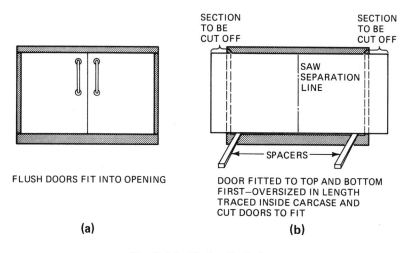

Fig. 6-54. Fitting flush door

Fig. 6-55. Lipped doors

Hinges

Butt hinges. These are among the least expensive and simplest to install. The length of the hinge is the distance from end to end of the leaves, as measured along the pin or barrel of the hinge [Fig. 6-56(c)].

The most common method of installing butt hinges is to cut a gain (recess) between the door edge and the carcase or carcase frame. This is suitable for flush doors that fit into the opening. The total gain depth is equal to the thickness of the hinge barrel. The gain can be cut completely into the door stile or the carcase frame [Fig. 6-56(a)]. An alternate method is to cut one-half of the gain required into each surface [Fig. 6-56(b)].

A simple installation method for this type of butt hinge is described below. With minor variations, other types of hinges can be installed in a similar manner.

1. Lay out and cut the hinge gains on the door stile then fasten hinges to door stiles [Fig. 6-57(a)].

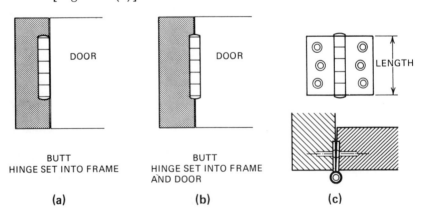

DOOR

DOOR

LENGTH

BUTT
HINGE SET INTO FRAME

BUTT
HINGE SET INTO FRAME
AND DOOR

(a)

(b)

(c)

Fig. 6-56. Butt hinges

2. Position the door in the opening, using a cardboard spacer to give the lower rail (edge) of the door the desired clearance [Fig. 6–57(b)].

3. With the hinge leaf positioned as shown in Fig. 6–56(b), trace along the edges of the hinge leaf with a pencil.

4. Remove the door and carry the lines drawn in step 3 around to the inside surface of the carcase or carcase frame using a try square [Fig. 6–57(c)].

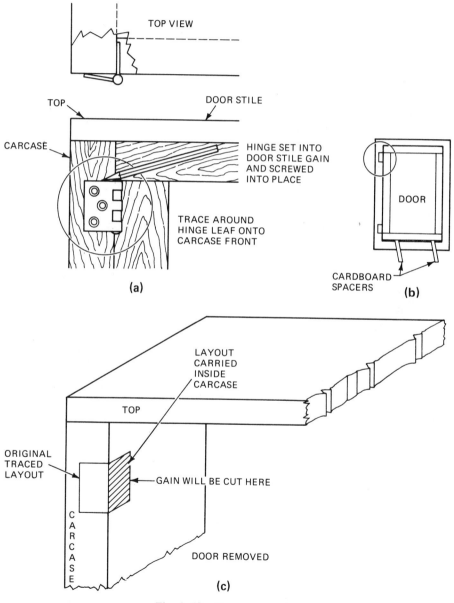

Fig. 6-57. Door removed

5. Using the hinge as a template, locate and drill the holes for the hinge. *Note:* When brass screws are to be used in hardwoods, mount the hinges with steel screws of the same size first. These will cut holes for the soft brass screws, which might otherwise twist apart in the hardwood.

Butt-hinge variations. *Loose-pin* butt hinges [Fig. 6–58(a)] allow the doors to be removed from a cabinet easily. If these hinges are installed upside down, the pins will eventually work out and the hinge will come apart. *Lift-off* butt hinges are similar in function to loose-pin butt hinges, except that the pin is permanently attached to the upper half of the hinge [Fig. 6–58(b)]. *Piano hinges* are long butt hinges which are cut to length as required. They are useful in stiffening long surfaces to be hinged and were designed to be used on piano tops [Fig. 6–58(c)].

Pivot hinges. Pivot hinges (Fig. 6–59) are commonly used in cabinet construction because they are easily installed and less visible than butt hinges. In addition, they allow the door to be swung back through 270° so that it can lie flat against the side of the cabinet.

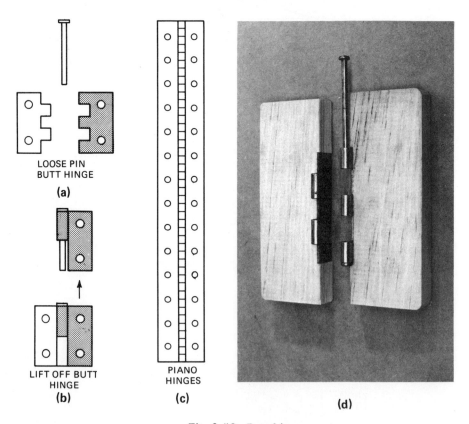

Fig. 6–58. Butt hinges

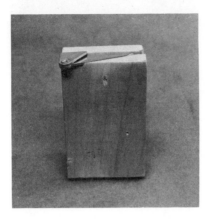

Fig. 6-59. Pivot hinges

Soss hinges. Soss hinges (Fig. 6-60) are invisible when the door is closed. They are difficult to install and are not commonly used on cabinet doors.

Mortiseless hinges. These hinges (Fig. 6-61) were developed for use on folding doors. They do not require a gain or mortise for their leaves because one leaf fits into an opening cut into the other.

Reversible screen hinges. Reversible screen hinges (Fig. 6-62) allow the hinged elements to fold in either direction. These hinges were designed for folding screens.

Surface hinges. Surface hinges [Fig. 6-63(a)] are commonly used on kitchen cabinets and on Colonial-style pieces. They are decorative, and installation is simple. The door half of the hinge is attached first; then the

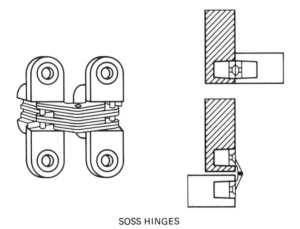

SOSS HINGES

Fig. 6-60.

Fig. 6-61. Mortiseless hinges

Fig. 6-62. Reversible hinges

door is positioned in the opening and the frame portion of the hinge is fastened. Some varieties require the door portion of the hinge to be attached to the inside surface of the door [Fig. 6-63(b)]. Hinges are available with built-in springs, which hold the door open or closed.

Catches

Magnetic catches. Catches are designed to hold doors closed. The simplest to install is the magnetic catch. This consists of a ferrite magnet, which is fastened to the carcase first [Fig. 6-64(a)], and a steel plate, which is attached to the inner surface of the door. After the magnet is loosely secured with screws, the striker plate is placed on the magnet [Fig. 6-64(b)]. The door is then closed, pushing the magnet and striker plate into the correct position. Now the doors are opened and the screws on the magnet are tightened, and the plate is attached with the screw provided.

(a)

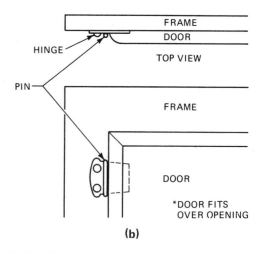

(b)

Fig. 6-63. Surface hinges

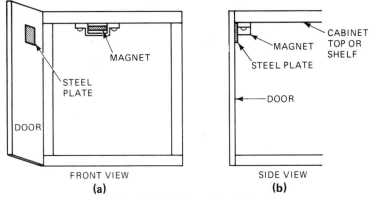

FRONT VIEW
(a)

SIDE VIEW
(b)

Fig. 6-64. Magnetic catches

Friction catches. Friction catches consist of two basic components, the catch and the stud (Fig. 6-65). They are installed in a manner similar to that described for magnetic catches. More force is required to close a door with a friction catch than to close one with a magnetic catch.

Roller catches. The roller catch is a variation of the friction type, and its installation is similar. Its principal advantage is relatively quiet operation (Fig. 6-66).

Bullet catches. The bullet catch is used where other types of catches would be unsightly or would interfere with the use of the cabinet. The bullet portion fits into a hole bored into the cabinet door (Fig. 6-67). The striker is mounted on the carcase frame or on a shelf (Fig. 6-67). One disadvantage of this type of catch is that it is not a positive stop. The cabinet door can override the strike catch, and the door can swing past its intended position.

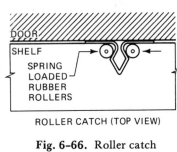

ROLLER CATCH (TOP VIEW)

Fig. 6-66. Roller catch

Fig. 6-67. Bullet catch

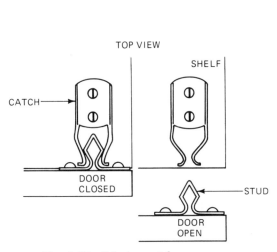

Fig. 6-65. Friction catches

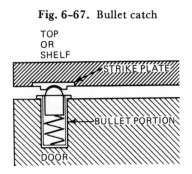

SECTIONAL FRONT VIEW

Stays

Stays are mechanical devices designed to hold, drop, or lift doors in the open position [Fig. 6–68(a) and (b)]. In Colonial pieces, desk falls were frequently supported by rails which pulled out to provide support [Fig. 6–68(c)].

Drawer Construction

Drawers are boxlike units which fit into recesses in the face of a cabinet. In the evolution of furniture, drawers came on the scene fairly late because they require a high degree of skill to construct. The quality of furniture is often judged by the type and quality of the drawers.

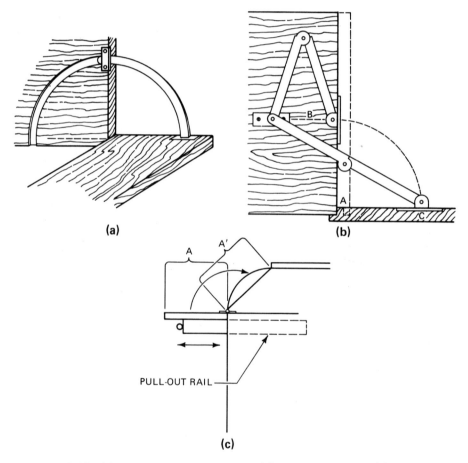

(a)

(b)

PULL-OUT RAIL

(c)

Fig. 6–68. (a) Quadrant support for flap. (b) Desk fall support. (c) Pull-out rail support

Characteristics of Well-Made Drawers

1. Ease of operation. Well-made and -fitted drawers should slide in and out with a minimum of effort. The drawer should not tip forward unduly when it is pulled all the way out. Lateral movement should be minimal, and stops that limit draw travel should be provided.

2. The materials used should be of high quality. Ideally, fronts should be of solid wood 3/4 in. thick, although hardwood plywood is acceptable. Particle board is not suitable. Sides should be of hardwood 1/2 in. or 3/8 in. thick. Oak is often used. Bottoms can be made of plywood or hardboard.

3. Multiple-dovetail joinery should be used to join sides to fronts. Lock joints should be employed to fasten sides to the backs.

Drawers are essentially flat, open boxes. The simplest drawers (e.g., those fabricated for built-on-the-job kitchen cabinets) often utilize nailed butt joints and extra-thick materials to provide the durability required. In fine furniture, multiple-dovetail construction may be used for joining sides to both fronts and backs. Bottoms are fitted into grooves cut into the sides and front. The drawer travels on a fairly complex guide framework.

Drawer Front Fit Types

1. Flush fit. In this type of construction [Fig. 6–69(a)] the drawer front fits into an opening. This is the most difficult type of drawer to fit because fitting on four surfaces is required.

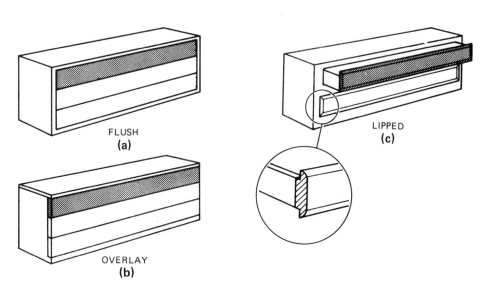

Fig. 6–69. Drawer fronts

2. Overlay. In this method of construction the ends of the drawer front cover the edges of the cabinet sides [Fig. 6–69(b)]. This type requires fitting drawer front edges to the opening. The ends overlap the edge of the cabinet's sides.

3. Lipped drawer. [Fig. 6–69(c)]. In this construction the opening is covered by a flange-like lip which extends around the drawer front on all sides. The actual fit of the drawer is hidden. Colonial-style furniture often has this type of drawer construction.

Joining Drawer Fronts to Sides

The simplest joinery method, other than the butt joint, is the rabbet joint [Fig. 6–70(a)]. In flush-drawer construction this type of joint is fairly durable because the major stress on the joint develops when the drawer is opened. If it were used in lipped construction [Fig. 6–70(b)] where the drawer front is used as the drawer stop, the joint would open in a very short time.

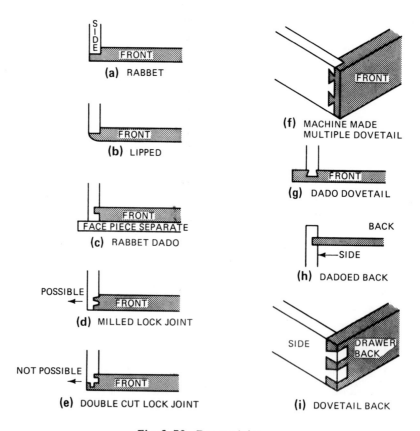

Fig. 6–70. Drawer joinery

Rabbet dado. Among the lock joints, the simplest is the rabbet dado [Fig. 6–70(c)]. This joint is commonly used in fastening backs to sides, but it can also be used for fronts if the drawer is to be faced with a separate piece. Although this method of drawer construction is not considered to be of top quality, it is used commercially and it can reduce many drawer-fitting problems for the novice.

Figure 6–70(d) and (e) illustrate two joints which are used in manufactured work. The lock joint [Fig. 6–70(e)] is assembled by sliding the pieces together with a vertical motion. The milled joint [Fig. 6–70(d)] is fashioned on the shaper and does not restrict side-to-side movement.

Multiple dovetail. The blind, multiple dovetail is machine-made and is considered to be one of the finest types of drawer joints [Fig. 6–70(f)]. Its resistance to forces pulling or pushing the front of the drawer depends on the inherent strength of the materials used.

Dado dovetail. The dado or slip dovetail is often used when the drawer front extends past the drawer sides, as in a lipped drawer [Fig. 6–70(g)]. This type of dovetail is not comparable to the multiple dovetail in strength or durability.

Joining Drawer Backs to Sides

The dado joint is commonly used in accomplishing this assembly [Fig. 6–70(h)]. The joint is simple to make and provides adequate holding power against the forces involved. The sides of the drawer are usually left oversize in length so that the short grain of the dado is strengthened. In situations where a drawer fits into a wide unit, such as a desk, the extra-long sides can be used as stops. In light drawers, such as desk top drawers, the extra-long sides also provide some insurance against tipping if the drawer is pulled out too far. In some high-quality pieces, the backs are through-dovetailed to the sides [Fig. 6–70(i)].

Drawer-Bottom Construction

Bottoms are usually fitted into grooves cut at least 1/4 in. up from bottom edges. In some types of construction, the bottom continues to the ends of the sides and is glued to the edge of a narrower back (Fig. 6–71). This assembly is easier to accomplish than one in which all of the sides must be assembled around the bottom.

Drawer Supporting Systems

Drawer supports have one basic function, that is, to support the drawer when it is in a closed or open position. In some antique pieces, the drawers simply fit into an opening made up of the carcase sides, top, and a horizontal

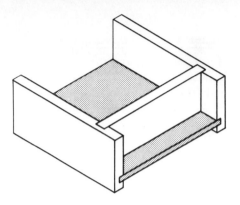

Fig. 6-71. Drawer bottom construction

Fig. 6-72. Drawer supporting systems

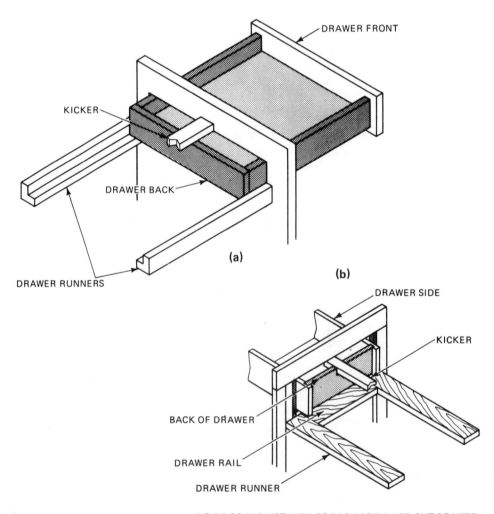

KICKER

DRAWER FRONT

DRAWER BACK

DRAWER RUNNERS

(a)

(b)

DRAWER SIDE

KICKER

BACK OF DRAWER

DRAWER RAIL

DRAWER RUNNER

INSIDE OF CABINET VIEW OF BACK OF PULLED OUT DRAWER

DRAWER KICKER

shelflike component. In such an arrangement, binding between all surfaces of the drawer and the interior of the cabinet is possible. In framed construction, runners are used to support the lower edges of the drawer sides [Fig. 6–72(b)]. A second set of top runners is sometimes installed to keep the drawer from kicking up as it is pulled out.

Kickers. In many instances, when a drawer is installed in a framed carcase, two draw guides with an L-shaped cross section are installed to guide the lower edges of the drawer [Fig. 6–72(a)]. A kicker above the drawer keeps it from tipping when it is pulled out [Fig. 6–72(a)].

In some built-on-the-job cabinets, the drawer travels on the drawer rails and is supported on drawer runners [Fig. 6–72(b)]. The runners do not keep the drawer back from moving from side to side, however. This is accomplished by means of the kicker which fits into a cutout in the drawer back [Fig. 6–72(b)].

One type of construction utilizes a metal kicker track, which mounts in the bottom of the drawer opening, a follow plate and rod, and two nylon bearings [Fig. 6–73(a) and (b)]. The follow plate and rod is attached to the center of the drawer back and it, together with the track, guides the travel of the drawer and prevents it from tipping. The nylon guides reduce friction between the lower edges of the drawer and the drawer rails.

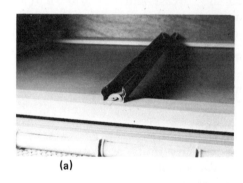

(a)

Fig. 6–73. Drawer slide hardware. (a) Drawer bottom kicker track. (b) Follower plate and rod. (c) Side-mounted metal slides (d) Roller supports

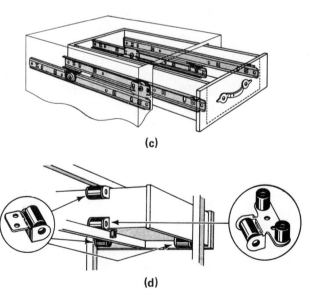

(b)

(c)

(d)

Fig. 6–74. Side-mounted wooden slides

Another type of drawer guide utilizes a runner rail mounted on the top and bottom of the drawer. Rollers mounted on the drawer engage the runner rail and provide smooth operation. They also prevent the drawer from tipping or traveling too far out of the cabinet [Fig. 6–73(a)].

Side-mounted guides. Metal, side-mounted guides are available for providing both guide and kicker action [Fig. 6–73(c)]. These units are designed so that half of the guide is attached to the carcase and the other half is mounted on the drawer side. These guides allow the drawer to operate in much the same fashion that file-cabinet drawers do.

Wooden side mountings. If a slot or groove is cut into the drawer sides and a corresponding strip is fastened to the carcase side, drawers can be provided with a simple antikick type of support (Fig. 6–74).

Fitting Drawers

Fitting side-mounted drawers before auxiliary fronts are installed. This method of fitting drawers into a carcase can be used to advantage by the novice. The carcase must be rigid and stable enough not to require reinforcement by drawer rails or guides. The directions given are suitable for flush-fitting drawers.

1. Fabricate the required number of drawers for the existing carcase so that each drawer will have approximately 1/2 in. of clearance on all sides [Fig. 6–75(a)].
2. Cut 3/4-in.-wide grooves, half-depth, into the sides of each drawer along the centerline of the sides.
3. Fabricate hardwood guide strips which are slightly less than 3/4 in. wide and approximately 1/2 in. thick. Test the strips (two on one drawer) to make sure they slide freely, but are not loose, in the drawer-side grooves.

4. Insert two of the over-length-drawer-guide strips into the drawer grooves as shown. Position the drawer horizontally, using the strips to lift and position the drawers. Clamp the strips in place, or tack them in position temporarily [Fig. 6–75(a)].

5. Install each of the other drawers in the same way.

6. When the drawers are correctly positioned and they slide freely, glue and fasten the side strips permanently.

7. Now fabricate the fronts of the drawers from 1/2-in.-thick material, and attach them to the drawers [Fig. 6–75(b)].

8. Attach the carcase back after trimming off the excess material from the runners.

This method allows free adjustment of the drawers during installation and permits the drawer fronts to be installed and fitted separately.

Hand-fitting drawers. In cabinets where drawers are to be flush-fitted, the following procedure may be followed before assembling drawers:

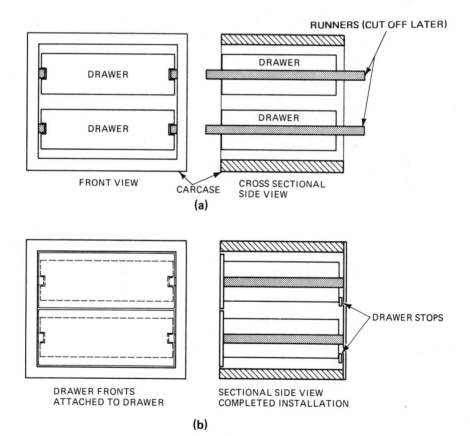

Fig. 6–75.

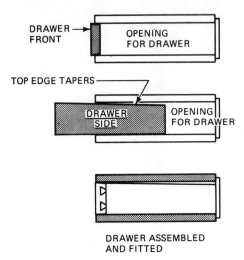

DRAWER FRONT → OPENING FOR DRAWER

TOP EDGE TAPERS

DRAWER SIDE OPENING FOR DRAWER

DRAWER ASSEMBLED AND FITTED

Fig. 6-76. Fitting drawers

1. Square-up drawer fronts to match the openings to which they will be fitted. These fronts should be oversize by approximately 1/16 in. in width and length. Bevel each end and edge slightly so that the front fits about half-way into the opening (Fig. 6-76).

2. Cut the sides with the top edge tapering slightly toward the back end so that the drawer sides fit half their length into the opening.

3. Perform the normal joinery processing and assembly.

4. After assembly, fit the drawer to the opening by slowly paring, planing, and scraping high spots until the desired fit is obtained.

Drawer Stops

The interior travel of drawers must be limited so that when they come to rest, their fronts will be in the desired location. This can be accomplished by installing stopblocks at the rear of the drawer guides, in line with the drawer sides [Fig. 6-75(b)]. Figure 6-77 shows a drawer stop designed to keep drawers from being pulled out too far.

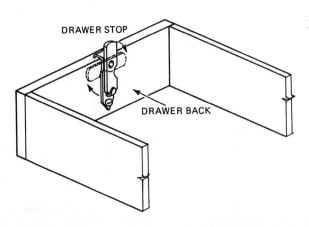

DRAWER STOP

DRAWER BACK

Fig. 6-77. Drawer stops

CHAIRS

Traditional chairs are difficult to fabricate (Fig. 6–78). This is true because of the many curved components, the angles of joined pieces, and the strength and lightness required in good chair construction.

Design

Although chair heights and shapes vary, a good rule of thumb is to make chair seats approximately 17 in. high. If the seat is tilted, it should not require the knee to bend to more than a 90° angle with the feet on the floor (Fig. 6–78). Chair seats should also be about 17 in. deep. Greater depth interferes with comfort. The widths of chairs vary considerably, with 20 in. being a common size. Arms should be about 9 in. above the seat. A back that is 18 in. high provides good support for most people. Chair backs often curve backward. The center of these curves should be about 8 in. above the seat.

Chair drawings should be made full size so that transferring shapes is simplified. Existing samples of well-designed and comfortable chairs should be studied as an aid in designing well-proportioned and comfortable pieces.

Joinery

Chair joints are subjected to high levels of stress and must therefore be well designed and constructed. Mortise and tenon joints still predominate in well-made pieces. Reinforced dowel joints can be used in some cases.

Traditional chair. In Fig. 6–79(a) through (i), the rear legs and the chair back are a single unit. This type of construction is typical because it provides the strength required when a chair is tipped back by someone seated in it. The upper horizontal portion of the chair back serves two purposes. It sup-

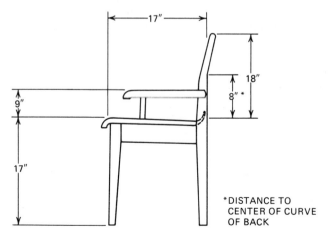

Fig. 6–78. Traditional chair

17"

18"

8" *

9"

17"

*DISTANCE TO
CENTER OF CURVE
OF BACK

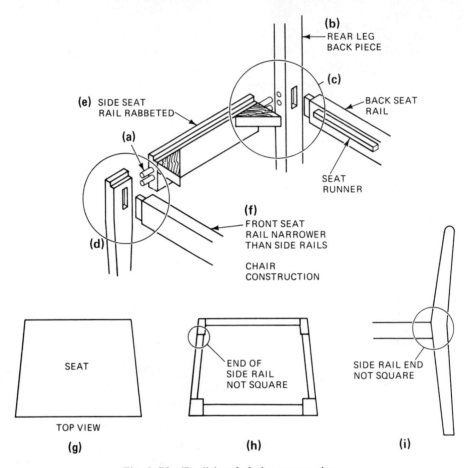

Fig. 6-79. Traditional chair construction

ports the back of the person seated in the chair and it ties the upper ends of the back posts together.

The rear seat-rail provides the major link between the back posts; this is why a mortise and tenon joint, reinforced with a corner block, is used [Fig. 6-79(c)]. The front legs are jointed to the forward chair rail in a similar manner [Fig. 6-79(d)]. Dowels can be used in tying the front and back frames into the side seat-rails [Fig. 6-79(a) and (c)]. In this case, the side rails are rabbeted to receive the seat. Note that the rear seat-rail is not rabbeted, but has a runner screwed to it [Fig. 6-79(e)]. A rabbet in this location would weaken the rail.

The front rail is narrower than the side rails, so that the seat rests on top of it and provides more comfort for the chair user [Fig. 6-79(f)]. Note that the top view of the seat in Fig. 6-79(g) shows that the seat is wider in front than in back. A seat of this shape makes the chair more comfortable since a seated person sits with legs slightly apart.

The ends of the chair rails, at the point where they meet the back post, are not square [Fig. 6-79(i)]. The forward ends of the chair side-rails are square. The cross section of the legs (front) is altered to accommodate these rails [Fig. 6-79(h)].

The grain direction of the corner brace must run as shown, to provide adequate strength. The seat base should be of plywood and must fit snugly into the framed recess provided by the chair seat-rails.

Contemporary easy chair. The contemporary piece shown in Fig. 6-80(a) is simpler, in terms of joinery, than the more traditional chair discussed above. Many of the joints are right-angle joints. Note the use of the open mortise and tenon joint on the armrests.

In this piece the armrest strengthens the legs while functioning as an arm support [Fig. 6-80(b)]. Side units are constructed first. The back is not part of the rear leg assembly. The extra-wide chair rails provide adequate gluing area to allow the back sides to be tied to it. The armrests provide additional support for the chair back. Dowels or mortise and tenon joints are suitable for the leg-rail joints.

This basic design can be altered as required. The chair arms (Fig. 6-80), which are square in cross section, can be widened or sculpted to provide more comfortable support. The cushions are made of foam rubber covered with a stretchable fabric.

Fabrication Procedure

Common practice is to build the chair back and front first. These are then joined together with the side seat-rails. In contemporary pieces, sides are sometimes fabricated as units and then joined together, using back and seat rails.

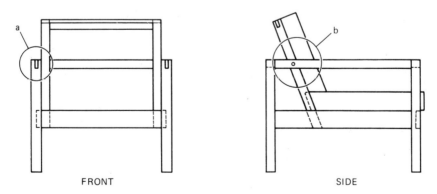

FRONT   SIDE

Fig. 6-80. Contemporary easy chair

PLASTIC LAMINATES

Heavily used surfaces, such as counter and dresser tops, are often protected by a plastic laminate. The plastic used for such purposes is manufactured by soaking several (usually seven) layers of heavy paper in a liquid plastic resin, and then combining them under heat and pressure to form a continuous sheet. The color or pattern of a particular laminate is determined by the top sheet of paper, which has a pattern printed on it.

Plastic laminate is available in two standard thicknesses, 1/16 in. and 1/32 in. The 1/16-in. material is designed for heavily used horizontal surfaces such as counter tops. The thinner material is intended for vertical or light-use applications.

A variety of sheet sizes are available, including 2-, 3-, and 4-ft widths and 3-, 4-, 6-, 8-, and 12-ft lengths. The material is available in many colors, patterns, and finishes, ranging from solid glossy to patterned slate.

Estimating Quantity Required

A simple way to estimate the quantity of any sheet material is as follows:

1. Lay out the surfaces to be covered to scale on graph paper. That is, assign a convenient value, such as 1 in. or 1 ft, to each square, and draw each of the surfaces to be covered on graph paper.

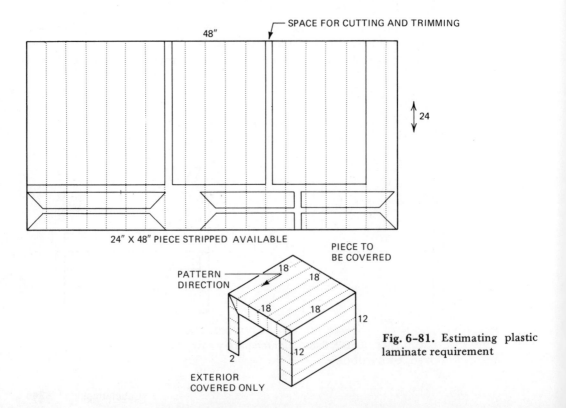

Fig. 6-81. Estimating plastic laminate requirement

2. Cut out the shapes drawn on the graph paper, and indicate pattern direction on each if necessary (Fig. 6–81). If a directional pattern such as a stripe is to be used, it is important to determine how the pattern will be oriented on each piece. If a solid pattern is used, the cutouts can be placed in almost any position.

3. On another sheet of graph paper, using the same scale, draw rectangles representing several standard sizes of plastic laminate sheet. Indicate pattern direction on the sheets if necessary (Fig. 6–81).

4. Arrange the cutouts prepared in step 2 on the sheet, starting with the largest pieces. Where appropriate, align the cutouts with the pattern direction on the larger sheets representing the stock pieces of plastic laminate. Align the straight edges of the pattern pieces with the edges of the plastic laminate to reduce the number of cuts required (Fig. 6–81). Allow scrap material for cutting out and trimming. A minimum of 1/2 in. should be left around each piece, with 1-1/2 in. between pieces (Fig. 6–81). This is necessary if a router bit is to be used for cutting the material. If a saw is to be used, somewhat less space can be left between pieces.

5. After determining the minimum-size sheet that can be used, purchase the material and begin the actual layout cutting.

Rough-Cutting Plastic Laminate to Size

Several methods can be used to cut plastic laminate to rough dimensions.

The ideal method involves using a carbide-tipped saw blade with small teeth (designed to cut plastic laminates) on the circular saw. For infrequent cutting, a 10-in. hollow-ground blade with eight points to the inch will provide smooth cutting of plastic laminate. Such a blade will cut approximately 150 ft before sharpening is required. Band-sawing can be accomplished with a metal or standard blade of suitable width for the radii being cut. Such a blade should be of 20-gauge thickness and have four to seven teeth per inch. Cutting should be done with the blade moving at 6500 ft per minute.

A router with a straight-cutting, carbide-tipped, ball-bearing follower can be used to rough-cut the material [Fig. 6–82(a)]. If straight edges are required, the cutter can be guided by a straight-edged piece of wood which is clamped to the plastic laminate.

It is also possible to break the plastic laminate along fairly straight lines after scribing the lines on both surfaces of the plastic laminate with a hardened steel scribe [Fig. 6–82(b)]. The scribed lines should be made as deep as possible, and the piece should be supported along the break line, as shown in Fig. 6–82(b). This method is not suitable for interrupted cuts or curved cuts.

Preparing the Object to be Covered

Contact cement adheres to almost any surface, porous or nonporous. In this discussion, we assume that a material such as solid wood, plywood, particle board, or hardboard is being covered.

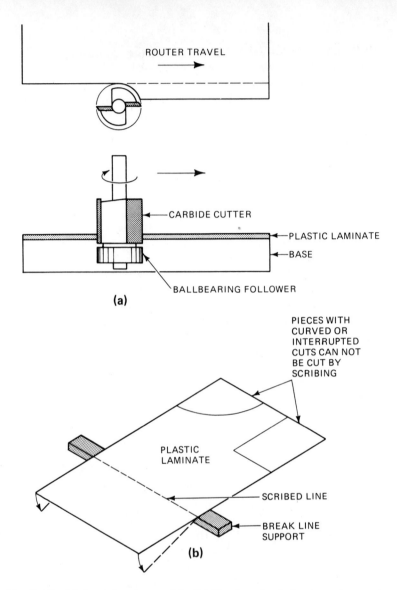

ROUTER TRAVEL

CARBIDE CUTTER

PLASTIC LAMINATE

BASE

BALLBEARING FOLLOWER

(a)

PIECES WITH
CURVED OR
INTERRUPTED
CUTS CAN NOT
BE CUT BY
SCRIBING

PLASTIC
LAMINATE

SCRIBED LINE

BREAK LINE
SUPPORT

(b)

Fig. 6–82. (a) Straight trimmer bit. (b) Cutting plastic laminate by scoring

The object being covered should be soundly constructed of appropriate materials. The plastic laminate will mask the surface, but will not normally increase the strength of joints. The surface to be covered should be flat and devoid of high and low areas. High spots tend to raise the plastic laminate, and the pattern layer will wear away more quickly in that area. Even relatively narrow edges of 1/2 in. can be successfully covered. Edges must also be carefully checked and treated because adhering failures are most common at these points of stress.

Adhering Plastic Laminate

Plastic laminates are adhered to surfaces by contact pressure adhesives known as contact cements. These materials are similar to rubber cement in composition and use. Both of the surfaces are coated. After drying, they are brought together and they adhere instantly.

Before starting, read the manufacturer's directions printed on the contact-cement container. Provide adequate ventilation and turn off any devices which produce sparks or open flames. (Latex-based cements are available which do not present a fire hazard.)

1. Wipe the surfaces with a rag saturated with lacquer thinner to remove dust, grease, and any other substances which might interfere with the adhesion of the contact cement.

2. Determine which surfaces are to be covered first. For example, in the case of a counter top, the edges are normally done first [Fig. 6–83(a)].

3. Following the manufacturer's directions, apply a coat of contact cement to the first surface to be covered and to the underside of the plastic laminate to be adhered to it. A brush or suitable roller can be used for this purpose. In most cases it is desirable to apply a second coat to each surface after the first coat is dry. To test for dryness, touch a piece of kraft (brown wrapping) paper to the surface. When it stops sticking to the surface, the cement is dry.

4. Apply the plastic laminate to the surface within 20 minutes after the last coat of cement is applied. Generally, the piece of plastic laminate is oversize in all dimensions. This allows all of the edges to be trimmed flush to the surface [Fig. 6–83(a)]. If, however, the particular installation requires that a straight-edged piece of plastic laminate be aligned with the straight edge of an existing surface, the method illustrated in Fig. 6–83(b) can be utilized.

5. Apply pressure to the laminate using a special hard-rubber roller designed for that purpose, or use a mallet and a block of wood. The aim here is to make sure that the plastic laminate and the surface being covered have come into complete contact.

If a large area such as a counter top is to be covered, a piece of kraft paper should first be placed on the contact-cement-coated surface to be covered. Then the contact-cement-coated surface of the plastic laminate sheet should be placed down on the kraft paper. The contact cement will not adhere to the kraft paper, so the plastic sheet can be adjusted until it is in the desired position. At this point approximately one-third of the sheet of paper is withdrawn, allowing a portion of the plastic laminate to adhere to the surface being covered. This locks the sheet of plastic laminate in position. Now the kraft paper can be completely withdrawn, and the surface can be pressurized.

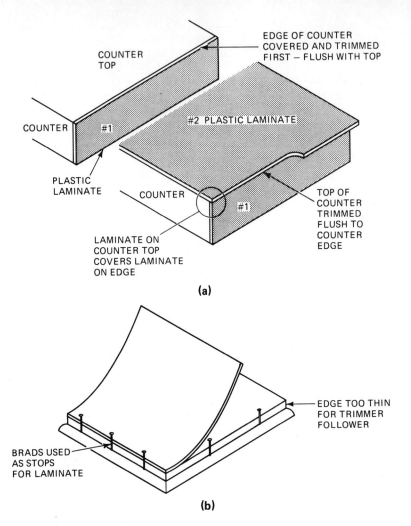

Fig. 6-83. (a) Laminating adhering sequence. (b) Fitting laminate pre-cut on surface where it cannot be trimmed

Trimming

The most common method of trimming involves the use of a standard power router and a special carbide bit fitted with a ball-bearing guide. Two types of bits are available, the straight bit [Fig. 6-82(a)] and the bevel bit [Fig. 6-84(a)]. The ball-bearing guide travels along the surface adjacent to the one being trimmed and trims the plastic laminate flush with that surface. *Any irregularity in the surface being followed will be reproduced* in the trimmed plastic laminate. In addition, the surfaces might be at right angles (90°) to each other or the finished surface of the plastic laminate will be marred [Fig. 6-84(b)]. If the surfaces are not square, a special router with a tiltable base must be used.

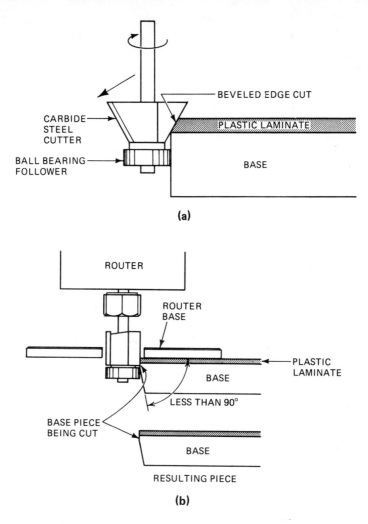

(a)

(b)

Fig. 6–84. (a) Bevel trimmer for plastic laminate. (b) Problems caused trimming plastic when surfaces are not square to each other

If conditions permit, it is desirable to wait 24 hours before trimming the laminate. This will allow the contact cement on the exposed portion of the plastic laminate to dry completely, thereby reducing the buildup of contact cement on the router bit. If time or conditions do not permit, trimming can be done immediately after adhering, and the bit will have to be cleaned with lacquer thinner as required.

1. Install the straight-trimming bit into the router so that approximately 1/8 in. of the router bit cutting edge will be involved in cutting.
2. Place the base of the router on the surface adjacent to the one covered with the plastic laminate, turn the router on, and travel it toward the

work until the follower contacts the surface. Travel the router to the right and trim off the excess laminate.

3. When trimming is complete, dust off the next surface to be covered and repeat the procedure.

In trimming the horizontal surface of a counter, a beveled trimmer is usually used [Fig. 6–84(a)].

When the trimming is complete, it is advisable to sand the edges lightly with No. 280 paper wrapped around a sanding block. This will eliminate the razor sharpness of the trimmed edges.

In trimming cutouts or interior corners, a radius is left in the corner by the router bit. If this is objectionable, the corner can be squared by filing with an appropriate metal-cutting file.

A carbide-tipped blade installed in a block plane can also be used to trim plastic laminates. Sanding materials and equipment can be used to treat the edges of plastic laminates when necessary. Where required, holes can be drilled through the plastic laminate with standard wood or metal drills.

Treating Backs of Components with Plastic Laminate

Unsupported units such as doors should have both faces coated with plastic laminate rather than just the show face. If this is not done, warping is likely to occur. Though standard material can be used for this purpose, low-cost backing plastic laminates are available.

Mitered Corners

In covering units like the table shown in Fig. 6–81, a miter joint allows two fairly small pieces of material to be utilized. This miter is obtained by clamping the pieces to a mitered guide piece as shown. If the pieces do not

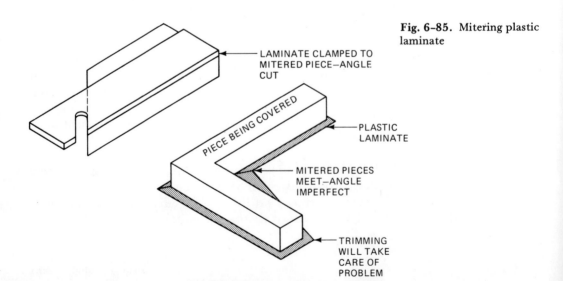

Fig. 6–85. Mitering plastic laminate

LAMINATE CLAMPED TO MITERED PIECE—ANGLE CUT

PIECE BEING COVERED

PLASTIC LAMINATE

MITERED PIECES MEET—ANGLE IMPERFECT

TRIMMING WILL TAKE CARE OF PROBLEM

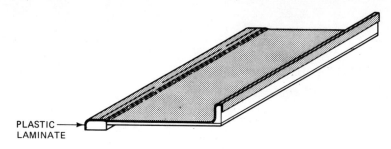

PLASTIC
LAMINATE

Fig. 6-86. Postformed counter top

have a directional pattern and are oversize in width, a perfect miter joint can be obtained even if the angle cut is not precise (Fig. 6-85). The edges are trimmed after adhering as usual.

Postformed Counters

Postformed counters are available for use on counter tops. These counters have the advantage of a continuous unbroken surface which facilitates cleaning. In addition, the raised area just above the edge helps to keep spilled liquids from running over the edge (Fig. 6-86). Such counters are sold by the running foot. Preshaped end caps are available for use with these counter tops.

WOODBENDING AND LAMINATION

The bendability of wood has been recognized and utilized by man for almost as long as wood itself has been harvested and used. Even the casual observer of nature has seen tree limbs and branches sway in the wind. For centuries, archers have used the natural spring of wood to propel their arrows. In spite of this awareness of wood's ability to bend, the student and craftsman too often think of wood as a rigid, unyielding material which must be assembled in pieces using complex and inherently weak joints. This chapter tells how to take advantage of the bendability of wood. The techniques described will enable the student and craftsman to take a fresh look at project design and fabrication and to design and construct more creatively than is possible with traditional methods of fabrication.

Many woodworkers have been faced with the problem of making curved components for various pieces. For example, the chair back requires a curved shape because the human spine is curved. The most obvious approach to this problem might be to take a block of wood of suitable dimensions and lay out and cut out the required curved piece. The resulting piece would be curved, but also very weak and fragile because in cutting the curve from a solid piece, it would be necessary to cut across grain lines (Fig. 7-1).

A much stronger piece could be made if the solid piece of wood could be bent in some way. One way to accomplish this is by steaming the piece, which would soften the wood fibers and allow the piece to be bent to shape in a suitable mold.

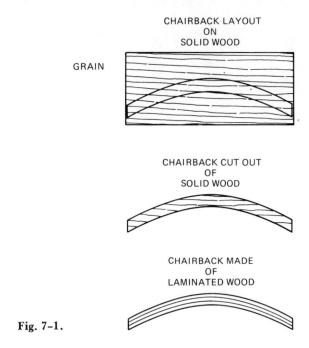

CHAIRBACK LAYOUT
ON
SOLID WOOD

GRAIN

CHAIRBACK CUT OUT
OF
SOLID WOOD

CHAIRBACK MADE
OF
LAMINATED WOOD

Fig. 7-1.

Still another solution is possible. Suppose thin pieces of wood are stacked and glued with the grain running in the same direction. If the stack is then placed in a sandwich-like mold, and the mold is clamped to bend the stack of thin pieces to conform to its shape, the resulting piece would be curved and very strong because the grain would be parallel to the curvature of the piece. This process is wood lamination bending.

A *wood lamination* is any piece of wood that has been made by gluing layers of wood together, with the grain of each layer going in the same direction. The thickness of the layers can vary and the piece may be flat or curved.

In a *bent wood lamination,* pieces of wood are stacked one on another, with their grain running in the same direction, and are then placed in a device which holds them in a curved shape until the glue between the layers has set.

TYPES OF MOLDS

Sandwich Mold

A mold formed from a single piece of wood by making a curved saw cut or a pair of parallel saw cuts is known as a *sandwich* mold (Fig. 7-2). A sandwich mold is useful for making a variety of simple shapes. It is a good device to use to gain experience with the laminating process because of its

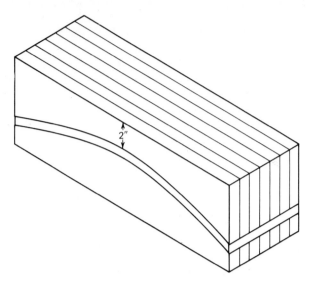

Fig. 7-2. Sandwich-type mold

simplicity and because it can use several different types of woods for laminating. Projects such as drawer pulls, salad servers, and coat hooks can be made using sandwich molds.

Designing a sandwich mold.

1. Sketch the piece to be produced. Two views are required: a side or profile view and a top view.

2. Square a block of wood of suitable size for the mold. A hardwood such as maple works well. The length of the mold block should be 2 in. longer than the lamination to be produced. The width of the block should be 1 in. wider than the width of the finished lamination at its widest point. The thickness of the mold block should provide at least 2 in. of material between the curve to be cut and the edge of the block (Fig. 7-2).

3. Lay out the curve along the midline of the block. If the curve is fairly flat, only one cut is required. If the curve is more abrupt, a pair of parallel saw cuts must be made. The distance between these parallel saw cuts should be equal to the thickness of the desired lamination because as the two sides of the curve form a more acute angle, space between the mold halves is reduced when the mold halves are mated (Fig. 7-3).

Using a sandwich mold.

1. Select and prepare material to be used for the lamination. Straight-grained wood is the most suitable, and wood from the scrap box may be resawed and surfaced for this purpose. The practical thickness limit in this processing method is about 1/8 in. Wood of this thickness can be bent

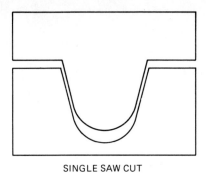 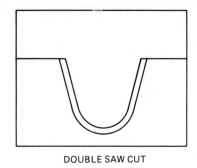

SINGLE SAW CUT   DOUBLE SAW CUT

Fig. 7-3. Mold design

around a minimum radius of 5 in. if a hardwood is used and 7-1/2 in. if a softwood is used. These radii are determined by multiplying the thickness of hardwoods by 40 and of softwoods by 60. Thus:

$$1/8 \times 40 = 40/8 = 5 \text{ in.} \quad \text{and} \quad 1/8 \times 60 = 60/8 = 7.5 \text{ in.}$$

An alternate method is to test scrap wood in the mold to see if it fails when the mold is clamped. Cabinet veneers can be used in place of processed stock. This material is 1/28 in. thick; so the minimum usable radius is 1.4 in. for hardwoods and 2 in. for softwoods.

2. If desired, line the mold with a piece of sheet metal or waxpaper.

3. Apply glue to the surface of the first piece of veneer. The glue used for small areas can vary. Polyvinyl glue works well for areas of approximately 30 sq in. or less. For larger areas, for thicker laminations, or where more than 15 minutes is required for glue application and clamping, plastic resin glue mixed 3 to 1 by volume dry glue to water is a better choice. The glue can be applied with a brush over small areas; for larger areas, a roller works more efficiently.

4. Place the best pieces of material on the outside of the lamination. If the grain is not parallel to the edges, arrange the pieces as shown in Fig. 7-4.

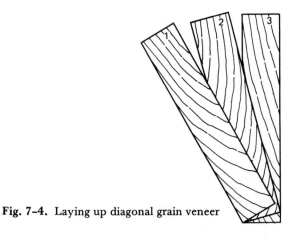

Fig. 7-4. Laying up diagonal grain veneer

5. After the glue is applied, place the lamination in the mold and pressurize.

6. Small molds can be placed in a vise and pressurized. Larger ones can be placed in hand-screw or C clamps. Some molds tend to slide horizontally when pressurized, but this can often be overcome by applying a bar clamp to the ends of the mold (Fig. 7-5).

Processing the lamination.

1. Remove the clamps from the mold and remove the lamination. Strip away any paper or excess dried glue.

2. Transfer the top-view layout of the piece from the paper to the lamination. A convenient way to do this is to cut out the top view and cement it to the lamination blank with rubber cement.

3. Cut the piece to shape using a band saw or a jigsaw. If power equipment is used, be sure to provide adequate support for the work to avoid binding during cutting.

4. The edges of the piece may be rounded by sanding with a drum sander. Surface sanding should be done with care because it is very easy to sand through the thin layers of material which make up the lamination.

5. The resulting piece can be a project in itself (e.g., a salad server or drawer pull) or it can be combined with other pieces to make a more complex project. If the piece is to be used alone, apply a suitable finish. For example, salad oil is a suitable finish for a salad server.

Limitations of Sandwich-Type Molds

Although sandwich-type molds are easy to build and work well for small pieces with gentle curves, they do have some limitations. Only a limited variety of pieces can be produced. Pieces which require more of a curve are

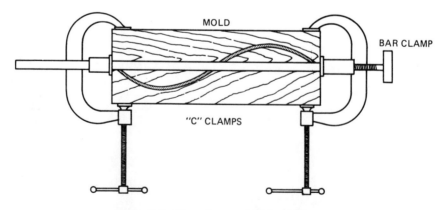

Fig. 7-5. Clamping sandwich molds

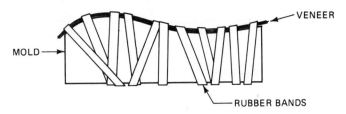

Fig. 7-6. A one-piece mop

difficult to handle during clamping. Thus, sandwich-type molds are limited to small productions with large-radius curves.

One-Piece Molds

If the lamination required is narrow (1-1/2 in. or less), a simpler mold can be used.

1. Design the lamination and transfer the profile curve to a block of suitable size.
2. Cut the block along its layout line using the band saw.
3. Retain the positive portion of the cut block for use as the mold.
4. Prepare the veneer layers to be used and apply glue to them.
5. Place the veneer stack on the mold and secure it with strips of rubber. Old inner tubes can be cut up for this purpose (Fig. 7-6).
6. After the glue has set, remove the lamination blank and process it in the usual way.

The obvious advantage of this method is that it requires no clamps. Although its use is limited to narrow laminations, fairly complex shapes can be made by this method.

THE VARIABLE LAMINATOR

Because of the limitations of the sandwich-type mold, the author developed the *variable laminator* described below. This device is capable of producing a variety of shapes of various thicknesses (Fig. 7-7). Actually, an infinite number of angular shapes can be produced. Although the radius provided by the laminator described is 2 in., any radius larger than 2 in. is possible if the diameter of the cylinder on the movable arm of the laminator is increased to the desired size. The width of the pieces produced in the laminator described is 4 in.; however, wider laminations can be made if the widths of the laminator parts are increased. The basic curved shapes produced by the laminator can be combined with other laminated pieces or solid wood pieces.

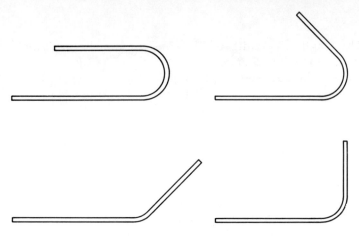

Fig. 7–7. Lamination shapes

They can also be added to table tops to serve as legs. In short, a whole new range of design possibilities is provided by this variable laminator.

The variable laminator described here can be built using supplies and equipment available in the typical noncommercial shop. A typical setup requires four No. 1 or 2 hand-screw clamps and four 8-in. C clamps with a 3-1/2-in. throat.

All of the projects shown as samples were made in the variable laminator using standard 1/28-in.-thick cabinet veneers. This material is highly suitable for use in the laminator, and suppliers can provide smaller pieces of veneer at low cost for this purpose. The variable laminator described here requires pieces of veneer up to 40 in. long and 4 in. wide. Such small pieces are considered waste by many veneer suppliers. Since only the outermost layers of veneer show on the finished lamination, less exotic veneers of lower quality and smaller size may be used for inside layers. An additional design possibility exists in the possible use of alternating layers of dark and light veneer in the lamination.

The craftsman or student experienced with more traditional methods of design and construction can begin working with wood lamination by making one-piece lamination projects such as the one shown in Fig. 7–28. Later, simple angular laminations can be combined with other parts made of solid wood in the conventional way to produce pieces such as the one shown in Fig. 7–30. Each laminator requires approximately 8 cu. ft. of storage space.

Building the Variable Laminator

The steps outlined below are provided as a guide and can be varied to suit each individual situation. Dimensions can be changed to increase or decrease the size of various components within certain limits. The diameter of the cylinder which gives the lamination its curve should not be reduced below 2 in. since this is the minimum radius for softwoods 1/28 in. thick.

The length and width of the arms can also be increased or decreased. However, remember that any very large increase in these dimensions greatly increases the time required to apply glue to the layers of veneer. This glue application time is limited by the setting period of the glue used. The glue recommended for use here begins to set in about 30 minutes; so a practical limit is set on the size of the area to be covered.

The movable arm. Figure 7–8 illustrates the movable arm (part T).

1. Cut a piece of 1-in.-thick maple, or other hardwood, so that it measures 4 in. wide and 20 in. long.

2. Turn a cylinder of maple, or other hardwood, on the wood lathe so that it measures 4 in. long (this dimension is equal to the width of both jig arms, the caul, and the lamination producible on the jig) and 4 in. in diameter (2-in. radius).

3. Cut the cylinder along its axis so that the arm (T) described in step 1 will fit into the cylinder (I) as shown in Fig. 7–8.

4. Use dowels and glue to fasten parts T and I together.

5. Bore a hole of 1-1/4-in. diameter 1 in. into the bottom of the cylinder at its center. This hole accommodates the pivot pin (J), which is 1-1/4 in. in diameter and 1-3/4 in. long. Glue the pivot pin into the cylinder.

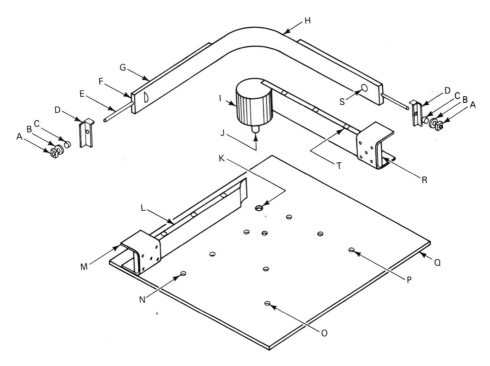

Fig. 7–8. Variable laminator parts

6. Reduce the end of the movable arm in width from 4 in. to 3-3/4 in., as shown in detail R of Fig. 7–9b.

7. Fashion the jig arm brackets [M, Fig. 7–8; detail M, Fig. 7–9(a)] from half-hard aluminum 1/8 in. thick. Attach them to the cut-away ends of the jig arms (L and T), using five steel flathead wood screws (1 in. No. 12). Drive the screws into the inside faces of L and T (Fig. 7–8).

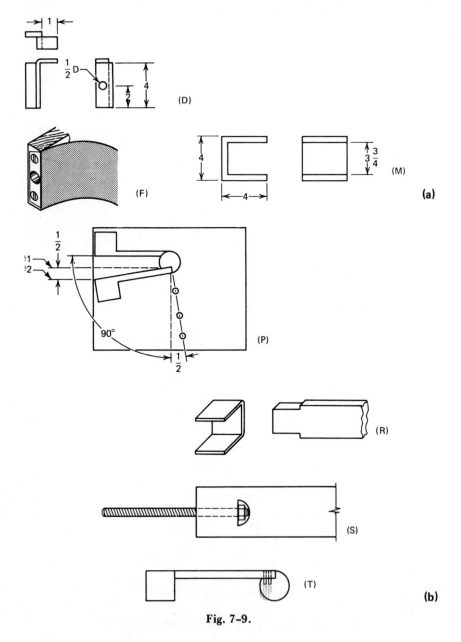

Fig. 7–9.

The fixed arm. Figures 7-8 and 7-9 show the construction details for the fixed arm (part L). Its construction is very similar to that of the movable jig arm (T).

1. Shape the end of the fixed arm, opposite the end with the jig arm bracket attached, on the band saw so that it fits against the cylinder block (I), as shown in Fig. 7-8.
2. In the edges of the fixed arm (L) and the movable arm (T), bore a series of 1/2-in-diameter holes through from edge to edge as shown in Fig. 7-8 and as described in Fig. 7-9. These holes receive 3/8 in. by 6 in. bolts that anchor each of the arms to the baseboard.

The base. Figure 7-8 shows the base (part Q) of the variable laminator.

1. The base of the variable laminator measures 30 in. by 40 in. Cut it from 3/4-in.-thick plywood, good on one side. These dimensions permit the accommodation of veneer strips up to 40 in. in length. The base may be faced with a plastic laminate if desired. This will eliminate any problems caused by glue seepage.
2. Position the fixed arm (L) on the base (Q) as shown in Fig. 7-8, 4 in. away from the edge and parallel to it. Clamp the arm to the base.
3. Use the holes in the fixed arm as a jig to bore three 1/2-in.-diameter holes through the base.
4. Bolt the fixed arm to the base using three 3/8 in. by 6 in. bolts, washers, and nuts.
5. Locate hole K (Fig. 7-8) and bore through the base using a 1-1/4-in.-diameter bit.
6. Place the movable arm (T) in position against the cutout section of the fixed arm (L). The pivot pin (J) should fit into hole K (Fig. 7-8).

Locating holes for the movable arm for various angular settings of the jig.

1. Set the movable arm (T) at the desired angle to the fixed arm (L) as shown in Fig. 7-9 detail P.
2. Move the movable arm away from the fixed arm 1/2 in., as shown in Fig. 7-9, detail P.
3. Clamp the movable arm to the base (Q), and use the holes in the movable arm as a jig to bore three 1/2-in.-diameter holes through the base. Follow this procedure for any angle desired. Detail P (Fig. 7-9) illustrates the procedure for making three angular settings: U-shape, 45°, and 90°.

The additional 1/2 in. added to the angle is equal to approximately 3°. Experience has shown that bent laminated pieces, unlike bent solid wood components, tend to close during the first 10 days after removal from the laminating device.

The caul. A caul is a mold component which is used to distribute pressure evenly along the material being laminated. In sandwich molds the caul is rigid. In this variable laminator, the caul is flexible and can conform to the various angular settings of the laminating jig.

1. Using tin snips, cut a strip of 14-gauge galvanized steel into a rectangular shape 4-1/2 in. wide and 43 in. long.

2. Bend each end of the caul band (H) to an angle of 90° along a bending line 5/8 in. in from each end (Fig. 7–9(a), detail F, and Fig. 7–10).

3. Punch two holes to accommodate 3/4 in. No. 8 self-tapping screws. After the caul rods (E) are inserted, fasten the caul band (H) to the caul blocks (G) with screws [Fig. 7–9(a)].

4. Prepare two maple blocks measuring 1 in. by 4 in. by 17 in. [part G, Fig. 7–8; detail G, Fig. 7–9(a)].

5. Cut a D-shaped hole through the face of each of the caul blocks (G), on center, and 4 in. in from one end of each block. See Fig. 7–10 for details and dimensions.

6. Bore a 1/2-in.-diameter hole into the end of each caul block on center, through to the D-shaped hole cut in step 5 (Fig. 7–10).

7. Insert the caul rods into each of the holes bored in step 6. Hold the caul rods [Fig. 7–9(b), detail S] in place with a nut positioned in the D-shaped hole in the caul blocks.

8. Fabricate two pressure bars [D, Fig. 7–8; detail D, Fig. 7–9(a)] from 1/8 in by 1 in. angle iron.

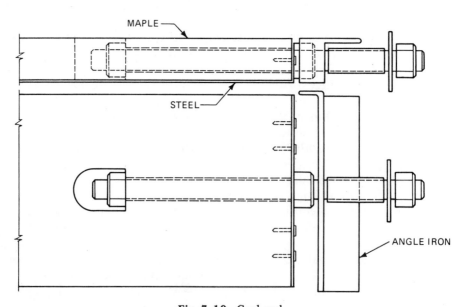

Fig. 7–10. Caul end

9. Position the pressure bars over the caul rods as shown in Fig. 7–8.

10. Cut two 1-1/2-in.-long metal sleeves (C) from metal pipe of 1/2-in. inside diameter.

11. Place the metal sleeves over the caul rods and against the pressure bars, as shown in Fig. 7–8.

12. Complete the assembly of the caul by adding steel washers (B) and steel nuts (A) to the caul rods.

When the laminating jig is in use, the pressure bars fit over the jig arm brackets. As the caul nuts are drawn up, the caul band is drawn up tightly against the veneer stack which is in position against the two arms of the variable laminator.

Preparing the Material for Use

Veneer is generally available in pieces which measure 2 to 3 ft wide and up to 15 to 20 ft long. Shorter and narrower pieces are available from some suppliers, in units of 100 sq ft, at considerable savings.

Cutting with the grain can be accomplished by sawing along a wooden straightedge with a curved veneer saw, or by ripping several pieces at a time on the band saw. When ripping on the band saw, a table fence should be used. Circular-saw cutting is not recommended because it usually causes excessive splintering of the veneer.

1. Once the veneer has been cut to usable size, check for splits and remove any tape found. Tape is used by veneer manufacturers to contain splits, and it would interfere with gluing later in the process.

2. Split pieces can be used on the inside of laminated pieces. Splits should be staggered so that they do not weaken the piece.

3. Short pieces can be used by butting them end to end on inside layers. Avoid having these joints positioned in the stack at a point where the bend will be made. If several butt joints are formed, they should also be staggered. To ensure a well-matched butt joint, the pieces to be joined should be overlapped and cut simultaneously at about a 45° angle to the edges of the strips. This will result in a perfect joint.

4. Note that the thickness of the lamination will, for all practical purposes, be equal to the sum of the thicknesses of the veneer layers used. The glue adds no thickness to the lamination.

5. If the visible outer faces of the lamination are to remain intact, a minimum of finish sanding is permissible. Therefore, the outer layers of veneer should be selected with care to ensure a sound and attractive appearance. When a laminated piece is joined to a solid piece with a scarf joint, the two pieces should be as close to the same thickness as possible. If one piece is thicker than the other, it should be the solid piece, because solid material can be sanded to thickness after joining—the lamination cannot.

6. Grain pattern should be checked on each piece of veneer to be used in the stack. If the grain is not parallel to the edges of the piece, the pieces should be alternated so that one layer has grain running off one edge, and the next layer has grain running off the opposite edge (Fig. 7-4). This will reduce the tendency of laminated pieces to deform by twisting while drying.

Any veneer that is to be stored for a period of more than 1 week should be placed on a flat surface, weighted or clamped to keep it from warping, and wrapped in plastic to keep its moisture content constant.

Adhesive Selection, Preparation, and Use

Satisfactory gluing in wood lamination depends on several important factors. The first is the setting time of the glue. It must be possible to coat the required area with glue in less than the setting time of the glue. Therefore, fast-setting glues such as polyvinyl are generally not satisfactory for larger laminations. A second important characteristic of the glue is its viscosity or thickness. Premixed liquid glues tend to be thin and runny. Dry glues such as plastic resin can be mixed to the desired viscosity. Finally, the glue should have good filling properties so that any minor voids in the lamination will be filled by the glue. Plastic resin glue has all of these desirable characteristics. Weldwood plastic resin glue mixed with water in a ratio of 3 to 1 by volume remained workable on the material being laminated for a minimun of 25 minutes at 75° F.

Mixing glue.

1. Calculate the area of one side of one full piece of the veneer to be used. Multiply this by the number of pieces to be glued.
2. One cup of dry glue mixed with 1/3 cup of water produces enough glue to cover approximately 1700 sq in. of surface, which is equivalent to ten pieces of veneer measuring 4 in. by 40 in. Determine the amount of glue needed for the area to be covered.
3. Measure out the dry glue required into a round plastic container. Measure out the water required and add it all to the dry glue. Mix with a round stick until all lumps are broken.

Applying glue.

1. Arrange the stack of veneer, with the pieces stacked in their final relative positions.
2. Place the top piece on a strip of newspaper and apply an even layer of glue to its surface with a 3-in. paint roller. When the glue is applied properly, it has an orange-peel appearance. A piece 4 in. by 40 in. should require the roller to be dipped into the glue three times.

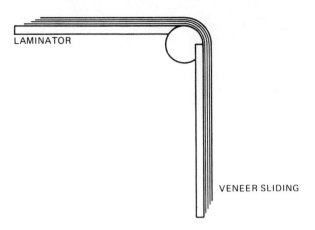

LAMINATOR

VENEER SLIDING

Fig. 7-11. Veneer sliding during bending

3. Place the second piece on top of the piece just coated with glue and apply glue to its surface.

4. Continue until the last piece has been put in position. *Do not apply glue to it.*

5. Place the stack in the variable laminator *with the layer of veneer coated with glue first, against the arms of the jig.* The last veneer layer coated should be closest to the caul. This is important because the last layers of veneer coated with glue have set the least, allowing the layers to slide on each other as the stack of veneer is bent around the variable laminator arms (Fig. 7-11). Since those closest to the caul will have to slide the most, this placement of the veneer stack is critical.

Setting and Using the Variable Laminator

1. Set the variable laminator arms to the angle desired. Figure 7-12 shows the arms set to a 90° angle.

2. Place the glued veneer stack in the laminator, with the piece of veneer first coated with glue against the fixed arm, in the horizontal position, as shown in Fig. 7-12(a).

3. Place the caul against the veneer stack so that the stack is sandwiched between the caul and the horizontal fixed arm of the mold [Fig. 7-12(a)]. Place a snug clamp (clamp 1) in position as shown in Fig 7-12(a).

4. Rotate the free end of the caul and the free end of the veneer stack down until they come into position against the vertical movable arm of the mold [Fig. 7-12(b)]. Place a second snug clamp (clamp 2) as shown in Fig. 7-12(b).

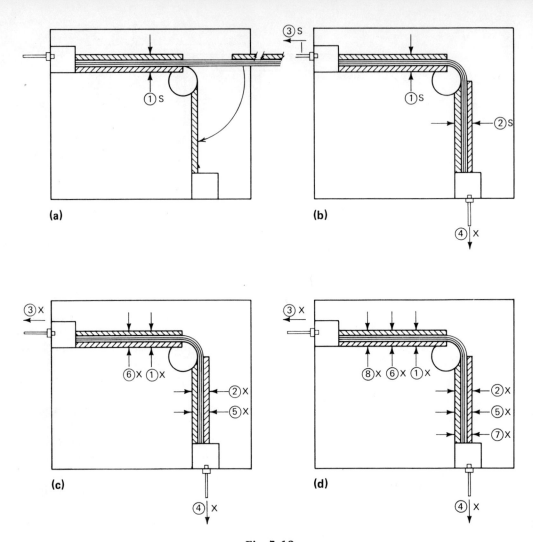

Fig. 7–12.

5. Prepare the caul clamping system by adjusting the position of the steel nuts on the caul rods to permit the caul pressure bars to fit over the jig arm brackets. Tighten each of the steel nuts [Fig. 7–12(b) and (c)] until glue seepage is detected between the layers of veneer in the bent section of the veneer stack. If no glue seepage is seen, tighten the clamp until a moderate amount of pressure on a 6-in. wrench is felt at each nut. Be sure to check the position of the caul on the veneer stack before tightening the caul nuts. The caul should be in place over the entire veneer stack. If this is not the case, reposition the caul over the veneer stack by traveling the nuts on the caul rods until the caul is correctly positioned—an approximately equal distance will exist between the nuts and the ends of the threaded rods.

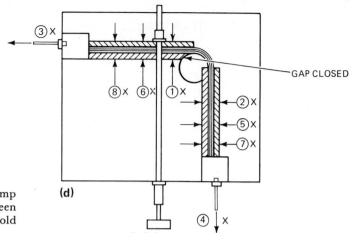

GAP CLOSED

Fig. 7-13. Use of bar clamp if space develops between fixed and movable mold components

(d)

BAR CLAMP

6. Tighten clamps 1 and 2; add clamps 5 and 6 and tighten them [Fig. 7-12(c)].

7. Add clamps 7 and 8 and tighten them [Fig. 7-12(d)]. Where possible, No. 2 hand-screw clamps should be used because of their large contact surface. However, C clamps may be substituted if necessary.

8. Leave the veneer stack in the laminator for at least 12 hours.

Possible problems. A minimum amount of glue seepage should be seen. No glue seepage may mean that not enough glue was used. Excessive glue seepage generally indicates that too much water was added to the dry glue, or too much glue was applied.

After the clamps are applied, the caul nuts may be relieved of pressure, since the other clamps will hold the caul in place. If a space is seen between the cylinder block and the curved end of the fixed arm, the caul has been overtightened. Release some of the pressure; then apply a bar clamp from the edge of the baseboard and the fixed arm, and apply moderate pressure until the gap is closed. For the U setting, a large hand-screw clamp can be applied to the arms to accomplish this (Figs. 7-13 and 7-14).

Fig. 7-14. Clamping mold in "U" setting

CLAMP APPLIED AT ARROWS

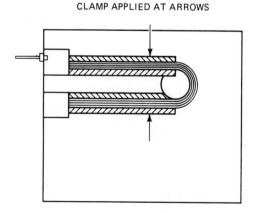

Processing the Lamination

As noted earlier, the laminations tend to close approximately 3° after curing takes place. This process takes about 10 days for completion. Therefore, processing can be started on the lamination immediately after it is removed from the laminator, but assembly and finishing should be postponed until setting is complete.

1. Remove the lamination from the laminator and scrape away any excess dried glue with a cabinet scraper.
2. Install a plywood saw blade in the table saw. (If such a blade is not available, any small-toothed blade will suffice.)
3. Set the rip fence at a distance from the saw blade equal to the width of the lamination, minus 1/4 in.
4. Place the truest edge of the lamination against the fence. This is usually the edge that was in the bottom of the laminating jig. Turn the saw on and trim both straight sections of the lamination. Now pivot the curved section of the lamination so that the saw blade cuts through it (Fig. 7–15).
5. Trim the second edge to final width.

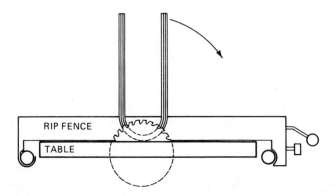

Fig. 7–15. Trimming "U" shaped piece on the circular saw against the rip fence

6. The faces of the lamination should not require any processing other than light sanding.

Joinery

The laminated angular pieces produced by the variable laminator all but eliminate right-angle joints. Most of the joints required will be located in the straight sections of various components. The technique described below is for the scarf joint (Fig. 7–16).

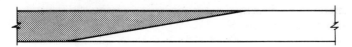

Fig. 7-16. Scarf joint

1. A special miter box can be constructed for making this joint using handtools (Fig. 7-17). Because the two pieces to be joined are cut at the same time, the cut surfaces always match exactly. Set a sliding T bevel to match the angle of the saw cut in the miter box.

2. Lay out the angle on the two pieces using the T bevel.

3. Place the pieces in the miter box with their layout lines aligned.

4. Secure the pieces with the wedges designed to hold them in position in the miter box. The wedges are expendable and therefore can be cut as the joint is cut, if necessary.

5. Place a crosscut saw in the miter box slot and cut through the pieces.

6. Apply glue to the cut surfaces and place the cut surfaces together. Place waxpaper around the joint and place two straight pieces of wood, approximately 12 in. long and equal in width to the pieces being joined, on each side of the joint. Place two hand-screw clamps over the two straight pieces and apply pressure (Fig. 7-18).

7. After the glue has set, remove the straight pieces and waxpaper, and sand the edges of the pieces until they are smooth and in alignment. Light hand sanding on the faces may be done if necessary.

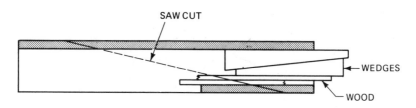

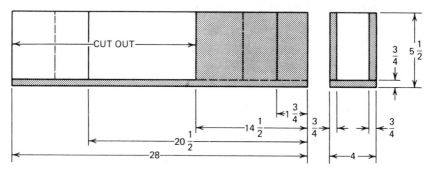

Fig. 7-17. Scarf joint miter box

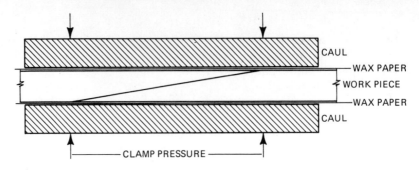

Fig. 7–18.

Machine Method of Making a Scarf Joint

1. Clamp a straight-edged piece of wood to the table of a 6-in. belt sander.

2. Set the piece of wood at an angle to the face of the belt sander equal to the angle to be produced on the pieces to be joined (Fig. 7–19). The width of this auxiliary fence should be approximately equal to the width of the pieces.

3. Lay out the angles to be cut on the workpieces with a T bevel.

4. Turn the sander on and feed the workpiece in against the fence and the sanding belt until the layout line is reached.

5. Repeat steps 3 and 4 on each of the pieces to be joined.

6. Glue the pieces together following steps 6 and 7 above (Joinery).

No precutting of the pieces is necessary if a coarse belt, No. 40 grit is used. However, rough cutting of the pieces can be accomplished on the band saw if desired.

Partial Sawing

Certain projects, such as water skis and chair arms, require a straight piece with a fairly short bent section at one end. In partial sawing, a portion of the solid piece is made flexible by a series of saw cuts parallel to the face

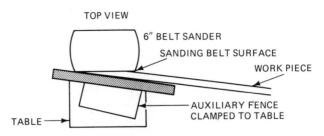

Fig. 7–19. Using 6″ belt sander to fabricate scarf joint

of the workpiece in one end of the piece (Fig. 7-20). The thin layers of wood thus produced are flexible for the same reason that layers of thin veneer are flexible. The space between the layers produced by the sawing are filled with layers of veneer coated with glue. The piece is then clamped in a mold until the glue sets. The piece retains the shape given it by the mold. The variable laminator can be used as the mold, and the procedure for cutting the layers and inserting the veneer is as follows:

1. Select a solid piece of wood free of defects and of appropriate size for the project.
2. Square-up the piece so that it is 1 in. wider than the finished piece desired.
3. Set the saw blade square to the saw table and elevated to a point that will leave approximately 1/8 in. of the material uncut (Fig. 7-21).
4. Position the rip fence so that the first cut into the piece will be into the edge and parallel to the face, leaving a layer of wood approximately 1/28 in. thick (Fig. 7-21). Then make the first cut.
5. Reposition the fence so that the next cut will leave a second layer of wood 1/28 in. thick on the piece.
6. Repeat the procedure in step 5 until the entire width of the piece has been cut into a series of such layers.
7. Place the workpiece face down on the table saw. Position the fence so that the uncut portion of the workpiece can be ripped off; then rip off the uncut portion (Fig. 7-21). This uncut section kept the layers of wood in place as succeeding layers were cut. If the uncut section had not been left,

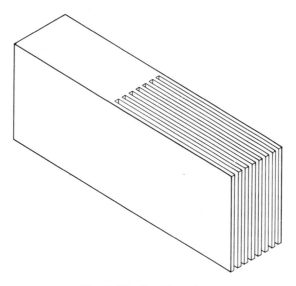

Fig. 7-20. Partial sawing

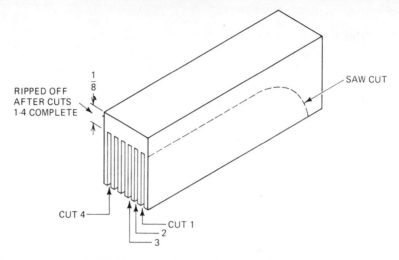

Fig. 7-21. Processing partially sawed material

the layers would have deflected during cutting and been torn out by the blade.

8. Select an appropriate number of layers of veneer to fill all of the spaces cut into the workpiece. Cut these layers of veneer to the width of the workpiece.

9. Shape the ends of the veneer layers to fit the curve produced in the piece by the saw blade (Fig. 7-22). To accomplish this, select a scrap piece that is equal in width to the workpiece. Cut into its face, with the opposite face against the rip fence, to a point where the saw blade will cut out a gain

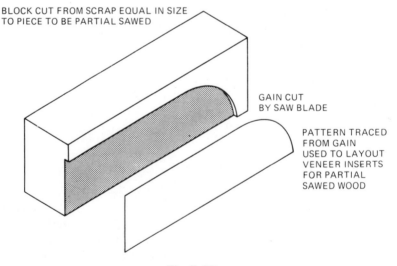

Fig. 7-22.

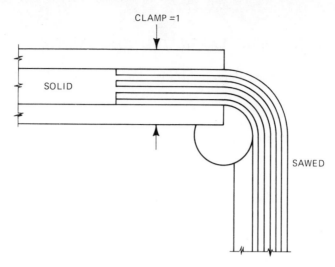

Fig. 7–23. Schematic diagram of partially sawed material in variable bending device

as shown in (Fig. 7–22). Now use this gain as a pattern in cutting the ends of the pieces of veneer to shape (Fig. 7–22).

10. Apply glue to each of the layers of veneer (both faces), and insert the layers into the slots in the workpiece.

11. Place the workpiece in the variable laminator so that *at least 3 in. of the layered section of the workpiece is in the straight portion of the mold.* See Fig. 7–23.

12. Place the caul in the horizontal position (Fig. 7–23) and apply a clamp to the caul, mold, and workpiece as shown. Tighten the clamp.

13. Complete the installation of the clamps and the positioning of the caul in the normal fashion. The correct placement of this first clamp is essential because it keeps the pieces of veneer from sliding as the caul is bent.

14. Process the piece to final size and shape after it is removed from the laminator.

Resawing a Lamination to Produce Two or More Identical Pieces

If a number of identical narrow laminations are required, a single wide laminated piece may be resawed parallel to its edges to produce them.

Edge-to-Edge Joining of Laminated Pieces

For certain applications, the student or craftsman may wish to fabricate pieces that are wider than can be produced in the variable laminator. In such cases, edge-to-edge joining may be used. The lamp shown in Fig. 7–29 is made of two identical curved laminated pieces joined edge to edge. Dowels can be used for joining.

PIECES UTILIZING BENT LAMINATED COMPONENTS

The productions depicted and examined here all use bent laminated pieces in their construction and are included to suggest design possibilities for the reader.

Sandwich Mold Pieces

>   *Piece:* Salad Server
>   *Materials:* Mahogany Cabinet Veneer
>   *Dimensions:* Thickness, 3/8 in.; Width, 2-1/2 in.; Length, 12 in.
>   *Source:* Author's Production
>   *Finish:* Corn Oil

Construction details. The piece shown in Fig. 7-24 contains seven layers of mahogany cabinet veneer. The piece was shaped in a sandwich mold using plastic resin glue. After sanding, five coats of corn oil were applied and rubbed into the surface of the piece. This project is an example of producing a single basic shape in a sandwich mold.

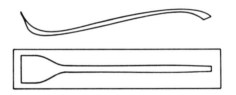

Fig. 7-24. Salad server

>   *Piece:* Trivet or Serving Tray
>   *Materials:* Mahogany and Poplar Scrap
>   *Dimensions:* Thickness, 5/8 in.; Width 9 in.; Length, 18 in.
>   *Source:* Author's Production
>   *Finish:* Deft Brushing Lacquer

Construction details. The piece shown in Fig. 7-27 contains 72 pieces of wood measuring 3/4 in. by 1/8 in. by 13 in. in size. These strips were prepared by ripping mahogany and poplar scrap 3/4 in. thick into strips 1/8 in. wide. The pieces were coated with plastic resin glue and shaped in a simple sandwich mold. An alternating pattern of dark and light strips was produced by alternating pieces of mahogany and poplar in the stack. The mold was pressurized with three bar clamps (Fig. 7-25). The piece was surfaced to 5/8 in. in thickness and then ripped in half lengthwise (Fig. 7-26). The edge of the piece (the concave edge) was ripped again to remove the concave surface. The two remaining pieces were reassembled edge to edge as shown in Fig. 7-27. The finished piece was removed from the clamps, sanded, and finished with five coats of brushing lacquer.

CLAMP PRESSURE
SANDWICH MOLD

Fig. 7-25. Trivet lamination

A
B

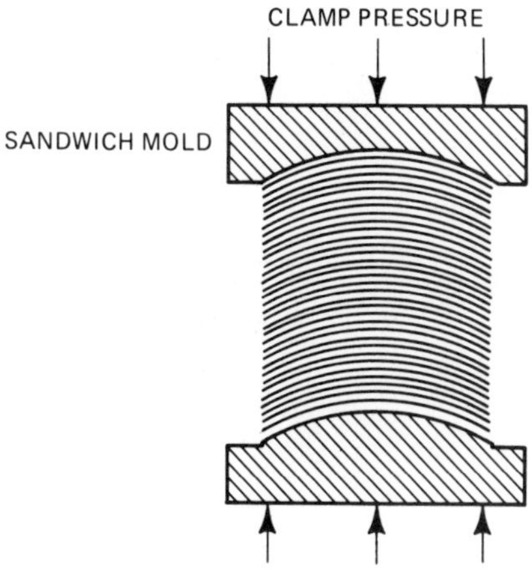

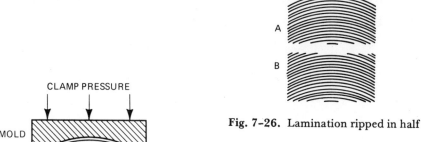

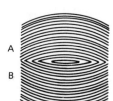

Fig. 7-26. Lamination ripped in half

A
B
PIECE "B" REVERSED AND REGLUED
TO PIECE "A"' THEN OUTSIDE EDGE
CURVED ON BAND SAW

Fig. 7-27. Trivet processing lamination

This project utilizes a single reprocessed lamination, produced in a sandwich mold, to make a more complex production which appears to be made from two basic combined shapes.

Variable Laminator Pieces

Piece: Decorative Lamp
Materials: Mahogany Veneer, Brass Tubing, Lamp Socket, Wire, Switch, and Plug
Dimensions: Thickness, 1/2 in. (15 Layers of Cabinet Veneer); Width, 2-3/4 in.; Height, 18 in.
Finish: Deft Brushing Lacquer (Five Coats)

Construction details. The piece shown in Fig. 7-28 contains 16 layers of mahogany cabinet veneer. It was shaped in the variable laminator, with the laminator arms set to form a U-shaped piece. The strips of veneer used were 40 in. long. This project is an example of the use of a single lamination, produced in the variable laminator, in project construction.

Piece: Table or Desk Lamp
Materials: Mahogany Veneer, Mahogany (5 in.), Milk-Glass Globe, Wire, Lamp Socket, Plug, and Cord Switch
Dimensions: Thickness, 1/2 in.; Width, 4-3/4 in.; Height, 14 in.
Source: Author's Production
Finish: Oil

Fig. 7-28. Lamp

Construction details. The piece shown in Fig. 7-29 contains 16 layers of mahogany cabinet veneer. The piece was shaped in the variable laminator set to produce a 40° angle. The pieces of veneer used were 33 in. long. Two laminations were made, each 3 in. wide. This piece is an example of a project produced by combining two identical bent laminated components.

The pieces discussed up to this point were fabricated almost exclusively from laminated parts. These pieces would be suitable as separate experiences in the use of laminated components in project construction. In the following section, the productions involve the use of solid wood construction combined with laminated parts. These pieces could serve as transitional experiences for advanced students who have had considerable experience with standard cabinet construction.

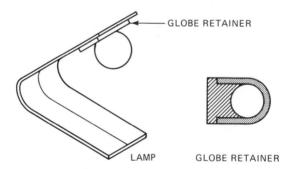

Fig. 7-29. Globe retainer

PIECES FABRICATED WITH SOLID WOOD
AND LAMINATED PARTS

> *Piece:* Table
> *Materials:* Mahogany Cabinet Veneer, Mahogany
> *Dimensions:* Length, 22-1/2 in.; Width, 22-1/2 in.; Height, 16 in.
> *Source:* Author's Production
> *Finish:* Deft Brushing Laquer

Construction details. The tabletop (Fig. 7–30) contains six pieces of solid wood joined edge to edge using dowel construction. These pieces were approximately equal in width. The four legs were laminated from 16 layers of mahogany cabinet veneer and were shaped in the variable laminator set to produce a 90°-angle lamination. The legs were joined to the edges and ends of the solid wood top using dowel construction. Holes, 1/4 in. in diameter, were bored into the tabletop, three for each leg, using a self-centering dowel jig. The matching holes in the legs were located with dowel centers which were inserted into the holes (bored in the edges and ends) of the tabletop. The legs were glued to the tabletop after it had been processed as described below.

After the tabletop was assembled, it was cut into a square measuring 22-1/2 in. on each side, using the table saw. The faces of the top were sanded flat and true with a portable belt sander; at this point, the tabletop was approximately 3/4 in. thick.

The blade on the table saw was tilted to 10°. The rip fence was set at a distance from the blade that would reduce the edge of the tabletop to 1/2 in. in thickness (Fig. 7–31). The blade was elevated to a point 2 in. above the table. The top face was placed against the fence, and each edge and end was reduced to 1/2 in. in thickness by this bevel cutting.

The top of the table appears to be equal in thickness to the laminated legs attached to it. Yet, it is really a full 3/4 in. thick and will resist warping. No rail system was included in the design, since the horizontal portions of

Fig. 7–30. Magazine table

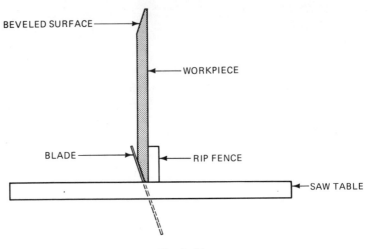

Fig. 7-31.

the legs stiffen the top in place of the traditional apron rail. In addition, the same horizontal portions of the legs add to the usable table surface.

It is important that the legs be carefully aligned with the tabletop, because the faces of the bent legs cannot be sanded into alignment with the tabletop. The 1/28-in.-thick layers of veneer are subject to sanding through very quickly. Face sanding of laminated components should be limited to light, careful hand sanding.

This piece illustrates how the unique properties of bent laminated wood can simplify construction and thereby add to the design economy of the piece. It also shows how solid wood parts can be combined with single laminated components.

Piece:	Table
Materials:	Mahogany and Ash
Dimensions:	Length, 22-1/4 in.; Width, 22-1/4 in.; Height, 15 in.
Source:	Author's Production
Finish:	Deft Brushing Lacquer

Construction details. The tabletop contains several pieces of mahogany joined edge to edge using dowel joints (Fig. 7-32). The actual thickness of the top is 3/4 in. however, the edges and ends of the tabletop are 1/2 in. thick. This was accomplished by cutting away 1/4 in. of thickness along the ends and edges of the top (Fig. 7-31).

The leg substructure was constructed of four L-shaped laminated pieces which were produced in the variable laminator with the arms set to produce a 90° angle. The three outer layers of each leg are ash, and the ten inside layers of veneer are mahogany. This combination results in a banded edge, which adds a decorative element to the piece.

Fig. 7–32. Table

The legs were attached to the top with blind dowels. No apron rail was used to stiffen the tabletop, since the thickness of the material was sufficient to keep the top flat. The rounded corners of the top have the same radius as the bend in the legs. This is a design device used to unify the top and the legs visually.

The "chaser" arrangement of the legs causes the legs to be offset with respect to the corners of the tabletop. This was done for visual interest. The chaser arrangement of the legs was secured with dowels. The legs could have been made of three pieces instead of four. If two of the L's were combined to make a U (via a scarf joint), the other two L's would meet the U at its midpoint and could be fastened to it with dowels.

The piece was sanded and finished with five coats of brushing lacquer.

Piece:	Coffee Table
Material:	Mahogany
Dimensions:	Length, 41-1/2 in.; Width, 17-1/2 in.; Height, 14-1/2 in.
Source:	Author's Production
Finish:	Deft Brushing Lacquer (Five Coats)

Construction details. The top contains several pieces of solid mahogany joined edge to edge using dowel construction. The edges and ends of the top are rabbeted to make the visible edge of the top the same thickness as the laminated rails, 1/2 in. thick. Rabbeting was selected instead of beveling because the rails are fastened to the underside of the tabletop, and a beveled surface would make this complicated to accomplish. The top is 3/4 in. thick (Fig. 7–33).

The leg-rail system was made of eight L-shaped pieces of mahogany, which were fabricated in the variable laminator from 16 layers of cabinet

Fig. 7–33. Coffee table

veneer. The laminator was set to produce pieces with a 90° bend. The rails and the tabletop were separated from each other by means of wooden spacers 3/16 in. thick. These spacers are circular disks 1 in. in diameter and they create a space, which appears as a black line, between the top and the rails. The legs were also separated with these disks.

The straight sections of the rails were made of solid wood, equal in thickness to the laminated legs. The end rails were fastened to the legs with end lap joints.

This piece illustrates how several laminated pieces can be combined using scarf joints. (The two legs on each side of the table were made of two L's and one U fabricated from two L's with a scarf joint.) In addition, it also demonstrates how solid wood and laminated pieces (the end rails and the side leg-rail system) can be combined.

Piece:	Bench
Material:	Walnut
Dimensions:	Circular Top, 33-in. Diameter; Seat Height, 15 in.; Back Height, 22 in.
Source:	Author's Production
Material:	Mahogany

Construction details. This bench is complex because it is fabricated of many small pieces of material (Fig. 7–34). The legs are made of three L-shaped laminated walnut pieces. Two of the pieces were spliced together (using a scarf joint) to form a U. The third L was attached to the U at its midpoint to form a T, using dowel joint construction. The leg assembly was attached to the underside of the bench, again with dowel joint construction. Three rubber pads were fastened to the underside of the legs to provide three points of contact between the piece and the floor. This made the piece more stable.

Fig. 7-34. Bench

An alternate method, which provides more stability, involves ripping the L-shaped piece into two L's of equal width, and then fastening these to the U at right angles, spaced about 12 in. apart.

This piece was included because it illustrates how laminated pieces may be combined to create a base. This base is a good basic unit for use with a variety of tabletops and seating units. It can also be used in the reverse position, with the flat portions of the base under the tabletop and the legs extending down to the floor in the traditional manner.

Piece:	Child's Chair
Materials:	Mahogany
Dimensions:	Seat Height, 17-1/2 in.; Back Height, 24 in.; Width, 12 in.
Source:	Author's Production
Finish:	Deft Brushing Lacquer

Construction details. The substructure of the chair (Fig. 7-36) is made of two Z-shaped pieces which, in turn, are made of two 45° laminations. The laminated parts were fabricated in the variable laminator. The two 45° pieces were joined together using scarf joints. The two Z units were connected together by two solid mahogany transverse rails. These rails were half-lapped to the laminated Z-shaped units. The seat back is supported by two L-shaped laminated pieces which were fastened to the top sections of the Z-shaped units with three No. 10 1-in. flathead wood screws. The laminated L's were fashioned in the variable laminator. The chair back itself was fabricated from 16 plies of veneer which were shaped by an internal steel bar. The bar is a piece of cold-rolled steel measuring 1/8 in. by 1 in. by 16 in. (Fig. 7-35). This method of shaping laminated wood is an interesting one which the reader may wish to experiment with.

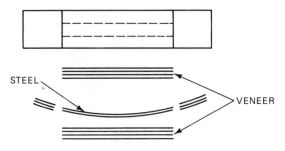

STEEL   VENEER

Fig. 7–35. Stacking arrangement used for "moldless" lamination bending

Despite the fact that the Z-shaped laminations are only 5/8 in. thick and joined at the point of greatest stress by scarf joints, the chair has supported persons who weighed close to 200 pounds. This piece was included because it illustrates the great strength of laminations and scarf joints and because it utilizes the natural spring of laminated wood. Finally, it shows an approach to a seating problem with laminated wood. The piece, or a modification of it, could easily be enlarged to be suitable for adult use.

SOLID-WOOD BENDING

Solid-wood bending has been in use for a much longer period of time than lamination bending because the technology required to prepare large quantities of veneer has only recently been developed. Solid-wood bending generally requires some prior treatment of the wood that renders it more flexible and makes bending to small radii practical. Among the objects bent wood was used for are the D-handled shovel, barrel staves, and pitch forks.

Fig. 7–36. Laminated chair

Kerf Bending

Possibly the simplest solid-wood bending method is saw kerf bending. In this process, the material is prepared by making a series of evenly spaced saw cuts across the grain of the piece. The saw kerfs are then filled with glue and the piece is bent to shape and restrained in a clamp until the glue sets. The resulting piece is relatively weak and its use is generally limited to decorative applications.

Kerf Bending Procedure

1. Prepare the material to be bent by reducing it to the desired thickness, width, and length.

2. Lay out a line across the grain of the face of the piece at a distance from the end equal to the radius of the desired bend (Fig. 7–37).

3. Make a saw cut through the line so that approximately one-sixteenth of material remains uncut.

4. Secure the piece to a flat surface, saw kerf up, and lift the end of the piece until the saw kerf closes. Measure the space between the face of the piece and the surface to which it is clamped. This distance is the saw kerf spacing interval (Fig. 7–37).

Fig. 7-37. Saw kerf bending

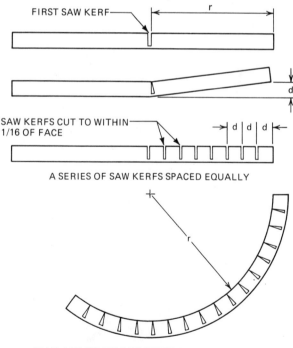

FIRST SAW KERF

SAW KERFS CUT TO WITHIN 1/16 OF FACE

A SERIES OF SAW KERFS SPACED EQUALLY

GLUE APPLIED TO SAW KERFS

5. Lay out the lines for the saw cuts at the interval determined in step 4, and make the cuts with the circular saw.

6. Apply glue to the piece so that the saw kerfs are filled.

7. Bend the piece so that the saw kerfs close. Place the piece in a clamp until the glue sets.

An Analysis of the Stresses Developed During Bending

When a piece of wood is bent the fibers on the upper face, outside the bend, are stretched or put under tension. The fibers on the lower face, inside the bend, are compressed. Steamed wood fibers can tolerate up to 30 times more compression than tension. Thus the problem in woodbending is to avoid stretching the outer fibers (Fig. 7–38).

Untreated wood can be bent to a minimum radius of 40 times its thickness for hardwoods, and 60 times its thickness for softwoods. This fact is taken advantage of in laminated-wood bending, where cabinet veneers 1/28 in. thick can easily be bent to a radius of between 1-1/2 and 2 in.

This 40 times–60 times rule of thumb is valid because of the forces at work during bending. In a thick piece of wood, 1 in. from face to face, the inside fibers compress during bending while the outside fibers stretch. At some point, the inside fibers begin to act as a pivot point and the outer fibers overstretch and fail. Thus, if a bent piece of wood fails, it is the outer fibers that generally fail first (Fig. 7–38).

Material Suitable for Solid-Wood Bending

Certain species of woods are more suitable for solid-wood bending than others. Among the suitable woods are beech, white oak, and ash. Moisture content is critical in woods intended for bending. The ideal moisture content

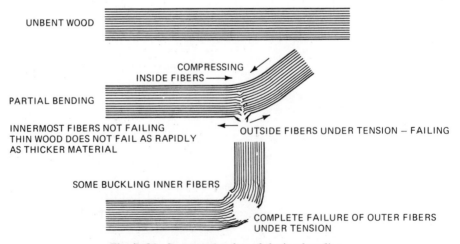

Fig. 7–38. Stresses developed during bending

is about 25 percent, which is frequently the moisture content of air-dried material. Kiln-dried woods are generally too dry for successful bending and should be avoided.

Material Preparation and Selection Prior to Plasticizing

1. Cut the material to be bent to size with about a 1/8- to 1/4-in. allowance added to all dimensions for finishing and final shaping. The ends of the material must be square.

2. Seal the ends of the material with a water-resistant coating.

3. Make the width of the piece larger than the thickness, if possible.

4. Use a support strap the same length as the length of the material.

5. Use woods that are free of defects, such as knots and checks, and as straight-grained as possible.

Plasticizing

The purpose of plasticizing is to render the fibers more tolerant to compression and stretching. This can be accomplished in a number of ways, for example, by steaming, boiling, or applying chemical softening agents. Steaming and boiling are the most practical and are discussed below.

The purpose of steaming and boiling is to raise the temperature of the wood without changing its moisture content. This is the reason the ends of the workpiece are sealed. Dry heating tends to cause excessive drying at the surface and cause failure during bending. Steaming is an ideal method of plasticizing because it allows a fairly small quantity of water to be heated to produce steam. Boiling requires a vessel large enough to hold the piece to be bent. A simple steaming device is illustrated in Fig. 7–39.

Approximately 1 hour of steaming or boiling is required for each inch of thickness of the workpiece. This plasticizing treatment increases the wood's tolerance for bending (in compression) approximately tenfold.

The Bending Device

The bending devices used to curve steamed solid wood pieces are designed to put the piece being bent in a condition of compression. The outer surface of the workpiece is in constant contact with a metal band which helps to keep the outside fibers from stretching. The ends of the workpiece are also pressurized to eliminate any possibility of the outside fibers stretching as the piece is bent. The inner surface is bent around a form which gives the piece its final shape. The procedure for bending follows.

1. Steam or boil the prepared material 1 hour for each inch of thickness.

2. Remove the workpiece from the steamer or boiler and place it against the strap of the bending device. The pith (Fig. 7–40) face of the stock should be positioned to be on the concave side of the bent piece. The workpiece

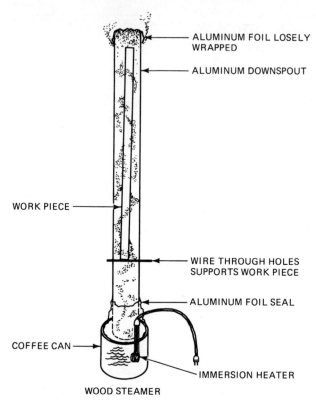

ALUMINUM FOIL LOSELY WRAPPED

ALUMINUM DOWNSPOUT

WORK PIECE

WIRE THROUGH HOLES SUPPORTS WORK PIECE

ALUMINUM FOIL SEAL

COFFEE CAN

IMMERSION HEATER

WOOD STEAMER

Fig. 7–39.

should fit snugly between the handles attached to the support strap (Fig. 7-40).

3. Place the workpiece against the mold portion of the bending device and bend the piece to shape. Insert the pins designed to hold the support strap handles in position. Insert the wedge at the center of the curve (Fig. 7-40).

Setting—Curing

The bent workpiece must be held in its bent position until it has cooled. After approximately 1 hour, the restraining strap may be removed. However, the bent piece should be kept in shape by means of retaining strips fastened to the workpiece before the restraining strap is removed.

Keep the retaining strips on until the piece has completely dried out (Fig. 7-41). Once the retaining strips are removed, the workpiece can be processed. Some spring back will occur during the first few days after bending. This is unavoidable and must be allowed for in designing the mold

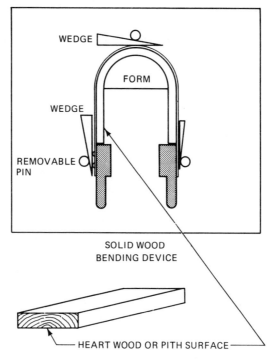

METAL SUPPORT STRAP

HANDLES PRESSURIZE
ENDS OF WORK PIECE

WORK PIECE

WEDGE

FORM

WEDGE

REMOVABLE
PIN

SOLID WOOD
BENDING DEVICE

HEART WOOD OR PITH SURFACE

Fig. 7–40.

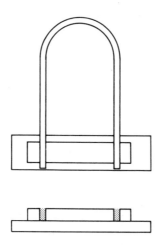

Fig. 7–41. Retainer for bent wood

or in processing the bent piece after bending and curing. It is likely that 25 percent or more of the pieces bent may fail either completely or partially during bending. This is normal and to be expected. Partial failures can sometimes be salvaged by careful processing. The bent pieces can be handled as though they were normal material. Fastening, joinery, and finishing are accomplished in much the same way as for unbent material.

Woodbending is an interesting and challenging activity which may appeal to advanced woodworking craftsmen.

8

FINISHING

FINISHING SAFETY PRECAUTIONS

The two major hazards connected with wood finishing are fire and inhalation of dangerous fumes.

1. Do all finishing in well-ventilated or fan-exhausted areas.

2. Extinguish open flames and remove spark-producing devices from any finishing area where combustible fumes are produced.

3. Dispose of rags or papers used in finishing in special approved fire-proof metal containers that are emptied daily. This will help to prevent spontaneous combustion, which can result from the oxidation of rags soaked in various oils and solvents.

4. Store solvents in approved fire-safety containers stored in metal cabinets.

5. Always wear eye protection when transferring solvents.

6. Paint and varnish removers and bleaches are powerful agents and should be used with great care. Use eye and hand protection and suitable protective clothing. Pay careful attention to the manufacturer's directions for handling.

FINISHING PROCESS

The finishing process involves applying materials to the wood that can protect the wood from moisture, enhance its appearance, and protect it against staining and abrasion. Finishes range from simple one-step wipe-on types to very complex multilayer finishes that require a high degree of skill to apply successfully.

Surface Preparation

The condition of the surface to be finished varies according to the processing that the wood has gone through up to the point where finishing begins. In new work, the craftsman should handle his material with care so that it is not unduly damaged or marred during processing. Most finishing operations begin with sanding.

Sanding with a coated abrasive, such as flint sandpaper, prepares the surface by abrading away dirt and tool marks and exposing new wood. As sanding proceeds with progressively finer abrasives, the scratches in the surface gradually become smaller and less visible. The finished, sanded surface should be blemish-free.

Abrasives

Abrasives are substances that are harder than the material they are designed to abrade. For wood sanding, several common coated abrasives are popular, including flint, garnet, and aluminum oxide.

Flint is a form of silicon dioxide. Quartz and sand are chemically the same material. Flint paper is coated with crushed quartz. This type of coated abrasive has a tan color and is graded from fine to coarse (Fig. 8–1). Flint paper does not last very long, but its low cost makes it popular as an abrasive.

Garnet-coated paper is much more durable and more expensive than flint paper. Like flint, it is a natural abrasive, and it is processed from the mineral almandine, a ferroaluminum silicate. The garnet crystals have a characteristic reddish-brown color. The abrasive cuts fast because of its many sharp cutting edges. The brittle nature of the substance causes it to fracture in use, thereby presenting new sharp cutting edges to the work.

Aluminum oxide is a brown material frequently used for machine applications. Its extreme toughness makes it ideal for sanding hardwoods. Although aluminum oxide is a natural material, the form used for abrasive grains is manufactured.

Silicon carbide is one of the hardest materials available to man. Its extreme hardness makes it very brittle. Silicon carbide abrasives are manufactured and are used mainly for sanding finishes between coats.

In the manufacture of abrasives, the abrasive grains are separated into various degrees of coarseness when they are passed through a series of pro-

FIGURE 8–1. SANDPAPER GRADING SYSTEMS

Word Identification	Number Identification	Fraction Identification
	600	12/0
	500	11/0
Extra fine	400	10/0
	360	
	320	9/0
	280	8/0
Very fine	240	7/0
	220	6/0
	180	5/0
Fine	150	4/0
	120	3/0
	100	2/0
Medium	80	0
	60	1/2
Course	50	1
	40	1 1/2
	36	2
Very course	30	2 1/2
	24	3
	20	3 1/2
Extra course	16	4
	12	

Fig. 8–1. Sandpaper grading systems

gressively finer screens. The number assigned to a particular grade of abrasive grain is derived from the screen that retains it. The coarsest screen is No. 12. This screen has 12 openings per 1-in. section of screen (Fig. 8–2). The finest abrasive is No. 600. In the upper range of grain sizes, the screens would be impossible to construct because they are so fine. These very small grains are air-separated. They are dropped into a device which allows a high-speed air stream to come into contact with the falling mixed grains (Fig. 8–3). The heavier and larger grains are blown a relatively short distance, while the lighter and smaller particles are blown farthest. The table shown in Fig. 8–1 compares the three grit identification systems in use.

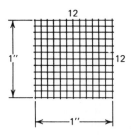

Fig. 8–2. Sieve numbers

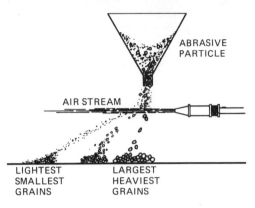

Fig. 8–3. Air separation

Backing materials. In the production of coated abrasives, the abrasive particles are applied to a glue film, which has been applied to the backing material. If both the adhesive and the backing are water-resistant, the paper is labeled wet-and-dry paper. This type of paper can be used wet to reduce its cutting speed, which is a common practice when smoothing between coats.

Various types and weights of paper and cloth are used for backing. Among the weights of paper available are A, the lightest weight used for finishing paper; C and D, which are heavier and are called "cabinet papers"; and E, which is the heaviest backing and is used for heavy-production paper. These letters, together with the grit number, are printed on the back of the abrasive (Fig. 8–4).

Cloth backings are used for machine abrasives like those used on belt sanders. J is the lighter of the two grades; X is heavier and is used for products like disks.

Abrasive paper types and packaging. Abrasive papers, or coated abrasives, are sold in several sizes and forms. The most common is the 9 in. by 11 in. sheet. The sheets are sold in sleeves containing 50 or 100 sheets. Abrasive papers are also sold in rolls.

Disks are also available for use on the various sanding machines, and range in diameter from 4 to 12 in. Sleeves, consisting of cardboard tubes with the abrasive adhered to the outside surfaces, are also available in various diameters for drum sanders (Fig. 8–5). Cloth-backed belts are manufactured for use on portable and stationary units. The width and length of the belt must be specified when purchased.

Abrasives are available in open or closed coated forms. Open-coat paper has abrasive grains spaced at greater intervals than in standard paper. This open-coat paper is most suitable for softwoods such as pine, which tend to be gummy and load the paper quickly.

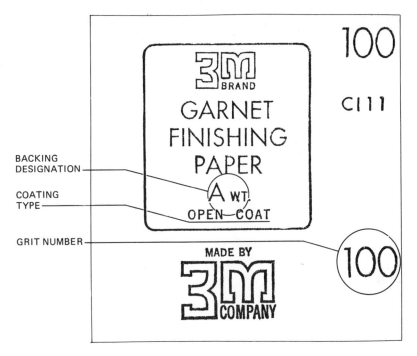

BACKING DESIGNATION

COATING TYPE

GRIT NUMBER

Fig. 8-4. Information printed on the back of a sheet of sandpaper

Sanding procedure—hand operations. Careful handling of material during fabrication can reduce the amount of sanding necessary during the finishing process. Steaming with a soldering iron and a piece of wet cloth can be used to swell any crushed fibers on the material back to their original position. In addition, pencil layout lines can be erased with a standard ink eraser before sanding.

When sanding begins, the paper selected should be suitable for the condition of the surface to be sanded. Normally, unfinished wood is sanded first with No. 80 grit paper. The sandpaper itself should be limbered up before sanding by running the paper over a rounded corner of a workbench in two directions, with the abrasive side up [Fig. 8-6(a)]. This breaks the layer of glue into small pieces, which are much less likely to peel away from

Fig. 8-5. Drum sander. (Courtesy of *Delta Div., Rockwell Corp.*)

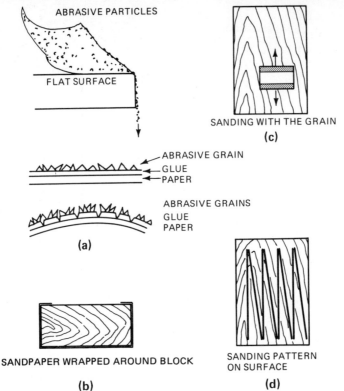

Fig. 8-6. Hand sanding

the paper backing. The paper is usually wrapped tightly around a sanding block. This is especially important if flat surfaces are to be maintained [Fig. 8-6(b)].

Sanding should be done along the direction of the grain wherever possible [Fig. 8-6(c)]. As the sandpaper is moved forward and back, it should also be moved from left to right across the surface being sanded [Fig. 8-6 (d)]. This lateral movement reduces the tendency of the individual grains of abrasives to cut grooves in the surface.

When the initial sanding has removed all visible tool marks, other blemishes, and dirt, the sandpaper is exchanged for one of a finer grade. The initial sanding takes the longest to complete. All sanding after that takes much less time because the only function of the sanding at this stage is to remove the scratches made by the first sandpaper used. The process is continued through No. 200 or No. 220 paper.

Powdered Abrasives

In the finishing of wood, loose abrasives are sometimes used. The two most common loose abrasives used in wood finishing are *pumice* and *rottenstone*. These abrasives are used to smooth the final layer of finishing material when a satin finish is desired. Pumice is used first because it is more coarse than rottenstone. It is usually applied with a felt pad dampened with oil or water. Rubbing is done along the grain direction, and when the desired degree of smoothness is obtained, the surface is wiped clean. The rottenstone is used in the same way. These abrasives are sold by the pound and are available from paint suppliers.

TRANSPARENT FINISHES

Most fine furniture is protected by a transparent finish, which allows the natural beauty of the wood to show through. If the color of the wood is to be altered, the first step after sanding and wiping is staining. Wiping is done after every sanding operation. Tack rags, which are ideal for this purpose, are available in paint and hardware suppliers' stocks.

Materials Handling

It is good practice to test all finishing materials before using. This will enable the user to determine the handling qualities and other characteristics of the finish.

Avoiding contamination. It is economical to purchase finishing materials in relatively large units. Paint, for example, costs almost twice as much when bought in quarts, than when it is bought in gallons. One problem with large containers is the possibility of contamination. A way to avoid this problem is to pour just the amount of the material required for a particular job into a smaller container and work from that container. Though large quantities are economical, remember that most finishing materials have a limited shelf life. An unused portion of a finishing material in a large can that spoils is not economical at all.

Opening, closing, and pouring. Before opening a new container, read the directions for use and clean off the rim. Dust left on the rim may fall into the finish and contaminate it. After opening, carefully punch three or four holes in the rim as shown in Fig. 8-7(a). These holes will allow any material collected in the rim to drain back into the can. If this is not done, the material will spill over the outside of the container when it is closed.

Before storing a material such as varnish or oil-based paint, which dries through oxidation, transfer the material to a smaller container so that the volume of air in the container is reduced [Fig. 8-7(b)].

When closing cans, place the lid on the can, place a piece of newspaper on the lid, and then stand on it. This will force the lid down completely without splashing and without damaging the lid.

When transferring liquids, such as solvents, from a full can, spillage can be reduced if the can is held as shown in Fig. 8-7(c) during pouring.

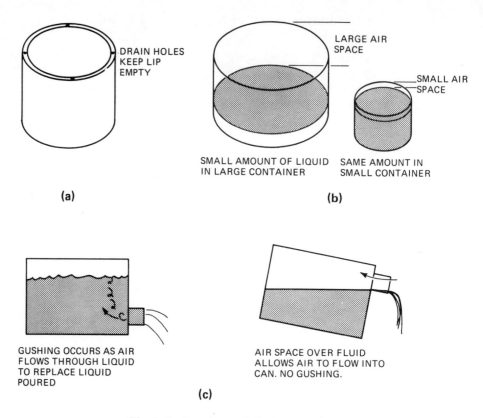

(a)

(b)

LARGE AIR SPACE

SMALL AIR SPACE

SMALL AMOUNT OF LIQUID IN LARGE CONTAINER

SAME AMOUNT IN SMALL CONTAINER

DRAIN HOLES KEEP LIP EMPTY

GUSHING OCCURS AS AIR FLOWS THROUGH LIQUID TO REPLACE LIQUID POURED

AIR SPACE OVER FLUID ALLOWS AIR TO FLOW INTO CAN. NO GUSHING.

(c)

Fig. 8-7. Opening and closing containers

Stains and Staining

Stains are colorants which are used to give the wood the appearance of some other darker wood. By themselves, stains do not protect or preserve wood. The only way to determine how a particular stain will look on a particular piece of wood is to apply some of it to a sample of the wood.

Although a walnut stain can color a piece of pine a brown color that is very similar to the brown color of walnut, it cannot change the grain pattern of the pine. Fine furniture is seldom stained. Rather, the desired color is obtained by using a wood which will give the desired effect.

Oil Stains. Two basic types of oil stains are used, penetrating and pigmented. Both types have oil *vehicles*. A vehicle is a liquid which either dissolves the solids or carries them in suspension. For oil stains, a turpentine-oil mixture is a common vehicle. A third, newer type is the gelled stain. This type of stain is prepared in a pastelike form which eliminates the spilling and splashing problems common with liquid forms of stain.

Pigmented stains contain a vehicle like turpentine and oil and a ground color similar to those used by artists. These ground colors are solids which tend to settle out of the vehicle if the stain is not stirred constantly. The presence of solids in the stain tends to muddy or mask the grain of the wood to a certain extent. Scratches or other depressions in the surface will collect more of the solids and become much more obvious.

Before staining the end grain of a piece, precautions must be taken. Even if the end grain of a piece is sanded very thoroughly, it is still more absorbent than either edge or face grain, and it will stain a darker color than these surfaces. To reduce this darkening, the end of the piece should be wiped with boiled linseed oil before staining. The oil-filled pores will not absorb as much stain and will not darken excessively.

Pigmented oil stain can be applied with a brush or a rag. After application, the excess is immediately wiped off with a clean rag. The pigment in the stain allows a certain amount of color blending or toning when additional stain is applied with a partially saturated rag. Pigmented oil stains do not generally bleed through finishing materials applied over them.

Penetrating stains. Penetrating stains are made of light oils colored with dyes. No solids are present in these preparations. Such stains allow the grain of the wood to show through quite clearly. Although the absence of pigment reduces the amount of darkening caused by scratches, these scratches do absorb more stain and appear to be darker. Nonpigmented stains are generally more uniform in appearance than pigmented stains.

Penetrating stains tend to bleed into finishing materials applied over them and therefore must be sealed. Shellac can be used for this purpose. Penetrating stains also have a tendency to fade in the presence of strong sunlight. Application by brush or cloth is possible, but dipping or spraying is commonly used for large areas.

Water stains. Water stains are dyes dissolved in hot water. They are available in powdered form and must be mixed with hot water before use. These stains penetrate deeply and produce a clear, uniform, color-fast surface. One problem with water stains is their tendency to raise the grain of the wood on which they are applied. For that reason, the wood to be water-stained is usually dampened after sanding is completed. This step causes the grain of the wood to rise. When the wood is dry, it is then resanded with the final grade of sandpaper. It is important to sand *before* the stain is applied because sanding after staining removes some of the stain.

After this final sanding, the water stain is applied. It penetrates deeply because it dries slowly. If any area of the surface is coated twice with the stain, it will appear darker than areas coated only once.

Since the vehicle of the stain is water, subsequent coatings of finishes which have lacquer or oil bases will not dissolve the stain, and bleeding will not occur.

Spirit stains. Spirit stains have an alcohol vehicle. Some of the powdered stains can be mixed in either water or alcohol. They are applied in much the same way that water stains are; however, they are not generally as resistant to fading. The problem of obtaining a uniform coating can be solved, to some extent, by rubbing overly dark areas with a soft cloth dampened with alcohol. This cloth redissolves some of the stain and spreads it out over a larger area.

Spirit stains are especially suitable for refinishing applications because they tend to adhere to surfaces which may not have been completely stripped of the original finish. Spirit stains sometimes bleed through, and into, other finishes.

Shading stains and varnish stains. Varnish stain or colored varnish is not a true stain. It is varnish which has been colored by the addition of a dye. This material tends to mask the grain of the wood to which it is applied.

Lacquer stains are available in pressurized spray cans. This material can be used for giving surfaces a shaded or blended appearance. Like varnish stain, it tends to mask the surface if applied too heavily.

Wood Fillers and Wood Filling

If a transparent finish, such as lacquer or varnish, is to be used over an open-grained wood like oak, walnut, or mahogany, a wood filler should be used to fill the pores and dents in the wood so that the final finish will be flat and free of depressions. In some cases, fillers of contrasting colors are used to produce special effects. An example of such an effect is the limed oak finish, where a white filler creates white lines and dots which contrast with the tan color of the finished oak.

Paste fillers. Paste wood fillers are either slow or fast drying. The slow-drying types have been in use for many years and consist of boiled linseed oil and silex (crushed quartz). Turpentine is used to thin the filler, and a small amount of drier (oxidizing agent) is added to speed the drying of the linseed oil.

The newer, fast-drying types of fillers have a synthetic alkyd resin, instead of the linseed oil, and these dry in as little as 10 minutes. Linseed oil fillers take 24 hours to dry.

Fillers are available in several colors, including natural, white, and various wood colors such as mahogany. The natural filler has a medium tan color compatible with most medium wood colors. White is used for special effects like liming. Colored fillers act as stains if they are applied to unsealed woods. If a colored wood filler is applied over a stained surface of a different color, the surface should be sealed before the filler is applied.

Application of wood fillers. If a paste wood filler is applied to unstained surfaces, the wood should be sealed first. Sealing prevents the vehicle (linseed oil) from darkening the wood. If the wood has been stained with an oil stain, the tendency of the raw wood to absorb the sealer oil has already been satisfied, and sealing is probably not required.

1. Always read the manufacturer's directions before using any commercially prepared product.

2. Be sure the filler is in condition to be used. Discard any filler that has hardened to the point where it can no longer be mixed smoothly into a paste.

3. Be sure that the filler is thin enough to apply correctly. If it is not, thin it as required, using the thinner recommended by the manufacturer.

4. Apply the filler with a padded rag, working in a circular motion across the grain. Wiping with the grain will rub the filler out of the pores of the wood. Do not leave an excessive amount of filler on the surface because it may harden and become very difficult to remove. Allow the surface of the work to dry until a dull appearance develops. Do not wait more than 10 or 15 minutes for this dulling to develop.

5. Rub across the grain with a padded piece of burlap, or other stiff material, to bring the surface of the filler even with the surface of the wood [Fig. 8-8(a)].

6. When the filler is completely dry, perform the next step in the finishing process.

Filling surface holes and defects. Although a paste wood filler can fill small voids in the surface, larger holes must be filled with other materials.

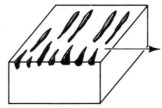

FILLING FILLS DEPRESSIONS IN THE SURFACE GRAIN.
WIPING WITH THE GRAIN WOULD REMOVE THE FILLER.
WIPING ACROSS THE GRAIN LEAVES THE FILLER IN PLACE.

(a)

| BEFORE SEALING SANDING HAS LEFT A VELVETY SURFACE OF FLEXIBLE FIBERS | SEALER COATS AND STIFFENS FIBERS WHICH ARE NOW INFLEXIBLE AND FEEL ROUGH. | ADDITIONAL SANDING REMOVES THE COATED FIBERS LEAVING THE SURFACE GLASSLIKE. |

(b)

Fig. 8-8. Sealing and filling

Ideally, a hole should be filled with wood. In some cases a defect can be drilled out and filled with a plug made from the same wood. Such a plug should be selected for grain match and color match.

Some craftsmen use a mixture of glue and sawdust to fill holes. This method can be used for small voids, especially if the surface around the hole is resanded lightly immediately after application of the glue and sawdust mixture.

Water putty can also be used to fill holes. One advantage of this material has over many others is that it is stainable. The material is mixed according to the manufacturer's directions and applied with a putty knife. After only a few minutes of drying, the material can be sanded flush with the wood around it.

For external applications, white lead putty is useful. This material is water-resistant, stays flexible for quite a long period of time, and can be painted with an oil-based paint.

Sealers and Sealing

The function of a sealer is, as the name indicates, to seal a surface so that it cannot be penetrated or affected by subsequent applications of finishes. Sealers are usually applied to the surface of wood after staining. If stain is not used, then the sealer is applied after sanding.

When a sealer (e.g., a wash coat of shellac) is applied to a sanded surface, a surface that felt velvetlike before sealing will feel rough after the sealer dries. This happens because sanding leaves semifree fibers on the surface [Fig. 8-8(b)]. These fibers, which are very fine, react in much the same way that the surface of a piece of velvet reacts when it is touched. Once the sealer is applied, the fibers absorb the sealer and stiffen as the sealer dries. Sanding removes these stiffened fibers and results in a glass-smooth surface.

Sealing reduces the amount of finish required because the sealed wood absorbs less of the finish. If the wood contains knots or pitch pockets, the sealer locks in the excess sap and helps to prevent bleeding through the finish later. If a filler is used, the sealer is generally applied after the filler is wiped and dried. The sealer protects the filler from the loosening action of subsequent applications of finishes such as lacquer.

The selection of a sealer depends largely on the finish to be used after sealing. Shellac is a popular sealer because it is compatible with almost any finish. It can be coated with lacquer or varnish without interacting with either. If shellac is used, it is diluted with alcohol until it is very thin. Three-pound-cut shellac should be mixed half and half by volume with alcohol. Application is usually by brush. The shellac should be allowed to dry for 24 hours before light sanding with No. 220 or No. 280 paper is attempted.

If varnish is used, sealing can be done with shellac or varnish thinned half and half with turpentine. Lacquer can also be used as its own sealer when it is thinned half and half with an appropriate thinner. However, the vehicle in brushing lacquers is very likely to loosen fillers and to dissolve stains. For this reason, a shellac sealer is preferred. Stains and fillers are available which are designed to be used with lacquer. In such cases, the lacquer can be used as its own sealer.

Transparent Coated Finishes

Shellac. Shellac is a natural product obtained from the excretions of an insect called the lac bug. The excretions (raw lac) are dissolved in alcohol, purified, and sold in liquid or dry form.

The natural color of shellac is orange. White shellac is orange shellac that has been bleached. White shellac tends to darken until it is orange in color after several years of exposure to light.

When shellac is sold in liquid form, it is prepared in mixtures described as cuts. Five-pound-cut shellac, a common thickness, is made by dissolving 5 pounds of dry shellac in enough alcohol to make a volume of 1 gallon. For most purposes a 5-pound cut is too thick. Adding approximately one part alcohol to three parts of 5-pound-cut shellac will give a good working consistency. For sealing purposes, a one-to-one mixture of alcohol to 5-pound-cut shellac can be used.

The most important advantages of shellac are its rapid drying and its relative stability as a sealer under a variety of other finishes. It is popular for floor finishing because of its rapid drying, its relatively low cost, and its easy removal by sanding. Most other clear finishes soften under the action of the belt sanders commonly used in resurfacing floors. Shellac does not, and thus it allows the belts to be used for a longer period of time.

Its lack of resistance to water and alcohol makes shellac unsuitable for use as a general wood-finishing material. Shellac has a limited shelf life, that is, it tends to deteriorate if kept in liquid form over a long period ot time. If the quality of shellac is suspect, test it on a piece of scrap wood before it is used on the piece to be finished. If the shellac does not dry in half an hour, it is spoiled and should be discarded.

Most shellac is brush-applied, though a roller can also be used. In floor finishing, a moplike device is used for application. Shellac dries by evaporation of its vehicle. For this reason, if shellac is brushed over excessively, especially if it is not completely dry, the solvent in the fresh shellac may redissolve the shellac already on the surface. The result may be a thinly coated area. This problem is especially prevalent with brushing lacquer.

Lacquer. Lacquer can be thought of as a plastic dissolved in a solvent. Actually, lacquer is a complex mixture of ingredients designed to produce a material that has specific desirable characteristics. Most lacquers are composed of nitrocellulose dissolved in a mixture of thinners, often including acetone, amyl acetate, and ethyl acetate. In addition, some lacquers have resins added to give the lacquer certain desirable properties such as resistance to weathering. Many wood lacquers contain 5 to 10 percent alkyd resin to improve their durability.

Most lacquers are applied with a spray gun. In commercial practice, hot lacquers have found increasing use because this process allows quick drying without baking equipment. It also allows a more rapid buildup of the coating, with less solvent required to accomplish this.

Brushing lacquers like Deft® and Satinlac® are available to the craftsman who wants to use a brush-on technique. One problem that often arises with brushing lacquers is thin spots. These spots develop when partially dry finished areas are rebrushed with a lacquer-loaded brush. This causes the finish to redissolve, and thin spots develop. The correct procedure is to apply a single coat without recoating any area until after the entire area has dried.

Varnish. Varnish is one of the oldest finishes in use. It consists of a natural resin or gum combined with an oil like linseed oil that acts as a drier. The oil changes chemically as it dries through oxidation.

The oil content of varnish has an effect on its ultimate use and drying time. *Long-oil* varnishes contain the highest proportion of oil to gum or resin. This increased amount of oil causes the varnish to dry slowly and to form a tough and elastic film that is quite durable. Marine spar varnish is of this type. In marine finishes, linseed oil is largely replaced by tung oil, because tung oil is highly resistant to water.

Medium-oil varnishes contain an intermediate proportion of oil to resin and produce a varnish that dries faster than spar varnish. In addition, the film produced is tougher and less elastic than that formed by long-oil varnishes. Medium-oil varnish contains approximately one-third of the oil that a long-oil varnish does. Varnish of this type is used for floor finishing.

Short-oil varnish contains approximately one-tenth of the oil in long-oil varnish and about one-fourth the oil in medium-oil varnish. This type of varnish is used for cabinet-rubbing purposes and provides a hard, brittle finish which can stand up to the abrasives used in rubbing and polishing.

Varnish dries through oxidation of its oil vehicle and evaporation of the solvent (turpentine) in the vehicle. Turpentine speeds the drying process because it absorbs oxygen from the air. The oxygen is then available for oxidizing the oil in the varnish. Driers, added to speed oxidation, are metallic salts of cobalt or manganese.

Synthetic resins are also used in the manufacture of varnishes. The synthetic varnishes are similar in general composition to other types, except for the substitution of synthetic resin. Among the synthetic-resin varnishes is polyurethane varnish. This finishing material imparts a very hard, durable finish to wood and is used for tabletops and other surfaces where resistance to wear is important. Because of its wear-resistance, it is often used for floor finishing. It is also extremely weather- and corrosion-resistant and is therefore used for marine and other outdoor uses. Polyurethane dries rapidly and gives a clear, almost colorless finish. Its alkali resistance makes it suitable for use on masonry and swimming pools.

Varnish dries slowly and can be worked with a brush until the desired finish is obtained. The slow drying of varnish does present another problem, namely, dust collecting. Ideally, a dust-free environment is required for varnishing.

The varnish film gradually builds up thickness after several coats, and it then becomes possible to flatten the coating through proper abrasive rubbing techniques. Wet-and-dry No. 600 paper, backed by a block, can be used to produce a flat, ripple-free surface. This can be followed by rubbing with a pad that is moistened with water or oil and has pumice applied to its surface. After a second rubbing with rottenstone, the result is a satin finish of depth and durability.

Oil finishes. The simplest oil finishing material is one made of equal parts of boiled linseed oil and turpentine. This finish is applied with a soft padded cloth, which is rubbed with moderate pressure across the grain. The oil is applied liberally and allowed to stand for 30 minutes. Then the excess oil is wiped away with a dry rag. This process is repeated daily for about 2 weeks until a finish of the desired depth is built up. If excess oil collects in the inside corners, it can be removed with a cloth dampened in turpentine.

Oil finishes are easy to maintain because they penetrate the wood and do not built up a thick film which has to be restored in the event of scratching or other marring. Wiping with a cloth dipped in the oil-turpentine mixture hides most blemishes.

Oil finishes work best on close-grained woods such as walnut and teak. However, some of the commercial penetrating oils like Watco® and Minwax® antique oil finish can be used with success on other species of woods.

Stain can be applied before the oil, or colors-in-oil can be mixed with the first coat of the oil to provide staining action. Usually, one or two applications of these commercial oil finishes are required. Linseed-based oil finishes are not weather-resistant and should be used only on interior surfaces.

Waxes. Waxes can be used as a finish; however, they are more commonly used to provide a protective coating for surfaces finished with some other material. Most waxes are derived from the distillation of petroleum. They are essentially paraffin, or paraffinlike, compounds blended with solvents and other materials that make them soft enough to apply easily. Some waxes contain *carnuba* wax, which is derived from a plant grown in South America. Carnuba wax is more durable than paraffin-based waxes. In addition, it is less "slippery," which is a very desirable characteristic in floor waxes. When using wax, the manufacturer's directions should be followed carefully.

Paints

The most common types of opaque finishes are paints. Paints consist of a vehicle, such as linseed oil, and pigments to give them color and opacity. The first paints were nothing more than boiled linseed oil mixed with pigments such as white lead. Such a paint could still provide a durable finish on exterior work.

Enamels are formed by adding pigments to varnish. The body of the paint and its protective properties are provided by the varnish, and the pigment makes it opaque and gives it color. Colored lacquers are made in much the same way.

Paints are available in several finishes, including *flat, semigloss,* and *high gloss.* Flat paints dry with a somewhat rough, nonreflective finish. This kind of surface diffuses any light that strikes it and tends to mask irregularities in the surface. For this reason, flat paints are commonly used on walls and ceilings, which frequently contain irregularities. A rough surface is more difficult to wash free of dirt than smoother surfaces are.

Gloss or enamel surfaces are very smooth and highly reflective, and they tend to highlight irregularities. A smooth finish makes a surface easier to wash free of dirt or grease; therefore gloss paints are generally used on surfaces that must be washed frequently.

Semigloss paints are about halfway between gloss and flat paints. Their characteristics also enable surfaces to be cleaned fairly easily.

Pigments. Pigments are generally metal oxides which give paint both color and hiding power. Much of the cost of paints is determined by the quality and type of pigments used.

White pigments include lead carbonate and titanium dioxide. White lead, as the carbonate is called, is among the very best of white pigments because of its durability. Unfortunately, when lead carbonate is exposed to sulphur dioxide, a common air pollutant, it forms a blackish compound, lead sulfide. Another problem with lead is its ability to build up in body tissues, causing a disease known as lead poisoning. This fact has greatly reduced the use of lead in interior paints.

Most of the white paints on the market contain titanium pigments. Titanium provides excellent hiding power and resistance to chalking. Chalking is the condition which leads to the streaking of areas below painted surfaces on the exterior of buildings.

The pigments which are used to provide hiding power and to give color are known as *active* pigments. Other solids, *extender* pigments, are added to paints to keep the active pigments in suspension and to provide other desirable characteristics. Extender pigments are usually composed of silicon magnesium and aluminum silicates. Minerals such as talc and mica are also used as extender pigments.

Vehicles. The vehicle is the fluid portion of the paint that carries the pigment and develops into the film, which ultimately provides protection for the surface coated. Forty percent of the weight of high-quality oil-based paints is provided by the vehicle, and 75 or 80 percent of the vehicle is drying oil. The remaining 20 or 25 percent of the vehicle consists of solvents and driers which speed drying through oxidation.

Linseed, soya, and other vegetable and fish oils are used as paint vehicles. Each has a characteristic set of properties it imparts to the coating. Linseed oil is considered to be one of the highest-quality vehicle oils.

Oil-based paints dry through a combination of evaporation of the solvent, absorption by the material being coated, and oxidation of the drying oils.

Exterior Paints

Exterior surfaces can be left unpainted, treated with special stains or varnishes, or painted. In most cases an opaque paint finish is used, for several reasons. Most woods, with the exception of woods like cedar and redwood, deteriorate rapidly if left unfinished. Although varnish does provide some protection in exterior application, it is of short duration. Most spar varnishes have to be reapplied every 6 months. Stains are popular on contemporary-styled homes, but their low hiding power often limits their use to first or second applications. The ability of paint to dramatically alter the appearance of a structure makes it a very desirable finish. This, together with the relative durability of the painted surface, contributes greatly to its popularity.

Until fairly recently, oil-based exterior house paints were the most commonly used. Water-based paints, with their easy-cleanup feature, have largely displaced oil-based paints. However, many professional painters still use oil-based exterior paints for initial applications on new wood. In general, oil-based paints seem to be somewhat more weather-resistant than water-based types.

One of the best ways to judge the quality of exterior oil-based paints is to determine the relative quantities of pigment and vehicle. High-quality paints contain approximately 60 percent pigment to 40 percent vehicle, by weight. Water-based paints can be compared by weighing. The heavier the paint, the higher its quality. This is true because the resin provides most of the weight in water-based paints.

Water-Vehicle Paints

The original water-vehicle paints used latex as the coating-former and color-giver. The word "latex" has almost become generic for all types of water-vehicle emulsion paints. These paints clean up with water, dry quickly, have little or no odor, and are not combustible. In addition, they are excellent in their hiding action and are relatively economical. When compared to oil-based interior paints, their durability and resistance to abrasion are somewhat lower than those of good-quality oil-based paints.

Interior latex paints contain a variety of resins, including butadiene-styrene and polyvinyl acetate. For exterior applications, acrylic latex emulsion paints are the most commonly used. Since all of these paints contain considerable quantities of water, they should never be used directly on raw wood. All new wood should be treated with some oil-based primer which completely seals the surface. As the water evaporates from the water-based coating, the emulsion deteriorates and the particles that make up the emulsion move together to form a tough, continuous film on the surface.

Because water-based emulsion paints are formulated with water, they can be applied to damp surfaces without the problem of peeling later. This property makes such coatings highly suitable for masonry and damp exterior surfaces.

METHODS OF APPLICATION

Brush Applicators

Brushes are among the oldest of coating applicators. Several factors influence the quality of the brush. Among these are the length and type of bristle and the quality of the bond between the bristles and the handle. The primary classification of a brush is determined by the brush width and the kind of bristles or fibers used [Fig. 8-9(a)].

Nylon and other synthetic-fiber brushes are suitable for use with water-based finishes. They can also be used with oil-based finishes, but they tend to be too hard and stiff for use with materials like varnish. Natural-bristle brushes contain a variety of natural fibers, including hog bristles, camel hair (actually, squirrel hair), and horsehair, or vegetable fibers such as tampico or palmetto. The stiffest of these fibers (horsehair, tampico, and palmetto) are used for brushes designed to clean, sweep or scrub surfaces rather than to apply finishing materials. The softer fibers (camel and badger hair) are used for applying fine finishes like varnish. Natural bristles are not generally used for water-based coatings because they absorb water and become limp.

Brush use. After preparing the material to be applied and selecting the appropriate brush, begin by dipping the first one-third of the brush into the finishing material. Wipe both faces of the brush on the can lip to remove excess material [Fig. 8-9(b)]. Apply the finish with continuous, even-pressure strokes, utilizing the tip of the brush. It is best not to attempt to

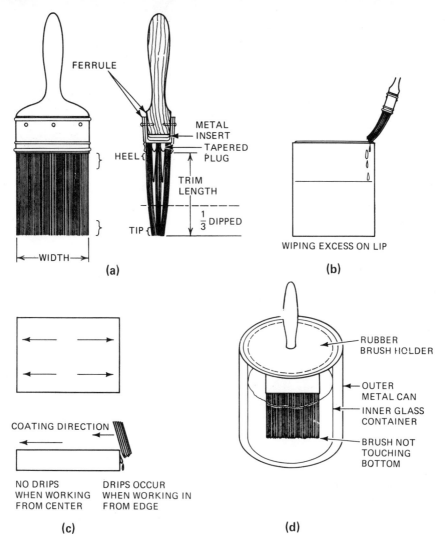

Fig. 8–9. Brush use

spread the material on the brush too far. When the brush stops coating properly, redip the brush into the finish. When coating objects such as the one shown in Fig. 8–9(c), the best results can be obtained by working from the inside of the surface toward the corners. This practice prevents runs by keeping the corners from wiping excess finish from the brush. Special care must be taken not to apply excessive amounts of materials on surfaces that are not horizontal, or runs may result.

Brush storage and care. When using a brush, dip only about one-third of the brush into the finish Fig. 8–9(a). This will prevent the finishing material from getting into the area around the ferrule. If the finishing material does

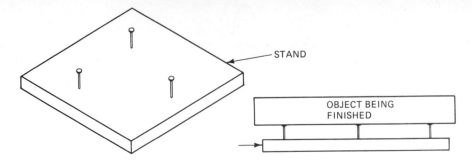

Fig. 8-10. Drying stands

get into this area, it eventually hardens and, in effect, shortens the working length of the bristles.

Brushes should be washed in a suitable thinner immediately after use. Several changes of thinner should be made during cleaning, and cleaning should continue until the thinner remains clean after the brush is worked in it. After cleaning, the brush should be dried and wrapped in paper until it is needed again. This wrapping will help to keep the brush in shape.

In ongoing finishing operations, where the brushes are used over an extended period of time, they can be stored as shown in Figure 8-9(d). The jar can be used to store the finishing material itself or to hold an appropriate solvent for the finish. If the solvent is used in the container, the brush must be dried carefully before it is dipped into the finishing material, or it will thin out the material. If the finish itself is used in the storage container, care must be taken to avoid contamination of the material. The metal can [Fig. 8-9(d)] gives some protection against breakage of the glass jar. The jar is used because its contents can be seen clearly and because it does not react with any finish or finishing solvent. Note that the tip of the brush is suspended above the bottom of the container [Fig. 8-9(d)]. This keeps the bristles from being bent out of shape during storage.

Drying stands. Small workpieces can be supported conveniently on locally produced stands. Three or four nails partially driven into a piece of scrap wood of suitable size, as shown in Fig. 8-10, can be used to support the workpiece while the upper surface is being coated.

Hand-Roller Applicators

Rubber rollers have been in use for many years in the machine application of coatings to sheet materials such as metals. The hand paint roller is a recent offshoot of this rubber roller. Among the advantages of roller applicators for paint are:

1. Relatively low cost as compared to a quality brush of the same size.
2. Speed of application and coverage.
3. Uniformity of film applied.
4. Variety of sizes, shapes, and types of rollers for various applications.

Cover types. Most manufacturers label roller covers to indicate the type of finishing material and surface for which the particular roller was designed. Four materials are commonly used in the production of roller covers (Fig. 8-11):

1. Mohair—Useful where a very smooth finish is required, as in the application of enamels.
2. Wool—High paint-holding capacity and low splattering. Often used in combination with other materials.
3. Nylon—Used together with other synthetic materials to produce a cover that is ideally suited for water-based paints.
4. Dynel—Used with nylon for water-based paints. Nonabsorbent and easily cleaned.

Covers are available with different nap lengths. Long-nap roller covers are used for very highly textured surfaces. Those with shorter naps are suitable for smoother surfaces. Covers containing wool tend to texture the surface and give a stippled appearance. This type of surface has excellent hiding power because it diffuses the light striking the surface and tends to camouflage irregularities.

Roller covers usually have a plastic cylinder as a base. The cover is designed to fit onto a metal tube, which is attached to a handle. The covers are available in sizes ranging from 3 to 12 in. in length, with 1-1/2 in. being the most common inside diameter of the cover.

Fig. 8-11. Paint roller covers

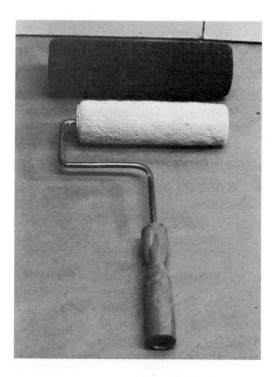

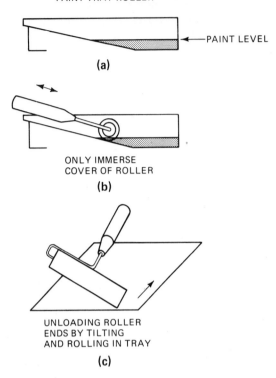

PAINT TRAY-ROLLER

←—PAINT LEVEL

(a)

ONLY IMMERSE
COVER OF ROLLER

(b)

UNLOADING ROLLER
ENDS BY TILTING
AND ROLLING IN TRAY

(c)

Fig. 8-12. Paint application with a roller

The finishing material is usually placed in a tray with a slanting surface, which allows the excess material from the roller to return to the reservoir at the bottom of the pan (Fig. 8-12).

Application.

1. After the finish is properly mixed, pour enough of the finishing material into the tray to fill the reservoir to about one-third of its capacity.

2. Roll the roller down into the liquid so that its *cover* is immersed [Fig. 8-12(b)]. If the roller is rolled into the liquid too far, it will collect the finishing material inside the cover and will tend to leak during application.

3. Repeat step 2 until the entire cover is coated.

4. Apply the roller to the surface to be coated.

5. Since the ends of the roller tend to load up with paint, unload it periodically by tipping the roller as shown in Fig. 8-12(c).

Cleaning.

1. First roll the roller on an absorbent surface until it stops coating the surface.

2. Wash the roller in a pan, using a suitable solvent. The empty paint tray can be used for this purpose.

3. Dry the roller with paper towels or a clean rag, and *place it on end* until it dries. This position prevents a flat spot from developing on the surface of the cover.

Although the roller applicator is often used to apply paints, other finishes such as varnish can also be applied with a roller. Try the roller and finish on scrap material before attempting application on the workpiece itself.

Pad Applicators

Pads of various types, covered with a nap similar to that found on rollers, are available for finishing applications (Fig. 8–13). These pad applicators have handles of various types which make their use convenient. The pads have several advantages over rollers for paint application. Among these are:

1. Ability to work up close to other surfaces in corners.
2. Usefulness on textured surfaces such as striated shingles.
3. Absence of the spray generated by rapidly spinning rollers.

Pad applicators are usually sold with special applicator trays.

Spray Finishing

Spraying is the most commonly used industrial finishing method, primarily because of its speed of application. Spraying is especially efficient for coating uneven or highly textured surfaces. Certain fast-drying finishing materials, such as lacquer, can best be applied by spraying. Although some

Fig. 8–13. Pad applicators

very complex and expensive equipment is used for spraying, the basic technique can be used with inexpensive pressurized spray cans.

Spraying should be done in a well-designed spray booth. Such booths have air filters which reduce the problem of contamination of the wet coating. Booths are also provided with an exhaust system that keeps the air in the booth free of the material being sprayed. This eliminates the danger of explosions and fire and keeps the air suitable for breathing. The paint spray operator should always wear a mouth and nose mask for protection against inhalation of finish particles.

Pressurized Spray Cans

A great variety of finishing materials are available in pressurized spray cans. Though these cans have limitations, they are useful for spraying small articles.

It is important to read the manufacturer's directions carefully, especially with regard to safety and permissible time between coatings. If a can indicates that the finish is fast-drying (5 minutes or less), there is a strong possibility that the finish contains lacquer thinners, which soften oil-based coatings. In any case, before coating an existing finish using a spray can, try a small area in a hidden spot to test the compatibility of the materials.

Principles of operation. Spray cans contain a liquified propellant gas, such as Freon. Cans of pigmented finishes contain a metal ball which stirs up the ingredients when the can is shaken. A plastic tube extends from the bottom of the can to the plastic valve at the top. When the valve is depressed, the gas (in vapor form) above the liquid forces the finishing liquid up through the tube and out of the valve (Fig. 8–14). When the liquified gas mixed with the finishing material is released from the valve, it instantly vaporizes. This action helps to disperse the droplets of finish more effectively. The droplets then fall on the surface to be coated and combine into a continuous film.

Use of spray cans.

1. After reading the manufacturer's directions carefully, shake the can as directed to mix the ingredients.

2. Position the arrow on top of the valve so that it points toward the area to be sprayed. Try the spray on scrap material. If possible, position the surface to be coated so that it is horizontal. This will reduce the tendency for runs to develop.

3. Depress the valve and pass the spray over the work using a slow, sweeping motion. Try to stay parallel to the surface being sprayed while maintaining the recommended distance, usually 8 to 12 in.

4. Continue sweeping the article from left to right as you work from the top of the article to the bottom.

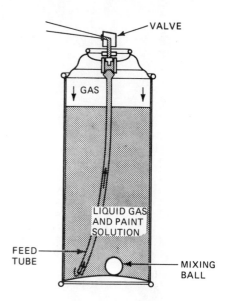

Fig. 8-14. Spray can construction

5. When the first coat is completed, apply the second as soon as recommended by the manufacturer. Avoid coating the article too quickly. This leads to excessive buildup of the coating, and running will develop.

Remember that adequate ventilation is essential for the safe use of any sprayed material. Inhalation of built-up material in the air can injure the spray user. Many spray-can ingredients are explosive when mixed with the air in certain proportions. Therefore, *open flames and spark-producing devices must be removed from spray areas.*

Even when carefully used, sprays tend to float to areas and objects at some distance from the object being sprayed. Care should be taken to mask the areas around the section to be sprayed. Spraying out of doors should be done on days when little or no wind is present.

Dispose of spray cans carefully. The remaining gas in an "empty" spray can will cause the can to burst if it is burned or thrown into an active incinerator.

Compressed-Air Units

Air compressors of various types are available for use with spraying equipment. The compressing unit should be matched to the requirements of the spraying equipment. In larger units, the compressed air is stored in a tank so that a reserve of air pressure can be developed. In smaller portable units, the compressed air is delivered directly to the spray gun and no real reserve capacity is available.

In tank-type compressors (Fig. 8-15), the unit is fitted with a pressure-regulating device which functions as an automatic switch. The regulator is

Fig. 8-15. Air compressor (Courtesy of De Vilbiss Corp.)

set to the desired limits by the operator. Many units are also equipped with a device known as an *extractor*. The extractor removes oil and water vapor from the air before it is delivered to the gun. The valve on the bottom of the compressor tank should be opened periodically to drain the tank of water.

Siphon Feed Gun

The siphon feed gun is a fairly common type of unit used in small installations where a limited quantity of spraying is done [Fig. 8-16(a)]. The fluid to be sprayed is held in a container attached to the gun. When the trigger valve is squeezed, the flow of air through the gun causes a partial vacuum to develop in the feeder tube, and the finishing material travels up the tube and into the airstream. As the finishing liquid is forced through the nozzle [Fig. 8-16(a)], it is atomized (broken into droplets) by the action of two airstreams on either side of the nozzle. This action is known as *external mixing*. The spray pattern is determined by the relative positions of these two airstreams. Turning the nozzle makes the pattern variable. The droplets fall on the surface to be painted and flow together to form a continuous coating.

Characteristics of the siphon feed gun.

1. The material to be sprayed must be thinned to approximately the consistency of water. Heavy liquids cannot be sprayed successfully.

2. The air flow is intermittent, and both the air and liquid are controlled by a single valve.

3. The amount of finish in the gun is usually limited to a quart.

4. The hole in the cap of the can allows atmospheric air to replace the liquid sprayed. It is essential to keep this hole open, or else the gun will stop functioning.

5. Only external-mix-type spray guns are used in nonbleeder units.

Pressure- or Bleeder-Type Guns

In this type of gun, the air flows continuously through the nozzle. For this reason, it can be used with compressing units which do not have storage tanks. When the trigger switch is squeezed, air is diverted into the paint container [Fig. 8-16(b)], and the fluid in the container is forced up the delivery tube and through the nozzle. In external-mix guns, the stream of finishing material is then mixed with streams of air from the nozzle. In internal-mix guns, the air and finish are mixed inside the cap and atomized as they emerge.

Some commercial pressure-spray units have a large container holding the finishing material isolated or remote from the gun. This sytem allows several

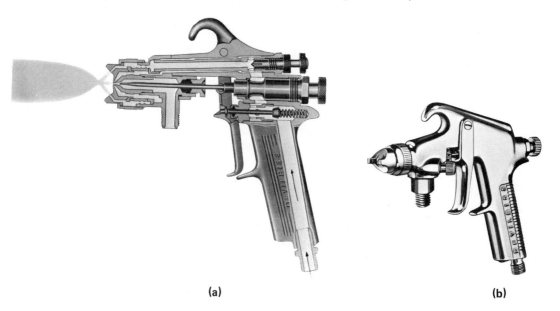

(a)   (b)

Fig. 8-16. (a) Suction or siphon feed gun with external mix air cap. (b) Pressure feed gun. (Courtesy of De Vilbiss Corp.)

guns to draw from one large container. It also allows the guns to be more maneuverable, since they do not carry the weight of stored finishing material.

Characteristics of the bleeder or pressure gun.

1. Relatively heavy materials can be sprayed. Liquids such as house paint can be sprayed with pressurized units.

2. The flow of air is continuous, and the gun trigger valve controls the flow of finishing material.

3. Finishing materials can be stored in a large, remote container (Fig. 8–15).

4. Containers are air-tight and have no holes to allow outside air to flow into the gun to replace the liquid lost in spraying.

5. Bleeder guns can be used with a compressor without a storage tank or pressure regulator.

6. Pressurized guns can be of either the internal- or external-mix type.

Preparation of materials.

1. Strain all liquids to be used in the gun. Small particles easily clog the gun and interrupt spraying operations.

2. If possible, use the material to be sprayed at can consistency. Over-thinning creates problems in the application of many finishes. In any case, attempt to use the material as it comes from the can unless it is obviously too heavy for the equipment being used.

Spraying technique.

1. Hold the gun 18 in. from the surface to be sprayed [Fig. 8–17(a)].

2. Aim the spray nozzle at an imaginary point 2 or 3 in. to the left of the upper left corner of the object. Depress the trigger.

3. Starting at the upper left end of the object, travel the gun to the right *while keeping its path parallel* to the surface being coated. This traverse should be slow and steady and should continue until the spray goes beyond the object at the right end of the traverse.

4. As the spray approaches the end of the first traverse, gradually release the trigger. Then reverse the direction of travel and sweep the gun to the left, gradually depressing the trigger so that the spray is full as the gun reaches the object again. Overlap the first stroke by about one-half [Fig. 8–17(b)].

5. Continue this process until the first coat is completed.

6. Repeat until the desired coating is applied.

Cleaning the gun. When spraying is completed, empty the remaining finishing material into a storage can. Fill the gun can one-third of the way with a suitable thinner, and rotate the gun horizontally to wash the inside of the gun can. Then spray the thinner out until the gun is empty.

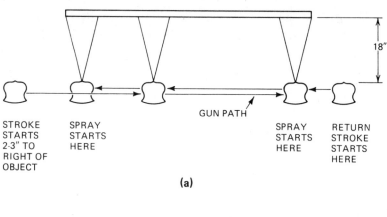

STROKE STARTS 2-3" TO RIGHT OF OBJECT

SPRAY STARTS HERE

GUN PATH

SPRAY STARTS HERE

RETURN STROKE STARTS HERE

18"

(a)

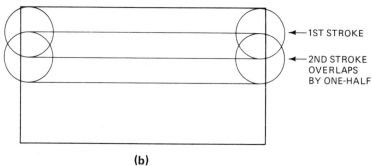

1ST STROKE

2ND STROKE OVERLAPS BY ONE-HALF

(b)

Fig. 8–17.

RECOMMENDED PRESSURES FOR SPRAYING SOME COMMON MATERIALS

Varnish	Nonbleeder gun—30 psi
Lacquer	After thinning as recommended by manufacturer— nonbleeder gun—30 psi
Stains	Bleeder or nonbleeder type—15 psi
Oil-based paints	Pressure-type gun—20 psi
Latex-based (not gelled type)	Pressure-type gun—25 psi

PROBLEMS AND REMEDIES

Runs or sags	Finish too thin or coats too heavy— move gun more rapidly or thin finish less
Orange-peel surface	Low air pressure or unmixed thinner
Dull finish or blush (whitish appearance)	Moisture in air or in finishing material

FINISHING SYSTEMS

The finishing systems outlined below are suggested procedures. It is always wise to follow the manufacturer's directions carefully. Where a system conflicts with the manufacturer's instructions, follow the manufacturer's instructions.

A large number of variables exist in any finishing situation. Among these are the finish used, the applicator selected, the wood to which the finish is applied, and the environment in which the finishing is to be carried out. Because such variables exist, it is important to test all finishes on sample pieces under conditions similar to those likely to be encountered in the actual finishing process.

FINISHING SYSTEM I

Finish Type: Opaque Antique Finish
Finishing Material: Oil- or Water-Based Semigloss Enamel and Gloss Enamel Paint
Surface Condition: Raw Wood or Previously Finished Wood

Step Description	Drying Time	Cautions
1. Apply a coat of sealer (water-thin shellac is suitable). If piece is finished, skip this step.	24 hr	
2. Sand lightly with No. 250 or No. 280 paper. Wipe dust off.	none	
3. Apply first coat of semigloss paint, working from the center of surfaces toward outside edges.	24 hr	If roller is used, stippled surface may result. Try roller on test surface first.
4. Sand surface lightly with No. 250 or No. 280 paper. Wipe dust off.	none	
5. Apply second coat of semigloss enamel.	24 hr	
6. Apply water-thin coat of accent color paint, enamel, with a cloth pad. Wipe surface with another pad until desired pattern develops on the surface.		
7. The antique finish is now visible and may be left at this point.	24 hr	
8. If added durability is desired, apply a coat of semigloss or satin varnish.	24 hr	

FINISHING SYSTEM II

Finish Type:	Transparent
Finishing Materials:	Varnish, Cabinet Rubbing, Gloss, Semigloss, or Matt
Surface Condition:	Raw Wood Sanded through No. 220 Paper and Wiped

Step Description	Drying Time	Cautions
1. Apply stain.	24 hr	If water stain is used, raise grain by wetting, allow 24 hr to dry, and resand with No. 220 paper before staining.
2. Apply paste wood filler if required.	24 hr	Required on open-grain woods like oak. For others, skip step 2.
3. Apply sealer—water-thin shellac or brushing lacquer may be used.	24 hr	Lacquer tends to cause most stains to bleed. Use only on un-stained woods.
4. Sand lightly with No. 250 or No. 280 paper until surface feels glass smooth. Wipe dust off.	none	Avoid sanding outside corners because stain can easily be sanded off.
5. Apply varnish as it comes from container, using good-quality soft brush.	24 hr minimum	Stir carefully. Try not to mix air bubbles into varnish. If bubbles appear on surface and do not disappear in 1–2 min, blow lightly on surface.
6. Sand lightly with No. 250 or No. 280 paper and wipe.*	none	
7. Apply second coat of varnish.	24 hr minimum	
8. Sand lightly with No. 250 or No. 280 paper and wipe.*	none	
9. Apply third coat of varnish.	24 hr minimum	
10. Sand lightly with No. 600 wet-and-dry paper.	none	No sanding block necessary. If semigloss or flat varnish is used, skip steps 10–12 and go on to waxing.
11. Apply powdered pumice to a felt pad dampened with water or very thin machine oil and rub lightly with the grain. Wipe clean with a damp cloth.		
12. Repeat step 11, using another dampened felt pad and powdered rottenstone. Wipe clean and allow to dry.		If oil is used, wipe surface clean with cloth dampened with turpentine.
13. Apply paste wax and buff.		

*The purpose of sanding between coats is to roughen surface so that subsequent coats will adhere, and to flatten coat. Use sanding block to level surface during sanding.

Finish Type:	Transparent
Finishing Material:	Brushing Lacquer, Gloss, Semigloss, or Flat
Surface Condition:	Raw Wood Sanded through No. 220 Paper and Wiped

Step Description	Drying Time	Cautions
1. Apply stain if desired.	24 hr	If water stain is used, raise grain before staining by wetting surface. Allow 24 hr to dry, then resand with No. 220 paper. Apply stain to wiped surface.
2. Apply paste wood filler if required.	24 hr	Required on open-grain woods like oak. For others, skip step 2.
3. Apply sealer—water-thin shellac or the lacquer itself may be used.	24 hr	If stain or wood filler was used which is not specifically designed to be used with lacquer, use a shellac sealer to prevent bleeding into lacquer.
4. Sand lightly with No. 250 or No. 280 paper until surface feels glass-smooth. Wipe dust off.	none	Avoid sanding outside corners because stain can easily be removed. Sanding roughens the surface so that subsequent coats will adhere, and flattens the coat applied. Use a sanding block to flatten surface during sanding.
5. Apply brushing lacquer as it comes from container. Do not sand between this coat and the next.*	30 min	Apply a thin coat. *Do not go over missed areas.* This practice will remove undried finish and result in bare spots. Coat missed areas on next application.
6. Apply second coat of lacquer.	24 hr	
7. Sand lightly with No. 220 or No. 250 paper and wipe.	none	Hard-use surfaces require application of several more coats.
8. Apply third coat.	24 hr	
9. Apply wax and buff.		If a gloss lacquer is used, it can be made satinlike by rubbing with pumice and then rottenstone. See Finishing System I, steps 11 and 12.

*When lacquer is applied in thin coats, the buildup of finish between coats is very slight. For this reason, time can be saved by not sanding between coats 1 and 2. Sanding on any finish which has dried for only 30 min is risky because a surface skin may give the false indication that the coat is dry. Sanding will break through the skin and expose a sticky, undried layer.

FINISHING SYSTEM IV

Finish Type:	Transparent*
Finishing Material:	Boiled Linseed Oil and Turpentine Mixed Half and Half
Surface Condition:	Raw Wood Sanded through No. 220 Paper and Wiped

Step Description	Drying Time	Cautions
1. Apply oil mixture.	24 hr	Rub oil in liberally. After 30 min remove excess with dry rag.
2. Apply oil mixture.	24 hr	Same as above. Repeat daily, until desired depth of finish develops—10 to 15 applications required. Thereafter, repeat every 3 months.
		If excessive buildup develops, remove by wiping with cloth dampened with turpentine.

*This finish is most suitable for woods like walnut and teak.

FINISHING SYSTEM V

Finish Type:	French Polishing on the Lathe
Finishing Material:	Shellac and Oil
Surface Condition:	Raw Wood Sanded through No. 220 Paper

Step Description	Drying Time	Cautions
1. Saturate a soft absorbent pad with boiled linseed oil and squeeze "dry." Sprinkle a few drops of 3-pound-cut shellac on the pad. Apply the pad to the workpiece as it rotates while mounted on the lathe. Travel the pad along the work, adding shellac to the cloth periodically. If cloth begins to stick to the work, remove it, and add oil. Continue until desired buildup of finish develops.	immediate drying	Be sure to add shellac frequently or an oil finish will result. The test of finish quality and build-up is a glossy finish which lasts more than 24 hr. Additional finishing can be done anytime before wax is applied.
2. Apply paste wax if desired.		

BUILDING CONSTRUCTION

Most organized instruction in woodworking is related to fine woodworking. Cabinetmaking and accessory construction are the primary areas of interest of the typical craftsman and student of woodworking. This is understandable because such activity is interesting, project-centered, and manageable both in the school setting and in the craftsman's shop. However, when one considers occupational opportunities in woodworking, building construction immediately stands out as the area where most of the jobs exist. A case can be made for the study of building construction for the person who is interested in woodworking as a craft or avocational activity. Most small dwellings in this country are constructed of wood and are of light frame design. Since all of us are potential homeowners, an understanding of such construction is of importance to us. A home represents the single largest purchase made by the average consumer, yet very few people have any understanding of the essential components of even the most basic frame structure.

Many homeowners do undertake renovations of wood frame structures, and an understanding of the design of the structure can help the homeowner to make more intelligent decisions. Even apartment dwellers should know about wall construction, basic plumbing, and wiring so that they can live within their housing environment in a more satisfactory way.

The basic design of the frame structure has not changed in any significant way for the last century. Although some new materials and methods of construction have been devised, the basic components of the typical light frame structure remain unaltered. This seems to be a paradox in this era of highly developed technology and mass production. However, many small frame dwellings are built by relatively small contractors using basic equipment and designs. This is increasingly true as large, undeveloped tracts of land become less and less available. Although high-rise apartments have been and will continue to be built, many people still desire the relative privacy afforded by the one-family home in the suburbs.

In the last decade, some factory-produced housing has become available. The mobile-home industry has developed to the point where two or more units are transported to a site and combined to form a single structure that approaches the size and comfort of the traditional built-on-the-site structure. Modular construction has also grown. In such construction, wall units are plant-fabricated complete with insulation, utilities, and finished surfaces and then shipped to the site where they are assembled into a functioning home. Many of these units are designed so that additions and rearrangements can easily be made to the original structure. In spite of these developments, the traditional frame structure remains a highly significant part of the housing picture.

Most frame structures built today utilize a style of framing known as *Western* or *platform* framing. In this type of construction a complete platform, consisting of floor joists and subflooring, is built at each level of the structure. This provides a secure surface for the worker to walk on and utilizes framing material of relatively short lengths. Wall studs, for example, are approximately 8 ft long (Fig. 9–1).

A century ago, many multistory structures were fabricated using a framing system known as *balloon* framing (Fig. 9–2). In this type of construction the wall members (studs) went from the sills to the top plates of the second floor, which supported the rafters. Since each floor had a ceiling height of 10 or even 12 ft, these studs had to be 20 to 24 ft long.

THE PLANNING PHASE

The amount and kind of planning required for construction begins with an idea in the head of the amateur builder and proceeds all the way to architect-drawn plans that are submitted to, and approved by, a building department. In some rural areas no building codes or building inspectors exist. In general, as the population of an area increases, the amount and degree of building control increase.

Building codes are rules which set minimum standards for construction. They are designed to protect the consumer and the community, in general, and ensure that structures are safe and functional. In many large cities, a professional licensed architect must attest to the fact that the plans for a structure conform to the building code of the community in which the structure is to be built.

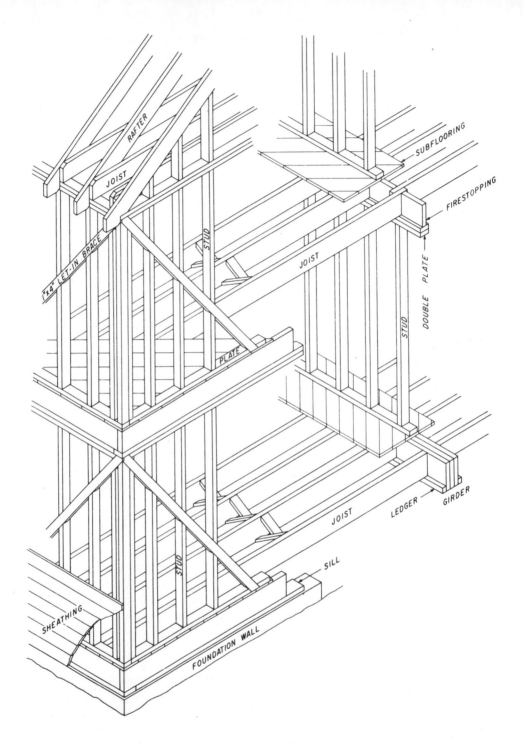

Fig. 9-1. Platform frame construction

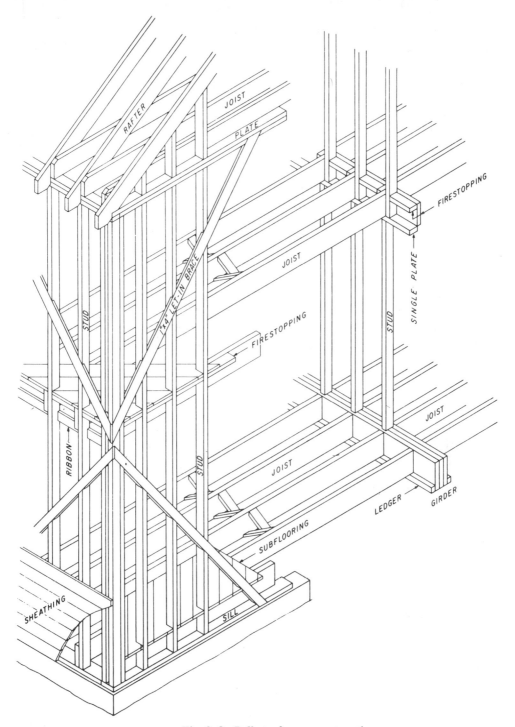

Fig. 9-2. Balloon frame construction

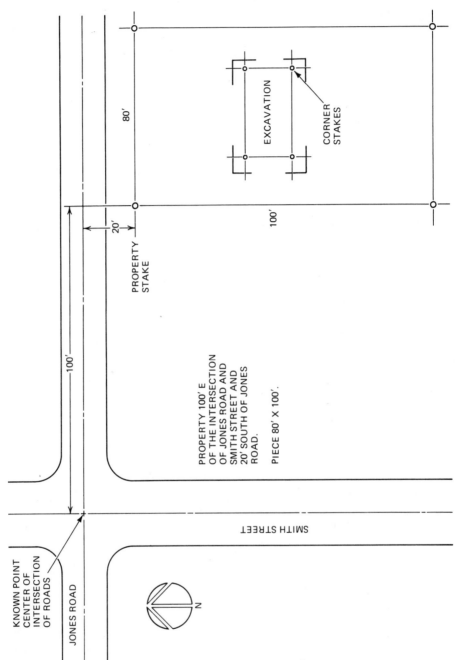

Fig. 9-3. Site survey

If the builder does not wish to consult an architect, he can buy complete plans for homes designed by architects for a nominal fee. Most communities do require that a building permit be obtained before construction is started. This permit is issued after the building inspector has approved the plans submitted by the builder. The permit itself is then posted in some visible spot on the building site.

When the structure is finished and the building, plumbing, and electrical inspections are completed, the building department issues a *certificate of occupancy*. This is the document that certifies that the structure has been completed and conforms to the building code. At this point the structure can be occupied and the tax assessor determines the tax value of the building.

Any intelligent building planner has a site survey made of the property on which the building is to be built. This is very important because such a survey accurately locates the boundaries of the site. These boundaries determine the maximum size of the structure to be built and its location on the site. An error at this point in the planning can be very costly. For example, most communities specify the minimum distances permitted between a roadway and a structure and between one structure and another. If these guidelines are not adhered to, the structure may have to be torn down.

In performing a site survey, the surveyor locates the four corners of the lot by working from some known geographic point such as a street centerline intersection (Fig. 9-3). Property stakes are usually driven in at the four corners of the site. Then the surveyor locates the house on the site and drives corner stakes at these points (Fig. 9-3). All this is accomplished by the survey team, using a transit for measuring angles, and a steel tape for measuring distances.

If the structure is to have a basement, an excavation will be made within the area defined by these stakes. Since digging such a hole would dislodge these important stakes, a more flexible and durable system is used to keep the location of the foundation under control. This system commonly involves the erection of four fencelike *batter boards*. These batter boards (Fig. 9-4) have lines (strings) attached to them which form a frame that outlines the outer limits of the foundation. The lines are located by placing them into saw cuts on the batter boards. This makes the removal and replacement of the lines simple and accurate. The batter boards themselves are located at least 4 ft away from the corner stakes.

FOUNDATION

Excavation

Once the batter boards are set up, the excavation of the foundation can begin. A bulldozer is often used to accomplish this. A ramp is formed at one end of the excavation (Fig. 9-5), and the earthmover scoops the earth out of

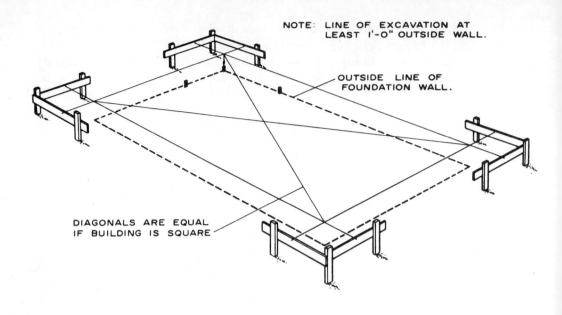

NOTE: LINE OF EXCAVATION AT LEAST 1'-0" OUTSIDE WALL.

OUTSIDE LINE OF FOUNDATION WALL.

DIAGONALS ARE EQUAL IF BUILDING IS SQUARE

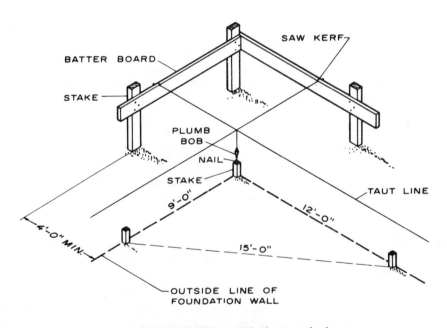

SAW KERF

BATTER BOARD

STAKE

PLUMB BOB

NAIL

STAKE

9'-0"

12'-0"

TAUT LINE

4'-0" MIN.

15'-0"

OUTSIDE LINE OF FOUNDATION WALL

Fig. 9-4. Staking and laying out the house

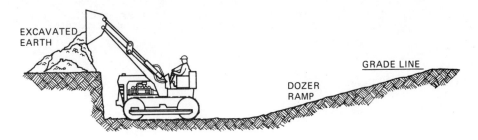

Fig. 9-5. Excavation

the area inside the batter boards. The depth of the excavation depends on the headroom required in the basement and the portion of the basement that is to be above grade. In some homes, the basement is designed to be used as living space and most of the basement is above grade (Fig. 9-6). This allows full-sized windows to be used in the basement walls. A more typical basement would have a minimum headroom of 7 ft, 4 in., though the 8-ft minimum is frequently used. A minimum of 8 in. of the foundation wall should be visible above the final grade of the earth around the structure.

The depth of the excavation can be checked with a transit or level and a rod, which is a type of ruler (Fig. 9-7).

The final part of the excavation is for the *footings,* which will form the foundation on which the house rests. The corners of the foundation can be accurately located by dropping a *plumb line* (a weighted string) from the intersection of the lines attached to the batter boards. The footings themselves are usually dug with a shovel in virgin soil. Such soil has a high load-

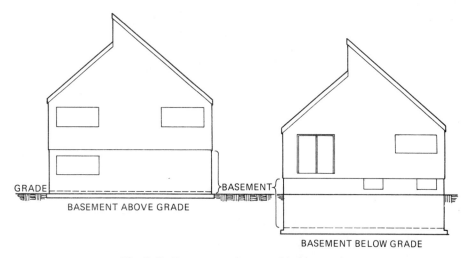

Fig. 9-6. Basements above and below grade

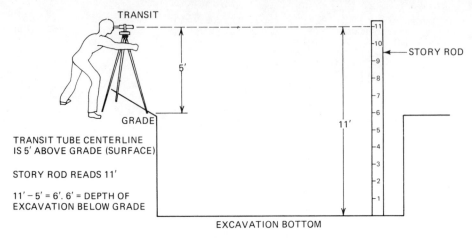

TRANSIT

STORY ROD

5'

11'

GRADE

TRANSIT TUBE CENTERLINE
IS 5' ABOVE GRADE (SURFACE)

STORY ROD READS 11'

11' − 5' = 6'. 6' = DEPTH OF
EXCAVATION BELOW GRADE

EXCAVATION BOTTOM

Fig. 9-7.

bearing capacity because it has been compacted by the weight of the soil that was in place above it before excavation.

Footings must be placed below the *frost line,* which is the average depth to which the soil freezes during the coldest part of the year. A 4-ft depth is generally considered safe for footings in most parts of the country. The size of the footings may be specified in the building code and, in such cases, the building inspector inspects the footings to make sure that they conform to the standards set by the code. Since the function of the footings is to transmit the load of the entire structure, including its contents, to the soil below, they must be carefully constructed and capable of supporting the house load. Solid concrete footings are usually from 6 to 8 in. thick. A rule of thumb is to make the footing thickness at least equal to the foundation wall thickness. For example, when block construction is used in the foundation wall, the footings are 8 in. thick because the blocks are 8 in. thick. The width of the footings is generally twice the wall *thickness.* If the load-bearing capacity of the soil is low, reinforcing steel may be used in the foundation footings (Fig. 9-8).

Fig. 9-8. Reinforcing and draining footing

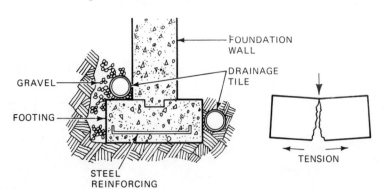

GRAVEL

FOOTING

FOUNDATION
WALL

DRAINAGE
TILE

STEEL
REINFORCING

TENSION

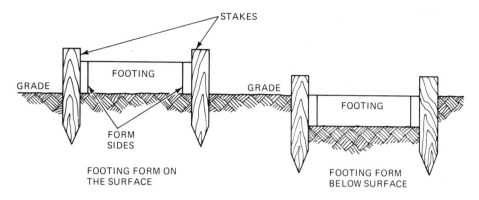

Fig. 9-9. Footing form on and below the surface

The forms for the footings can be erected on the surface (Fig. 9-9) or they can be cut into the soil to form a trench. In either case, the sides of the forms must be secure enough to support the fluid concrete until it sets.

Column Footings

In most light frame structures, intermediate floor support is provided by a girder. This girder frequently requires support by columns placed under it. The columns rest on footings which are subject to the same general rules as the foundation wall footings (Fig. 9-10).

Foundation Walls

Foundation walls are usually made of masonry materials. Either cast concrete or blocks are used in the fabrication of a foundation wall. Masonry materials are suitable for use below grade, where moisture and insect prob-

Fig. 9-10. Concrete footing

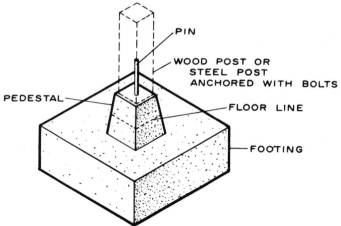

lems would normally render wood unsuitable. Many contractors use block construction, where codes permit, because they do not require forms to be erected and are generally less costly. Block foundations are satisfactory if properly built, but they are subject to cracking along their many joint lines. When cracks develop, water and termites can enter.

Poured concrete foundations. Concrete foundations are cast from 6 to 10 in. in thickness. The forms constructed to shape the walls are really molds. Several types are used, including carpenter-built forms and resusable forms.

In some cases, a carpenter builds the concrete forms, as shown in Fig. 9–11. These forms must be strong enough to hold the fluid concrete in place until it hardens. Snap ties can be used and serve a dual function. They spread the form to keep the sides apart before the concrete is poured and, together with their shoes, they restrain the form when it is loaded with the concrete mix (Fig. 9–12). After the concrete cures, these ties are snapped off. The portion of the tie in the foundation wall remains in it.

Window or door openings in the foundation walls are provided for by the installation of boxes which leave voids as required (Fig. 9–13).

Many contractors fabricate reusable forms from plywood and framing material and use these forms, with appropriate bracing and snap ties, to

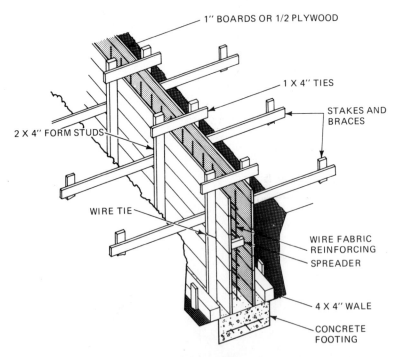

Fig. 9–11. Wooden form for concrete "carpenter built."

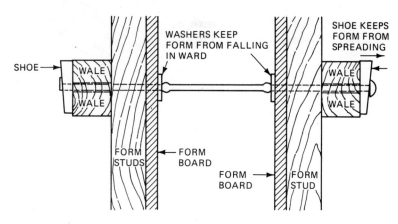

Fig. 9–12. Cross section of a form utilizing "snap ties"

shape concrete foundation walls (Fig. 9–14). Other builders rent steel forms which are held together with removable steel pins (Fig. 9–15).

Anchoring the structure to the foundation. In some instances, the structure is not fastened to the foundation walls. The weight of the building is depended upon to keep it in place. When a structure is anchored to the foundation, the methods described below may be used.

Anchor bolts are L-shaped rods that are threaded on the straight end. In poured foundations, these anchor bolts are placed in the top of the form, with the bent portion extending down into the form (Fig. 9–16). The threaded portion of the anchor passes through the sill and is held in place

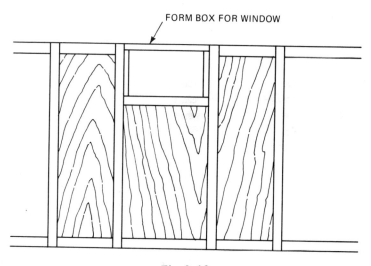

Fig. 9–13.

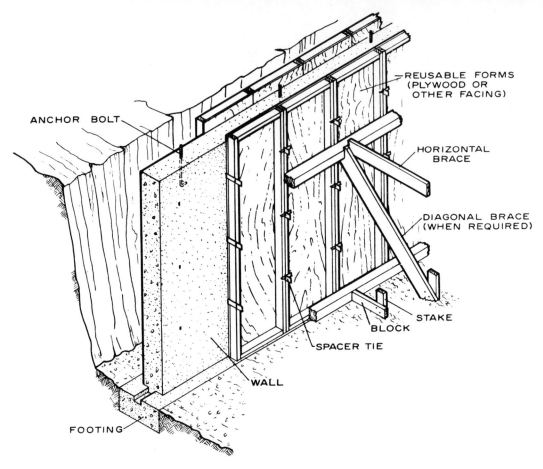

Labels on figure:
ANCHOR BOLT
REUSABLE FORMS (PLYWOOD OR OTHER FACING)
HORIZONTAL BRACE
DIAGONAL BRACE (WHEN REQUIRED)
STAKE
BLOCK
SPACER TIE
WALL
FOOTING

Fig. 9-14. Forming for poured concrete walls

by a nut and washer. Another method used in poured foundations is to install a two-by-four in the top of the form (Fig. 9-17). This is held in place by the concrete which surrounds it.

Block foundations. Blocks are usually constructed of cinders held together with a cementlike binder. These blocks come in various sizes, with the most common size approximately 8 in. by 8 in. by 16 in. The blocks are held in position with mortar, which is a special cement mix containing lime. Block walls should be capped with 4 in. of solid masonry or reinforced concrete. This helps to distribute the load more uniformly between the structure and the blocks, and it makes the wall more water-resistant.

Waterproofing

Where soil drains poorly because of a high clay content, for example, drainage tiles are installed along the inside and outside of the footings. These

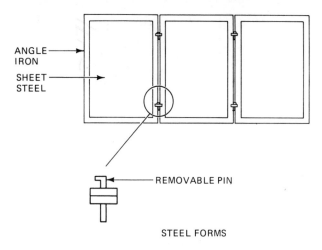

ANGLE IRON

SHEET STEEL

REMOVABLE PIN

STEEL FORMS

Fig. 9–15.

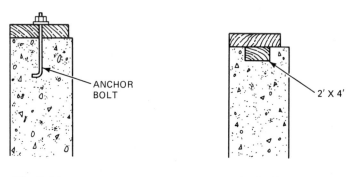

ANCHOR BOLT

Fig. 9–16.

2' X 4'

Fig. 9–17.

tiles carry water away from the structure to a dry well or into a storm-sewer system (Fig. 9-8).

Concrete walls are usually waterproofed by coating the exterior of the foundation wall with tar or asphalt. Block walls can be waterproofed in a similar way, or a membrane can be applied to the exterior of the foundation wall. The wall is first coated with hot tar or asphalt, and then a membrane of roofing felt or other material is applied. Finally the membrane is coated with tar or asphalt.

Brick Veneer Walls

In some construction, one or more exterior sides of the structure are covered with brick one course deep. To support the brick, a shelflike projection is cast into the foundation (Fig. 9-18). The width of the projection allows an air space to be left between the brick and the building wall. The air

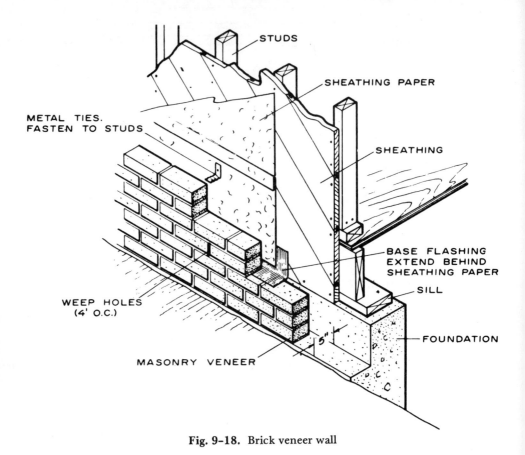

Fig. 9-18. Brick veneer wall

space insulates the wooden wall from the brick, which can conduct water through capillary action to its inner surface. The brick wall is tied to the wooden wall with metal strips that are nailed to the wooden sheathing and are also cemented into the mortar between the bricks.

Termite Shields

In most areas of the United States, termites can invade wooden structures. The nest of the termite is in the earth close to its source of food. If a crack develops in a foundation wall, below grade, the termites can use it to gain entry to the house. If the foundation is sound, the termites can construct a paper tube on the surface of the masonry up to the wooden portion of the structure. Termite shields can prevent this entry of termites (Fig. 9-21).

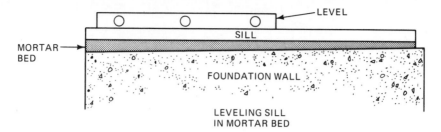

Fig. 9-19. Leveling sill in mortar bed

PLATFORM CONSTRUCTION

Sill Installation

Sills are commonly 2 in. by 6 in. framing material laid flat (face down) on the foundation wall (Fig. 9-19). The sills must be level, or else the structure built upon them will not be level. The sills on adjacent foundation walls must be at right angles to each other (Fig. 9-20). If a transit level is available, it can be used for this purpose.

One or two sills may be used, depending on the design of the structure. The edge of the sill is usually set back about 3/4 in. from the exterior surface of the foundation to allow space for the sheathing (Fig. 9-21). The siding

Fig. 9-20. Squaring sills to each other

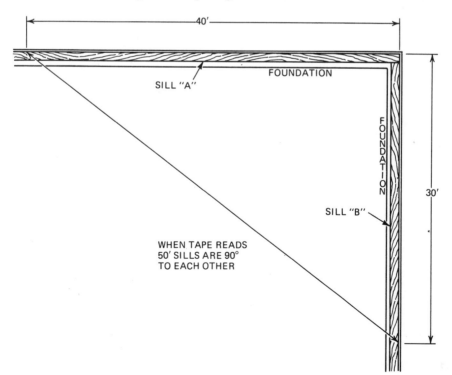

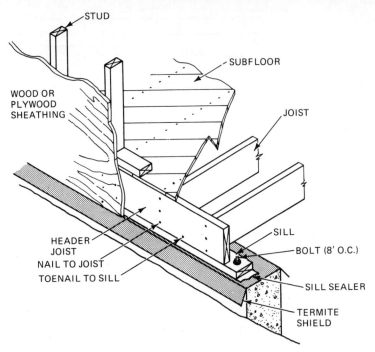

Fig. 9-21. Platform construction and sills

can then extend down over the foundation wall, reducing the possibility of water seepage into the basement from runoff coming down the exterior wall.

Girder

A girder is an intermediate member which supports the ends of the floor joists (Fig. 9-22). The ends of the girder are supported by cutouts in the foundation walls at least 4 in. deep. Note that the ends of the girder do not touch the masonry wall. This reduces the tendency of the girder to absorb moisture into its ends. The upper surface of the girder is flush with the upper face of the sill (Fig. 9-22). This is necessary so that the floor joists will be level.

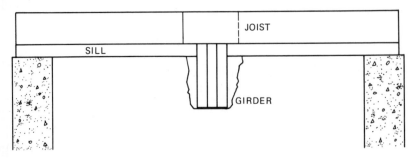

Fig. 9-22. Girder

The girder usually consists of three 2-in.-thick pieces of framing material nailed together as staggered end joints (Fig. 9–23). A wide-flange steel I beam can also be used as a girder. The three two-by-eight built-up girder is commonly used with posts at 8-ft intervals. See Fig. 9–23 for girder construction.

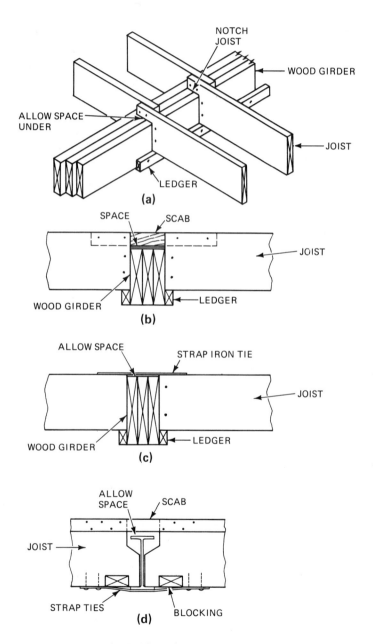

Fig. 9–23. Joists girder meetings

Joist Installation

Floor joists are commonly two-by-eights placed on edge and spanning the basement area from foundation wall to girder. At the girder, the floor joists overlap (Fig. 9-22) and are nailed face to face. This fastening helps to stiffen the joists and enables them to resist deflection during loading. In general, any two-by-eight floor joist over 16 ft long requires an intermediate support such as a girder.

The most common spacing of framing members is 16 in. on center (Fig. 9-24). This spacing provides the support required and also allows sheet materials such as plywood and gypsum board to be fastened to it easily (Fig. 9-24). Floor joists are placed on 16-in. centers, with bows and any defects such as knots facing up (Fig. 9-25). This positioning results in the bowed members being flattened when the subflooring is in place. Defects such as knots are placed in compression when the joist is loaded (Fig. 9-25).

Where extra loads are likely, as with partition walls running parallel to the joists, double joists are used (Fig. 9-24). Where joists are interrupted (e.g., where openings in the floor must be cut for stairways), double joists are placed on each side of the opening. The cut-off joists are supported by *headers* (Fig. 9-26), which carry the end load of the joists to the full double

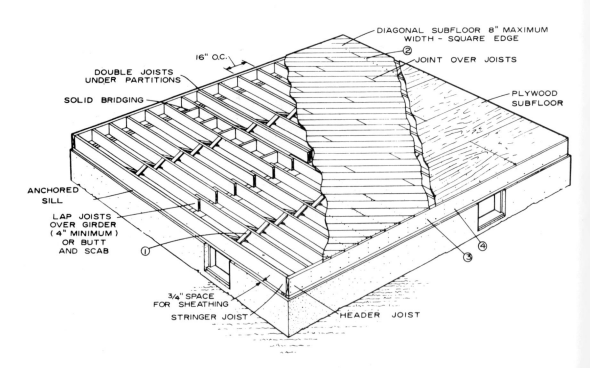

Fig. 9-24. Floor framing: (1) Nailing bridging to joists; (2) nailing board subfloor to joists; (3) nailing header to joists; (4) toenailing header to sill

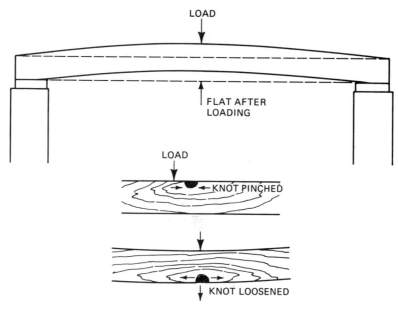

Fig. 9-25.

joists on each side of the opening. (The ends of the joists are covered by a header joist, which rests on the sill, with its outer face flush with the edge of the sill (Fig. 9-24).)

Bridging

It is common practice to install bridging when joists are over 10 ft long. The bridging ties the floor joists together laterally so that when one joist is loaded, its load is transmitted to the joists around it. In addition, the bridging also helps to keep the floor joists vertical.

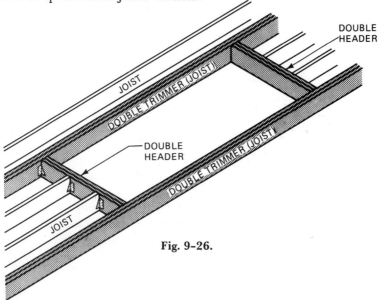

Fig. 9-26.

Wooden cross-bridging. In older structures, wooden cross-bridging is common. This bridging is constructed of one-by-fours nailed in an X pattern as shown in Fig. 9–24. The top of the bridging is nailed to the upper faces of the joists before the subflooring is installed but the lower ends are left unfastened until after the subfloor has been installed. This procedure allows any bowed joists to be flattened before the bridging is secured at the lower face of the joists; otherwise, the floor will be uneven.

Steel cross-bridging. Steel cross-bridging is frequently used in place of wooden cross-bridging because it takes less time to prepare and install.

Solid bridging. Solid bridging is sometimes used in place of cross bridging. When used, it should be installed after the subflooring is in place (Fig. 9–24).

Subflooring

The floor joists are covered with wooden subflooring. It is called subflooring because it is the floor beneath the hardwood finish flooring. If solid wood is used for subflooring, one-by-sixes or one-by-eights are used. They can be tongue-and-groove or plain, and they can be laid at right angles to the joists or in a diagonal pattern (Fig. 9–24). In many structures, plyscore is used for the subflooring. This is a rough material that is between 1/2 and 3/4 in. thick.

WALL FRAMING

Exterior walls serve several functions. They support the roof and carry its load down to the platform and the foundation. Walls create an interior space that is insulated from the exterior environment, and they provide an anchoring surface for the interior walls. The *interior walls* are of two types, *load-bearing* and *non-load-bearing*. Load-bearing walls run at right angles to the floor joists and carry part of the ceiling load down to the floor joists [Fig. 9–27(c)]. Non-load-bearing walls are laid out parallel to floor joists and are not required to support ceiling joists.

Wall framing is similar for all walls in the structure [Fig. 9–28(a)]. All of the framing members, except for the headers over openings, are two-by-fours. The horizontal member resting on the subfloor is called the *sole plate*. These plates anchor the walls to the platform.

The vertical members, spaced on 16-in. centers, are the *studs*. For an 8-ft first-floor ceiling height, the studs should be 7 ft, 9 in. long. This would be correct if the plate's actual thickness is 1-1/2 in.

Double plates are used at the upper ends of the studs. The plate in direct contact with the ends of the studs is called the *top plate,* and the one

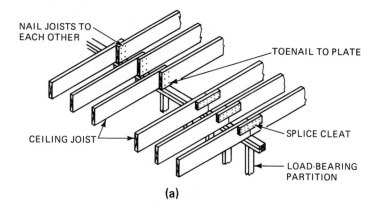

(a)

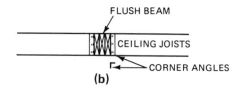

(b)

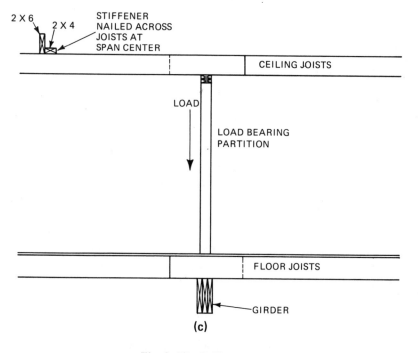

(c)

Fig. 9-27. Ceiling joists

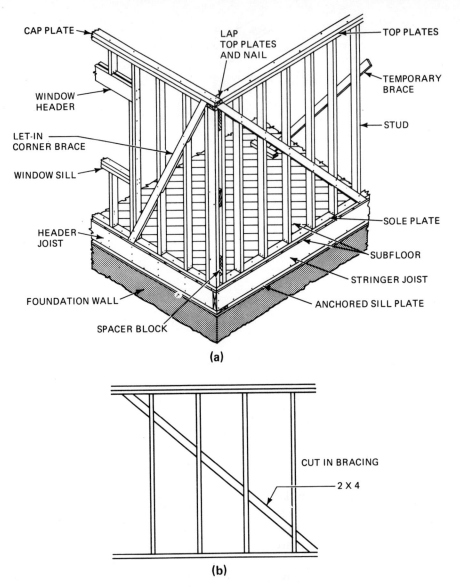

Fig. 9-28. Exterior wall framing

above it is called the *cap plate*. These plates stabilize the studs, support the rafters (or the second story), support the ceiling joists, and provide a fastening surface for the interior and exterior wall coverings. [Fig. 9-28(a)].

Openings in the Wall

Exterior door openings are usually 36 in. in width and 6 ft, 8 in. (80 in.) in height. Interior door openings are usually 2 ft, 6 in. wide and 80 in. high (Fig. 9-29). The load above the doors is carried laterally by headers that are

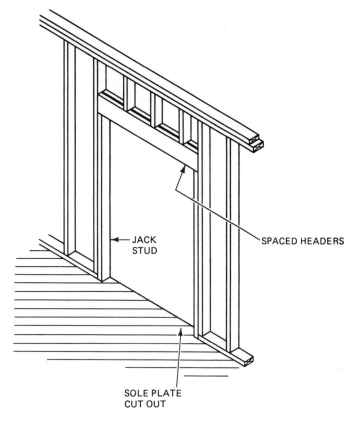

JACK STUD

SPACED HEADERS

SOLE PLATE CUT OUT

Fig. 9–29. Door opening framing

a minimum of 2 in. by 4 in. Two headers are used with a spacer inserted between them to make their combined thickness equal to that of the studs supporting them (Fig. 9–29). The headers are supported by a jack stud, which rests under the header, and by the full studs on both sides of the opening. The sole plate is cut away (actually, left out) so that the floor can remain flat.

For window openings, the width of the headers increases as the width of the opening increases. Windows up to 36 in. wide use two-by-fours for the headers. If the window is between 36 and 54 in. wide, two-by-sixes are used; if it is between 54 and 76 in. wide, two-by-eights are used.

If window or door openings are over 36 in. in width, additional studs are added to each side of the opening to carry the load down to the platform. The number of additional studs required depends on such factors as the width of the opening and the roof or ceiling load over the opening (Fig. 9–30). The horizontal member, which supports the lower portion of the window, is the sill. One or two two-by-fours, laid flat, make up the sill. The sill is supported by cripple studs, which are sometimes spaced on 10-in. rather than 16-in. centers.

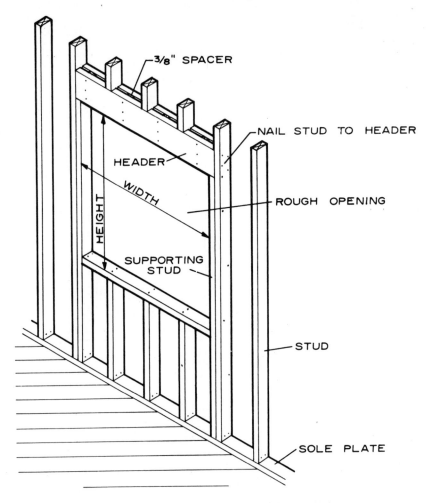

Fig. 9-30. Headers for windows and door openings

Corner Posts

When two walls meet at right angles, it is necessary to provide nailing surfaces in the corner for the application lath or gypsum board. The arrangement illustrated in Fig. 9-31 provides two solid inside surfaces for nailing.

Bracing

Bracing is used when additional stiffening of a wall is required. The most common type of bracing is let-in bracing [Fig. 9-28(a)], in which a one-by-four is set into a gain (recess) cut into the edges of the studs. Another type of brace is the cut-in brace illustrated in Fig. 9-28(b).

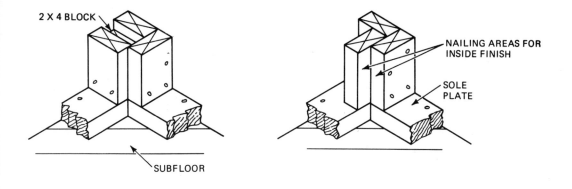

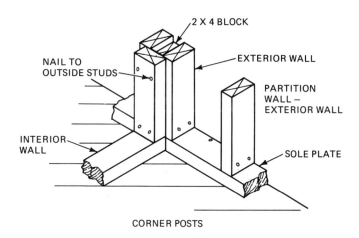

Fig. 9-31. Corner post construction

Wall Fabrication Procedure

Walls can be fabricated in a number of ways. In one method, sole plates are fastened to the platform first; then the top plate and studs are assembled on the floor, using through nailing. The wall is raised and the lower ends of the studs are toenailed into the sole plate.

Another method involves assembling the wall on the platform floor with or without the window and door openings complete. The wall is checked for squareness by adjusting the frame until the diagonals are of equal length. Temporary bracing is applied to keep the frame square, and the wall is raised.

Side walls are usually raised and braced first because these walls are generally the longest. When a wall is raised, it is checked for plumbness (verticality). This can be done with a level or with a plumb bob (Fig. 9-32). The temporary bracing holds the wall in position until the end walls are

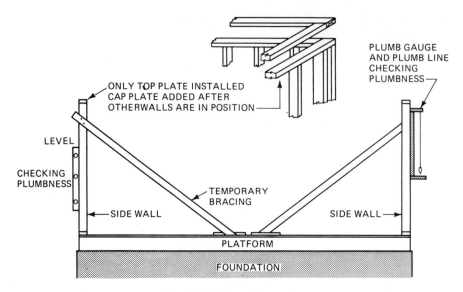

Fig. 9-32. Plumbing walls

raised. End walls are raised after side walls because the braced side walls hold the end walls in position. In Fig. 9-32, note that the cap plates have been left off the walls. These are added last and are used to form a kind of lap joint at each corner and wall intersection. Once the exterior walls are plumbed and braced, the interior walls (partitions) are laid out, and the walls are installed. Smaller rooms are done first.

ROOF FRAMING

Ceiling Joists

Ceiling joists support the ceiling of the structure. In multistory structures, the ceiling joists of the first floor become the floor joists of the second floor. If the space above the ceiling is not designed for expansion, two-by-sixes are commonly used as ceiling joists.

Typically, the ceiling joists rest on a load-bearing wall in much the same way that the floor joists rest on the girder. Where large open areas prevent the installation of load-bearing walls, a flush beam is used [Fig. 9-27(a) and (b)].

Roof Structure

Flat roof. The flat roof is the simplest type of roof because the ceiling joists double as roof supports. For this roof, the ceiling joists have to be strong enough to support any anticipated snow load. Although the flat roof saves a considerable amount of material, in comparison to other roof types, it is highly susceptible to leaking [Fig. 9-33(a)].

Shed roof. The shed roof is basically a roof with a single slope [Fig. 9-33(b)]. It is less likely to leak than the flat roof, but its span is somewhat limited.

Gable roof. The gable roof is the simplest type of multipitched roof. Its great inherent strength makes it highly suitable for use in a variety of climates [Fig. 9-33(c)]. Since the gable roof is the basic roof, its rafter layout is described in detail below.

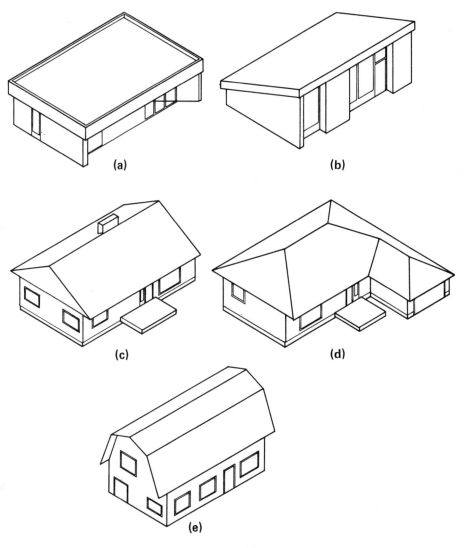

Fig. 9-33.

Hip roof. The hip roof has four sloping surfaces [Fig. 9-33(d)]. In this type of construction, all of the building walls carry some of the roof load. The hip roof allows all of the exterior building walls to have an overhang, which helps to protect them from the elements.

Gambrel roof. The gambrel roof allows the space above the ceiling joists to be used more readily [Fig. 9-33(e)].

Roof Rafters

A gable roof can be thought of as being constructed of two right-angle triangles placed against each other as shown in Fig. 9-34. The horizontal base of each of the triangles is known as the *run* of the rafter. The rafter is the sloping member of the roof represented by the hypotenuse of the triangle shown in Fig. 9-34. The *run* of the rafter is the *horizontal distance* covered as a point moves along the rafter from one end to the other. The total horizontal distance covered by both rafters is called the *roof span*. In most cases, the rafter run is equal to one-half of the building width or one-half of the roof span. The vertical side of each of the roof triangles is known as the *rise* of the rafter. It can be thought of as the vertical distance covered as a point moves from one end of the rafter to the other (Fig. 9-34).

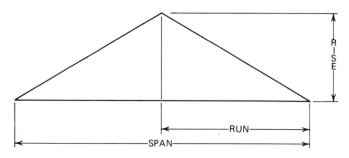

Fig. 9-34. Roof structure terms

When a more complete diagram of the roof structure is studied (Fig. 9-35), other components are visible. The upper ends of the rafters butt against a *ridgeboard*. Each of the rafters has a cutout which allows it to sit on the cap plate of the walls on each side of the structure. This cutout is known as the *bird's-mouth* or *seat cut*. In some gable roofs, the rafter extends out past the wall of the structure. This part of the rafter is called the *rafter tail*.

The slope of the roof is designated in two ways. One designation involves the calculation of *roof pitch*. This is the fraction obtained by dividing the *rise* by the *span*. Therefore, if a roof has a *rise* of 10 ft and a *span* of 40 ft, then rise/span = 10/40 = 1/4 pitch.

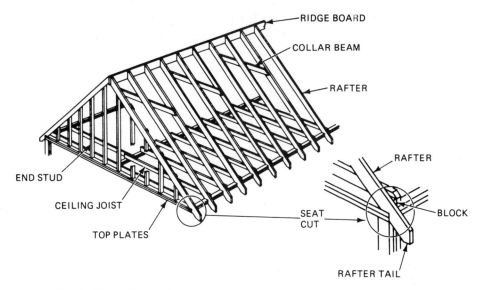

Fig. 9-35. Ceiling and roof framing: Overall view of gable roof framing

The second way to designate roof slope is to draw a *roof slope triangle,* as shown in Fig. 9-36. This triangle appears on the building plan. The horizontal number is always 12, because the unit of rafter run is the foot and there are 12 in. in a foot. The vertical leg of the triangle has another number, for example, 8, as shown. This roof is said to have a roof slope of 8 in 12, which means that for each foot of rafter run, 8 in. of rafter rise is covered (Fig. 9-36).

Rafter Layout Procedure

To lay out a rafter, the length of the rafter must be known or determined. In an actual roof structure, the slope of the triangles shown in Fig. 9-34 is replaced by the centerline of the rafter (Fig. 9-37). The horizontal leg of the triangle is now represented by the lower edge of the ceiling joist,

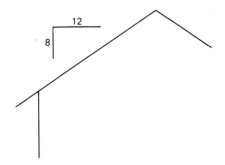

Fig. 9-36. Slope triangle

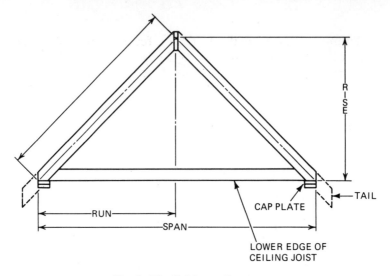

Fig. 9-37. Gable roof structure

which rests on the cap plates of the wall (Fig. 9-37). The vertical leg of the triangle is represented by an imaginary vertical line running from the lower edge of the ceiling joists up through the center of the ridge (Fig. 9-37).

Mathematical method for determining rafter length. In the diagram shown in Fig. 9-38, the roof slope triangle indicates a slope of 5 in 12. The rafter run is 24 ft and the rafter rise is 10 ft. Using the formula $a^2 + b^2 = c^2$, where a and b are the legs of the triangle at right angles to each other and c is the hypotenuse (Fig. 9-38), we calculate:

$$a^2 + b^2 = c^2$$

$$10^2 + 24^2 = c^2$$

$$100 + 576 = 676$$

$$c = \sqrt{676}$$

$$c = 26 \text{ ft}$$

Thus the rafter length is 26 ft.

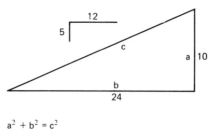

$$a^2 + b^2 = c^2$$
$$100 + 576 = 676$$
$$c = \sqrt{676}$$
$$c = 26'$$

Fig. 9-38. Calculating rafter length

Framing square method (table) for determining rafter length. On the front of the framing square blade is a horizontal table marked Length Common Rafters per Foot of Run. To use this table, follow this method:

1. Find the number that represents the unit rise from the slope triangle on the roof diagram. In this case, the number is 5. See Fig. 9–39(b).

2. Locate the number 5 on the upper edge of the framing square blade among the inch markings [Fig. 9–39(a)]. This number is the 5-in. mark in this case.

3. Look directly below the number 5, and find the number 13 in the horizontal table (Fig. 9–39). This means that for each foot of rafter run, 13 in. of rafter length is required. In the diagram of the framing square shown in Fig. 9–40, the ruler is positioned on the number 12 on the tongue, and on the number 5 on the blade. The hypotenuse of the triangle, the ruler, measures 13 in. The ruler also indicates the actual roof slope. Note that the numbers in the table to the right and left of the number 13 have four digits, like 12.65 and 13.42. These are read "twelve and sixty-five one-hundredths of an inch of rafter length per foot of rafter run," and "thirteen and forty-two one-hundredths of an inch of rafter length per foot of rafter run," respectively.

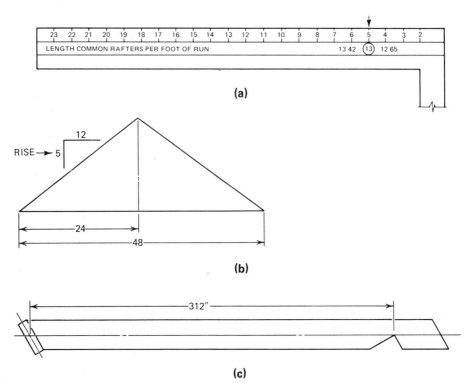

Fig. 9–39. Determining rafter length using rafter table

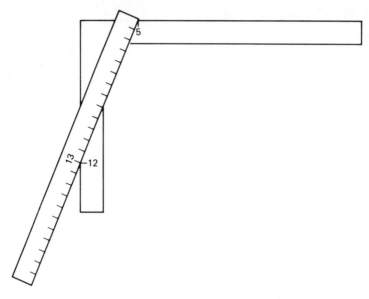

Fig. 9-40. Unit of rafter length in a 5-12 slope

4. Since the rafter run in this case is 24 ft [Fig. 9-39(b)], the number 13, found in step 3, is multiplied by 24 ft.

$$13 \text{ in.} \times 24 \text{ ft of run} = 312 \text{ in. or } 26 \text{ ft}$$

The rafter is 312 in. or 26 ft long [Fig. 9-39(c)].

The step-off method (using the framing square) for determining rafter length.

1. Select a piece of framing material to be used as a rafter and position the framing square as shown in Fig. 9-41A. Note that the 12-in. marking represents *horizontal* measurement or *rafter run* and the 5 represents *vertical* measurement or *rafter rise*.

2. Make the markings on the rafter as shown in Fig. 9-41. Note that line A will be vertical or plumb when the rafter is in position. Then position the framing square as shown in Fig. 9-41B. At this point, 1 ft or 12 in. of horizontal distance has been covered. Repeat this step until the 24 ft of rafter run has been covered. [Fig. 9-41(D)].

3. At this location, draw a plumb line (E) as shown in Fig. 9-41. This line will be aligned with the outside of the building wall (Fig. 9-37). If the rafter is to have a *tail,* lay out and cut a *seat cut* or *birds's-mouth* as shown in Fig. 9-41F. The depth of the bird's-mouth is indicated on the drawing provided. The plumb cut is generally at least deep enough to cover both of the top plates and, in this instance, it lies on the centerline.

4. Add the tail and lay out a plumb cut for the end of the rafter. If a *soffit* is to be installed, lay out a line for this purpose, as shown in Fig. 9–41G. This line becomes a level surface when the rafter is in place.

5. Now the rafter is the correct length, except for the necessary allowance for the ridgeboard. Subtract half the thickness of the ridgeboard from the rafter length as shown in Fig. 9–41H, and make the plumb cut for the ridgeboard.

This method is commonly used by carpenters because it requires a minimum amount of calculation. To improve its accuracy, a pair of stops (stair fixtures) can be clamped to the square to maintain the correct angle during layout.

In laying out a rafter whose length has been determined mathematically or from the table on the framing square, the same basic procedure is followed (Fig. 9–42).

In practice, a pair of rafters are cut as described and then fitted, together with a ridgeboard, to the structure to determine whether or not the layout is accurate. If it is, these rafters are used as templates for laying out the other rafters to be used in constructing the roof.

Rafters are installed in pairs against the ridgeboard, which is temporarily braced in position. One rafter in each pair is through-nailed and the other toenailed.

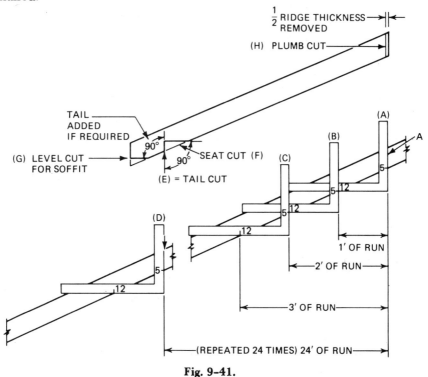

Fig. 9–41.

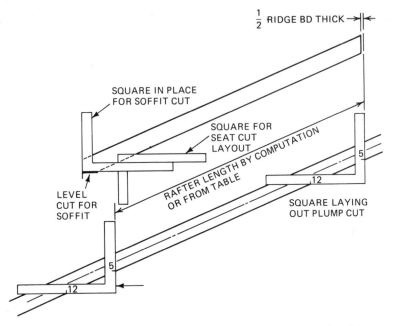

Fig. 9-42. Rafter layout when length is computed or found in table

SHEATHING

Wall Sheathing

Sheathing is the material that is part of the "skin" that covers the skeletal frame of the structure. It serves several purposes: It stiffens and reinforces the walls; it serves as a foundation for the siding which will be applied to it; and it helps to keep exterior air out and interior air in, by enclosing the structure.

A number of materials can be used as sheathing. In older homes, one-by-sixes or one-by-eights were nailed, either diagonally or horizontally, to the wall frame. Square-edge, shiplap, or tongue-and-groove material was used (Fig. 9-43). The shaped material formed a more effective barrier against air infiltration.

In current practice, sheet materials are commonly used. Plywood, ranging in thickness from 5/8 to 1/2 in., is the most commonly used. This material is installed with the outside grain running vertically. All ends and edges must be located over the framing members and nailed at 6-in. intervals (Fig. 9-44).

Various types of man-made composition sheathing are also available, including fiberboard and gypsum sheathing faced with a black, waterproof

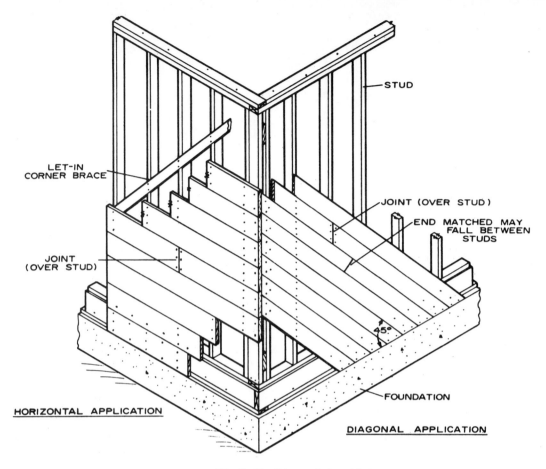

STUD

LET-IN CORNER BRACE

JOINT (OVER STUD)

END MATCHED MAY FALL BETWEEN STUDS

JOINT (OVER STUD)

45°

FOUNDATION

HORIZONTAL APPLICATION

DIAGONAL APPLICATION

Fig. 9–43. Diagonal sheathing

material. These sheet materials are generally available in either 24 in. by 96 in., or 48 in. by 96 in. panels, and they are usually about 1/2 in. thick (Fig. 9–44).

Roof Sheathing

For roofs, either plywood or solid wood sheathing can be used. One-by-six or one-by-eight solid wood or 5/8 to 1/2-in. plywood can be used. With plywood, an exterior glue line is used because of its ability to withstand moisture.

Cornice Construction

In designing a structure, the architect decides whether or not the building should have a roof with an overhang. Overhangs provide several advantages. First, they protect the walls and windows from the elements. Rain

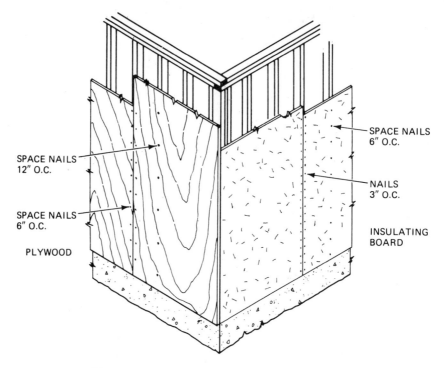

SPACE NAILS
12" O.C.

SPACE NAILS
6" O.C.

PLYWOOD

SPACE NAILS
6" O.C.

NAILS
3" O.C.

INSULATING
BOARD

Fig. 9-44. Insulating board and plywood sheathing

is carried out beyond the building wall by the overhang at the eaves of the roof. Second, they usually enhance the appearance of the structure. Finally, when properly designed, they shade the building interior from the hot summer sun which rises high in the sky, and yet allow the warming winter sun to penetrate the windows.

In most instances, the space between the roof eave edge and the side wall of the house is enclosed. This enclosure is called a *cornice*. Some of the various types of cornices are the wide box cornice (Fig. 9-45), the open cornice (Fig. 9-46), and the closed cornice (Fig. 9-47).

ROOFING

Wood Shingles

Originally, wood shingles were used extensively because of their relatively low cost, ease of installation, and lightness. Today, they are much less commonly used because they are expensive, less fire-resistant, and more expensive to install than asphalt shingles. They are generally made of edge-grain cedar or redwood. Roofing felt is not generally required under wood shingles, and spaced roof sheathing is typical. The minimum recommended roof slope for wood shingles is 4 in 12 (Fig. 9-48).

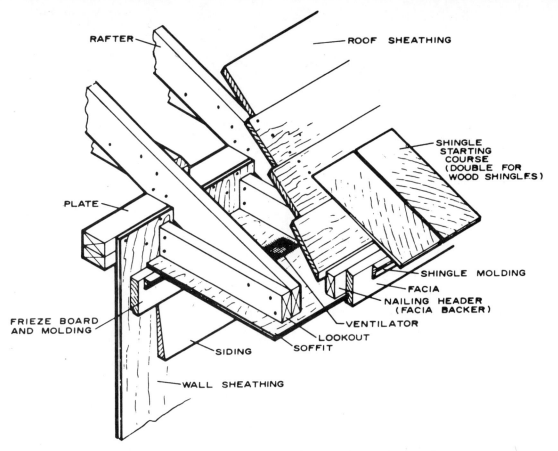

RAFTER

ROOF SHEATHING

SHINGLE STARTING COURSE (DOUBLE FOR WOOD SHINGLES)

PLATE

SHINGLE MOLDING

FACIA

NAILING HEADER (FACIA BACKER)

FRIEZE BOARD AND MOLDING

VENTILATOR

LOOKOUT

SIDING

SOFFIT

WALL SHEATHING

Fig. 9-45. Wide box cornice (with horizontal lookouts)

Fig. 9-46. Open cornice

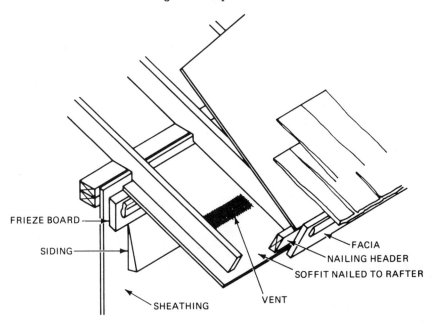

FRIEZE BOARD

SIDING

FACIA

NAILING HEADER

SOFFIT NAILED TO RAFTER

SHEATHING

VENT

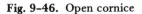

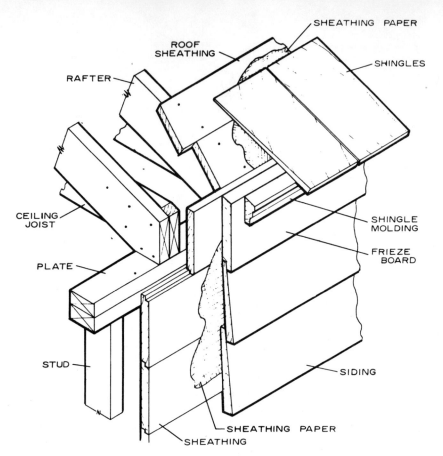

Fig. 9–47. Closed cornice

Asphalt Shingles

Asphalt shingles are popular because of the great variety of colors and types available and because of their ease of installation and relatively low cost. A properly installed asphalt shingle roof lasts about 20 years. The present recommended weight for asphalt roofing is 235 pound for square-butt strip shingles. The weight refers to the weight of a square (100 sq ft) of shingles, and three bundles make a square.

Self-sealing shingles have a spot of asphalt cement under each tab, which helps the shingles to resist wind action during periods of high wind velocity. *Square-butt* shingles (Fig. 9–49) are a standard 12 in. wide by 36 in. long. In most cases, the shingles are installed with a 5-in. exposure.

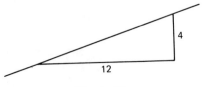

Fig. 9–48.

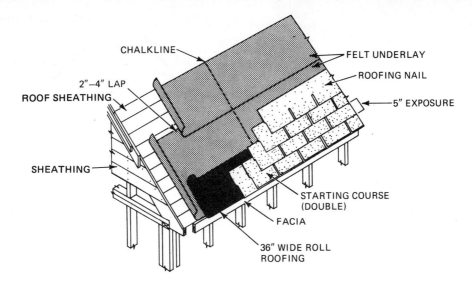

Fig. 9-49. Roofing installation eave end of roof

Before the shingles are nailed into position, roofing felt is applied to the roof sheathing. This *underlayment* is made of a feltlike paper that is saturated with asphalt. Fifteen-pound felt is recommended. The felt is laid horizontally with a 2- to 6-in. overlap.

At the eave end of the roof, a 36-in.-wide strip of smooth roll roofing is applied over the roofing felt. This helps to resist damage from ice damming (Fig. 9-49) which results when melted snow reaches the gutter or the cooler roof area of the overhang and refreezes. As the ice collects, it traps water which can seep under the shingles and leak into the living space below, damaging walls and ceilings. The 36-in.-wide strip of roll roofing provides additional waterproofing for this area.

Flashing and counterflashing are applied to chimneys, and flashing is applied to dormers (Fig. 9-50). Valleys are also flashed for additional protection. Most flashing is installed before shingles are applied.

Fig. 9-50. Flashing around dormer

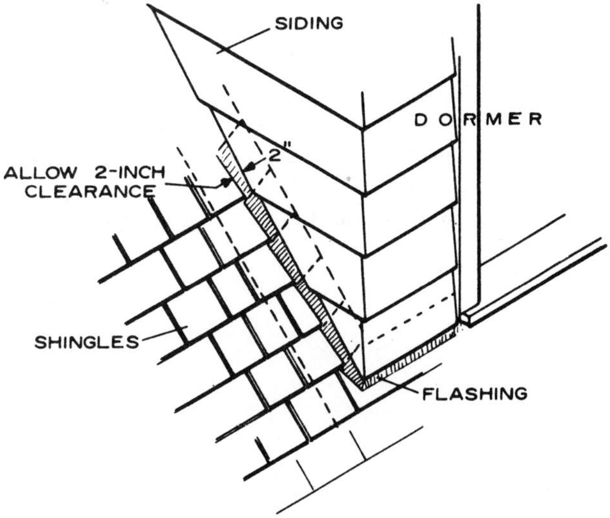

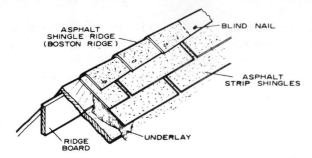

Fig. 9-51.

Shingle application starts at the eave edge of the roof. Each shingle is attached with four or six 1-in. galvanized roofing nails. The ridge or hip of the roof is usually finished off with a row of individual shingles which are nailed into position (Fig. 9-51). This is known as a *Boston ridge*.

Slate Roofs

Slate roofs are very durable and very expensive. Each piece of slate has two holes drilled in it to receive nails. In addition to their durability and beauty, slate roofs are fireproof.

Built-up Roofs

Built-up roofs are commonly used on flat roofs. In such installations, several layers of roofer's felt are applied to the roof, with tar or asphalt mopped on between layers. The final layer is mopped and covered with crushed stone.

WINDOWS

Windows are installed after the sheathing has been applied but before the siding is added to the structure. This sequence is used because the siding is fitted against the window frames.

Windows serve two primary functions: They allow light to enter the structure and they permit ventilation. To determine the minimum window area required in a room, the designer uses the rule of thumb that says that window area should equal approximately 10 percent of the floor area of a room for proper light. An open-window area equal to approximately 4 percent of the floor area should be provided for ventilation.

Types of Windows

Windows are of several types. Among the most commonly used types are double-hung [Fig. 9-52(a)], casement [Fig. 9-52(b)], stationary [Fig. 9-52(c)], sliding [Fig. 9-52(d)], and awning [Fig. 9-52(e)] windows.

Double-hung windows. Double-hung window units are widely used in construction. This type of window consists of two glazed frames or sashes which slide up and down in side jambs (frame). The upper sash overlaps the lower when the window is closed, making it waterproof. The sashes are held in position by counterweights (found mostly in older structures), by springs, or by compression weather stripping. Weather stripping consists of metal strips that fit into grooves in the sash to make the window more resistant to the flow of air around the sash. Double-hung windows can provide a maximum of 50 percent of their area for ventilation purposes.

Fig. 9–52.

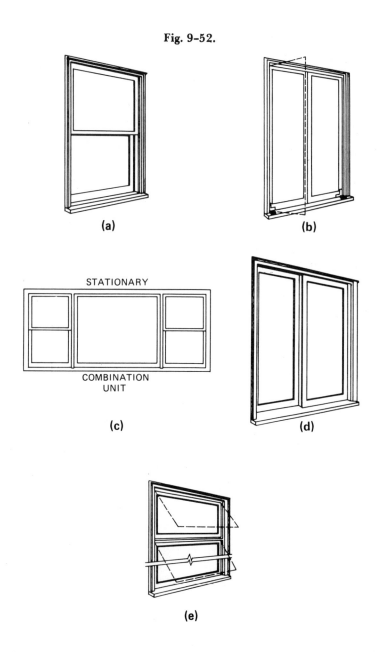

(a)

(b)

STATIONARY

COMBINATION
UNIT

(c)

(d)

(e)

Casement windows. Casement windows consist of a frame fitted with a single or double window sash unit. The windows are side-hinged and swing out like a door. They can be made of wood, vinyl-covered wood, or metal [Fig. 9-52(b)].

The principal functional advantage of the casement window is its capacity to be fully opened, permitting 100 percent ventilation.

Stationary windows. Stationary windows cannot be opened for ventilation and therefore are often combined with other types which can be opened [Fig. 9-52(c)].

Sliding windows. Sliding windows consist of sashes which slide horizontally when being opened or closed. These units are usually made of metal and can provide a maximum opening of 50 percent. One advantage of the sliding window is the ease with which the sashes can be removed by lifting and swinging the bottom inward [Fig. 9-52(d)].

Awning windows. Awning windows usually consist of several sashes which are hinged at the top and are opened together by a rotary handle [Fig. 9-52(e)]. These windows allow 100 percent ventilation.

Window Installation

The area around a window opening is usually covered with building felt to inhibit the passage of air. Window units are generally purchased as a complete unit which fits into a rough opening. Flashing is installed above the window and extends down over the drip cap. This allows any water that seeps through the siding to travel down and away from the window frame. (Fig. 9-55).

DOORS

Exterior doors are at least 36 in. wide and 80 in. high. Rear doors are usually 30 in. wide. Door units are available partially assembled with hardware installed (Fig. 9-53). These units are installed in much the same way that window units are. Note that the sloping sill of the exterior door requires that the joists and subflooring be sloped to accommodate the sill [Fig. 9-53(c)].

Storm doors are commonly used to provide extra protection against air infiltration around and through exterior doors [Fig. 9-53(a)]. Metal insulated doors are available which can be used without storm doors.

SIDING

The purpose of siding is to provide added protection for the structure. In most cases it is applied to the sheathing after window and door units have been installed. A great variety of siding types are available.

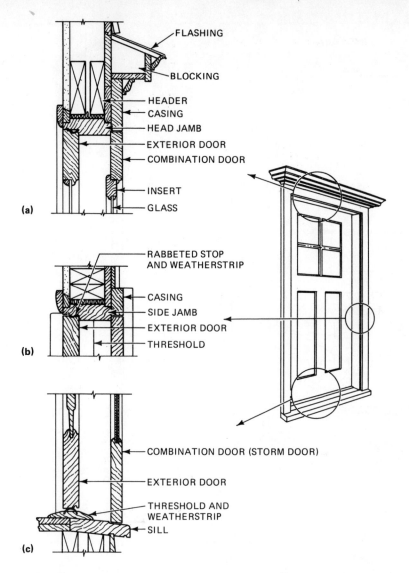

Fig. 9-53. Exterior door and frame. Exterior-door and combination-door (screen and storm) cross sections: head jamb; side jamb; sill

Wood Siding

Wood shingles are still commonly used as siding material. Various types are available, including hand-split shakes and striated (Fig. 9-54). Shingles made of cedar or redwood can be left unpainted, since they develop a natural color through weathering. Shingles are applied singly over a covering of horizontally lapped building felt and are nailed into position with at least two rust-resistant nails.

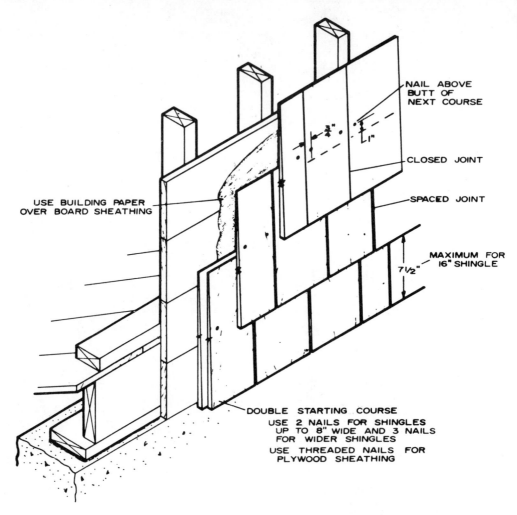

NAIL ABOVE
BUTT OF
NEXT COURSE

CLOSED JOINT

SPACED JOINT

MAXIMUM FOR
16" SHINGLE

7½"

USE BUILDING PAPER
OVER BOARD SHEATHING

DOUBLE STARTING COURSE
USE 2 NAILS FOR SHINGLES
UP TO 8" WIDE AND 3 NAILS
FOR WIDER SHINGLES
USE THREADED NAILS FOR
PLYWOOD SHEATHING

Fig. 9-54. Single-coursing of sidewalls (wood shingles - shakes)

Horizontal sidings of various types are available, but the familiar clapboards or bevel siding is still commonly used. A variety of other horizontal types are shown in Fig. 9-55. When installing horizontal siding, care must be taken to provide a waterproof covering for the structure. If shingles are used, joints between the shingles should be staggered to help prevent water seepage. Building felt under the shingles also provides protection against water. In other types of horizontal sidings, the overlapping nature of the material helps to keep water out.

Vertical sidings of various types are also used. Board and batten (Fig. 9-56) consists of relatively wide boards nailed to the sheathing, with vertical joints covered with narrow boards or battens.

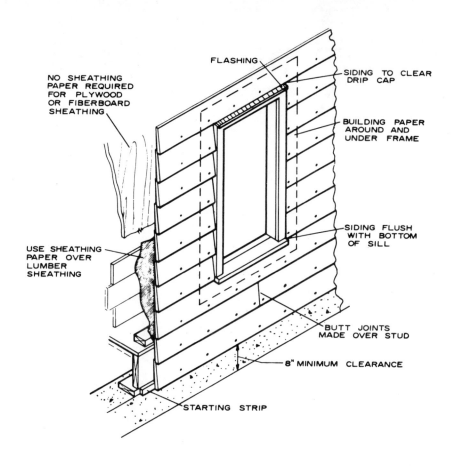

NO SHEATHING PAPER REQUIRED FOR PLYWOOD OR FIBERBOARD SHEATHING

FLASHING

SIDING TO CLEAR DRIP CAP

BUILDING PAPER AROUND AND UNDER FRAME

USE SHEATHING PAPER OVER LUMBER SHEATHING

SIDING FLUSH WITH BOTTOM OF SILL

BUTT JOINTS MADE OVER STUD

8" MINIMUM CLEARANCE

STARTING STRIP

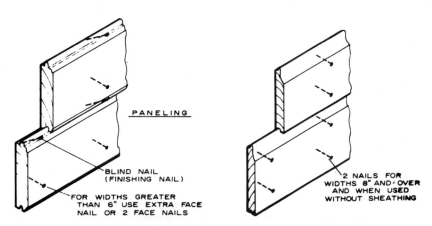

PANELING

BLIND NAIL (FINISHING NAIL)

FOR WIDTHS GREATER THAN 6" USE EXTRA FACE NAIL OR 2 FACE NAILS

2 NAILS FOR WIDTHS 8" AND OVER AND WHEN USED WITHOUT SHEATHING

Fig. 9-55. Installation of bevel siding and nailing of siding

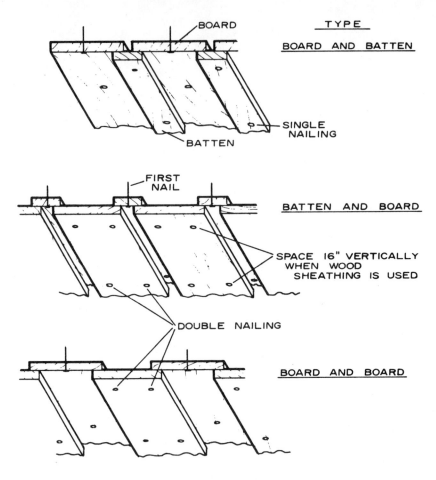

Fig. 9-56. Vertical siding

Sheet materials are available which speed up installation and which are designed to imitate some of the other types of sidings, like board and batten. One type of plywood used for siding takes the place of both the sheathing and the siding, but this material must be thick enough to perform both functions. Material that is 1/2 to 3/4 in. thick is recommended for such single-layer applications.

Nonwood Sidings

Many of the nonwood sidings were developed for installation over existing siding for the home-improvement market. However, many builders use these materials as primary sidings.

Asbestos-cement siding is one of the older materials on the market. These shingles are made of an asbestos-cement material and are nailed into place in much the same way wood shingles are. One of their positive features is resistance to weathering, which makes painting unnecessary for protection. However, the shingles tend to become discolored and are often painted to improve their appearance. Another feature is that these shingles are fireproof. On the negative side, the shingles are somewhat brittle and will fracture if struck a hard blow.

Aluminum siding is a very popular siding material because it installs quickly, comes prepainted, and is often provided with fiberglass insulation. A variety of patterns are available, including types that look like clapboards or shingles. The finish is durable and normally does not require repainting for as long as 10 years. Among the disadvantages of aluminum siding are its tendency to dent and its interference with electronic reception when indoor antennas are used.

Plastic siding is also available. This material is frequently made of vinyl and works easily with common woodworking tools. It has the advantages of dent-resistance, uniform color, and no negative electrical properties. One drawback of plastic siding is that it is difficult to paint; so color cannot be changed easily.

Masonry sidings of various types are used, including brick veneer and stucco.

UTILITIES

Once the exterior of the structure is enclosed, electrical work and plumbing are installed before the plaster walls or dry walls are applied, because the installation of pipes and cables requires access to the framing members of the structure. For major pipes and heavy fixtures, steps are taken during framing to provide for their installation (Fig. 9-57). Additional floor support is provided for bathtubs, extra-wide plates are installed for soil stacks, and reinforcing scabs are installed when framing members are cut. Holes in joists should be limited to 2 in. in diameter, with a minimum of 2-1/2 in. between a hole and the edges of the joist [Fig. 9-57(d)].

Plumbing System

The plumbing system in a structure can be divided into two major components: the *supply system* and the *drain-waste system*.

Supply system. The supply system originates at a well or water main. Water from either of these sources is carried to the house supply system through pipes. In most cases, the pipe comes through the foundation wall closest to the street and enters a water meter. In many systems a valve is

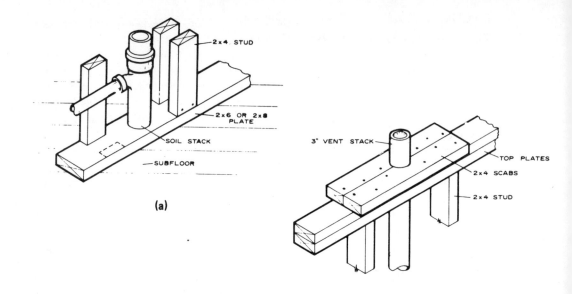

(a)

—Plumbing stacks: A, 4-inch cast-iron stack;
B, 3-inch pipe for vent.

(b)

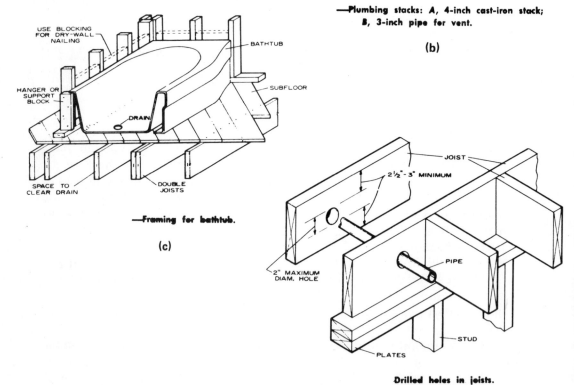

—Framing for bathtub.

(c)

Drilled holes in joists.

(d)

Fig. 9-57.

installed between the meter and the house supply system. This valve allows the water supply to the entire system to be cut off.

From the meter, the water is carried by pipes throughout the house to various taps. One of the pipes in the system delivers water to a water heater, where it is heated and stored until used. Dwellings have two sets of delivery pipes: cold water pipes and hot water pipes. Pipes of 1/2- or 3/4-in. diameter are normally used for delivery supply lines. Brass or copper pipe is commonly used since galvanized or plain iron pipe eventually builds up a layer of oxide on its interior walls, causing the pressure and rate of water flow to be gradually reduced. Copper tubing is sometimes used because its installation requires fewer fittings and because it is easy to work with. Joints are sweat-soldered and changes in the system are easy to accomplish.

It is a good idea to install individual shutoff valves at all fixtures (sinks, bathtubs, and showers). This makes it possible to change washers and make other repairs without turning off the main water supply system. The supply system should be installed so that horizontal runs have a slight incline to enable the system to be drained completely if necessary. This is necessary if a house is to be left unheated during the winter, since any water left in the supply system might freeze, causing pipes to split [Fig. 9–58(a)].

Drain-waste system. Once the water is delivered to the various taps in the system, it must be disposed of. The drain-waste system accomplishes this job. In addition to carrying the unwanted water to a sewer system or septic tank, the system must protect the occupants of the house from sewer gases [Fig. 9–58(b)]. Traps keep sewer gases from escaping by maintaining a body of water in the trap between the fixture drain and the drain-waste system. As new water flows into the trap, the water that was in the trap overflows into the drain-waste system. In toilets, the trap is an integral (built-into) part of the ceramic toilet.

The drain lines lead away from the fixtures at a slope of 1/4 in. vertical drop for each foot of horizontal run [Fig. 9–58(b)]. If the incline is any sharper, the solid waste in the system will tend to settle out and clog the pipes. If it is any less steep, the drainage will be sluggish and may lead to sewerage backup.

As shown in Fig. 9–58(b), a vertical *soil stack* is the most prominent feature of the system. This stack is 3 or 4 in. in diameter and usually made of cast iron. It terminates in a roof vent at one end, and connects to the sewer system or septic tank at the other end. The soil stack serves two functions. It carries the wastewater away, and it provides a vent for the system.

The venting function is very important. The open end of the stack keeps the entire drain-waste system at atmospheric pressure, which prevents vacuum or excessive suction from building up. If a milk carton is filled with water and inverted, the water will gush out in spurts rather than in a steady stream. However, if the carton is vented by a hole punched in its bottom, the water will flow out of the carton in a strong, steady stream without

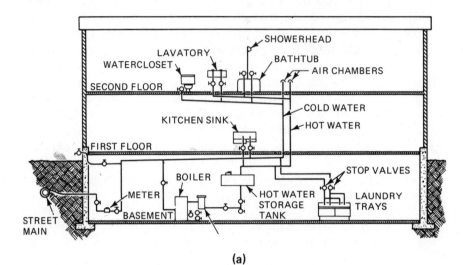

(a)

Fig. 9-58A. Water supply system

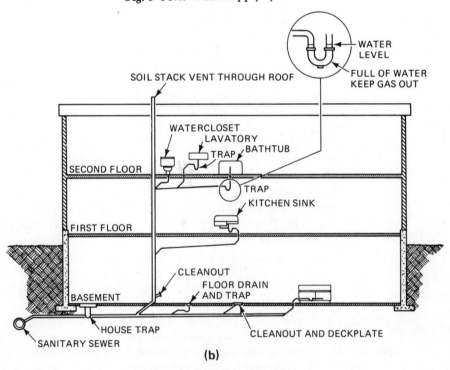

(b)

Fig. 9-58B. Drain waste system

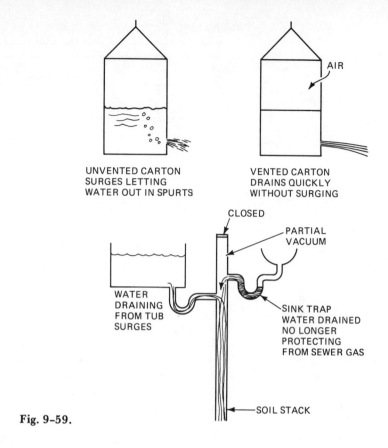

UNVENTED CARTON
SURGES LETTING
WATER OUT IN SPURTS

VENTED CARTON
DRAINS QUICKLY
WITHOUT SURGING

AIR

CLOSED

PARTIAL
VACUUM

WATER
DRAINING
FROM TUB
SURGES

SINK TRAP
WATER DRAINED
NO LONGER
PROTECTING
FROM SEWER GAS

SOIL STACK

Fig. 9-59.

surging or creating a vacuum [Fig. 9-59(a)]. In a plumbing system, an un-vented waste line would create a similar condition. If the vacuum were strong enough, as when a toilet is flushed, the traps in the system could be drained by the suction developed. This would leave the system unprotected against sewer gas until the traps were refilled [Fig. 9-59(b)].

Installation. The pipes of the supply system are run through framing members, where required, or attached to them with metal straps. The drain-waste system, if it is cast iron, requires special framing supports (such as metal straps) at various points (Fig. 9-57). All pipes are installed before the interior is complete, but fixtures (tubs, sinks, etc.) are not installed until the interior is more nearly complete.

WIRING AND THE ELECTRICAL SYSTEM

Power is usually delivered to a structure through overhead wires (Fig. 9-60) but sometimes underground cables are used. A modern home should have a minimum of 100 amperes (ideally, 200 amperes) and a maximum of 240 volts available. The ampere, or amp rating, is an indication of the quantity or

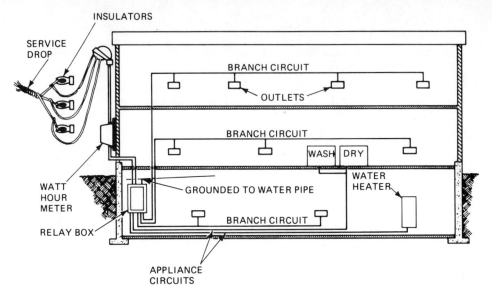

Fig. 9–60.

total amount of electricity which can be delivered to the house. Most electrical devices require 110 volts; however, heavy consumers such as air-conditioners and electric heating devices frequently require 240 volts.

Protective Devices

The fuse or circuit-breaker box contains a number of fuses or circuit breakers which control the flow of electricity to various parts of the house. Each of these devices is connected to a *branch* circuit in the house. The fuse or circuit breaker has a number on it indicating the maximum amount of amperage it will allow to flow (Fig. 9–60). If this number is exceeded, the fuse will blow or the circuit breaker will snap open, cutting off current to that branch. Thus, these circuit breakers and fuses are protective devices. If they were not in the system and too much current was allowed to flow to a branch circuit, the wires in the circuit would overheat and might cause a fire.

The fuse stops current flow when the metal strip inside the fuse melts because of excessive current flow. It must be replaced after the problem in the branch circuit is corrected. The circuit breaker is a magnetic switch that is activated by an excessive current flow through its coil. Once the problem in the branch circuit is corrected, the circuit breaker is reset by flipping the switch closed.

Installation of Wiring

The wiring installation plan is determined by the designer of the structure, who is guided by building-code requirements. The two most commonly used types of wiring are Romex (a plastic-covered wire) and Bx or armored cable (a metal-covered wire) [Fig. 9–61(a)]. Romex is easier to install but does not provide the protection to the wire that the metal-covered Bx does [Fig. 9–61(b)].

The diameter of the wires in a branch circuit determines the capacity of the circuit. No. 12 wire is used for moderate to heavy loads. No. 14, which is thinner, is the minimum-size wire permissible.

Fig. 9–61. (a) Plastic covered cable (Romex). (b) Romex entering junction box mounted between studs. (c) Outlet box flush with plaster or gypsum board.

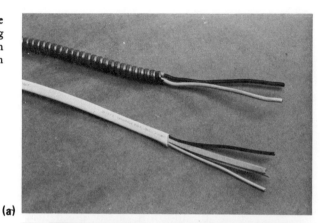

(a)

(b)

(c)

Switch and outlet boxes are located and installed in the house first. These attach to the framing members and are positioned so that when the plaster or gypsum board is installed, the box edges will be flush with the surface [Fig. 9-61(c)]. The various branch circuits are then installed, with the cables passing through framing members or stapled to them as required. If the electrical system is to be inspected, the wires are left unconnected in the various boxes for inspection and testing. The final installation of outlet switches and lighting fixtures is completed after the walls are in.

INSULATION

All exterior walls and ceilings should be insulated. Insulation is installed between the studs and joists before plaster or gypsum board is put up. The insulation of ceiling areas can await the application of ceiling covering materials.

Insulation makes heating and cooling a structure less costly. Heat that is normally lost through ceilings because of convection (the flow of air caused by heated air rising because it is lighter) can be significantly reduced by installing a vapor barrier and insulation to the spaces between ceiling joists. Heat loss around windows and through walls can also be reduced by insulation. In addition, many condensation problems caused by moisture-laden warm air coming into contact with cooler walls and ceilings can also be reduced by the proper installation of insulation and vapor barriers.

Insulating materials provide dead air space. The normal flow of air through spaces is reduced or stopped by filling these spaces with materials which trap air. The air itself acts as the insulator. Materials such as fiberglass and rock wool are commonly used for this purpose.

Vapor barriers are materials, usually in sheet or film form, which are applied to reduce the flow of air carrying water vapor through walls and ceilings. Plastic film, aluminum foil, and asphalt-laminated paper are among the materials used for this purpose.

Roll Insulation

Roll or blanket insulation is sold in rolls of various thickness with a width that allows the material to fit between studs spaced on 16-in. centers (Fig. 9-62). This material is available with an aluminum-foil or asphalt-paper vapor barrier. The blanket is attached to the studs by stapling tabs on the material directly to the framing members. The foil or paper side of the insulation is installed facing the heated area of the structure [Figs. 9-63(a) and (b)]. A maximum insulation thickness of 3 in. is normally used. A 3/4-in. space should be left between the vapor barrier and the wall-covering material. Areas around window and door openings should be carefully treated with a vapor barrier to reduce air infiltration.

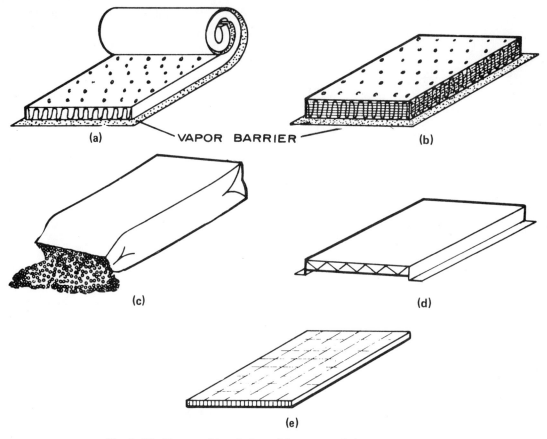

Fig. 9-62. Types of insulation: (a) Blanket; (b) batt; (c) fill; (d) reflective (one type), (e) rigid

Batt Insulation

Insulation of ceilings usually requires a minimum of 6 in. of insulation. Such insulation does not lend itself to roll-type packaging. The insulation is packaged in batts or matts of manageable size. This material is installed between the ceiling joists in much the same fashion as roll material is installed between studs. It can also be laid in place after the plaster has been installed (Fig. 9-63(e)].

Loose-Fill Insulation

Loose-fill insulation is supplied in bags whose contents can be poured into air spaces [Fig. 9-63(c)]. In existing finished structures, it is sometimes blown into spaces. Rock wool, glass wool, and vermiculite are among the materials used for this purpose.

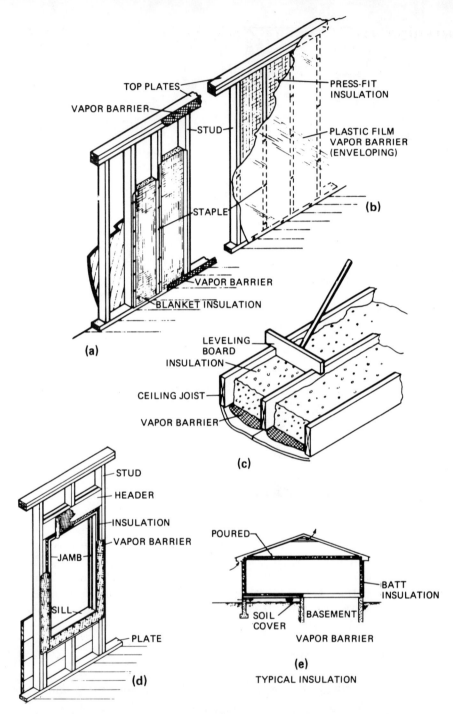

Fig. 9–63. Application of insulation: (a) Wall section with blanket type; (b) wall section with "press-fit" insulation; (c) ceiling with full insulation; (d) window insulation; (e) typical insulation

INTERIOR WALL AND CEILING COVERINGS

Once the utilities and insulation have been installed, the interior surfaces can be dealt with. The most common ceiling and wall coverings used in residential construction are plaster or dry-wall plaster boards. The internal wall and ceiling coverings allow the interior of the structure to be decorated with paint or wallpaper.

Lath and Plaster

Lath and plaster are relatively expensive to install because of the time required for the plaster to dry and because of the skill required to install it. Gypsum lath is made in the same way that gypsum board is—a layer of plaster is sandwiched between two layers of paper. The surface of the board is pierced with holes which help to keep the plaster, applied to the surface of the board, in place (Fig. 9–64). Gypsum lath is available in sheets 16 in.

Fig. 9–64. Plaster grounds: (a) At doorway and floor; (b) strip ground at doorway; (c) ground at window

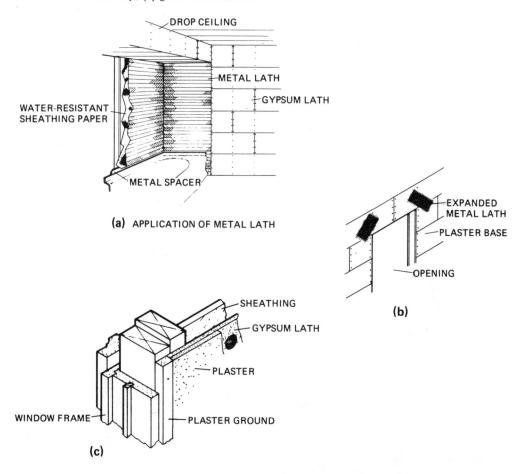

by 48 in., and 3/8 in. thick. Fiberboard lath, of similar construction, has the same dimensions, but with a 1/2-in. thickness. Wire lath, a type of expanded steel, is available in sheets 27 in. wide and 96 in. long [Fig. 9-64(a)]. Wire lath is commonly used in bathrooms, where it is applied over a waterproof barrier which is already in place over the wall studs [Fig. 9-64(a)]. In places of probable stress (e.g., areas around openings and outside corners), metal lath is applied for extra strength [Fig. 9-64(b)].

Plaster is made from a mixture of sand, lime, plaster, and water. The first coat applied is called the scratch coat, and it is normally 1/2 in. thick.

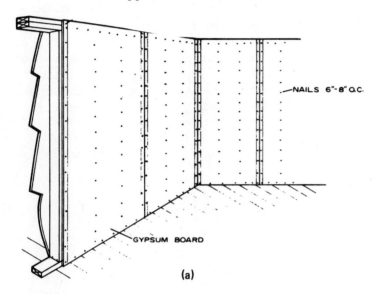

NAILS 6"-8" O.C.

GYPSUM BOARD

(a)

Fig. 9-65. Application of gypsum board finish

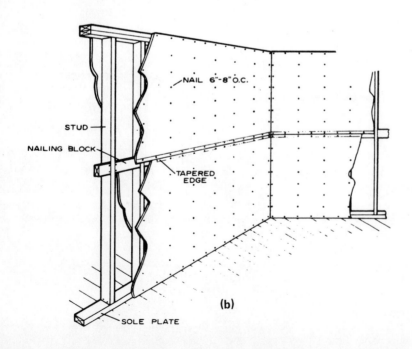

NAIL 6"-8" O.C.

STUD

NAILING BLOCK

TAPERED EDGE

(b)

SOLE PLATE

The surface of this coat is roughened or scratched to provide a good bond with the next coat. The second coat is the brown or leveling coat which eliminates any irregularities in the walls or ceilings. The final coat is either the sand-float (a slightly textured finish) or the putty coat (a very smooth finish). The plaster is applied and smoothed with a trowel by an experienced and skilled plasterer [Fig. 9–64(c)].

Dry-Wall Construction

Dry-wall finishing is probably the most commonly used interior wall and ceiling covering. It applies quickly, requires no drying time, and is relatively inexpensive.

Surfaces on which dry-wall is to be applied, must be flat. Any irregularities in the surface will deform the sheet material applied to them. Since the dry-wall is held in place with nails, the framing material must be relatively dry or the nails will tend to work out as the wood dries.

Gypsum Board

Gypsum board, Sheetrock, and plaster board are one and the same material. The board consists of a layer of plaster or gypsum sandwiched between two layers of paper. Sheets are usually 4 ft by 8 ft in size, but lengths up to 16 ft are available for horizontal and ceiling applications. The two most common thicknesses are 3/8 in. and 1/2 in. The long edges of the sheets are tapered to allow for taping [Fig. 9–65(b)].

Ceilings are installed first. Nails are driven at 5- to 7-in. intervals (1-5/8-in. nails for 1/2-in. material, and 1-3/8-in. nails for 3/8-in. material). Special nails which resist popping are used. The nail heads are driven slightly below the surface of the material, but do not break the paper coating [Fig. 9–66(d)].

After the ceiling is completed, the walls are covered, using a horizontal or vertical position for the sheets of material (Fig. 9–65). If the two-ply method is used, one layer of 3/8-in. thick material is placed horizontally and cemented to the first layer.

Joint Treatment

Seams are taped and spackled. Premixed taping compound is normally used over and under perforated paper tape. The following procedure is used on seams:

1. Apply a thin layer of compound, 1/16 in. thick, to the seam, starting at the top and working downward. Use a 5-in. spackling knife with a flexible blade. Hold the knife at about a 45° angle [Fig. 9–66(c)]. This application fills the recess formed by the tapered edges of the gypsum board about halfway.

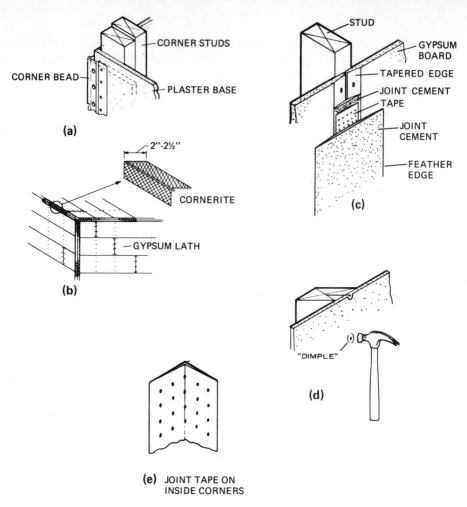

(e) JOINT TAPE ON INSIDE CORNERS

Fig. 9-66. Reinforcing of plaster at corners: (a) Outside; (b) inside

2. Measure, cut, and press a strip of perforated joint tape into the layer of compound with the knife held at a 45° angle as it travels from top to bottom.

3. Apply a thin layer of compound to *completely cover the tape.* At this point, the strip of compound is about 4 in. wide. Excessive spreading leads to "cratering (formation of crater-like depressions)." A single pass with the knife is recommended.

4. Cover the nail heads with a single application of compound, and allow to dry. No tape is used.

5. After drying, lightly sand the dry compound. Remove the compound dust produced with a damp cloth or sponge.

6. Apply a second, wider coat with feathered edges [Fig. 9-66(c)]. Repeat step 5, and apply a third coat if necessary. Then sand after drying.

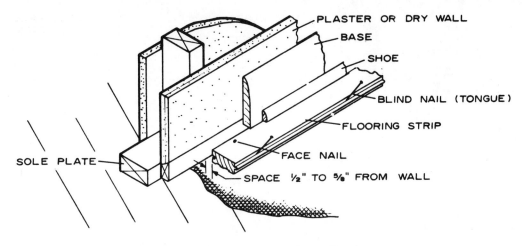

Fig. 9-67. Application of strip flooring

It is important to wear a dust-filtering mask when sanding taping compound. Some of this material contains asbestos and the inhalation of this substance is very dangerous.

Outside Corners

Outside corners have a metal strip applied to them which provides reinforcement and a rounded straight corner [Fig. 9-66(a)]. Inside corners are taped and spackled with a corner trowel. The nail heads at the base of the wall are usually covered by a baseboard and do not require covering.

When gypsum board is used in areas where moisture is a problem, a special water-resistant type of Sheetrock should be installed. This material is clearly marked or colored to indicate its moisture resistance.

FLOORS

After the walls and ceiling have been installed, the floors are completed. In many cases, hardwood flooring is applied over the subflooring. Vinyl or linoleum is often applied to kitchen floors. This material is usually placed on an adhesive, which holds it in place. Bathrooms usually have tile-, vinyl-, or linoleum-covered floors. Baseboard and other trimmings are applied after the finish flooring is installed (Fig. 9-67).

PRODUCTION

PRODUCTION IN MANUFACTURING FACILITIES

One of-a-kind pieces of furniture are still designed and built by cabinet-makers. Such work is usually limited to either the work of craftsmen in small shops or to specialty cabinetmaking firms that produce architectural work.

The bulk of furniture manufacturing today is carried out in large manufacturing plants. Large plants can produce quality pieces at relatively low cost because they can afford to invest in automatic and semiautomatic equipment which greatly speeds up production. In addition, workers who operate automatic machinery generally require less skill than workers using basic, nonautomatic machinery. Another basic cost-saving factor is related to the purchasing of materials. Large manufacturers can take advantage of quantity buying.

PRODUCT DEVELOPMENT

A discussion of the development of a product and its eventual manufacture has to be carried out in general terms. Each manufacturer operates independently. Each has particular methods of determining when new products are to be introduced and how they are to be manufactured. The process described here is fairly typical of that followed in industry.

Identifying a Need for a New Product

In some ways the furniture industry is unique. It rarely introduces new types of furniture. Most of the production is given over to the manufacture of standard pieces like chairs, tables, and sofas. The demand for furniture is relatively predictable.

One manufacturer may identify a changing selling pattern for a product, and this could lead to a decision to increase the production of the better-selling pieces and to explore the possibility of developing another line of lower-cost chairs. Another way of identifying a need for a new product can arise from changes in styling preference.

In some industries, once the need for a new product has been identified, a formal program of *market research* is carried out by specialists in that field. This process includes surveying consumers and test marketing. The results are then analyzed scientifically to determine more precisely what the public is likely to buy.

Industrial Design

Once the decision is made to produce a new product, the manufacturer turns to the industrial designer. The industrial designer is a commercial artist who is familiar with the design requirements of a product from both the consumer's and the manufacturer's viewpoint. In many instances, a full-size nonworking model of the proposed product is produced first. This *mock-up* is true in every external detail, but does not have operating parts. Later, after changes have been made, the mock-up is useful in helping to produce the *prototype*. This is a full-size working model of the piece. The prototype is used to develop special tools and sample parts which will be used in the actual mass production of the piece.

Industrial Engineering

Industrial engineering is concerned with the whole process of planning and executing the manufacture of a product. Included in the planning carried out by the industrial engineer are studies of the material requirements, special tools and cutters needed, material flow, and the number and location of work stations.

Manufacturing

After the product design has been determined, planning for actual full-scale production begins. As part of this phase of the operation, detailed plans and samples are made for each part of the piece. Alterations in the product are made if substantial savings in production costs can be realized. Materials and special or additional equipment are obtained. Engineers design and have special tools and fixtures made.

A master bill of materials, which lists all of the materials required for the piece to be produced, is prepared. An individual routing sheet for each part is prepared from this master bill of materials. These routing sheets are like a map; they show how the materials will move from machine to machine, and which operations are to be performed at each station. Copies of the routing sheets stay with the piece as it moves along and indicate to the operators what is to be done to the piece.

Routing sheets are useful in controlling certain variables in production. If a manufacturer is building a basic dresser with three different types of fronts and finishes, the routing sheets will control the number of each type manufactured. Perhaps the first five pieces produced will have Colonial fronts, while the next eight will be contemporary. In the assembly room the assemblers are guided in assembling the pieces by the routing sheets. In addition, the routing sheets also control the production of fronts so that the correct number and type of fronts are ready when needed.

In modern manufacturing, data-processing equipment improves the quality of control. The number of parts actually made at any moment can easily be determined by means of this equipment. In addition, inventories of materials on hand can be easily and quickly checked so that shortages do not develop. Waste in the form of unused materials can also be reduced through the use of data-processing equipment.

THE MANUFACTURING PROCESS

Many of the larger manufacturers buy unseasoned lumber and then season and prepare it for use in their own facilities. This is done to save money, which would otherwise be spent to have middlemen do some of this processing. On-site processing allows the manufacturer to have closer control over the condition of the material before it is processed into furniture. This preprocessing usually consists of air- and kiln-drying the lumber. After this treatment is completed, the lumber is put in storage or kept at the plant itself.

CUTTING ROOM OR ROUGH MILL SECTION

The rough mill is the first section of the plant to which the material goes. In the rough mill, material is crosscut to length and ripped to width. Surfacing on at least one face takes place here. The material is then prepared for future processing and cut into manageable lengths and widths.

Cutting Room Equipment

In addition to the automatic machinery in the cutting room, the basic, primary woodworking machinery such as the band saw, circular saw, and the jointer are also available.

Crosscut saws. Most of the crosscutting done in the cutting room involves long pieces which must be reduced to shorter lengths. The ideal machine for this purpose is the radial arm or cutoff saw. In this type of machine, the workpiece remains stationary while the saw blade travels across it.

The *sliding ram cutoff saw* is a power-operated version of the radial saw (Fig. 10-1). This saw can be programmed for repeated cuts, and after each cut, the work is advanced automatically. Clamping and operation are often pneumatically controlled.

The *swing saw* is an older type of machine which is still common in lumber yards and is used in some rough-cutting operations (Fig. 10-2).

Ripsaws. In some installations, standard primary table saws are fitted with powered chain feeders that speed up the ripping process. In modern operations, machines like the *straight-line ripsaw* are used for this purpose (Fig. 10-3). This machine is basically a large table saw which is fitted with an over-table pressurizing unit and an in-table chain feeder. The chain mechanism holds the work securely, and no side or edge guiding is required.

Fig. 10-1. Sliding ram cut-off saw. (Courtesy of Ekstrom, Carlson & Co.)

Fig. 10-2. Swing saw. (Courtesy of Fairfield Engineering and Manufacturing Co.)

Gang ripsaws. Gang saws are used to rip the workpiece into several narrow pieces. This saw mounts several identical ripping blades on one arbor. The spacing of the blades determines the width of the pieces produced. These machines generally have automatic feeders, which function in a way similar to that described for the straight-line ripsaw (Fig. 10-4).

Band resawing machines. In some installations, band saws are used for some ripping operations. Band saws do not have deformation problems when cutting through thick material. Modern machines with automatic feeds can rip workpieces into slabs of a given thickness automatically once the unit is loaded and set up.

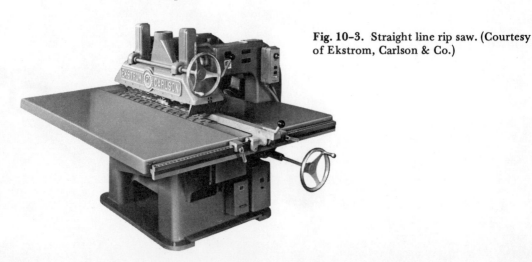

Fig. 10-3. Straight line rip saw. (Courtesy of Ekstrom, Carlson & Co.)

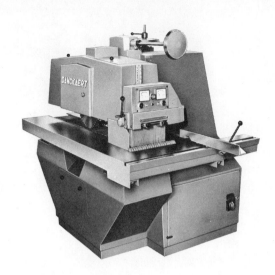

Fig. 10-4. Multiple straight line or gang ripsaw. (Courtesy of Danckaert Corp.)

Automatic curve cutter. Another version of the band saw has an auxiliary unit which guides the workpiece by means of a template (Fig. 10-5).

Jointers. In the cutting room, it is often required to joint edges and to combine small pieces into larger panels. One type of power-feed jointer (Fig. 10-6) consists of two vertical cutter heads and a pair of powered feeding units. Two operators are needed to operate this machine. One feeds the workpiece into the near end of the machine and the other receives it as it exits the machine at the far end. Material that is to be glued to form a panel can easily be prepared for gluing in this unit. For this reason, these machines are often known as *glue jointers.*

Fig. 10-5. Automatic band saw. (Courtesy of Tannewitz, Inc.)

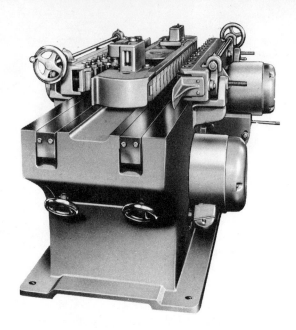

Fig. 10-6. Glue jointer. (Courtesy of Diehl Corp.)

Surfacers. Standard single surfacers are used in cutting rooms for producing a smooth face and for reducing thickness. Double surfacers, and double surfacers and planers, can surface two faces and two edges of a workpiece in a single pass through the unit (Fig. 10-7). Most units can be fitted with hopper-fed automatic feeders, which feed one piece after another through the surfacer and deliver it to a conveyer, which moves the piece to the next work station (Fig. 10-7).

The *facing planer* is a version of the surfacer that can flatten cupped or wound material. It does this by supporting the workpiece on a movable bed that can adjust itself to any irregularities of the piece (Fig. 10-8).

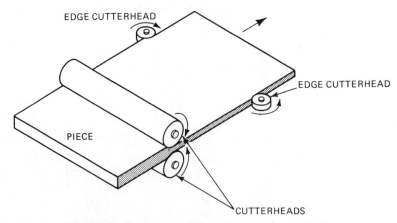

Fig. 10-7. Schematic of double surfacers and edges

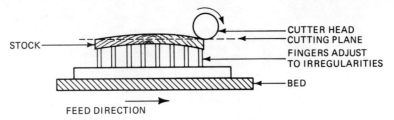

Fig. 10–8. Facing planer

MACHINING SECTION

Once the pieces have been cut to rough sizes, they are ready for more re-fined shaping. This part of the processing takes place in the machining section of the plant. In the fabrication of tables, for instance, legs are shaped and mortised and the rails are cut to width and tenoned. Tabletops are finished by having frames applied to their edges and ends and then shaped to conform to the plans.

The equipment and operations performed in the machining section are described in the following sections.

Shapers

The primary tenoning machine is known as the *single-end tenoner*. This unit consists of two cutterheads mounted horizontally. The space be-tween the cutterheads determines the thickness of the tenon (Fig. 10–9). A lipped door or drawer front can be produced on a version of this unit. When a shaped shoulder is required on the workpiece, as in certain panel frames (Fig. 10–10), shaper heads known as *cope* heads are used to accomplish this operation.

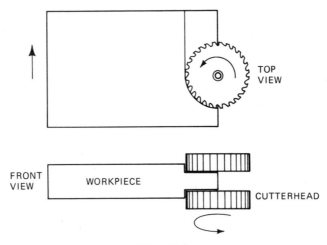

Fig. 10–9.

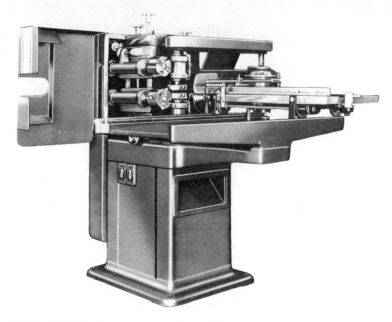

Fig. 10–10. Single tenoner with cope heads and cut-off saw. (Courtesy of Powermatic Machine Co.)

The *double-end tenoner* is really made up of two large single-end tenoners that have been combined into a single multipurpose unit. The schematic in Fig. 10–11 shows how the machine is organized. One of the tenoning units is fixed and the other is adjustable. The edges can be shaped and the panel reduced to finished width in one operation.

In more complex operations, other units can be added to the tenoner. One such unit is the rotating lathe cutterhead (Fig. 10–12) that can shape the face of a wide drawer front while tenoning units shape its end.

The simplest type of shaper is the *single-spindle shaper* which is commonly found in cabinet shops where basic millwork is done. *Double-spindle shapers* have two spindles which can be fitted with different cutters so that two operations can be performed, one after the other. In addition, if one

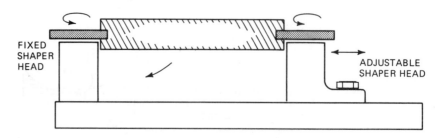

FIXED SHAPER HEAD

ADJUSTABLE SHAPER HEAD

Fig. 10–11. Double end tenoner

Fig. 10–12. Early American drawer fronts being cut with automatic lathe heads on a double end tenoner. (Courtesy of Wisconsin Knife Works.)

spindle rotates clockwise while the other rotates counterclockwise, changes in grain can be accommodated (Fig. 10–13).

Since hand-fed shapers are slow and dangerous, most manufacturing plants employ various types of automatic units. In the simpler type of automatic unit, the table and cutterhead are arranged in a manner similar to that of the standard hand-fed machine but the work is fed automatically. The shape of the piece is determined by the pattern piece to which the blank is fastened (Fig. 10–14). The pattern piece moves against a collar which keeps it at a fixed distance from the cutter.

Revolving-table shapers are really more like overarm routers than shapers. The table and the overarm to which the shaper-cutter is attached can be moved. Through the use of double spindles, hydraulic feeds, and various kinds of master pieces and followers, these machines can shape large and complex components.

BOTH SPINDLES CUTTING WITH GRAIN

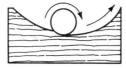

Fig. 10–13. Double spindle shaper

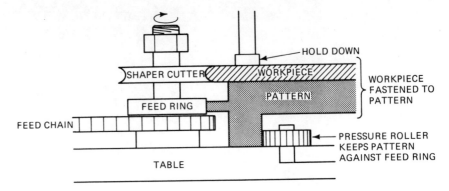

Fig. 10–14. Chain fed shaper utilizing pattern

Boring Machines

Precision of location is provided by various kinds of jigs and fixtures which position the workpiece under the boring tool (Fig. 10-15). As long as the workpiece is positioned against the stops, the hole will be bored in the same relative position in every piece. Speed is provided by having a number of spindles on the same machine (Fig. 10-16). This machine and the standard drill press are known as vertical boring machines (Fig. 10-16).

An independent multiple-spindle drill press (Fig. 10-17) consists of a number of separate spindles which operate independently of each other. An operator can bore a succession of holes in a workpiece using one spindle after the other.

The vertical boring machines described above are suited for boring fairly shallow holes into the faces of relatively thin materials. When holes are required in the ends or edges, the vertical machines are not as suitable. For

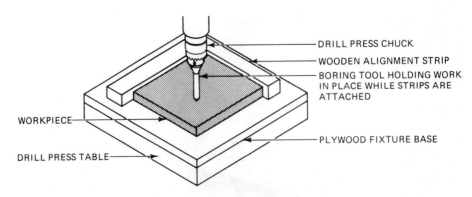

Fig. 10–15. Making a drill press fixture

Fig. 10-16. Single spindle vertical boring machine. (Courtesy of Cemco.)

Fig. 10-17. Independent multiple spindle drill press. (Courtesy of Cemco.)

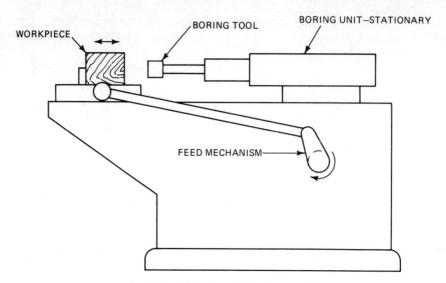

Fig. 10-18. Horizontal boring machine

these operations, *horizontal boring machines* are used. In a horizontal boring, both the workpiece and the spindle are horizontal (Fig. 10-18), which makes the boring of edge and end holes more manageable.

Mortising Machines

A special type of boring operation is required in mortising. A mortise is a rectangular hole which is shaped to receive a tenon. The hollow-chisel mortiser described in Chapter 5 produces such a hole by means of a hollow chisel fitted with an internal auger. Hollow-chisel machines can be made more efficient if they are provided with automatic features such as power feeds and power-operated rams. In any case, this type of machine tends to be relatively slow and inefficient.

Chain mortisers. Chain mortisers are very similar to chain saws in design. The rounded end of the saw is used to form a rounded-bottom mortise. This type of unit is highly efficient because it forms the mortise in a single thrust of the mortising cutter. The rounded bottom of the mortise limits its use to millwork frames and frames in general (Fig. 10-19).

Combination machines. In some operations a multispindle mortiser consists of chain and hollow-chisel units combined into a single machine. This type of machine can mortise a door stile in a single pass.

Oscillating-bit mortiser. The oscillating-bit mortiser consists of an over-arm router fitted with a bit which is equal in width to the mortise desired.

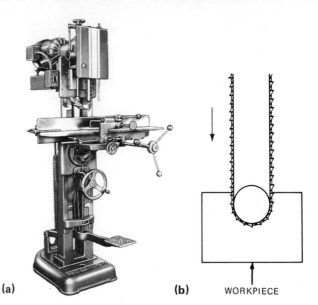

Fig. 10-19. Chain mortising machine. (Courtesy of Powermatic Machine Co.)　**(a)**

(b) WORKPIECE

The workpiece is traveled under the rotating bit a distance equal to the length of the mortise (Fig. 10-20). The result is a mortise with rounded edges.

Routing Machines

Overarm routers. Overarm routers are commonly used in production facilities. These machines are really a kind of shaper.

The overarm router consists of a head mounted on a rigid overarm and a movable table located below it. The table can be raised and lowered. In internal operations (Fig. 10-21), the workpiece is guided by a pin set in the table, which follows a pattern piece fastened to the underside of the workpiece.

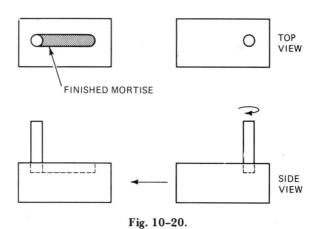

FINISHED MORTISE

TOP VIEW

SIDE VIEW

Fig. 10-20.

Fig. 10-21. Overarm router. (Courtesy of Danly Machine Corp.)

Multiple-spindle routers. These machines are used to generate dovetails in drawer work (Fig. 10-22). The required number of identical bits are positioned at fixed intervals, and the workpiece is traveled into the rotating bits to a preset depth. Thus, in one pass, the dovetails are cut into the end of the piece.

Radial arm routers. Radial arm routers (Fig. 10-23) are designed so that the router head can be traveled over the surface of a fixed workpiece. In addition, the arm is designed so that the router bit can be raised and lowered. This type of machine allows any point on the surface of the workpiece to be shaped.

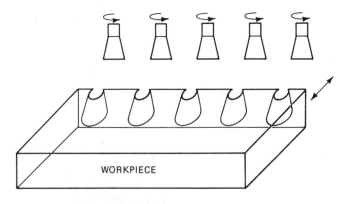

WORKPIECE

Fig. 10-22. Multiple spindle router

Fig. 10-23. Radial arm router. Courtesy of Ekstrom, Carlson & Co.)

Carving Machines

Carving machines are a version of the overarm router. These units usually consist of a number of carving heads guided by an operator who follows a master pattern with a follower. The motion is carried to the carving heads by means of a pantographlike device which ensures identical carving on all pieces (Fig. 10-24).

Turning Equipment

Back-knife lathes. The back-knife lathe is one of the production-turning machines which is similar in operation to the lathe. It has the same basic parts and the work is mounted between centers. The cutting operations are carried out in two separate phases. In the first phase, the shape to be cut

Fig. 10-24. Multiple carver. (Courtesy of Carver Division, Kurt Manufacturing Co.)

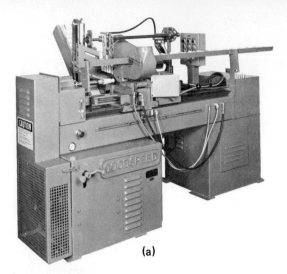

(a)

(b)

Fig. 10–25. (a) Back-knife lathe showing template. (b) Back-knife. (Courtesy of Goodspeed)

is roughed out by a cutter or cutters which follow a template [Fig. 10–25(a)]. A profile template guides the knives and roughs out the desired shape. In the second phase, the roughing knives are positioned out of the way of the back knife. The back knife is profile ground to conform to the desired final shape of the workpiece. As the workpiece rotates, the back knife is brought into contact with the preshaped spindle, giving it its final shape. [Fig. 10–25(b)] Modern back-knife machines have automatic features such as automatic centering, which increases the speed of operation.

Automatic turning lathes. Automatic turning lathes are complex machines which operate on a different principle than either the back-knife or the bench lathe. In these machines, the shaping is accomplished by high-speed, rotating, profile-ground cutters, which shape slowly revolving workpieces (Fig. 10–26). Such equipment is widely used in industry to produce baseball bats, bowling pins, and hammer handles.

Fig. 10–26. Automatic turning lathe. (Courtesy of Wisconsin Knife Works)

These machines can be made fully automatic: A hopper is loaded with blanks and the machine performs a programmed series of operations to shape each blank and deliver it to a second hopper. In some operations, turning-knife units are combined with other machines, such as the double-end tenoner (Fig. 10–12), to provide face shaping and edge shaping on the same machine.

Solid-Wood Bending Equipment

Chair manufacturers are among the principal users of solid bentwood parts. Chair backs, for example, are commonly made in this way. A wood like beech is plasticized by steaming (usually 1 hour per 1 in. of thickness) and then bent in a rim-bending press (Fig. 10–27). Note that the press is designed to support the inner and outer faces of the piece. The ends are also pressurized during bending to keep the outer surface, which is in tension, from failing. After the initial bending and setting takes place, the bent piece is placed in a retaining mold until setting is complete. Final shaping operations are usually carried out after bending has taken place. This procedure serves two purposes. First, it helps to prevent failing of the piece in bending. A shaped edge is more likely to split than a squared edge. Second, it saves money by reducing unnecessary machining. Since a significant percentage of bentwood pieces fail during bending, any machining performed on such pieces would be wasted.

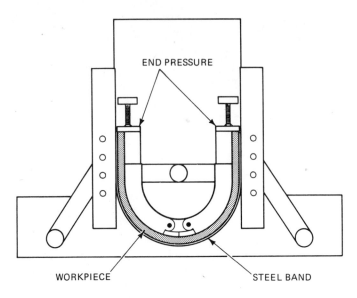

END PRESSURE

WORKPIECE   STEEL BAND

Fig. 10-27. Rim bender

Laminated-Wood Bending Equipment

Laminated parts are widely used in the manufacture of contemporary-styled pieces, which feature thin curved components. Shell-bending machines (Fig. 10-28) are used to fabricate such pieces. The required number of layers of veneer are coated with glue and stacked in the shell-bending press. Heated cauls or electronic glue-setting equipment sets the glue between the layers quickly. In the most modern equipment, shells can be fabricated in as little as 2 minutes.

Preshaping of the parts cuts down on the processing time required after forming. The use of high-quality veneers on the faces of the molded pieces reduces the time which would normally be spent in finishing operations. In addition to the time saved in processing and finishing, complex curved pieces allow one-piece construction. A laminated chair made of one or two molded parts represents a considerable savings in processing and assembly time over a chair made using traditional fabrication methods.

Sanding Equipment

The sanding equipment found in the machining section of a manufacturing plant is primarily intended for use in shaping operations. Although exceptions exist, this equipment is designed to remove considerable quantities of material in a short time. In contrast, finish sanders are designed to remove tool marks and scratches caused by shaping-sanding operations. In finish sanding, a minimum amount of material is removed.

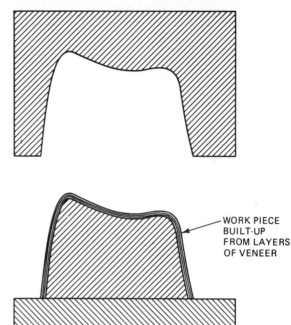

Fig. 10-28.

WORK PIECE
BUILT-UP
FROM LAYERS
OF VENEER

Most of the sanding equipment found in production facilities can be classified under one of the following categories: disk sanders, drum sanders, or belt sanders.

Disk Sanders. Disk sanders are used for a variety of purposes, including squaring ends and rounding over and smoothing corners and convex curves.

Spindle drum sanders. Spindle drum sanders are used for a variety of purposes, including sanding concave internal curved surfaces. In addition, they can be used to round off corners on parts shaped in other ways. These sanders function in much the same way as the drill press accessories described in Chapter 5.

Multiple-drum sanders. Multiple-drum sanders, arranged in machines that operate like surfacers [Fig. 10-29(a) and (b)], are used in sanding panels. Multiple-drum sanders have a series of abrasive drums, each with a finer grit abrasive, mounted one behind the other. As the panel passes into the machine, its surface is sanded first with a relatively coarse abrasive and then with a finer one, until the piece emerges completely sanded at the delivery end. The drums oscillate as they rotate [Fig. 10-29(a)], which helps to prevent the development of deep scratches in the surface of the piece. Among the advantages that the multiple-drum sander has over the surfacer is the absence of tearing out.

Belt sanders. Belt sanders perform many operations. Contoured surfaces can be smoothed after shaping, using a stationary belt sander and a shaped

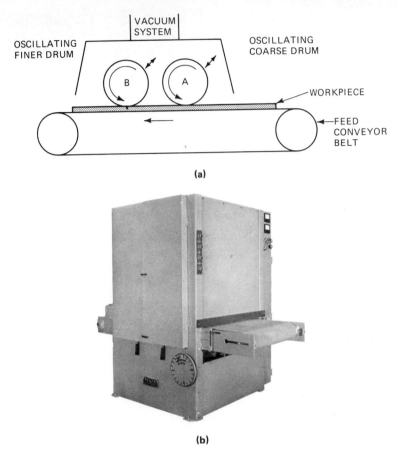

VACUUM
SYSTEM

OSCILLATING
FINER DRUM

OSCILLATING
COARSE DRUM

B   A

WORKPIECE

FEED
CONVEYOR
BELT

(a)

(b)

Fig. 10-29. (a) Drum sander. (b) 2 head drum sander. (Courtesy of Cemco.)

hand block.This type of unit is known as a *hand-block belt sander.* Other types of belt sanders use automatic or semiautomatic pressurizing of the belt as it passes over the surface to be sanded. These are known as *automatic belt-stroke* and *lever belt-stroke sanders* (Fig. 10–30).

Turning sanders. Turning sanders smooth the surfaces of turned objects. The flexibility required to sand an irregular, turned surface is provided by a slitted abrasive belt. Pressure which adjusts to the contours of the workpiece is provided by a brushlike device that keeps the slitted belt sections against the piece (Fig. 10–31).

CABINET SECTION

The cabinet section is the part of the plant where assembly takes place. Cabinet frames and carcases are assembled here using special gluing and clamping equipment. Power nailers and staplers and power screw-boring

Fig. 10-30. Lever stroke belt sander. (Courtesy of Norton)

and driving equipment speed assembly. Skilled workers fit drawers and doors to cabinets. Hardware is installed. In many instances, especially with case-goods, the pieces are temporarily attached to rough wooden bases (skids) to facilitate the handling of the assembled pieces. At some point before the assembled piece is moved into the finishing room, final sanding operations are carried out to remove scars and rough spots from the cabinet.

Gluing Equipment

Glue spreaders (Fig. 10-32) are used to apply glue to surfaces prior to assembly. These devices save time and material. In addition, they ensure uniform and adequate glue application, which is important for two reasons.

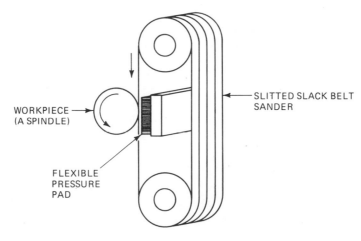

Fig. 10-31. Slitted belt turning sander

OPEN ROLL GLUE SPREADER

Fig. 10-32. Glue spreaders

First, inadequate glue application results in weak joints. Second, too much glue results in seepage which, in turn, requires a time-consuming cleanup and may interfere with finishing operations.

Fastenings

Fastenings are extensively used in furniture manufacturing because they speed up assembly by reducing the need for clamping.

Staplers. Power staplers are often pneumatically operated. Staples are widely used because they provide good holding power. Tack and nail drivers, of similar design, are used in upholstering operations.

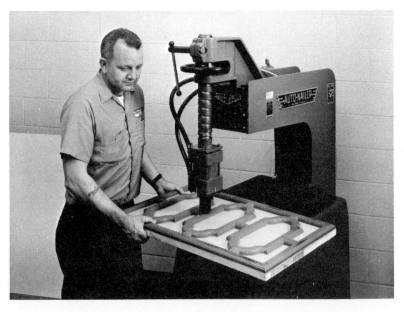

Fig. 10-33. Power nailer. (Courtesy of Bestich Division of Textron)

Stationary power nailers. Stationary power nailers are also used in assembly work (Fig. 10-33). These machines are either fed with nails from a reservoir, or they manufacture their own nails from a spool of wire.

Power screwdriving equipment. Power screwdrivers range from portable units which resemble electric drills to stationary machines which drive and position screws automatically.

Clamping Equipment

The main function of clamps is to hold components in position, under pressure, until glue sets. Standard bar clamps are sometimes used in manufacturing. However, problems arise when using such devices because they are time-consuming to apply and awkward to handle.

Various types of case clamps have been devised to replace individually applied bar clamps. In most machines, an entire case can be pressurized in one operation (Fig. 10-34). The smaller clamps at the top of the figure are designed to hold the workpiece in position and to prevent bulging. The major pressure is applied from the sides. Pressure is supplied by compressed air, which greatly reduces the time needed for clamping. The unit allows fast repositioning because it revolves.

Subassembles such as chair backs are assembled and clamped in units similar to the one shown in Fig. 10-35. Electronic glue-setting equipment can expedite the process.

Fig. 10-34. Case assembly machine. (Courtesy of Handy Manufacturing Co.)

Fig. 10–35. A revolving clamping machine. (Courtesy of Taylor)

FINISHING SECTION

After assembly, pieces are mounted on skids, which makes handling during the finishing process easier (Fig. 10–36). Inspection generally takes place throughout the production process, but it becomes even more critical as the pieces approach completion. Finish-sanding operations, using portable sanding equipment, are carried out prior to finish application, as required. It is important to note that as much sanding as possible takes place before assembly. The assembly process is designed to minimize the need for sanding after assembly.

The finishing process itself utilizes procedures that save time and materials. Slow-drying finishes are seldom used because they require excessive storage space for pieces during drying.

Fig. 10–36. Skid-mounted case work. (Courtesy of Dry Quik)

Spraying

Spraying has the major advantage of speed of application. A sprayed finish can be applied to all exposed areas rapidly. In the most basic setups, materials are applied by hand-held equipment in spray booths. In assembly-line installations, the pieces to be sprayed are traveled to the sprayer by means of a conveyer. Standard spray booths are impractical in such operations, so water-wash booths are used (Fig. 10–37).

Water-wash booths are designed to trap up to 95 percent of the oversprayed material in the recirculating water. The water is adjusted by means of additives, which cause particles of the trapped finish to float on the surface. It is possible to collect the oversprayed material, trapped in the water, and to recycle some of it.

Hot spraying. Hot-spraying units are frequently used in lacquer application. Such units thin the material to spraying consistency by heating. The heat eliminates the need for excessive quantities of solvents. In addition, the heated material dries very rapidly as it cools. Savings in solvent costs are significant.

Electrostatic spraying. In this process the article being sprayed is given an electrostatic charge. The spray droplets are given an opposite charge as they pass through a magnetic field. Since the oppositely charged spray particles are attracted to all parts of the object to be sprayed, very little overspraying results. This process lends itself to automatic operations. Because woods are nonconductive, they have to be precoated with a material which allows the wood to retain an electrostatic charge (Fig. 10–38).

Fig. 10–37. Water-wash spray booth. (Courtesy of DeVilbiss Corp.)

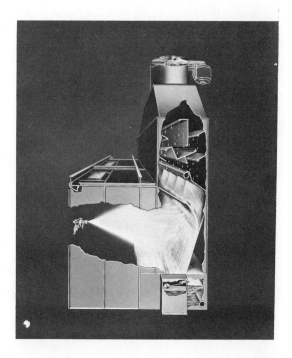

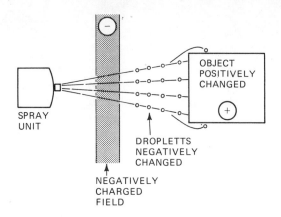

Fig. 10-38. Electrostatic spraying

In *airless spraying,* the coating is sprayed by means of a rotating disk. The charged disk flings the coating outward, toward its rim, by means of centrifugal force. As the coating leaves the disk, it breaks up into charged droplets, which are attracted to the oppositely charged objects to be sprayed (Fig. 10-39).

Tumble Finishing

Tumbling is a method of finishing that employs a tumbling barrel (Fig. 10-40). The articles most suitable for tumble finishing are small pieces like drawer pulls, which are difficult to finish individually.

The pieces and the finish are placed in the drum, and the drum is rotated slowly, usually about 30 revolutions per minute. The slow rotation of the drum is critical because it prevents the finish and the articles from being

Fig. 10-39. Rotating disk—airless spraying

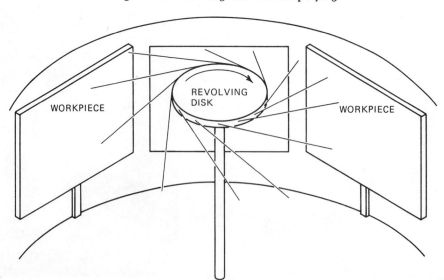

Fig. 10-40. Tumble finishing. (Courtesy of Baird Manufacturing Co.)

forced against the interior of the drum by centrifugal force. After about 10 to 15 minutes, the drum is emptied into a basket, which allows the articles to drain. After drying, often speeded up by baking, the articles are given an additional coating in the drum. The process is repeated until the articles are finished.

Drying

Infrared heaters speed drying by promoting solvent evaporation and by speeding up chemical action (Fig. 10-41). Forced-air drying is also used to cut drying time. This process speeds the evaporation of solvents by removing the solvent-saturated air around the pieces. In cases where oxidation is taking place, a continuous supply of oxygen is supplied by the air flow.

Fig. 10-41. Drying oven. (Courtesy of Dry Quik)

Hand Operations

Hand-finishing operations are sometimes required in processing. These are usually reserved for high-quality pieces and are usually limited to final rubbing operations. In the inspection process, some touching-up operations are carried out. Once the pieces are dry, they are moved to the packaging section, where they are packaged for safe shipping.

PRODUCTION IN NONMANUFACTURING FACILITIES

Most craftsmen engage in "mass production" at times, as required by their work. A person making a chest which requires several identical drawers usually produces all of the sides at one time and then may go on to the fronts. In school settings, line production experiences can be valuable and challenging.

Organizing a Group for Production

The committee approach can be used to organize a group for a production run. Three committees are suggested: a business committee, an engineering committee, and a production committee.

The business committee is charged with the following responsibilities:

1. Materials procurement.
2. Sales.
3. Fund raising.
4. Determination of all costs.
5. Disbursements and record keeping.

The production committee is responsible for:

1. Overall operation of the production run.
2. Determining operations and work stations needed.
3. Assigning available workers to work stations and training workers.
4. Providing for materials flow and transfer.
5. Eliminating production bottlenecks.
6. Reassigning workers to secondary jobs after primary jobs are completed.

The engineering committee is responsible for:

1. Devising means of producing the object.
2. Building the prototype and/or mock-up.
3. Determining the type and number of operations required.
4. Designing, building, and testing jigs and fixtures.
5. Determining the equipment needed.

Selecting a Design for Production

The commercial manufacturer determines the need for a product before designing it. A noncommercial group, whose principal reason for producing the object is to experience production, places less emphasis on this part of the process. The items considered in selecting or producing a design include the following:

1. Producibility of the object in the time allotted. If an "authentic" experience is desired, the time used for the actual production run should be short, one or two sessions at most. This will give those involved a feeling for the repetitive and somewhat pressurized nature of a production run. In most cases this time limitation dictates that a fairly simple one- or two-piece product be manufactured.

2. Utilization of as much of the existing equipment as possible. This is important because, in most cases, additional equipment is not readily obtainable.

3. Suitability of assembly and finishing for line production. In most cases this means that the piece can be assembled without the use of clamps. Finishes must be fast drying or of the one-application variety.

4. Appeal of the product to potential consumers. The cost of production, in terms of the materials required, is closely related to consumer acceptance. If a similar commercial item is available for less than the cost of the materials required, consideration should be given to producing a different item.

Jigs and Fixtures

Jigs and fixtures are very commonly used in production work. In the metalworking industries, a tool and die maker is the master machinest who produces these devices. Some of these devices, such as the dowel jig (Fig. 10-42) and the dovetail fixture (Fig. 10-43), have become standardized.

A jig is a device which holds and locates a piece of work and guides the tool or tools which work or operate on it. "Fixture" is a more general term

Fig. 10-42. Doweling jig. Courtesy of Stanley Tools)

Fig. 10-43. Dovetail fixture. (Courtesy of Stanley Tools)

and usually refers to a device which is more complex than the typical jig. The function of a fixture is to eliminate the individual fitting of parts in mass production, where interchangeable parts are required. Fixtures are usually attached to a machine and they position the workpiece (Fig. 10-44). Jigs often clamp to the workpiece and guide a bit or cutter, as in the use of the dowel jig.

Making a drill press fixture.

1. Install the boring tool in the drill press chuck.

2. Place the workpiece, with the center of the hole to be bored under the center of the boring tool, on a piece of plywood clamped to the drill press table (Fig. 10-44).

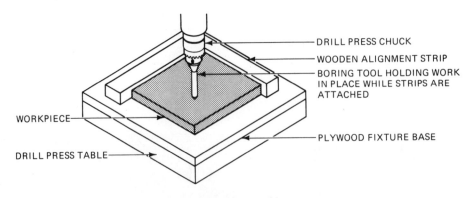

Fig. 10-44. Drill press fixture

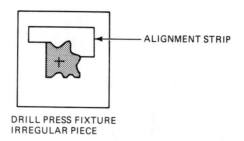

DRILL PRESS FIXTURE
IRREGULAR PIECE

ALIGNMENT STRIP

Fig. 10–45. Drill press fixture–irregular piece

3. Bring the boring tool down until it contacts the piece. Tighten the spindle clamp on the drill press.

4. Place strips of wood along two adjacent sides of the workpiece and nail them in place. Leave the nail heads above the surface for easy removal and adjustment.

5. Try the fixture on a scrap piece. Adjust if necessary. Drive nails all the way in.

If the piece has irregular surfaces, matching pieces may be required in place of the strips shown in Fig. 10-44. See Fig. 10–45. If the piece has more than one hole in it, the first hole can be used to locate the other holes (Fig. 10-46).

Making a router jig. If a round-ended mortise is required in a piece [Fig. 10-47(a)], it can be fashioned using the following procedure:

1. Lay out the required mortise on a sample piece of 1/4- or 1/8-in.-thick hardboard, which is 2 in. wider and longer than the actual workpiece [Fig. 10-47(a)].

2. Select and install an appropriate router bit in a router.

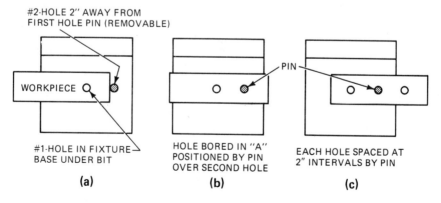

Fig. 10-46. Making a multiple hole drill press fixture

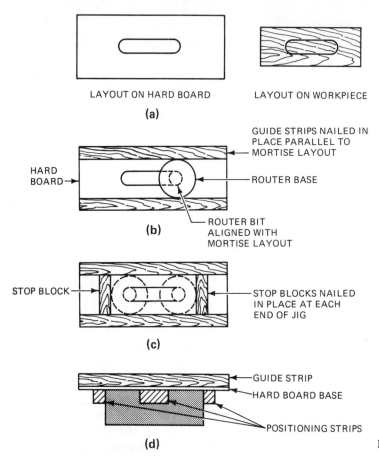

LAYOUT ON HARD BOARD LAYOUT ON WORKPIECE

(a)

GUIDE STRIPS NAILED IN PLACE PARALLEL TO MORTISE LAYOUT

HARD BOARD→

ROUTER BASE

ROUTER BIT ALIGNED WITH MORTISE LAYOUT

(b)

STOP BLOCK

STOP BLOCKS NAILED IN PLACE AT EACH END OF JIG

(c)

GUIDE STRIP
HARD BOARD BASE

POSITIONING STRIPS

(d)

Fig. 10-47. Router jig

3. Position the router at one end of the mortise layout.

4. Place a straight-edge guide strip on each side of the router base parallel to the mortise layout and tack each in position [Fig. 10-47(b)].

5. These two strips control the position of the router but do not limit the travel of the router between the strips. A block at each end of the jig can be installed for this purpose [Fig. 10-47(c)].

6. Now cut through the jig base with the router.

7. Place the jig on the piece to be mortised as shown, so that the cut-out area formed in step 8 matches with the mortise layout on the sample workpiece.

8. Attach positioning strips to the underside of the jig base as shown in Fig. 10-47(d). Test the jig and adjust if necessary.

When making jigs for stationary machines, consideration must be given to the fact that the workpiece, rather than the machine, must move. The jig maker should first determine the path of the workpiece by starting with a layout of the cut to be made (Fig. 10-48). Then a guide must be designed

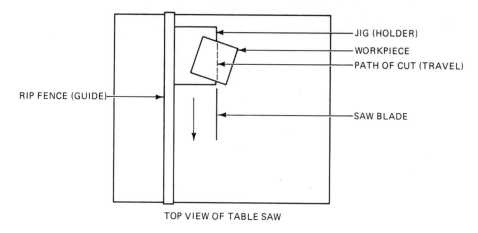

JIG (HOLDER)
WORKPIECE
PATH OF CUT (TRAVEL)

RIP FENCE (GUIDE)

SAW BLADE

TOP VIEW OF TABLE SAW

Fig. 10-48. Taper-cutting jig

to provide the travel required. It may also be necessary to design a holder for the workpiece. A taper-cutting jig is an example of such a holding or positioning device (Fig. 10–48). In the tapering jig, the rip fence is the guide. If a blind slot or groove is required, the jig would consist of stop blocks clamped to the rip fence. Straight-sided irregular pieces can be cut to shape using an auxiliary raised fence, attached to the rip fence, and a pattern block (Fig. 10–49).

In designing jigs and fixtures to be used with stationary equipment (e.g., the table saw and the band saw), consider attaching wooden pieces to components like the miter gauge (Fig. 10-50) or to the table itself. This procedure will make it easier to attach other jig and fixture components to the machine. The various slots in tables can also be used both in the positioning and in the traveling jigs and fixtures (Fig. 10-51).

In designing these devices, safety is of paramount importance. Be sure that fixtures hold workpieces securely and do not require the operator's hands to come too close to cutters. When clamps are used, be sure to check tightness frequently because machine vibration can quickly loosen such devices.

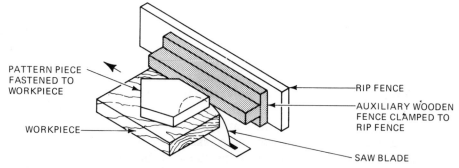

PATTERN PIECE FASTENED TO WORKPIECE

RIP FENCE

AUXILIARY WOODEN FENCE CLAMPED TO RIP FENCE

WORKPIECE

SAW BLADE

Fig. 10–49. Sawing after a pattern

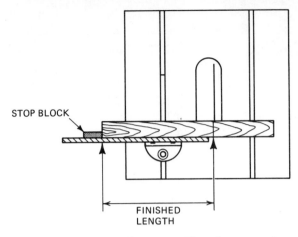

Fig. 10-50. Cross cutting using an auxiliary fence on miter gauge

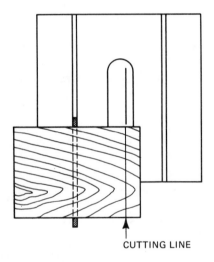

Fig. 10-51. Cross cutting using the table slot as a guide

A Typical Production Job

The piece shown in Fig. 10-52(b) is a commercially manufactured item which sold for $3.50. A check on the availability and cost of the ceramic shakers, and the cost of materials, indicated that the piece could be produced for less than the retail price.

The design was reworked to the form shown in Fig. 10-52(a). The groove in the handle was replaced with a hole. This was done because the groove required routing, which is more difficult and less safe than the boring operation. In addition, the bored hole could be used in fashioning the

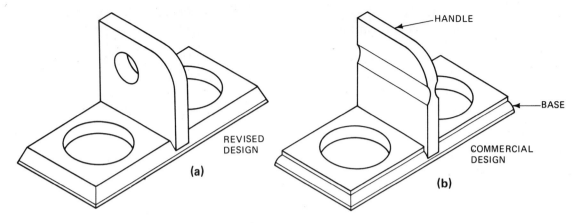

Fig. 10-52.

rounded corner. The shaped edge of the base was replaced with a chamfered base, which was simpler to fashion with the equipment available. The base was lengthened to make jointing operations safer. Finally, black walnut was used in place of stained poplar because a wipe-on oil finish could be used on walnut.

Operations and Sequence

As a result of experience gained in making the prototype, several potential problems were identified.

Base piece. Base pieces were "subcontracted." Each piece was cut double the finished length plus 1/2 in., and double the finished width plus 1/4 in.

Subcontracting is a device used to remove certain unsuitable operations from production. In this case, precutting the pieces allowed for a more uniform flow of materials because crosscutting capacity was limited. Other examples of subcontracting might include the purchase of nonwood project parts like the ceramic shakers.

Double-length bases were cut because the short bases could not be jointed safety on the jointer available. The jointing was necessary after the dado was cut because some tearing of the edge grain was noted during this operation. The pieces were made oversize in width by 1/4 in. to leave material for jointing. Another important consideration in determining these rough sizes was the width of the material available. Adjustments are often made so that waste is reduced in ripping operations.

1. The first operation was to cut the dado utilizing the miter gauge and stop rods. A suitable straight edge must exist on the subcontracted base pieces.

2. The second step was to joint the edge damaged during dado cutting while reducing the pieces to final width. A gauge can be used to check width. [Fig. 10–53(a)].

3. The third step was to cut bases apart using jig. The jig used for this operation uses the dado for positioning [Fig. 10–53(b)].

4. The fourth step was to sand ends to length on the disk sander using fixture [Fig. 10–53(c)]. The dado is used to locate the piece relative to the sanding disk.

5. The fifth step was to chamfer the base. The stationary belt sander and fixture were used to accomplish this [Fig. 10–53(d)].

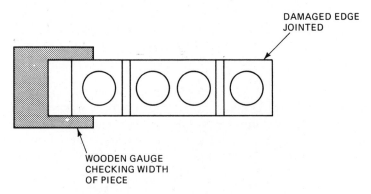

Fig. 10–53(a). Use of gauge in quality control;

Fig. 10–53(b). cutting to length using dado as a locating point;

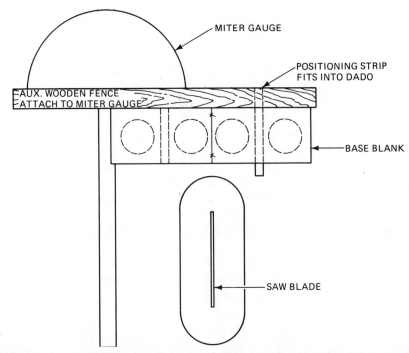

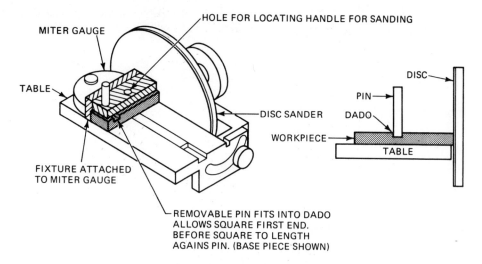

Fig. 10-53(c). dual jig used for base and handle;

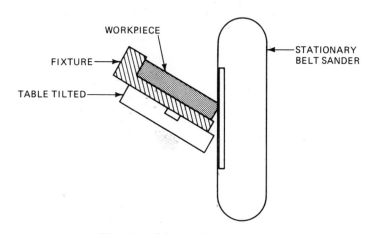

Fig. 10-53(d). sanding chamfers

6. Holes were bored for shakers on drill press using a jig similar to the one shown in Fig. 10-54(a).

7. The sanding was completed, using a hand or portable finishing sander.

8. The piece was inspected.

Handle. The blanks for the handle were subcontracted for cutting. They were cut to twice the required length, plus 1/4 in. Their width was equal to the finished width of the base.

1. Bore a finger-grip hole through the piece using the jig shown. In this case, a jig is used which permits the hole to be bored using a hand-held drill

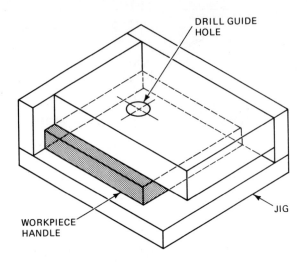

Fig. 10-54(a). Drilling jig;

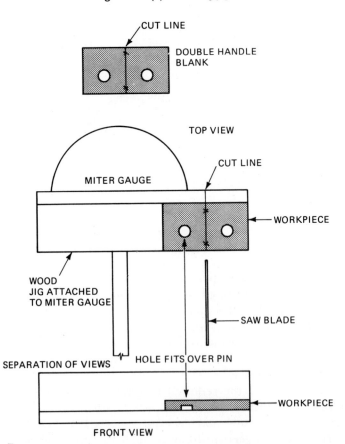

Fig. 10-54(b). cutting to length using hole in piece to position work;

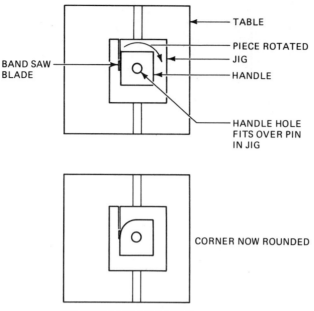

TABLE

PIECE ROTATED

JIG

HANDLE

BAND SAW BLADE

HANDLE HOLE FITS OVER PIN IN JIG

CORNER NOW ROUNDED

TOP VIEW BAND SAW TABLE

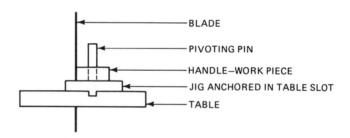

BLADE

PIVOTING PIN

HANDLE—WORK PIECE

JIG ANCHORED IN TABLE SLOT

TABLE

Fig. 10-54(c). circle cutting fixture;

[Fig. 10-54(a)]. This operation is done first because this hole will be used to position the piece during later cutting and sanding operations.

2. Cut the handles apart. Use the hole bored in step 1 to position the piece for this cut [Fig. 10-54(b)].

3. Sand the upper end, using the same jig used for the base in step 4 [Fig. 10-54(b)]. A pin fits the hole bored into the handle earlier, and it positions the piece.

4. Cut the curve on the band saw using the fixture shown in Fig. 10-54(c). Note that the radius is oversize to allow for sanding of the curve.

5. Sand the curve on the disk sander. If necessary, set up an auxiliary sander using the lathe as shown in Fig. 10-54(d) and (e).

6. Inspect the piece. Finish sanding it.

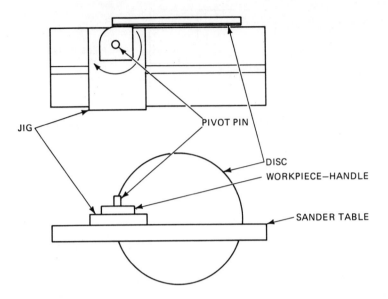

Fig. 10-54(d). curve sanding fixture;

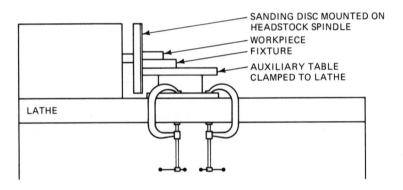

Fig. 10-54(e).

7. Apply glue and assemble. Note that a tight fit between the handle and base is required. This force-fit eliminates the need for clamping. The use of polyvinyl resin glue also ensures rapid setting.

8. Inspect, and apply an oil finish.

9. After the pieces dry, package and ship.

This brief description of the production sequence for a typical mass-produced piece can be varied to suit the equipment available in a particular facility. The sequence can be adjusted to more closely match the location of fixed equipment in a given shop.

Preliminary Procedures

In the actual execution of a job, the following steps might be followed before the actual production is attempted:

1. Outline a tenative production plan (described above).
2. Build and test jigs.
3. Train operators to use jigs.
4. "Dry run" several pieces through line. Determine transportation requirements of materials and identify bottlenecks. Serious bottlenecks can be broken by doubling up on an operation, i.e., have two workers drill holes instead of one, or redesign the piece to eliminate or simplify an operation.
5. Set up facility prior to actual production.
   a. Label stations in sequence: one, two, three, four, etc.
   b. Provide containers for parts to facilitate movement.
   c. Prefabricate a few pieces at various stages so that workers have pieces to work on when production begins.
   d. Provide for the shifting of workers in early operations to later operations, as production run winds down.

Calculating Unit Cost

One of the tasks performed by the business committee is the calculation of the unit cost of the items produced. This cost is a very significant factor in production because it really determines whether or not the product is marketable in terms of its cost to produce.

A number of factors determine this figure. One is *overhead,* which is defined as those costs, usually fixed, which are not directly connected to the cost of materials that go into the product. Such costs include:

1. Rental for the facilities used.
2. Cost of equipment and its depreciation.
3. Cost of labor, including fringe benefits.
4. Insurance.
5. Utilities.
6. Taxes on property and income.

In a hypothetical situation, rental cost can be determined by checking the cost of similar industrial space in the locality in which the production is being carried out.

The equipment cost is determined by checking suppliers' catalogs for prices, and then depreciating the equipment over a period of time, such as ten years. If a machine cost $1000 to purchase, it would cost $100 per year to own.

The cost of labor can be determined by checking local want ads to determine salaries offered for similar kinds of work. Local unions can also be checked to obtain the union rate for unionized workers.

Fringe benefits include health insurance, life insurance, etc., and should be comparable to benefits offered to other workers similarly employed.

Insurance costs for the plant and equipment can be obtained by talking to local insurance agents.

Utility costs can be computed by determining the power consumption of the machinery, as well as lighting and heating, used during production.

Taxes on the property can be determined by talking to the local tax-collection agency.

When all of the data are collected, the amount of each overhead item must be calculated for the length of the production run. For example, if the equipment depreciation cost for one year is $10,000, this would be divided by 250 (number of working days per year) and then by 8 (assuming the run takes 1 hour):

$$\frac{\$10,000}{250} = \frac{\$40}{8} = \$5$$

In a similar way, the 1-hour cost of each of the other overhead items can be determined. Let us say that these came out as listed:

Machinery depreciation	$5 per hour
Rental	2 per hour ($500 per month)
Labor (10 workers)	$50 per hour
Utilities	$1 per hour
Insurance	60¢ per hour
Taxes	50¢ per hour

Total overhead cost per hour	= $59
Materials (including subcontracted)	$10

Total cost per hour for 50 pieces produced:	$69
Estimated cost per piece to produce:	$1.38

Since the typical production run is of short duration, this production figure of 50 pieces per hour is likely to improve as the workers gain experience. But the figure does give the producer some idea of the actual cost of producing a single unit.

It should be noted that some of the overhead costs such as machinery depreciation, rental, and taxes are fixed. That is, they remain the same per week whether the plant runs 24 hours a day or 8 hours a day, as described here. So, if the pieces produced are sold in sufficient quantity, the unit cost can be lowered by operating three shifts (24 hours per day). This is why companies with high capital (plant and equipment) investments operate around the clock, when possible. This reduces their fixed costs per unit.

INDEX

Wood: *(Contd)*
cell structure, 12 *(See also* tree
growth)
characteristics, 15
classification, 14
defects *(See also* warping and
seasoning):
chipped grain, 24
compression wood, 20
fuzzy grain, 24
heart shakes, 21
raised grain, 24
reaction wood, 20
ring shakes, 21

Wood: *(Contd)*
surface, 401
tension wood, 20
dimensional stability, 10, 22
ecological advantages, 12
fillers, 400–402
fire resistance, 11
heat conduction, 12
permanence, 11
strength, 12
Working surfaces:
edges, 114
ends, 116
faces, 113